Protestantism in Latin America:

A Bibliographical Guide

OTHER WILLIAM CAREY LIBRARY BOOKS

ON LATIN AMERICA

The Emergence of a Mexican Church by James E. Mitchell,
   184 pp., $2.95p
*The Founding and Developing of Spanish Bible Institutes
   and Seminaries* by Janie Marie True, 208 pp., $8.95xp
A History of the Lutheran Church in Guyana by Paul B.
   Beatty, 136 pp., $2.45p
The Protestant Movement in Bolivia by C. Peter Wagner,
   264 pp., $2.95p
The Role of the Faith Mission: A Brazilian Case Study
   by Fred Edwards, 175 pp., $3.45p
Understanding Latin Americans by Eugene A. Nida, 164 pp.,
   $3.95p
*A Yankee Reformer in Chile: The Life and Works of David
   Trumbull* by Irven Paul, 174 pp., $3.95p

Protestantism in Latin America:

A Bibliographical Guide

AN ANNOTATED BIBLIOGRAPHY OF SELECTED REFERENCES
MAINLY IN ENGLISH, SPANISH AND PORTUGUESE AND
USEFUL BIBLIOGRAPHICAL AIDS TO ASSIST THE STUDENT
AND RESEARCHER IN THE GENERAL FIELD OF LATIN
AMERICAN STUDIES.

Edited by

John H. Sinclair

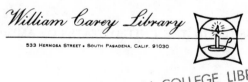

William Carey Library

533 HERMOSA STREET • SOUTH PASADENA, CALIF. 91030

In accord with some of the most recent thinking in the academic press, the William Carey Library is pleased to present
this scholarly book which has been prepared from an author-
edited and author-prepared camera-ready manuscript.

Library of Congress Cataloging in Publication Data

Sinclair, John H   1924-
    Protestantism in Latin America.

  1. Protestant churches--Latin American--Biblio-
graphy. I. Title.
Z7778.L3S57   016.280'4'098   73-12837
ISBN 0-87808-126-7

Published by the William Carey Library
533 Hermosa Street
South Pasadena, Calif. 91030
Telephone 213-799-4559

Dedicated to my wife, Maxine,
who continues to share enthusiastically
in our pilgrimage in the Americas . . .
and to our three sons, David, Paul, and John Mark,
whose lives have also been enriched
by Latin American friends and culture.

From the 1920's -

" . . . Desde Belén y el Calvario, Cristo pasó por Africa y
España en su largo viaje al occidente, hasta las pampas y las
cordilleras. Pero, ¿fué realmente El quien vino, o fué otra
figura religiosa que portaba el mismo nombre y algunas de
Sus marcas? Pienso a veces que el Cristo, de paso al occidente, fué encarcelado en España, mientras otro que tomó Su
nombre su embarcó con los cruzados españoles hacia el Nuevo
Mundo, un Cristo que no nació en Belén sino en Noráfrica.
Este Cristo se naturalizó en las colonias ibéricas de América,
mientras el Hijo y Señor de María ha sido poco más que un
extraño y peregrino en esas tierras desde los tiempos de
Colón hasta el presente . . ."

John A. Mackay, *El Otro Cristo Español*

From the 1970's -

" . . . América latina, de un ámbito marginal y olvidado de
la Iglesia, se va transformando en un auténtico laboratorio
de una nueva experiencia eclesial, de significación universal,
porque se vive la confrontación, el riesgo y las contradicciones propias de un estado de dependencia y de opresión
estructural de la que se comienza a tener conciencia . . .
El descubrimiento cultural y teológico de América latina
como oprimida y dependiente, permite repensar a la luz de la
fe el salir del aparente callejón sin salida de un eterno
subdesarrollo . . ."

Enrique D. Dussel, *Historia de la Iglesia en América Latina:
Coloniaje y Liberación, 1492-1972*.

Contents

PART ONE. 1967 EDITION

ix

PART TWO. 1976 EDITION

Abbreviations

ABS - American Bible Society, New York City.

ASTE - Associacão do Seminarios Teológicos Evangélicos, São Paulo, Brazil.

AURORA, La - Editorial y publicador "La Aurora," Buenos Aires, Argentina.

BFBS - British and Foreign Bible Society, London.

BWM - Board of World Missions, Presbyterian Church in the U.S., Atlanta, Georgia.

CCLA - Committee on Cooperation in Latin America, 1916-65. (Files and library now part of Latin American Working Group, NCCC).

CEC - Centro de Estúdios Cristianos, Buenos Aires, Argentina.

CEE - Confraternidad Evangélica del Ecuador, Quito, Ecuador.

CELAM - Consejo Episcopal Latinoamericano, Bogotá, Colombia.

CET - Comunidad Evangélica Teológica, Santiago, Chile.

CETIM - Centre Europe-Tiers Monde, Geneva, Switzerland.

CEPAE - Centro de Planificación y Acción Ecumenica, Santo
Domingo, D.R.

CHS - Church Historical Society, Austin, Texas. (Episcopal).

CIDOC - Centro Intercultural de Documentacion, Cuernavaca,
México.

CIF - Centro de Formacíon Intercultural, Cuernavaca, Mexico (Now
part of CIDOC).

CML - Columbus Memorial Library, Pan American Union, Washington,
D.C.

COEMAR - Commission on Ecumenical Mission and Relations, United
Presbyterian Church in the U.S.A., New York. (Now the
Program Agency of the United Presbyterian Church, U.S.A.).

CUPSA - Casa Unida de Publicaciones, S.A., Mexíco, D.F.

DMC - Day Missions Collection, Yale Divinity School, New Haven,
Conn.

DWME - Division on World Mission and Evangelism, World Council
of Churches, Geneva, Switzerland. (Now CWME - Commission
on World Mission and Evangelism).

EUSA - Evangelical Union of South America, London.

FERES - Federación Internacional de los Institutos Católicos de
Investigaciones Sociales y Socio-religiosas.

FET - Facultad Evangélica de Teología, Buenos Aires, Argentina.
(Now ISEDET, Instituto Superior de Estúdios Teológicos).

FUMEC - Federación Unida de movimientos estudiantiles Cristianos,
Lima, Perú.

ICG - Institute of Church Growth, Fuller Theological Seminary,
Pasadena, California.

IMC - International Missionary Council. (Now part of CWME of
the World Council of Churches, Geneva).

IRM - International Review of Missions, London.

ISAL - Iglesia y Sociedad en América Latina, Montevideo, Uruguay.

LACUT - Latin American Collection, Univ. of Texas, Austin, Texas.

LADOC - Latin America Documentation, U.S. Catholic Conference, Washington, D.C.

LAWG-NCCC - Latin American Working Group, National Council of Churches of Christ, New York. (Formerly Latin American Department - LAD).

LAGS - Latin American Gateway Series, Gainesville, Florida.

LARR - Latin American Research Review, Austin, Texas.

LEAL - Literatura Evangélica para la América Latina, Wheaton, Illinois.

LEE - Literatura Evangélica del Ecuador, Quito, Ecuador.

LWF - Lutheran World Federation, Geneva.

MARC - Missions Advanced Research and Communications Center, Monrovia, California.

MEC - Movimiento Estudiantil Cristiano, Buenos Aires, Argentina. (Now a part of FUMEC).

MEM - Missionary Education Movement of North America and Canada, New York.

MHL - Mennonite Historical Library, Goshen, Indiana.

ML - Maryknoll Library, Maryknoll, New York.

MRL - Missionary Research Library, Union Theological Seminary, New York.

MML - Methodist Mission Library, New York. (Now part of United Mission Library, New York).

OAS (OEA) - Organization of American States, Washington, D.C.

PAU - Pan American Union, Washington, D.C.

PHA - Presbyterian Historical Association, Montreat, North Carolina.

PHS - Presbyterian Historical Society, Philadelphia, Pa.

RBMU - Regions Beyond Missionary Union, London.

SEDOC - Sociedade de Estudios y Documentaçao, Petropolis, Río de Janeiro.

SEL - Servicio Evangélica de Literatura, Montevideo, Uruguay.

SEPR - Seminario Evangelico de Puerto Rico, Río Piedras, Puerto Rico.

SML - Speer Memorial Library, Princeton Theological Seminary, Princeton, New Jersey.

SPCK - Society for the Promoting of Christian Knowledge, London.

SPG - Society for the Propagation of the Gospel, London.

SVM - Student Volunteer Movement, New York.

TEF - Theological Education Fund, London and New York.

UAIM - United Andean Indian Mission, New York.

UCM - United Christian Movement, New York.

ULAJE - Unión Latinoamericana de Juventudes Evangélicas, Buenos Aires, Argentina.

UNELAM - Comisión de Unidad Evangélica Latinoamericana, San Juan, Puerto Rico.

UNESCO - United Nations Economic, Social and Cultural Organization, Paris.

UML - United Mission Library, The Interchurch Center, New York.

WCC - World Council of Churches, Geneva.

WCCE - World Council on Christian Education, Geneva. (Now the Commission on Education of the WCC).

WSCF - World Student Christian Federation, Geneva.

WCL - William Carey Library, South Pasadena, California.

Foreword

In these last years we have witnessed a spiritual drama in the lands south of the Rio Grande, a drama that gives special timeliness and significance to this unique Manual, which is an expansion of a previous study, and includes reference to books and pamphlets that portray developments in a purely secular perspective.

The drama in question may be described thus. There was a time and not so long ago, when two illusions were current regarding the religious situation in Latin America. One illusion was that this region was the most solidly Roman Catholic of all the great areas of the world. The other illusion was that Latin America is an area where Protestant Christianity has little significance. Recent dramatic events have brought both these illusions to an end.

Today Roman Catholic leaders in the Americas recognize that so far as the Mother Church is concerned, the great geographical area in the Western Hemisphere once acclaimed as a Roman Catholic paradise has been in reality a spiritual wilderness. The realistic acknowledgement of this fact, together with the evangelical renaissance now under way in large segments of world Catholicism including Latin America, have created, in informed Catholic circles, a mood of boundless appreciation and gratitude for the unique contribution of the Protestant witness in Latin American lands.

With the passing of a myth regarding the Protestant presence in Latin America, which is now recognized as potent, and with the advent of a new era in Protestant Catholic relations, the publication of *Protestantism in Latin America: A Bibliographical Guide*, by a well-informed student of Latin American affairs, will be hailed in religious and cultural circles of the Americas as a much needed pathway to a new world of reality.

John A. Mackay

Acknowledgments

The preparation of this bibliographical guide would not have been possible without the counsel, cooperation and contributions of many colleagues. I am particularly indebted to the following contributors and consultants who have provided invaluable original materials and critical comments for both Part One and Part Two.

Wilfrido Artús, Uruguay
R. Pierce Beaver, Mission history
Julio Barreiro, Church and Society
Beverly Chain, Mass Communications
Gonzalo Castillo Cardenas, Colombia
Richard A. Couch, Argentina
Gennett K. Emery, Argentina
J. Andrade Ferreira, Brazil
James E. Goff, Colombia
Justo L. Gonzalez
Heinz J. Held, Argentina
Warren Hornung, Chile
Fred A. Ineson, Brazil
John B. A. Kessler, Chile/Peru
Christian Lalive D'Epinay, Chile
Robert Joe Lee, periodicals
Gaspar Langella, Dominican Republic
Robert J. McIntire, Brazil
James W. McKaughn, Mexico

Marion C. McKechnie, Mexico
Richard L. Millett, Central America
R. Herbert Minnich, Jr., Mennonites in L. A.
Donald T. Moore, Puerto Rico
Gerson Meyers, Christian education
Paul McCleary, Bolivia
Wilton M. Nelson, Costa Rica
Harry Peters, Nicaragua
Irven Paul, Chile
Roger Perkins, Brazil
C. Arthur Phillips, Venezuela
H. Edwin Rosser, Mexico
L. A. Rutschmann, Rio de la Plata
W. Stanley Rycroft, Mission history
Aharon Sepsezian, Theological education
Theo Tschuy, Cuba
C. Peter Wagner, Peru/Bolivia
Wilkins B. Winn, Central America
William K. Wipfler, Dominican Republic
Lindolfo Weingartner, Brazil
Thomas E. Woodward, Dominican Republic

Mrs. Ellen Scott has worked hard and carefully on typing the manuscript. David M. Sinclair, my eldest son, did the thankless task of preparing the Index.

Introduction

Protestantism has a continuous history in Latin America of over 130 years. Early beginnings precede this period by over two centuries. Yet, despite the emergence of a *comunidad evangélica* in Latin America of nearly two million, only scant attention has been given to the development of adequate tools to study Protestant history and its contemporary life and thought.

A bibliographical guide is long overdue to encourage and assist students and researchers to explore the fascinating annals of Protestant history in Latin America. There is equally lacking a survey of an increasing flow of contemporary literature on this subject to enable the Christian world to understand the problems and challenges of this part of Christendom, perhaps the fastest growing part of world Protestantism. Seminary professors of church history -- both Roman Catholic and Protestant -- have asked for help in the preparation of course material on indigenous Protestant history in Latin America. Hopefully, the directors of centers of missionary training will derive benefit from this guide. In academic circles beyond the church, researchers and professors in Latin American studies expressed an interest in bibliographical tools in this field as they contemplate the emerging role of Protestant Christianity in present-day Latin America.

     This project has been limited by the time available to the
editor, to the inadequacy of budget for travel and the use of
volunteer contributors, many of whom carry full teaching and
administrative loads. It is also recognized that some sources
in secular institutions in Latin America and yet-to-be organized
archives of national churches have been virtually untouched. In
addition the primary sources are still to be surveyed (correspondence, personal diaries, manuscripts, reports, etc.) which
contain valuable and precise documentation. It is hoped that in
the near future a preliminary guide to missionary archives and
library manuscripts in the United States and Europe can be prepared to assist researchers in locating these primary sources.

     The scope of the geographical area is properly "Latin
America." The subgroups are primarily regional. The non-Latin
Caribbean (English and Dutch speaking areas) will be covered in
a future supplement. In the selection process we have tried to
include literature that is available in the major seminary
libraries, university libraries, the Maryknoll Library, the Day
Missions Collection in the Yale Divinity School Library, the
Hartford Seminary Foundation, and the Missionary Research
Library. Several works which are important, but are not easily
accessible, can be found in the important libraries which appear
in abbreviated form in the annotations. The bibliography is in
no sense exhaustive. The annotations are as extensive as space
and acquaintance with each work permit.

     Each Part of the Guide is divided into three Chapters. The
First and Fourth are to introduce the student who may have little
acquaintance with Latin American studies to the many useful
tools available to him. Included in these chapters are also
sections on various aspects of Roman Catholicism, contemporary
religions, and secular movements, together with the invaluable
reading list of Hubert Herring in his *History of Latin America*.
Chapters One and Four are only introductory. They were placed
in this *Guide* to facilitate Protestant researchers who have
limited competence in Latin American studies.

     Chapters Two and Five are more complete since they bring
together bibliographies, general literature, reports and periodicals which deal with Protestantism in two or more countries.
The reports of conferences are in chronological order and identified also by the location of the conference. The "Special
concerns of Protestantism" section does not include a separate
section on evangelism since this concern is articulated in some
way in the entire gamut of Protestant concerns.

Chapters Three and Six are the most complete sections. An
effort is made here to include most publications up to the limit
of the space available. After one or two general bibliographies
on each country, there is found a listing of general background
literature on each country. This is again very cursory and must
be supplemented by the Herring list in Chapter One, page 12.
Since permission was granted to reprint the entire reading list
from Hubert Herring's *A History of Latin America*, it is suggested
that the student first review this list and then turn to the
particular country listing under "General Background." These
works are listed only to supplement the Herring list or to provide the opportunity for further annotations by the editor.

Printed minutes, reports, minor denominational publications,
and missionary promotional material are not included, except in
special cases. The supplement on missionary archives (correspondence, diaries, etc.) in the United States and Latin America
will assist the researcher in locating denominational sources.
A few national churches in Latin America now have organized
their historical records and are usually found in the seminary
libraries of each denomination.

                                            John H. Sinclair

Minneapolis, Minnesota
Pentecost, 1975

Note to the Reader

The *Guide* follows the standards of style followed by the United
Nations Secretariat in the compilation of bibliographies with a
few exceptions. (Cf. *Manual of Bibliographical Style*. New York,
Dag Hammerskjold Library, 1963. 62 p.)

These standards attempt to set forth norms of bibliographical
usage that will be internationally acceptable. However, these
standards continue to lean heavily on certain existing sets of
rules, such as those of the American Library Association's
A.L.A. Cataloging Rules for Author and Title Entries and the
Rules of Descriptive Cataloging in the Library of Congress.

Each book with a known author or editor will appear with a
separate number. Only the section on General History on page
12 of Chapter One is not indexed in the Author/Editor Index.
The original 1967 Edition of the *Guide* includes numbers 1 through
2045. The 1976 Edition continues from 2046 through 3115.

Part One.
1967 Edition

Chapter 1.
Bibliographical Aids in the Field
of Latin American Studies

*"Somehow the people of the United States will do
anything for Latin America except read about it."*
(James Reston, THE NEW YORK TIMES)

BASIC RESOURCES AND STUDY TOOLS

Bibliographies and Indices on General Literature
See also p. 245.

1. Bayitch, S. A. Latin America: a bibliographical guide to
   economy, history, law, politics and society. Coral
   Gables, Fla., University of Miami Press, 1961. 350 p.

2. Bibliografía de América Latina. México, 1960. -- Sponsored
   by UNESCO. Contains and expands *its* Bibliografía de
   Centroamérica y del Caribe, 1952-59.

3. Boletim internacional de bibliografía luso-brasileira.
   Lisboa, Fundacão Calouste Gulbenkian, 1960-.

4. Boletín informativo sobre estudios latinoamericanos en
   Europa. Centro de Estudios y Documentación Latino-
   americanos, Nieuwe Doelenstraat 16, Amsterdam, 1965-.

-- A clearing house for all Latin American studies on the Continent in the field of the social sciences in the broadest meaning.

5. Comitas, Lambros. Caribbean 1900-65: a bibliography. Seattle, University of Washington Press, 1967. -- 8000 titles in English, French, Dutch, German, Spanish and Russian.

6. Del Toro, Josefina. A bibliography of the collective biography of Spanish America. Río Piedras, University of Puerto Rico, 1938. 140 p. -- See also Juan B. Iguinez. Bibliografía biográfica. México, 1930.

7. Fichero bibliográfico hispanoamericano. New York, Bowker, 1962. -- For the publisher, librarian and book dealer.

8. Focus: Latin America. New York, University Christian Movement, 1966. -- Brief but well chosen on contemporary publications.

9. Gale, Thomas M. Bibliography on urban Latin America. Lawrence, University of Kansas, 1963.

10. Gropp, Arthur E. A bibliography of Latin American bibliographies. 3. ed. 515 p. Metuchen, New Jersey, Scarecrow Press, 1968. Revision of the work of C. K. Jones by the director of the Library of the Pan American Union. Addition of 5000 items to bring total listings to over 8000 items. Also available is a 1971 supplement of 277 pages by the same publisher.

11. Guía de bibliotecas de la América Latina. Washington, D.C., Unión Panamericana, 1963. 165 p. (Bibliographic series no. 51). -- Helpful to locate libraries and identify the general quantity of material available.

12. Guide to national bibliographical information centers. 2. ed., Paris, UNESCO, 1962. 24 p.

13. Handbook of Latin American studies. Gainesville, University of Florida Press, 1935-. annual. -- No. 28 published in 1966. Earl J. Pariseay *and* Henry E. Adams, ed. The Handbook is a selective and annotated guide to recent publications on anthropology, economics, education, geography, government and international relations, law and sociology.

14. Humphreys, R. A. Latin American history: a selective

guide to the literature in English. London, Oxford
University Press, 1958. 197 p.

15. Indice bibliográfico. G. Arbaiza, dir. New York, Latin
    American Index. -- Quarterly listing of new publica-
    tions.

16. Indice general anotado de literature evangélica. Gonzalo
    Báez Camargo, comp. México, Comité de Literature
    Cristiana del Comité de Cooperación en la América
    Latina, 1948. 120 p. Cf. 309.

17. Indice histórico español. Barcelona, Universidad de
    Barcelona, Centro de Estudios Internacionales, 1953.
    -- Contains section on the Americas.

18. Jones, Cecil Knight. A Bibliography of Latin American
    bibliographies. 2. ed., rev. and enl. Washington,
    D.C., Library of Congress, Hispanic Foundation, 1942.
    i, 311 p.

19. Kidder, Frederick E. *and* Allen D. Bushong, comp. Theses on
    Pan American topics prepared for doctoral degrees in
    the universities and colleges. 4. ed. Washington,
    D.C., Pan American Union, 1962. 124 p. (Bibliograph-
    ical series no. 5, US$.75). -- In the introduction
    are found the sources from which the 1962 listings
    were compiled. Editions of 1931, 1933 and 1941
    included also masters theses. These previous editions
    are out of print. No seminaries are listed as having
    submitted data for those early editions. There is an
    up-dating of doctoral dissertations on Latin American
    topics which covers 1962-65.

20. Lateinamerika: bibliographie zum studium Lateinamericakis
    her entwicklungs probleme. 2. ed. rev. Frieburg, im
    Preisgay, Germany. Arnold-Bergstraesser, Institut für
    Kulturwissenschaftliche Forschung, 1964. 278 p.

21. Latin America: a bibliography of paper back books. David
    T. Andrews, comp. T. J. Hillman, ed. Washington,
    D.C., Library of Congress, Hispanic Foundation, 1964.
    38 p. -- For sale through Superintendent of Documents,
    U.S. Government Publications Office, US$.35. (See
    also Fleener and Seckinger, A preliminary guide to
    Latin American paperback literature, Gainesville,
    University of Florida Press, 1965. 25 p.)

22. Latin America: a guide to historical literature. Austin,

University of Texas Press, 1967. -- In preparation
under the direction of the Conference on Latin American History and Hispanic Foundation.

23. Latin America kyokai: survey of Japanese books of Latin
     American research and study. Tokyo, Sociedad Latino-
     americana, 1965. -- An annotated bibliography of
     about 1000 Japanese books of research and study on
     Latin America, 1868-1964.

24. Latin American prose in English translation: a biblio-
     graphy. Claude L. Hulet, comp. Washington, D.C.,
     Pan American Union, 1964. 19. p. Latin American
     Poetry in translation - a bibliography. Washington,
     D.C., Pan American Union, 1965. 192 p. (Basic
     bibliography series). -- For translation of Spanish
     see Alice S. Blackwell, Translations of some Spanish
     American poets, 1939; *and* Dudley Fitts, An anthology
     of contemporary Latin American poetry. Norfolk,
     Conn., 1942.

25. Latin American research at the University of Texas, 1893-
     1958. Austin, University of Texas Press, 1966. 67 p.
     -- All masters and doctoral dissertations and publica-
     tions of Latin American interest, 1941-58. Other
     major libraries such as the University of California,
     Stanford University have similar listings.

26. Lauerhass, Ludwig, Jr., ed. Communism in Latin America:
     a bibliography the past years, 1945-60. Los Angeles,
     Center of Latin American Studies, University of
     California, 1962. Vol. 1, 78 p.; Vol. 2 published in
     1967 covers period 1961-66.

27. Medina, J. T. Biblioteca hispanoamericana, 1493-1810.
     Amsterdam, N. Israel, 1962. 7 v. -- Facsimile
     editions of these classics of the greatest literary
     bibliographer in Latin America.

28. Mezirow, D. Jack *and* David Epley. Adult education in dev-
     eloping countries. Pittsburgh, Pa., University of
     Pittsburgh, School of Christian Education, 1965. --
     A bibliography with p. 77-98 dedicated to Latin
     America.

29. Okinshevich, Leo A., comp. *and* Robert G. Carlton, ed.
     Latin America in Soviet writings: a bibliography.
     Washington, D.C., Library of Congress, Hispanic
     Foundation, 1959. 2 v.

30. Parra, Germán y Rigoberto Jiménez Moreno. Bibliografía indigenista de México y Centroamérica, 1850–1950. México, Instituto Nacional Indigenista, 1954.

31. Reglas para la catalogación descriptiva en the Library of Congress. Trad. por Fermin Peraza Sarausa. Washington, D.C., Library of Congress, 1953. 174 p. -- Rules adopted by the American Library Association (LC.7:c28/2 Spanish).

32. Rubin, Selma F., ed. Survey of investigations in progress in the field of Latin American studies. Washington, D.C., Pan American Union, 1965. 103 p.

33. The seminars on the acquisition of Latin American library materials. Washington, D.C., Pan American Union, 1965. 326 p. -- First report and working papers. Reflects the growing discussion of this subject which is of such great interest to researchers.

34. Spanish and Portuguese translation of United States books, 1955–62; a bibliography. Washington, D.C., Library of Congress, Hispanic Foundation, 1963. 506 p. US$3.00 (LC24.7:8).

35. Trask, David F., Roger R. Trask *and* Michael C. Meyer. A bibliography of U.S. - Latin American relations since 1810. Lincoln, Nebraska, University of Nebraska Press, 1968. 441 p. A selected list of over 11,000 published references.

Guides to Archival Materials
See also p. 247.

North America

36. Harrison, John Parker. Guide to materials in Latin America in the national archives. Washington, D.C., General Services Administration, National Archives and Record Service, National Archives, 1961, 1967. 2 v. -- The first comprehensive guide to be published by the National Archives devoted to one area. A unit in the extensive series of guides projected by the International Council of Archives to cover material related to Latin America throughout the world.

37. Hilton, Ronald, ed. Handbook of Hispanic source material
     and research organization in the U.S.A. 2. ed. Palo
     Alto, Calif., Stanford University Press, 1956. xiv,
     448 p.

38. Mendoza, Gunnar. Guide to the historical sources on Latin
     America in the U.S.A. Initiated in 1963. 2 v. --
     The investigator will have researched the U.S. includ-
     ing the Library of Congress and the National Archives.
     A project of Archivo y Biblioteca Nacional de Bolivia.

39. Spell, Lota M. Research material for the study of Latin
     America at the University of Texas. Austin, Univer-
     sity of Texas Press, 1954. 107 p. -- Similar des-
     criptions are available on other major collections in
     the U.S.A.

                         Outside North America

40. De la Cámara, José María de la Peña. A list of Spanish
     residencias in the archives of the Indies, 1516-1775.
     Washington, D.C., Library of Congress, 1955. 109 p.
     -- Administrative judicial reviews of colonial
     officials in the American Indies, Canary Islands.
     US$.65.

41. Guía de los documentos microfotografiados por la unidad
     móvil de microfilm de la UNESCO. México, Instituto
     Panamericano de Geografía e Historia, 1963. 317 p.
     -- Documents of seven Latin American countries which
     were considered of special historical significance to
     be shared on microfilm. Microfilms are deposited in
     Mexico.

42. Hill, Roscoe R. The national archives of Latin America.
     Cambridge, Mass., Harvard University Press, 1945.
     169 p. -- Survey of archives of nineteen Latin
     American countries. Argentina founded its national
     archives in 1821, Ecuador in 1938.

                         Historiography

43. Bernstein, Harry. Brazilian historiography and Alexandro
     Herculano. New York, Gulbenkian Foundation, in

preparation since 1960. -- See also *his* A bookshelf
on Brazil. Albany, N.Y., State Education Dept.,
Foreign Areas Studies, 1964. v, 23 p.

44. Cline, Howard F., ed. Latin American History: essay on
its study and teaching, 1898-1965. Austin, University
of Texas Press. 2 v. -- One hundred essays which
trace the development of the specialized field of
Latin American history in the U.S.A. The editor is
the director of the Hispanic Foundation of the Library
of Congress. The book is the first in the series of
publications of the Conference on Latin American
History.

45. _____, comp. Historians of Latin America in the United
States. Chapel Hill, Duke University Press, 1966.
105 p. -- Biobibliographies of 680 specialists.

46. Garraghan, Gilbert Jos. *and* Jean Delanglez. A guide to
historical method. New York, Fordham University
Press, 1946. xv, 482 p.

47. Hanke, Lewis. Bartolomé de las Casas, historian: an
essay on Spanish historiography. Gainesville,
University of Florida Press, 1952. xiii, 125 p.

48. Potash, Robert A. Historiography of Mexico since 1821.
The Hispanic American historical review 40:3:383-424
August 1960.

49. Social Science Research Council. Theory and practice in
historical study. New York, 1946. -- Bulletin no.
54.

50. _____. The use of personal documents in history, anthropology and sociology. New York, 1945. -- Bulletin
no. 53.

51. Stein, Stanley J. The historiography of Brazil, 1808-89.
Hispanic American historical review 40, May 1960.

52. Wilgus, A. Curtis. Histories and historians of Hispanic
America. New York, Cooper Square, 1966. 144 p. --
For the graduate student in Hispanic American civilization and history. "The Medina type of individual must
now be replaced by a cooperating group of individual
specialists." This is the only biobiographical volume
in English which covers the histories and historians
of Latin America.

General Reference Materials
See also p. 249.

53. American universities field staff reports for foreign coun-
    tries. New York, 366 Madison Avenue, 1954-. (Mexico
    and Caribbean: east coast of South America: west
    coast of South America.)

54. Davis, A. E. Latin American leaders. New York, H. W.
    Wilson, 1949. 170 p. -- A biographical handbook
    listing statesmen and leaders of thought who have
    occupied important places in Latin American life.

55. Demographic yearbook. New York, Statistical Office of the
    United Nations, 1966. 808 p. -- See also J. M.
    Stycos *and* J. Arias, ed., Population dilemma in Latin
    America, 1966.

56. Directory, Washington, D.C., Organization of the American
    States.

57. Hilton, Benjamin, ed. Readings in Latin American civiliza-
    tions, 1492 to the present. Boston, Houghton, Mifflin,
    1965. 477 p. -- Many selections appear in English
    for the first time. An anthology broadly representa-
    tive of major Latin American creeds or ideals, politi-
    cal, social and literary.

58. Labelle, Ivan *and* Adriana Estrada, comp. Latin America in
    maps, charts and tables. Cuernavaca, Mexico, CIF,
    1963-64. 2 v. -- An introductory handbook-type work
    but lacking in documentation of sources.

59. National directory of Latin Americanists. Washington, D.C.,
    Hispanic Foundation, United States Library of Congress,
    1971. 684 p. -- Biographies of 2095 specialists in
    the social sciences and humanities.

60. Overseas programs of private non-profit American organiza-
    tions, no. 3. Washington, D.C., U.S. Government
    Printing Office, 1965. 54 p.

61. Pan American Associations in the U.S. Washington, D.C.,
    Pan American Union, 1966. 98 p.

62. Population bulletin. Washington, D.C., Population Research
    Bureau, Inc.

63. Rycroft, W. Stanley *and* Myrtle M. Clemmer. A factual study

of Latin America. New York, COEMAR, 1962. 241 p.

64. _____. A study of urbanization in Latin America. New York, COEMAR, 1963. 144 p.

65. Sable, Martin H., comp. Master directory for Latin America. Los Angeles, UCLA Latin American Center, 1965. 438 p. index. (Reference series no. 2). -- This directory contains ten sub-directories with names and addresses of U.S., Western European and Latin American organizations that are interested in aspects of contemporary Latin America. It also presents a survey of Latin American study programs of U.S. colleges and universities.

66. Situacão social de América Latina. Rio de Janeiro, Centro Latinoamericano de Pesquisas em Ciências Sociais, 1965. -- Extensive data on standards of living, working, educational levels, health conditions and demographic data. UNESCO project in cooperation with governments of Brazil and Mexico.

67. Statistical abstracts of Latin America. Los Angeles, UCLA Center of Latin American Studies, annual. -- General statistical information. Since 1955; 9. ed., 1965.

68. Statistical bulletin for Latin America. New York, United Nations.

69. United States-Latin American relations. Washington, D.C., U.S. Government Printing Office, 1960. 828 p. -- Compilation of studies prepared under the direction of the Subcommittee on American Republic Affairs of the Committee on Foreign Relations of the U.S. Senate.

Yearbooks and Handbooks
See also p. 250.

70. Editor and publisher: 1966 international yearbook. New York, Editor and Publisher, 1966. 589 p.

71. Guide to South America. Eugene Fodor, ed. New York, David McKay, 1967. 612 p.

72. Handbook of Middle American Indians. Robert Wauchope, ed. Austin, University of Texas Press. Seven volume series available. (Cf.2073)

73. Handbook of South American Indians. Julian H. Steward, ed.
    Washington, D.C., U.S. Government Printing Office,
    1946. 6 v. (Smithsonian Institute Bureau of American
    Ethnology bulletin, 193). -- Complete set with index
    volume now available, Cooper Square Publisher.

74. Indianist yearbook, 1962-. Mexico, Inter-American Indian
    Institute. -- Supersedes Boletín indigenista, 1941-
    61.

75. Latin American handbook. Claudio Véliz, ed. London,
    Anthony Blond, 1967. 872 p. (Handbooks to the modern
    world).

76. The Middle American handbook. New Orleans, Tulane Univer-
    sity Middle American Institute, 1966.

77. The South American handbook. Howell Davies, ed. London,
    Trade and Travel, 1924-. illus., maps. 18 v. --
    annual. Includes Mexico, Cuba, Central America.

78. The statesman's yearbook: statistical and historical
    annual of the states of the world...London, Macmillan,
    annually upon revision. -- 1966 ed., S. H. Steinberg,
    ed. New York, St. Martin's.

79. Statistical yearbook, 1965-. New York, United Nations,
    Statistical Office, 1965. 522 p. -- Free monthly
    bulletin from Inter-American Statistical Institute,
    Washington, D.C. Text in English and French.

80. West Indies and the Caribbean yearbook. Howell Davies, ed.
    London, Trade and Travel, 1935-. -- Prior to 1947 was
    the yearbook of the Bermudas, British Guiana, British
    West Indies and British Honduras. London, Canadian
    Gazette, 1926-. Publisher varies.

GENERAL BACKGROUND

General History
See also p. 251.

(See Historia de America y de los Pueblos Americanos. Ediciones
Salvat, 28 volumes, of which 14 have been published. An encyclo-
pedic work. See also Germán Arciniegas' A Cultural History of

Latin America, New York, Knopf, 1967, for a long-needed volume
to complement Herring's political history of Latin America. This
work includes a comparative chronology and a bibliography on the
fine arts and literature.)

Permission has been granted by Alfred A. Knopf, Inc., to reprint
the following comprehensive reading list found in Hubert Herring,
A History of Latin America, rev. 2. ed., 1961, p. 831-45. It
should be noted that this reading list surveys literature on
general history only up to 1960. The reading list is designed
to introduce the student to basic materials on Latin American
history and also to indicate sources for further information.
Emphasis is placed on books in English, although some sources
in Spanish and Portuguese are cited. Monographs and articles
are not included.

Bibliographies and Reference Guides

The student will find help from R. A. Humphreys, Latin
America: A Selective Guide to Publications in English
(London, 1949); C. K. Jones, A Bibliography of Latin
American Bibliographies (Washington, 1942); H. Keniston,
List of Works for the Study of Hispanic-American History
(New York, 1920); the annual Handbook of Latin American
Studies (now issued by the University of Florida Press);
Economic Literature of Latin America, 2 vols. (Cambridge,
Mass., 1935-36); Who's Who in Latin America, ed., Ronald
Hilton, 3rd ed. rev. (Stanford, 1950-51); P. H. Goldsmith,
A Brief Bibliography of Books in English, Spanish and
Portuguese, relating to the Republics commonly called Latin
American (New York, 1915).

Current Publications

Monographs, numerous and invaluable, are to be found in
Hispanic American Historical Review (1918-). Also see
Foreign Policy Reports and Foreign Policy Bulletin (For-
eign Policy Assn., New York); Americas (Organization of
American States, Washington, D.C.); Inter-American Economic
Affairs (Washington, D.C., 1947-); Foreign Affairs; The
Americas, Quarterly of the Academy of American Franciscan
History (Washington, 1944-). Useful for reference on

current developments is Hispanic American Report, ed. by
Ronald Hilton (Stanford, Calif., 1948-1963).

General Surveys

There are numerous *general surveys* which will reward the
the reader: John A. Crow, The Epic of Latin America (New
York, 1946); Dana G. Munro, The Latin American Republics:
A History, 2nd ed. (New York, 1950); J. Fred Rippy, Historical Evolution of Hispanic America, 3rd ed. (New York, 1945);
William L. Schurz, Latin America, a Descriptive Survey, rev.
ed. (New York, 1949) and, by the same author, This New World
(New York, 1954); Mary W. Williams, The People and Politics
of Latin America, rev. ed. (New York, 1955); Tom B. Jones
and W. Donald Beatty, An Introduction to Hispanic American
History, rev. ed. (New York, 1950); William Spence Robertson,
History of the Latin American Nations, 3rd ed. (New York,
1943); A. Curtis Wilgus, The Development of Hispanic America
(New York, 1941); Royal Institute of International Affairs,
The Republics of South America (London, 1937); J. F. Bannon
and P. M. Dunne, Latin America, an Historical Survey
(Milwaukee, 1947).   Other general surveys are F. A. Kirk-
patrick, Latin America: A Brief History (New York, 1939);
C. E. Akers, A History of South America, new edition with
additional chapters bringing the work up to 1930 by L. E.
Elliott (New York, 1930); Harry Bernstein, Modern and Con-
temporary Latin America (Philadelphia, 1952); C. E. Chapman,
Hispanic America: Colonial and Republican (New York, 1942);
Carlos Pereyra, Historia de la América Española, 8 vols.
(Madrid, 1920-26); Thomas C. Dawson, South American Repub-
lics (New York, 1903-04); R. A. Humphreys, The Evolution
of Modern Latin America (New York, 1946); John J. Considine,
New Horizons in Latin America (New York, 1958); Vera B.
Holmes, A History of the Americas, from Discovery to Nation-
hood (New York, 1950); Alfred B. Thomas, Latin America: A
History (New York, 1956); Donald E. Worcester and Wendell
G. Schaeffer, The Growth and Culture of Latin America (New
York, 1956).   Those who wish to know how the Communists
retell the story should read William Z. Foster, Outline
Political History of the Americas (New York, 1951).

For general treatment of *economic questions*, there is H. F.
Bain and T. T. Reed, Ores and Industry in Latin America
(New York, 1934); W. Feuerlein and E. Hannan, Dollars in
Latin America (New York, 1941); Wendell Gordon, The Economy
of Latin America (New York, 1940); Seymour Harris, ed.,
Economic Problems of Latin America (New York, 1944); D. M.
Phelps, Migration of Industry to South America (New York,
1936); J. F. Rippy, Latin America and the Industrial Age,

2nd ed. (New York, 1947); G. H. Soule, et al., Latin America in the Future World (New York, 1945); George Wythe, Industry in Latin America (New York, 1945); George Wythe, Outline of Latin American Economic Development (New York, 1946); Tom B. Jones, Elizabeth Z. Warburton and Anne Kingsley, comps., A Bibliography on South American Economic Affairs (Minneapolis, 1955); Clarence H. Haring, et al., eds., The Economic Literature of Latin America: A Tentative Bibliography, 2 vols., (Cambridge, Mass., 1935-36); Simon G. Hanson, Economic Development in Latin America: An Introduction to the Economic Problems in Latin America (Washington, 1951); Lloyd J. Hughlett, ed., Industrialization of Latin America (New York, 1946); Stacy May and Galo Plaza Lasso, The United Fruit Company in Latin America (Washington, 1958); National Planning Association, Technical Cooperation in Latin America: Recommendation for the Future (Washington, 1956).

For analysis of *educational and cultural forces*, see W. R. Crawford, A Century of Latin American Thought (Cambridge, Mass., 1944); Isaac Goldberg, Studies in Spanish American Literature (New York, 1920); C. C. Griffin, ed., Concerning Latin American Culture (New York, 1940); Pedro Henríquez Ureña, Literary Currents in Hispanic America, (Cambridge, Mass., 1945); A. Torres-Rioseco, The Epic of Latin American Literature, rev. ed. (New York, 1946). For general treatment of the Church, see J. Lloyd Mecham, Church and State in Latin America (Chapel Hill, N. C., 1934) -- revised ed. 1965, and E. Ryan, The Church in the South American Republics (Milwaukee, 1932).

For over-all *interpretation of Latin American life*, James Bryce, South America: Observations and Impressions, new ed. (New York, 1917), is a classic. See also Georges Clemenceau, South America Today (New York, 1911); Cecil Jane, Liberty and Despotism in South America (Oxford, 1929); Alfonso Reyes, The Position of America and Other Essays, tr. by Harriet de Onís (New York, 1950). A critical analysis by a Peruvian, Francisco García Calderón, Latin America, Its Rise and Progress, tr. by B. Miall (London, 1913), is required reading for those who would understand how many southern intellectuals feel about the United States. This same author tempered his earlier judgment in his En Torno al Perú y América (Lima, 1954).

For other *Latin American appraisals* see Germán Arciniegas, The State of Latin America (New York, 1952); Germán Arciniegas, ed., The Green Continent, Comprehensive View of Latin America by Its Leading Writers, tr. by Harriet de

Onís et al. (New York, 1944); Carlos Davila, We of the
Americas (Chicago, 1949); Galo Plaza Lasso, Problems of
Democracy in Latin America (Chapel Hill, 1955); Luis
Quintanilla, A Latin American Speaks (New York, 1943).

For studies of *government and jurisprudence*, Russell H.
Fitzgibbon, ed. The Constitutions of the Americas (Chi-
cago, 1948) is invaluable. Se also Austin F. Macdonald,
Latin American Politics and Government (New York, 1949);
Phanor J. Eder, A Comparative Survey of Anglo-American
and Latin American Law (New York, 1950); Gordon Ireland,
Boundaries, Possessions, and Conflicts in South America
(Cambridge, Mass., 1938), and Boundaries, Possessions,
and Conflicts in Central and North America and the Carib-
bean (Cambridge, 1941). Also, John J. Johnson, Political
Change in Latin America: The Emergence of the Middle
Sectors (Stanford, 1958); William W. Pierson and Federico
G. Gil, Governments of Latin America (New York, 1957);
Edwin Lieuwen, Arms and Politics in Latin America (New
York, 1960).

Part I., Foregrounds and Backgrounds

For studies of *geography*, see F. A. Carlson, Geography of
Latin America (New York, 1936); Preston E. James, Latin
America, rev. ed. (New York, 1950); Robert S. Platt, Latin
America: Countrysides and United Regions (New York, 1943);
Isaiah Bowman, South America: A Geography Reader (Chicago,
1915); C. F. Jones, South America (New York, 1930); E. W.
Shanahan, South America: An Economic and Regional Geo-
graphy (New York, 1927); R. H. Whitbeck, et al., The Econ-
omic Geography of South America, rev. ed. (New York, 1940);
A. Curtis Wilgus, Latin America in Maps, Historic, Econ-
omic, Geographic (New York, 1943).

On the *Indian Background of Mexico*, William H. Prescott,
The Conquest of Mexico, many editions, is still exciting
and revealing although subject to correction in the light
of subsequent archaeological study. Sylvanus G. Morley,
The Ancient Maya (Stanford, 1956) and George C. Vaillant,
The Aztecs of Mexico (New York, 1941) offer scholarly and
exciting introduction to those two civilizations. Also
see Herbert J. Spinden, Ancient Civilizations of Mexico
and Central America, 3rd rev. ed. (New York, 1928); J.
Eric Thompson, Mexico Before Cortés (New York, 1933) and
The Civilization of the Mayas (Chicago, 1936); Alfonso
Caso, The Aztecs, People of the Sun, tr. by Lowell Dunham,
il. by Miguel Covarrubias (Norman, 1958); J. Eric Thompson,
The Rise and Fall of the Maya Civilization (Norman, 1956).

On the *Indians of South America*, J. H. Steward, ed., Handbook of South American Indians, 6 vols. (Washington, D. C., 1946-50) has superseded earlier works. Readers will still turn to William H. Prescott, the Conquest of Peru, many editions, with profit and delight. Also see Philip A. Means, Ancient Civilizations of the Andes (New York, 1931) and J. Eric Thompson, Archaeology of South America (Chicago, 1936); Victor W. Von Hagen, ed., The Incas of Pedro de Cieza de León, tr. by Harriet de Onís (Norman, 1959).

On the *Iberian Background*, a standard history of Spain is Rafael Altamira y Crevea, Historia de España y de la civilización española, 6 vols. (Barcelona, 1900-30). Founded on Altamira's work is Charles E. Chapman, A History of Spain, tr. by Muna Lee (New York, 1949). Important for understanding Spain is Miguel Cervantes de Saavedra, Don Quixote de la Mancha; see the new translation by Samuel Putnam (New York, 1950). For interpretation of Spain and its people, see Havelock Ellis, The Soul of Spain (Boston, 1926); Martin A. S. Hume, The Spanish People: Their Origin, Growth, and Influence (New York, 1901); Salvador de Madariaga, Englishmen,Frenchmen and Spaniards: An Essay in Comparative Psychology (London, 1931); also Madariaga;s The Rise of the Spanish American Empire (New York, 1947); Ramón Menéndez Pidal, The Spaniards in Their History, tr. by Walter Starkie (London, 1951); Miguel de Unamuno, The Life of Don Quixote and Sancho, tr. by H. P. Earle (New York, 1927). Also invaluable is Roger B. Merriman, The Rise of the Spanish Empire in the Old World and the New, 4 vols. (New York, 1918-1934).

On *Portugal*, the material in English is scant. See H. Morse Stephens, Story of Portugal (New York, 1891); J. P. de Oliveira Martins, A History of Iberian Civilization, tr. by A. F. G. Bell (London, 1930); H. V. Livermore, Portugal and Brazil, An Introduction (Oxford, 1953); W. J. Barnes, Portugal, Gateway to Greatness (London, 1950); Charles E. Newell, A History of Portugal (New York, 1952).

The African Background: Much of the material on this subject is to be found in the various periodicals, especially the Hispanic American Historical Review, the Journal of Negro History, the Sociological and Social Review, and the American Anthropologist. Melville J. Herskovits has done pioneer work in the field contributing numerous valuable monographs. Among his books, The Myth of the Negro Past (New York, 1941) and Dahomey; An Ancient West African Kingdom, 2 vols. (New York, 1938),

are especially recommended. For the general anthropological background, see Alfred Louis Kroeber, Anthropology,
new ed. rev. (New York, 1948). On the ethnology of Africa,
C. G. Seligman, Races of Africa (London, 1939) and Wilfred
D. Hambly, Ethnology of Africa (Chicago, 1930) are both
useful. Fundamental to a study of the slave trade is
Elizabeth Donnan, Documents Illustrative of the Slave Trade
to America, 4 vols. (Washington, D.C., 1930); see espec-
ially Vols. I and II. A few books are indispensable to
the student of the Negro in the New World: Gilberto
Freyre, The Masters and the Slaves, tr. by Samuel Putnam
(New York, 1946); James G. Leyburn, the Haitian People
(New Haven, Conn., 1941); Fernando Ortiz, Hampa Afro-
Cubana -- Los Negros Esclavos (Havana, 1916); Donald
Pierson, Negroes in Brazil (Chicago, 1942); Arthur Ramos,
The Negro in Brazil, tr. by Richard Pattee (Washington,
D.C., 1939); and Frank Tannenbaum, Slave and Citizen, the
Negro in the Americas (New York, 1947); An ambitious and
important pioneer work is José Antonio Saco, Historia de
la esclavitud de la raza africana en el nuevo mundo y en
especial en los países américo-hispanos, 4 vols. (Paris,
1875-79). Valuable articles will be found in The Negro
in the Americas, Public Lectures of the Division of the
Social Sciences of the Graduate School, Howard University,
ed. by Charles H. Wesley (Washington, D.C., 1940).

Part II., The Iberians in the New World

Discovery and Conquest. F. A. Kirkpatrick, The Spanish
Conquistadores (New York, 1934) is excellent. E. G.
Bourne, Spain in America, 1450-1580 (New York, 1904) was
one of the first attempts to counter the leyenda negra.
See also Bernard Moses, The Establishment of Spanish
Rule in America (New York, 1898). For the conquest of
Mexico, Bernal Díaz del Castillo, True History of the
Conquest of New Spain (New York, 1958) is the fascinat-
ing account by one of Cortés's soldiers. William H.
Prescott, The Conquest of Mexico is a classic. For the
conquest of South America, Prescott's The Conquest of
Peru; Philip A. Means, The Fall of the Inca Empire and
tee Spanish Rule in Peru, 1530-1780 (New York, 1932);
and Agustín Edwards, Peoples of Old (London, 1929) --
the story of Chile -- are useful. There are some biogra-
phies of principal actors: Samuel E. Morison, Admiral
of the Ocean Sea, 2 vols. (Boston, 1942) is the best on
Columbus. Others include Morris Bishop, The Odyssey of
Cabeza de Vaca (New York, 1933); J. E. Kelly, Pedro de
Alvarado, Conquistador (Princeton, 1932); Kathleen Romoli,
Balboa of Darién (New York, 1953); R. B. Cunninghame

Graham, Pedro de Valdivia, Conqueror of Chile (London, 1926); the same versatile Cunninghame Graham wrote The Conquest of New Granada, being the life of Gonzalo Jiménez de Quesada (London, 1922) and The Conquest of the River Plate (New York, 1924). Three societies have concentrated on translating early chronicles, histories and narratives -- The Hakluyt Society (founded in Londin in 1846 and names after the sixteenth-century geographer), the Cortés Society (New York), and the Quivira Society (Los Angeles and Albuquerque). Their publications are useful to the student of this period. Also, Germán Arciniegas, Amerigo and the New World: Life and Times of Amerigo Vespucci, tr. by Harriet de Onís (New York, 1955); Frederick J. Pohl, Amerigo Vespucci, Pilot Major (New York, 1944); Stephen Clissold, Conquistador: the Life of Don Pedro Sarmiento de Gamboa (London, 1954); Lewis Hanke, Bartolomé de las Casas: An Interpretation of His Life and Writings (The Hague, 1951); Benjamin Keen, ed., Life of the Admiral Christopher Columbus by his Son Ferdinand (New Brunswick, 1958); Hernando Cortés, Five Letters, 1519-1526, tr. by J. Bayard Morris (London, 1928).

The Spanish Colonial Period

Among the numerous studies of this period, Clarence H. Haring, The Spanish Empire in America (New York, 1947) and Bailey W. Diffie, Latin American Civilization: Colonial Period (Harrisburg, Pa., 1945) are the most satisfactory recent treatments. Salvador de Madariaga, The Rise of the Spanish American Empire (New York, 1947) and The Fall of the Spanish American Empire (New York, 1948) offer eloquent apologia for Spain. Among early eyewitness accounts, Antonio Vásquez de Espinosa, Compendium and Description of the West Indies, tr. by Charles U. Clark (Washington, D.C., 1942) is notable for its penetrating comments on the Spanish American world of about 1600. Alexander von Humboldt, Political Essay on the Kingdom of New Spain, tr. and ed. by John Black, 4 vols. (London, 1811-22), describes Mexico at the end of the colonial era. Also, Philip W. Powell, Soldiers, Indians and Silver: the Northward Advance of New Spain, 1550-1560 (Berkeley, 1952).

Spain's government in America is dealt with by Lillian E. Fisher in her Viceregal Administration in the Spanish Colonies (Berkeley, Calif., 1926) and The Intendant System in the Spanish Colonies (Berkeley, Calif. 1929). Charles H. Cunningham, The Audiencia in the Spanish Colonies as Illustrated by the Audiencia of Manila,

1583-1800 (Berkeley, 1919) is valuable. Three biographies
should be noted: Arthur S. Aiton, Antonio de Mendoze,
First Viceroy of New Spain (Durham, N.C., 1927); A. F.
Zimmerman, Francisco de Toledo: Fifth Viceroy of Peru,
1569-1581 (Caldwell, Id., 1938); H. I. Priestley, José de
Gálvez, Visitor General of New Spain, 1765-1771 (Berkeley,
1916).

The role of *the Church in Spanish America* is treated in
J. L. Mecham, Church and State in Latin America (Chapel
Hill, N.C., 1934); C. H. Haring, The Spanish Empire in
America (New York, 1947); B. W. Diffie, Latin American
Civilization: Colonial Period (Harrisburg, Pa., 1945).
Also see Charles S. Braden, Religious Aspects of the
Conquest of Mexico (Durham, N.C., 1930); Peter M. Dunne,
Pioneer Missions in Northern Mexico (Berkeley, 1944);
R. B. Cunninghame Graham, A Vanished Arcadia: Being
Some Account of the Jesuits in Paraguay, 1607-1767, rev.
ed. (New York, 1924); Herbert E. Bolton, Rim of Christen-
dom: A Biography of Eusebio Francisco Kino, Pacific
Coast Pioneer (New York, 1936). A classic of inaccuracy
is Thomas Gage, Travels in the New World (Norman, 1958).

Man, his land and labor. An invaluable book is Lewis
Hanke, The Spanish Struggle for Justice in the Conquest
of America (Philadelphia, 1949). Also excellent are two
studies by L. B. Simpson: The Encomienda in New Spain:
forced native labor in the Spanish colonies, 1492-1550,
rev. and enl. ed. (Berkeley, Calif., 1950) and The
Repartimiento System of Native Labor in New Spain and
Guatemala (Berkeley, Calif., 1938).

Trade and economics. The following are important. C. H.
Haring, Trade and Navigation between Spain and the Indies
in the time of the Hapsburgs (Cambridge, Mass., 1918);
R. D. Hussey, The Caracas Company, 1728-1784 (Cambridge,
Mass., 1934); C. G. Motten, Mexican Silver and the Enlightenment (Philadelphia, 1950); W. L. Schurz, The Manila
Galleon (New York, 1939); A. P. Whitaker, The Huancavelica
Mercury Mine (Cambridge, Mass., 1941). Earl J. Hamilton
describes the effects of American silver upon Spain in
two books: American Treasure and the Price Revolution
in Spain, 1501-1650 (Cambridge, Mass., 1934) and American
Treasure and the Rise of Capitalism, 1500-1700 (London,
1929).

Intellectual and cultural. See John T. Lanning, Academic
Culture in the Spanish Colonies (New York, 1940); P. J.
Barth, Franciscan Education and the Social Order in

Spanish North America, 1502-1821 (Chicago, 1945); J. V.
Jacobsen, Educational Foundations of the Jesuits in
Sixteenth-Century New Spain (Berkeley, Calif., 1929);
I. A. Leonard, Don Carlos de Sigüenza y Góngora (Berkeley,
Calif., 1929); I. A. Leonard Books of the Brave (Cambridge,
Mass., 1949); I. A. Leonard, Baroque Times in Old Mexico
(Ann Arbor, 1959); Bernard Moses, Spanish Colonial Litera-
ture in South America (New York, 1922); A. P. Whitaker,
ed., Latin America and the Enlightenment (New York, 1942).

The Portuguese Empire in America

J. P. Calógeras, A History of Brazil, tr. and ed. by
P. A. Martin (Chapel Hill, 1939) is the best history
available in English. The poet Robert Southey's History
of Brazil, 3 vols. (London, 1817-1833) is a fascinating
but sometimes unreliable account of the colony. The
ablest history of the colony is F. A. de Varnhagen,
Historia geral do Brasil, 3rd ed., 5 vols. (São Paulo,
1927-30). Also Charles R. Boxer, The Dutch in Brazil,
1624-1654 (Oxford, 1957); Alexander N. Marchant, From
Barter to Slavery: The Economic Relations of Portuguese
and Indians in the Settlements of Brazil, 1500-1580
(Baltimore, 1942).

Part III., The New World Breaks With the Old

For understanding the forces which led to *the independence movement*, three books by Bernard Moses are impor-
tant: The Intellectual Background of the Revolution in
South America, 1810-1824 (New York, 1926); South America
on the Eve of Independence (New York, 1908); Spain's
Declining Power in South America, 1730-1806 (Berkeley,
Calif., 1919). Also see Lillian E. Fisher, The Background of the Revolution for Mexican Independence
(Boston, 1934); John Rydjord, Foreign Interest in the
Independence of New Spain (Durham, N.C., 1935); Alexander
von Humboldt, Personal Narrative of Travels to the
Equinoctial Regions of the New Continent during the years
1799-1804, tr. by Helen M. Williams, 7 vols. (London,
1814-1829). For the influence of other nations, see
A. P. Whitaker, The United States and the Independence
of Latin America, 1800-1830 (Baltimore, 1941); Alfred
Hasbrouck, Foreign Legionaires in the Liberation of
Spanish South America (New York, 1928); C. C. Griffin,
The United States and the Disruption of the Spanish
Empire, 1810-1822 (New York, 1937); C. K. Webster, ed.,
Britain and the Independence of Latin America 1812-1830,
2 vols., (London, 1928); William S. Robertson, France

and Latin American Independence (Baltimore, 1939); J. Fred
Rippy, Joel R. Poinsett, Versatile American (Durham, N.C.,
1935); J. Fred Rippy, Rivalry of the United States and
Great Britain over Latin America, 1808-1830 (Baltimore,
1929); William R. Manning, Diplomatic Correspondence of
the United States Concerning the Independence of the Latin
American Nations, 3 vols. (New York, 1925); R. A. Humphreys,
ed., British Consular Reports on the Trade and Politics of
Latin America, 1824-1826 (London, 1940); William Kaufmann,
British Policy and the Independence of Latin America, 1804-
1828 (New Haven, Conn., 1951); Benjamin Keen, David Curtis
DeForest and the Revolution of Buenos Aires (New Haven,
Conn., 1947); S. F. Bemis, The Latin American Policy of
the United States (New York, 1943).

For biographical studies -- all too scarce -- of the chief
actors *in the Spanish American struggle for independence*,
see W. S. Robertson, The Rise of the Spanish American
Republics as Told in the Lives of their Liberators (New
York, 1918). Among biographies of individuals, there is
W. S. Robertson, The Life of Miranda, 2 vols. (Chapel
Hill, N.C., 1929); Bartolomé Mitre, The Emancipation of
South America (London, 1893), a condensed translation by
William Pilling of Mitre's Historia de San Martín y de la
emancipación sudamericana, 2nd ed. (Buenos Aires, 1890);
R. B. Cunninghame Graham, José Antonio Páez (London,
1929); G. A. Sherwell, Antonio José de Sucre (Washington,
D. C., 1924); Ricardo Rojas, San Martín, Knight of the
Andes, tr. by H. Brickell and C. Videla (New York, 1945);
T. Cochrane, Narrative of Services in the Liberation of
Chile, Peru and Brazil, 2 vols., (London, 1859); V. A.
Belaúnde, Bolívar and the Political Thought of the
Spanish American Revolution (Baltimore, 1938); W. S.
Robertson, Iturbide of Mexico (Durham, N.C., 1952);
Sergio Bagú, Mariano Moreno: Pasión y vida del hombre de
Mayo (Buenos Aires, 1939). Among the numerous books on
Simón Bolívar, the most useful are H. Angell, Simón
Bolívar, South American Liberator (New York, 1930); G.
Masur, Simón Bolívar (Albuquerque, N. M., 1948); S. de
Madariaga, Bolívar (New York, 1952). Valuable material
on Bolívar will be found in Vicente Lecuna, comp.,
Selected Writings of Bolívar, tr. by Lewis Bertrand,
2 vols. (New York, 1951).

Part IV., Mexico

Of the many *general books* in Spanish, the following are
significant. For a conservative interpretation, Lucas
Alamán, Historia de Méjico desde los primeros movimientos

que preparan su independencia en el año 1808 hasta la
época presente, 5 vols. (México, 1849-52); Mariano Cuevas,
S. J., Historia de la nación mexicana (México, 1940); and
José Vasconcelos, Breve Historia de México, 4th ed., (Méx-
ico, 1938). For more dispassionate interpretation, Justo
Sierra, ed., México su evolución social, 3 vols. (México,
1900-02). For studies in English, Henry Bamford Parkes,
A History of Mexico (New York, 1938) is excellent; H. H.
Bancroft, History of Mexico, 6 vols. (San Francisco,
1883-1888) is still useful as is H. I. Priestley, The
Mexican Nation, A History (New York, 1930). W. H. Call-
cott, Liberalism in Mexico, 1857-1929 (Stanford, 1931);
E. Gruening, Mexico and Its Heritage (New York, 1940);
H. F. Cline, The United States and Mexico (Cambridge,
Mass., 1953); L. B. Simpson, Many Mexicos, 3rd ed., rev.
and enl. (New York, 1952) are all rewarding.

Biographies of the chief figures in Mexican history are
few. W. S. Robertson, Iturbide of Mexico (Durham, N. C.,
1952) is solid; W. H. Callcott, Santa Anna: the story of
an enigma that once was Mexico (Norman, 1936) is the best
on that tawdry hero; Vicente Fuentes Díaz, Gómez Farías
padre de la Reforma (México, 1948) hardly does justice to
that liberal, and readers are urged to watch for C. Alan
Hutchinson's forthcoming study; José Valadés, Alamán,
estadista e historiador (México, 1938) is the work of an
admirer. Benito Juárez is treated sympathetically by
Justo Sierra, Juárez, su obra y su tiempo (México, 1905-
06), and critically by Francisco Bulnes, El verdadero
Juárez (México, 1904); the best account in English is
Ralph Roeder, Juárez and his Mexico, 2 vols. (New York,
1947). Egon Corti, Maximilian and Charlotte of Mexico,
2 vols., tr. by C. A. Phillips (New York, 1928) is
excellent. F. A. Knapp, Jr., Life of Sebastián Lerdo de
Tejada, 1823-1889 (Austin, Tex., 1951) is the only book
in English on that neglected statesman. Carleton Beals,
Porfirio Díaz, Dictator of Mexico (Philadelphia, 1932)
is interesting but passionate. There is lack of sound
biographies on men since 1910. Harry Dunn, The Crimson
Jester, Zapata of Mexico (New York, 1933) is sketchy.
Nathaniel and Sylvia Weyl, The Reconquest of Mexico, the
Years of Lázaro Cárdenas (New York, 1939) is a leftish
account of that president. Also useful is Stanley R.
Ross, Francisco I. Madero, Apostle of Mexican Democracy
(New York, 1955).

Of *social and economic studies* of Mexico, the following
are significant. On agrarian questions: Tom Gill, Land
of Hunger in Mexico (Washington, D. C., 1951); G. M.

McBride, The Land Systems of Mexico (New York, 1923);
Eyler N. Simpson, The Ejido: Mexico's Way Out (Chapel
Hill, N. C., 1937); Frank Tannenbaum, The Mexican
Agrarian Revolution (New York, 1929); Frank Tannenbaum,
Mexico: The Struggle for Peace and Bread (New York,
1950); Nathan Whetten, Rural Mexico (Chicago, 1948).
On labor, Marjorie Clark, Organized Labor in Mexico
(Chapel Hill, N. C., 1934) is one of the few studies
available. Of sociological studies, the best are Robert
E. Redfield, Tepoztlán, a Mexican Village (Chicago,
1930); Robert E. Redfield, The Folk Culture of Yucatan
(Chicago, 1941); Oscar Lewis, Life in a Mexican Village:
Tepoztlán Restudied (Urbana, Ill., 1951). A revealing
book is Oscar Lewis, Five Families: Mexican Case Studies in the Culture of Poverty (New York, 1959). On
economic studies, the most significant is Sanford Mosk,
Industrial Revolution in Mexico (Berkeley, 1950).

Of the many travel books and eyewitness accounts of
events in Mexico, a few deserve mention: J. R. Poinsett,
Notes on Mexico made in the autumn of 1822 (Philadelphia,
1824); H. G. Ward, Mexico in 1827, 2 vols. (London, 1828);
Mme, Calderón de la Barca, Life in Mexico (Boston, 1843);
Waddy Thompson, Recollections of Mexico (New York, 1847);
C. M. Flandrau, Viva Mexico (New York, 1908); three
books by Edith O'Shaughnessy, Diplomatic Days (New York,
1917), A Diplomat's Wife in Mexico (New York, 1916); and
Intimate Pages of Mexican History (New York, 1920).
Graham Greene, Another Mexico (New York, 1939) is reveal-
ing.

Part V., Middle America

Among useful *general books* on the Caribbean area are
Dexter Perkin, The United States and the Caribbean
(Cambridge, Mass., 1947); J. Fred Rippy, the Caribbean
Danger Zone (New York, 1940); A. C. Wilgus, ed., The
Caribbean Area (Washington, D. C., 1934); A. C. Wilgus,
ed., The Caribbean at Mid Century (Gainesville, Fla.,
1951). Older, but still valuable, are C. L. Jones, The
Caribbean Interests of the United States (New York,
1916); C. L. Jones, The Caribbean since 1900 (New York,
1936). A colorful book is Germán Arciniegas, Caribbean:
Sea of the New World, tr. by Harriet de Onís, (New York,
1946).

Cuba's history is told in Charles E. Chapman, A History
of the Cuban Republic (New York, 1927). A popular and
sensitive description is Erna Fergusson, Cuba (New York,

1946). Analysis of the island's economy will be found
in R. L. Buell, et al., Problems of the New Cuba (New
York, 1935); L. H. Jenks, Our Cuban Colony; A Study in
Sugar (New York, 1928); Fernando Ortiz, Cuban Counter-
point: Tobacco and Sugar, tr. by Harriet de Onís (New
York, 1947); H. C. Wallich, Monetary Problems of an
Export Economy: The Cuban Experience, 1914-1947
(Cambridge, Mass., 1950). A biography of Cuba's chief
patriot is Jorge Mañach, Martí: Apostle of Freedom,
tr. by Coley Taylor (New York, 1950). R. H. Fitzgibbon,
Cuba and The United States, 1900-1935 (Menasha, Wis.,
1935) is an excellent analysis of the period. The best
book since the rise of Fidel Castro is Ruby Hart
Phillips, Cuba, Land of Paradox (New York, 1959).

Haiti's history and problems are best outlined in H. P.
Davis, Black Democracy, rev. ed. (New York, 1936), and
J. G. Leyburn, The Haitian People (New Haven, 1941).
M. J. Herskovits, Life in a Haitian Valley (New York,
1937) gives a sensitive analysis of the life of the
Haitian peasant. L. L. Montague, Haiti and the United
States, 1714-1938 (Durham, N. C., 1940), and R. W. Logan,
The Diplomatic Relations of the United States with Haiti,
1776-1891 (Chapel Hill, N. C., 1941) are careful studies.
An early traveler's report is Jonathan Brown, The His-
tory and Present Condition of St. Domingo (Philadelphia,
1837). A delightful retelling of Haitian history is
Selden Rodman, Haiti: The Black Republic (New York,
1954). Among biographies, Stephen Alexis, Black Libera-
tor; The Life of Toussaint Louverture, tr. by W. Stirling
(New York, 1949), and J. W. Vandercook, Black Majesty,
The Life of Christophe, King of Haiti (New York, 1928)
are interesting.

The Dominican Republic's history is told in Sumner Welles,
Naboth's Vineyard; the Dominican Republic, 1844-1924, 2
vols. (New York, 1928). The American intervention is
criticized in Melvin Knight, The Americans in Santo
Domingo (New York, 1928). The current dictatorship is
luridly described in Albert C. Hicks, Blood in the
Streets, the Life and Rule of Trujillo (New York, 1946).
A solid analysis of the Trujillo period is Jesús Galíndez,
La Era de Trujillo (Santiago, Chile, 1956).

The *history of Central America* is best told in Dana G.
Munro, The Five Republics of Central America (New York,
1918). C. M. Wilson, connected with the United Fruit
Company, has written ably and readably in Challenge and
Opportunity; Central America (New York, 1941); Empire

in Green and Gold: The Story of the American Banana Trade
(New York, 1947); Middle America (New York, 1944). The
United Fruit Company is treated critically in Charles D.
Kepner and Jay Soothill, The Banana Empire (New York,
1935) and Charles D. Kepner, Social Aspects of the Banana
Industry (New York, 1936). Invaluable light on early
days is shed by Ephraim G. Squier, Travels in Central
America, 2 vols. (New York, 1853), J. L. Stephens, Inci-
dents of Travel in Central America, Chiapas, and Yucatán,
new ed., by R. L. Predmore (New Brunswick, N. J., 1949).

There are few adequate books on the *individual republics
of Central America*. C. L. Jones, Guatemala, Past and
Present (Minneapolis, 1940) is admirable. E. Fergusson,
Guatemala (New York, 1937), and Vera Kelsey and L. de J.
Osborne, Four Keys to Guatemala (New York, 1948) are
sensitive interpretations of the people. Mary P.
Holleran, Church and State in Guatemala (New York, 1949)
is recommended. William S. Stokes, Honduras: An Area
Study in Government (Madison, Wisc., 1950) and Percy F.
Martin, Salvador of the Twentieth Century (New York,
19 1) are useful. C. L. Jones, Costa Rica and the Civ-
ilization in the Caribbean (Madison, Wisc., 1935) and
J. and M. Biesanz, Costa Rican Life (New York, 1944) are
the most satisfactory for that republic. There is a
scarcity of material on Nicaragua, but Isaac J. Cox,
Nicaragua and the United States, 1909-1927 (Boston, 1937)
is soundly done. Highly entertaining is William O.
Scroggs, Filibusters and Financiers: The Story of
William Walker and his Associates (New York, 1916).

The story of Panama and the Canal is well told in
Lawrence O. Ealy, The Republic of Panama in World Affairs,
1903-1950 (Philadelphia, 1951); Gerstle Mack, The Land
Divided: A History of the Panama Canal and other
Isthmian Canal Projects (New York, 1944); in two books
by Miles P. DuVal, Cadiz to Cathay (Stanford, Calif.,
1940) and And the Mountains Will Move (Stanford, Calif.,
1947). J. and M. Biesanz, The People of Panama (New
York, 1955) is the best analysis of that country.

Part VI., The Lands of the Spanish Main

Material on *Venezuela* will be found in the general books
cited earlier. There is no adequate history in English,
although W. E. and A. L. Marsland, Venezuela Through Its
History (New York, 1954) offers a popular introduction
to the subject. In Spanish, Carlos Pereyra, Historia de
la América Española, Vol. VI, is helpful; also José Gil

Fortoul, Historia constitucional de Venezuela, 2 vols.,
3rd ed., (Caracas, 1942). The best of the popular books
are E. Fergusson, Venezuela (New York, 1939) and T. R.
Ybarra, Young Man of Caracas (New York, 1941). For
brief biographies of Páez, Guzmán Blanco, Castro and
Gómez, see J. Fred Rippy in A. C. Wilgus, ed., South
American Dictators During the First Century of Indepen-
dence (Washington, D. C., 1937). Thomas Rourke (Pseud.),
Gómez, Tyrant of the Andes (New York, 1948) is readable.
George S. Wise, Caudillo: A Portrait of Antonio Guzmán
Blanco (New York, 1941) is the only biography in English
of that dictator. Edwin Lieuwen, Petroleum in Venezuela:
A History (Berkeley, 1954) is valuable as is his Vene-
zuela (New York, 1961).

Material on *Colombia* is scanty. J. M. Henao and G.
Arrubla, A History of Colombia, tr. by J. Fred Rippy
(Chapel Hill, N. C., 1938) is unsatisfactory but it is
the best available history. The reader must depend upon
the brief treatments in the general surveys cited earlier.
W. M. Gibson, The Constitutions of Colombia (Durham,
N. C., 1948) has good historical material. J. Fred Rippy
has brief essays on Mosquera, Núñez, and Reyes in A. C.
Wilgus, ed., South American Dictators, (Washington, D. C.,
1937). In Spanish, useful books are I. Liévano Aguirre,
Rafael Núñez, 2nd ed. (Bogotá, 1944); Rafael Núñez, La
reforma política en Colombia, 2 vols. (Bogotá, 1944);
Miguel Samper, Escritos politico-económicos, 2 vols.
(Bogotá, 1898); Luis E. Nieto Arteta, Economía y cultura
en la historia de Colombia (Bogotá, 1942); Luis López de
Mesa, De cómo se ha formado la nación colombiana (Bogotá,
1934); Kathleen Romoli, Colombia, Gateway to South America
(New York, 1941) is a popular and discriminating intro-
duction. E. T. Parks, Colombia and the United States,
1765-1934 (Durham, N. C., 1935) and A. P. Whitakes, The
United States and South America, the Northern Republics
(Cambridge, Mass., 1948) are excellent studies.

Part VII., The Indian Lands of the Andes

The history of *Ecuador* has never been adequately written.
In addition to the brief accounts in general books, see
Oscar Efrén Reyes, Breve Historia del Ecuador, 3rd ed.
(Quito, 1949); Charles R. Enock, Ecuador (New York, 1914);
George Blanksten, Ecuador: Constitutions and Caudillos
(Berkeley, 1951). Albert Franklin, Ecuador (New York,
1943) is a fine interpretation. For the Indian, see
Moisés Sáenz, Sobre el indio ecuatoriano (Mexico, 1933).
Richard Pattee, Gabriel García Moreno y el Ecuador de su

tiempo (Quito, 1941) is valuable. F. Hassaurek, Four
Years among Spanish Americans (New York, 1868) has useful
material on García Moreno. Teodoro Wolf, Geografía y
geología del Ecuador (Leipzig, 1892) is the work of a
German Jesuit. See N.A.N. Cleven, Dictator Juan José
Flores, in A. C. Wilgus, ed., South American Dictators,
(Washington, D. C., 1937). John Collier, Jr. and Anibal
Buitrón, The Awakening Valley (Chicago, 1949) is a
beautifully illustrated and over-optimistic introduction
to the Otavalo Indians. Elsie W. Parsons, Peguche,..
Ecuador: A Study of Andean Indians (Chicago, 1945) is
a significant study.

There is no adequate history of *Peru* in English. See
Charles R. Enock, Peru (London, 1925); Clements R. Mark-
ham, A History of Peru (Chicago, 1892); Percy F. Martin,
Peru of the Twentieth Century (London, 1911). Jorge
Basadre, Historia de la República del Perú, 1822-1908,
2 vols., rev. ed. (Lima, 1949) is excellent as is the
same author's Chile, Perú y Bolivia Independientes
(Barcelona, 1948), also his Perú: Problema y posibilidad
(Lima, 1931). N.A.N. Cleven, in A. C. Wilgus, ed., South
American Dictators (Washington, D.C., 1937) has brief
biographies of Gamarra, Orbegoso, Salaverry, and Santa
Cruz. Watt Stewart, Henry Meiggs, Yankee Pizarro (Durham,
N.C., 1946) is invaluable for the period from the 1860's
to the 1880's. W. J. Dennis, Tacna and Arica (New Haven,
Conn., 1931) is the best introduction to the war of the
Pacific. Manuel González Prada, Figuras y figurones
(Paris, 1948), Propaganda y ataque (Buenos Aires, 1939)
and other essays are brilliant analyses. Moisés Sáenz,
Sobre el indio peruano (México, 1933) is the best study
of the Indian. José Mariátegui, Siete ensayos de inter-
pretación de la realidad peruana, 2nd ed. (Lima, 1943) is
a Marxian interpretation of Peru's economy. Victor Raúl
Haya de la Torre, Adónde va Indoamérica, 2nd ed. (Santiago,
1935) introduces the APRA. Criticism of Haya de la Torre
will be found in Eudocio Revines, The Yenan Road (New
York, 1951). A. P. Whitaker, The United States and South
America: Northern Republics (Cambridge, Mass., 1948)
should be consulted. Thomas R. Ford, Man and Land in
Peru (Gainesville, Fla., 1955) is important. A sympathetic treatment of APRA is Harry Kantor, The Ideology and
Program of the Peruvian Aprista Movement (Berkeley, 1953).

Bolivia's history is recited briefly in the general sur-
veys already noted. The ablest history is Alcides Argüedes,
Historia general de Bolivia, 1809-1921 (La Paz, 1922).
A. P. Whitaker, The United States and South America:

Northern Republics (Cambridge, Mass., 1948) is helpful.
N.A.N. Cleven, in A. C. Wilgus, ed., South American Dicta-
tors (Washington, D.C., 1937) has a brief study of
Mariano Melgarejo. For current interpretation see
Harold Osborne, Bolivia, A Land Divided (London, 1955)
and Robert J. Alexander, The Bolivian National Revolution
(New Brunswick, 1958).

Part VIII., Chile

The best history in English is Luis Galdames, A History
of *Chile*, tr. and ed. by I. J. Cox (Chapel Hill, N.C.,
1941); in Spanish, Diego Barrios Araña, Historia general
de Chile, 16 vols., 2nd ed. (Santiago, 1940). Interpretative of Chilean history is Agustín Edwards, The Dawn
(London, 1931) and My Native Land (London, 1928). A
masterly analysis of the land problem is G. M. McBride,
Chile, Land and Society (New York, 1936). Also see I. J.
Cox, Chile, in A. C. Wilgus, Argentina, Brazil and Chile
Since Independence (Washington, D. C., 1935), and Jorge
Basadre, Chile, Perú y Bolivia independientes (Barcelona,
1948). For analysis of Chile's politics, see Alberto
Edwards, La fronda aristocrática (Santiago, 1945); J. R.
Stevenson, The Chilean Popular Front (Philadelphia, 1942);
G. Butland, Chile, An Outline (London, 1951). For bio-
graphies, see Francisco A. Encina, Portales, 2 vols.
(Santiago, 1934); Lewis Bealer, in A. C. Wilgus, ed.,
South American Dictators (Washington, D. C., 1937),
studies of Diego Portales and Balmaceda: Joaquim Nabuco,
Balmaceda (Santiago, 1914). For economic analysis, see
Oscar Alvarez Andrews, Historia del desarrollo industrial
de Chile (S tiago, 1936); Paul Ellsworth, Chile, an
Economy in Transition (New York, 1945). For travel
accounts, see María Graham, Journal of a Residence in
Chile, during the year 1822; and a Voyage from Chile to
Brazil, in 1823 (London, 1824); Erna Fergusson, Chile
(New York, 1943); Stephen Clissold, Chilean Scrapbook
(London, 1952). An important new study is La División
de la Tierra en Chile Central, by Gene Ellis Martin
(Santiago, 1960).

Part IX., The Republics of the Río de la Plata

The most useful books on *the history of Argentina* in
English are F. A. Kirkpatrick, A History of the Argentine
Republic (Cambridge, Mass., 1931); Ricardo Levene, A
History of Argentina, tr. and ed. by W. S. Robertson
(Chapel Hill, N.C., 1937); Ysabel Fisk Rennie, The
Argentine, Brazil and Chile Since Independence (Washington,

D.C., 1935); V. Fidel López, Historia de la República
Argentina, 8 vols. (Buenos Aires, 1949-50); Enrique de
Gandía, Historia de la República Argentina en el siglo
XIX (Buenos Aires, 1940). For political developments see
Ismael Bucich Escobar, Historia de los presidentes de
Argentina, enl. ed. (Buenos Aires, 1934); José Ingenieros,
La evolución de las ideas argentinas (Buenos Aires, 1946);
A. F. Macdonald, Government of the Argentine Republic (New
York, 1942); Leo S. Rowe, The Federal System of the Argen-
tine Republic (Washington, D.C., 1921). For economic and
social analysis, see Miron Burgin, The Economic Aspects of
Argentine Federalism, 1820-52 (Cambridge, Mass., 1946);
Simon G. Hanson, Argentine Meat and the British Market
(London, 1938); Madaline Nichols, The Gaucho (Durham, N.C.,
1942); Mark Jefferson, Peopling the Argentine Pampa (New
York, 1926); V. L. Phelps, The International Economic
Position of Argentina (Philadelphia, 1938); C. C. Taylor,
Rural Life in Argentina (Baton Rouge, La., 1938); Felix
Weil, Argentina, The United States and the Inter-American
System, 1880-1914 (Cambridge, 1957). A useful analysis is
George Pendle, Argentina (London, 1955). Also important,
Arthur P. Whitaker, Argentine Upheaval: Perón's Fall and
the New Regime (New York, 1956).

For biographies: Lewis W. Bealer in A. C. Wilgus, ed.,
South American Dictators (Washington, D.C., 1937) has
brief sketches on Rivadavia, Quiroga, Rosas and Urquiza:
Octavio Amadeo, Vidas Argentinas, 6th ed. (Buenos Aires,
1940) deals with Pelligrini, Roca, Alem, Sáenz Peña, etc.
Also see C. Galván Moreno, Rivadavia, el estadista genial
(Buenos Aires, 1940); C. Ibarguren, Juan Manuel de Rosas,
3rd ed. (Buenos Aires, 1940); and J. M. Ramos Mejía, Rosas
y su tiempo, 3 vols., 2nd ed. (Buenos Aires, 1907); A. W.
Bunkley, The Life of Sarmiento (Princeton, N.J., 1952);
Pablo Rojas Paz, Alberdi, el ciudadano de la soledad, 2nd
ed. (Buenos Aires, 1941); J. M. Niño, Mitre, 2 vols.
(Buenos Aires, 1906); Manuel Gálvez, Vida de Hipólito
Irigoyen, 2nd ed., (Buenos Aires, 1939); Raúl Larra,
Lisandro de la Torre (Buenos Aires, 1942). For studies
of the Perón regime, see R. J. Alexander, The Perón Era
(New York, 1951); G. I. Blanksten, Perón's Argentina
(Chicago, 1953). Of the many descriptions of Argentina
by travelers, the following are illuminating: Joseph
Andrews, Journey from Buenos Ayres, etc., 2 vols. (London,
1827); P. P. King, Robert Fitzroy, and Charles Darwin,
Narrative of the Surveying Voyages of His Majestys Ships
Adventure and Beagle, etc., 4 vols. (London, 1839); J.
Anthony King, Twenty-four years in the Argentine Republic
(Buenos Aires, 1939); Thomas Jefferson Page, La Plata,

the Argentine Confederation, and Paraguay (New York, 1859);
Woodbine Parish, Buenos Aires and the Provinces of Río de
la Plata (London, 1852); Thomas A. Turner, Argentina and
the Argentines, Notes and Impressions, 1885-1890 (London,
1892); Benjamín Vicuña Mackenna La Argentina en el año
1855 (Buenos Aires, 1936).

There is scant material on *Uruguay*. W. H. Koebel, Uruguay
(London, 1911) is the only general history in English.
See Pablo Blanco Acevedo, Historia de la República Orien-
tal del Uruguay, 6 vols. (1910). For modern description
and analysis, see George Pendle, Uruguay, South America's
First Welfare State (London, 1952); Simon G. Hanson, Utopia
in Uruguay (New York, 1938); and the excellent study by
R. H. Fitzgibbon, Uruguay, Portrait of a Democracy (New
Brunswick, N.J., 1954). For description of the country,
see W. H. Hudson, The Purple Land (various eds.).

The best history of *Paraguay* is H. G. Warren, Paraguay:
An Informal History (Norman, 1949). C. A. Washburn,
History of Paraguay, 2 vols. (Boston, 1871) is an attack
by a disgruntled United States official. For material on
Dr. Francia, see Guillermo Cabanellas, El Dictator del
Paraguay, Dr. Francia (Buenos Aires, 1946); the historical
novel by E. L. White, El Supremo (New York, 1916); J. P.
Robertson and W. P. Robertson, Letters on Paraguay, 3 vols.
(London, 1938-39); J. Rengger and I. Longchamp, The Reign
of Doctor Joseph Gaspard Roderick de Francia, in Paraguay
(London, 1927). Lewis W. Bealer in A. C. Wilgus, ed.,
South American Dictators (Washington, D.C., 1937) has
brief sketches of Francia, Carlos Antonio López, and
Francisco Solano López. Pelham H. Box, The Origins of
the Paraguayan War (Urbana, Ill., 1930) is an excellent
study. Among contemporary reports on the Paraguayan War,
see Richard F. Burton, Letters from the Battlefield of
Paraguay (London, 1870); G. F. Masterman, Seven Eventful
Years in Paraguay, 2nd ed., (London, 1870); G. Thompson,
The War in Paraguay (London, 1869). A fine analysis of
social conditions is Philip Raine, Paraguay (New Brunswick, N.J., 1956).

Part X., Brazil

General books on Brazil include João Pandiá Calógeras, A
History of Brazil, tr. and ed. by P. A. Martin (Chapel
Hill, N.C., 1939); J. Armitage, The History of Brazil
(London, 1836); L. F. Hill, ed., Brazil (Berkeley, 1947);
T. L. Smith and Alexander Marchant, eds., Brazil; Portrait
of Half a Continent (New York, 1951); Gilberto Freyre,

Brazil, An Interpretation (New York, 1945); Roy Nash, The
Conquest of Brazil (New York, 1926). For the economic
geography of Brazil, see Preston James, Brazil (New York,
1946). For cultural analysis, see Fernando de Azevedo,
Brazilian Culture; An Introduction to the Study of Culture
in Brazil, tr. by W. R. Crawford (New York, 1950). The
literature of Brazil is introduced in Samuel Putnam,
Marvelous Journey; Four Centuries of Brazilian Literature
(New York, 1948). José Francisco de Rocha Pombo, História
de Brasil, 10 vols. (Rio de Janeiro, 1905) is a serious
study. Two books by H. G. James are useful: The Consti-
tutional System of Brazil (Washington, D.C., 1923), Brazil
After A Century of Independence (New York, 1925). A popular interpretation is Hernane Tavares De Sa, The Brazilians:
People of Tomorrow (New York, 1947).

There are few adequate *biographies of Brazilians*. Sergio
Correa de Costa, Every Inch a King, tr. by Samuel Putnam
(New York, 1950) deals with Pedro I. Mary W. Williams, Dom
Pedro the Magnanimous, Second Emperor of Brazil (Chapel
Hill, N.C., 1937) is excellent. An important work is
Joaquim Nabuco, Um estadista do Império: Nabuco de Araujo,
sua Vida suas Opiniões, sua Epoca, 3 vols. (Paris, 1898-
1900). Carolina Nabuco, The Life of Joaquim Nabuco, tr.
and ed. by R. Hilton (Stanford, Calif., 1950) is the story
of the great abolitionist.

Among *economic and social studies of Brazil*, Gilberto
Freyre, Masters and the Slaves, tr. and ed. by Samuel
Putnam (New York, 1946) is notable. Other significant
books are C. Simonsen, Brazil's Industrial Revolution
(São Paulo, 1939); J. F. Normano, Brazil: A Study of
Economic Types (Chapel Hill, N.C., 1935); Donald Pierson,
Negroes in Brazil: A Study of Race Contact in Bahia
(Chicago, 1942); Arthur Ramos, The Negro in Brazil, tr.
by R. Pattee (Washington, D.C., 1939); T. Lynn Smith,
Brazil: Peoples and Institutions (Baton Rouge, La., 1946);
H. W. Spiegel, The Brazilian Economy: Chronic Inflation
and Sporadic Industrialization (Philadelphia, 1949).
Studies of *Brazil's international relations* include A. K.
Manchester, British Pre-eminence in Brazil, Its Rise and
Decline (Chapel Hill, N.C., 1933); L. F. Hill, Diplomatic
Relations between the United States and Brazil (Durham,
N.C. 1932). A fundamental economic study is George Wythe,
et al., Brazil, An Expanding Economy (New York, 1949).

Part XI., Latin America and the United States

Basic in importance for the study of *Latin American relations with the United States* are Samuel F. Bemis, The

Latin American Policy of the United States (New York,
1943); J. W. Gentenbein, ed., The Evolution of Our Latin
American Policy; A Documentary Record (New York, 1950);
William R. Manning, ed., Diplomatic Correspondence of
the United States: Inter-American Affairs, 1831-1860,
12 vols. (Washington, D.C., 1932-39); J. Fred Rippy,
Latin America in World Politics, 3rd ed. (New York, 1938);
J. B. Scott, ed., The International Conferences of American States, 1889-1928 (New York, 1931); Graham H. Stuart,
Latin America and the United States, 4th ed. (New York,
1931-43). To these should be added the invaluable studies
by Dexter Perkins: The Monroe Doctrine, 1823-1826 (Cambridge, Mass., 1927); The Monroe Doctrine, 1867-1907
(Baltimore, 1937), and his summary, Hands Off: A History
of the Monroe Doctrine (Boston, 1941). For Latin opinions
of the United States, see José de Onís, The United States
as Seen by Spanish American Writers, 1776-1890 (New York,
1952). (Note: See also Arthur P. Whitaker, The Western
Hemisphere Idea: Its rise and decline. Ithaca, New York,
Cornell University Press, 1954).

Among the studies of relations between the *United States
and individual Latin American nations*, note: J. M.
Callahan, American Foreign Policy in Mexican Relations
(New York, 1932); C. W. Hackett, The Mexican Revolution
and the United States, 1910-1926 (Boston, 1926); J. Fred
Rippy, The United States and Mexico, rev. ed. (New York,
1931); G. L. Rives, The United States and Mexico, 1821-
1848, 2 vols. (New York, 1931); Justin H. Smith, The War
With Mexico, 2 vols. (New York, 1919); Henry C. Evans,
Chile and its Relations with the United States (Durham,
N.C., 1927); C. H. Haring, Argentina and the United States
(Boston, 1941); E. T. Parks, Colombia and the United
States, 1765-1934 (Durham, N.C., 1935); L. F. Hill,
Diplomatic Relations Between the United States and Brazil
(Durham, N.C., 1932); A. P. Whitaker, The United States
and South America: The Northern Republics (Cambridge,
Mass., 1948). An invaluable study of Inter-American rela-
tions (1933-45) is Laurence Duggan, The Americas: In
Search for Hemispheric Security (New York, 1949). For
light on the workings of the Good Neighbor Policy, see
Josephus Daniels, Shirt-Sleeve Diplomat (Chapel Hill,
N.C., 1947); E. David Cronon, Josephus Daniels in Mexico
(Madison, Wisc., 1960) and Edward O. Guerrant, Roosevelt;s
Good Neighbor Policy (Albuquerque, 1950).

Roman Catholicism in Latin America

Bibliographical Aids
See also p. 252.

81. Agencias religiosas. Barcelona, J. Flors, 1964-65. 4 v.
    In Enciclopedia de orientación bibliográfica, v. 1.,
    sección 9, Misionología. -- Tomás Zumarriego, dir.

82. Delacroix, S., ed. Historie universelle des missiones
    catholiques. Paris, Libraire Grund, 1965-68. 4 v.
    -- See bibliographies at end of each volume.

83. Disch, Anastasius *and* J. Wils, ed. Critical bibliography
    of missiology. Nijmegen, Bestelcentrale der VSKB,
    Publ., 1960. v. 2 (E-2). (Bibliographia ad usum
    seminariorum). Dutch Assoc. of Seminary and Monastery
    Librarians (VSKB), ed. -- Bibliography on the study
    of non-European peoples and cultures. Does not include
    missiological books written on Protestantism or works
    dealing with Protestant missions, however, important
    as a basic bibliographical resource on non-European
    cultures and peoples.

84. Enciclopedia cattolica. Città del Vaticano, Ente per
    l'Enciclopedia cattolica e per il libro cattolico,
    1949-54. illus., maps. 12 v. -- Contains brief but
    helpful articles with maps, about the history and
    circumstances of the missions in each country; with
    statistics and some bibliographies.

85. Gibbons, Wm. Joseph. Basic ecclesiastical statistics for
    Latin America, 1959. Maryknoll, N.Y., Maryknoll Publi-
    cations, 1958. viii, 72 p. (World horizon reports,
    no. 4). -- Bibliography p. 68-72.

86. Guía apostólica de la América Latina. Bogotá, Consejo
    Episcopal de América Latins, 1965.

87. Lescrauweat, J. F., ed. Critical bibliography of ecumenical
    literature Nijmegen, Bestelcentrale ver VSKB, Publ.,
    1965. 7 v. -- Valuable, but limited source.

88. National catholic almanac. Paterson N.J., St. Anthony's
    Guild, 1959-. illus., maps.

89. New catholic encyclopedia... Wm. J. McDonald, ed. New York,
    McGraw-Hill, 1967. illus., maps. 15 v. -- 17,000

articles, updating 1907 publication. Includes decrees
of Vatican II Council.

90. Rommerskirche, Johannes, O.M.I., Giovanni Dindinger, O.M.I.
et al., ed. Bibliografia missionaria; unione missionaria del clero in Italia, Roma. Isola del Lira, Tip.
ed. M. Pisani, 1935-, annual. -- A basic work to keep
up on the Roman Catholic missionary movement.

91. Santos Fernández, Angel, S. J. Biografía misional.
Santander, España, Editorial Sal Terrae, 1965--
Parte doctrinal, 944 p. Parte II, a limited but
accurate section on Protestant literature in each
country, 1299 p.

92. Statistics on Roman Catholic missionary societies, 1966.

93. Streit, Carolus. Atlas hierarchus. Paderborn, Typographia
Bonifaciana, 1913. 3 v. -- Solid Catholic work.

94. Streit, F. D. Catholic world atlas. Paderborn, St.
Boniface, 1929. 2 v. -- An official publication of
the Society for the Propagation of the Faith.

95. Streit, Robert, O.M.I., G. Dindinger , G. Rommerskirchen,
O.M.I. Bibliotheca missionum. Münster, Aix-la-Chapelle,
1916-66. 22 v. -- Monumental work. Best major collection of missionary bibliography. v. 1. and 2. on
America, 1700-1919 period. v. 19, 20, 21 cover until
1950.

96. Vriens, Livinus, O.F.M., cap. Bibliographie analytique de
la missiologie. Nijmegen, Ed., Bestelcentrale der VSKB,
1962. 132 p. (Bibliographia ad usum seminariorum).
-- Includes missiology as well as mission history.

Roman Catholicism in Spanish America

97. Arcita Robledo, Gregorio. La orden franciscana en la
América meridional. Roma, Pontificio Ateneo Antoniano,
1948. xviii, 416 p. -- An official compilation.

98. Bayle, Constantino, S. J. El clero secular y la evangelización de América. Madrid, Consejo Superior de Investigaciones Científicas, Instituto Santo Toribio de
Mogronejo, 1950. xvii, 350 p.

99. _____, España en América. Madrid, 1942.

100. Bolton, Herbert E. The mission as a frontier institution
     in the Spanish American colonies. El Paso, Texas
     Western College Press for Academic Reprints, 1962.
     24 p. -- A reprint of Chap. 3 of *his* Wide horizons
     of American history. New York, Appleton-Century,
     1939. xv, 191 p.

101. _____, The rim of Christendom; a biography of Eusebio
     Francisco Kino, Pacific coast pioneer. New York,
     Russell and Russell, 1960. xiv, 644 p. -- Reissue
     of 1936 ed. An excellent biography of the Jesuit
     pioneer in Lower California, Sonora and Arizona.

102. Borges, Pedro, O.F.M. Los conquistadores espirituales de
     América. Sevilla, Escuela de Estudios Hispano-
     americanos, 1961. 187 p. -- A study of the image of
     the Spanish missionary to the New World.

103. _____, Métodos misionales en la cristianización de
     América, siglo XVII. Madrid, Consejo Superior de
     Investigaciones Científicas, Depto. de Misionlogía
     Española, (n.d.). 567 p. -- Excellent bibliography.
     p. 13-23.

104. Carbía, Rómulo D. Historia de la leyenda negra hispano-
     americana. Buenos Aires, Ediciones Orientación
     Española, 1943. 240 p.

105. Casas, Bartolomé de las. Del único modo de atraer a
     todos los pueblos a la verdadera religión. Méjico,
     Fondo de Cultura Económica, 1942. xliv, 593 p. --
     Intro. by Lewis Hanke. The papers and proceedings
     of the Conference in Observance of the 4th Centennial
     of Death of Fray Bartolomé de las Casas, October 1933,
     will be published by the Aquinas Institute of
     Theology, Dubuque, Iowa.

106. Coleman, William J., Father. The first apostolic delega-
     tion in Rio de Janeiro and its influence in Spanish
     America; a study of papal policy, 1830-40. Washing-
     ton, D.C., Catholic University of America Press, 1950.
     ix, 468 p.

107. Delacroix, S. ed. (no. 82). -- See v. 1, Chap. 9; 2,
     Chaps. 12, 13, 14; 3, Chap. 6; 4, Contemporary
     Missionology.

108. de Egaña, Antonio, S. I., ed. La Teoría del regio vicariato
     español en Indias. Roma, Apud Aeder Universitatis
     Gregorianae, 1948. xxviii, 315 p.

109. Figuero, G. La iglesia y su doctrina en la independencia
     de América. Caracas, 1960. -- An attempt to show the
     relationship between the doctrine of the Church and
     the ideals of the Independence.

110. Gómez Hoyos, Rafael. La iglesia de América en las leyes
     de Indios. Madrid, Instituto Gonzalo Fernández de
     Oviedo, Instituto de Cultura Hispano-americana de
     Bogotá, 1961. 234 p. -- A systematic explanation of
     the origin and development of the Church in Spanish
     America by a Colombian.

111. Hanke, Lewis. The Spanish struggle for justice in the
     conquest of America. Pittsburgh, University of
     Pennsylvania Press, 1949. xi, 217 p. -- A descrip-
     tion of the "encomendero" system for the evangeliza-
     tion of the new continent, of the problems it raised
     and of Bartolomé de las Casas' gallant fight against
     abuses. (Cf. no. 47).

112. Hernáez, Francisco Javier. Colección de bulas, breves y
     otros documentos relativos a la iglesia de América y
     Filipinas. Bruselas, Impr. de A. Vromant, 1879. 2 v.
     -- Reprint, 1964. This work has been republished in
     1964 and should be placed in every library which
     is interested in the study of the origins of Chris-
     tianity in America.

113. Junco, Alfonso. Inquisición sobre la inquisición.
     México, 1949. -- Examines the writings of historians
     who have attacked and defended the Inquisition. Some-
     what sympathetic to the institution.

114. La iglesia frente a la emancipación americana. Santiago,
     1960. -- This book includes among other works, the
     following: Encíclicas de los Papas Pío VII, León
     XII contra la independencia de la América española;
     also Barrios Araña D. La acción del clero en la
     revolución de la independencia de América. (See also,
     Francisco E. Trusso. El derecho de la revolución en
     la emancipación americana. Buenos Aires, Emile Ed.,
     1961. 105 p.).

115. Lea, Henry Chas. The inquisition in Spanish dependencies.
     New York, Macmillan, 1908. xvi, 564 p.

116. Leturia, Pedro, S.I., ed. Relaciones entre la santa sede
      e hispanoamérica. Caracas, Venezuela, Sociedad
      Bolivariana de Venezuela, 1959-60. 3 v.
      v. 1.: Epoca del real patronato, 1492-1800. Rev. by
              Antonio de Egaña, S.I., Caracas, Sociedad
              Bolivariana de Venezuela, 1959.
      v. 2.: Epoca de Bolívar, 1800-35. Rev. by Carmelo
              Sáenz de Santa María, S.I.
      v. 3.: Apéndices: documentos e índices. Rev. by
              Miguel Batllon, S.I.

117. Lewin, Boleslao. La inquisión en hispanoamérica: judíos,
      protestantes y patriotas. Buenos Aires, Editorial
      Proyección, 1962. -- (See also *his* El santo oficio en
      América... Buenos Aires, Sociedad Hebraica Argentina,
      1950. 224 p.). La inquisición has bibliography on
      p. 343-39.

118. Mecham, John Lloyd. Church and state in Latin America;
      a history of politico-ecclesiastical relations. 2.
      rev. ed. Chapel Hill, University of North Carolina
      Press, 1966. viii, 465 p. -- A monumental work.

119. Menéndez y Pelayo, Marcelino. Historia de los hetero-
      doxos españoles. 2. ed. rev. Madrid, Victoriano
      Suárez, 1911-32. 7 v.

120. Picón Salas, Mariano. Pedro Claver: el santo de los
      esclavos. México, Fondo de Cultura Económica, 1950.
      210 p.

121. Reuter, Frank Theo. Catholic influence on American
      colonial policies, 1898-1904. Austin, University of
      Texas Press, 1966. -- Refers primarily to Cuba,
      Guam, Puerto Rico and the Philippines. Of interest
      to students of religion, foreign policy and national
      politics, as well as to non-American historians.

122. Ryan, Edwin. The church in the South American republics.
      2. ed. Westminster, Md., Newman Book Shop, 1943.
      119 p.

123. Specker, Johann. Der einheimische klerus in Sp. Ameri.
      mit besonderer Berücksichtigung auf Kon. u. Synoden.
      Schöneck, 1950. -- An excellent analysis of the
      attempts of the Roman Catholic church to build up an
      indigenous ministry in Mexico and Peru during the
      colonial period, especially in the 16th Century.

124. _____, Die missionsmethode in Sp. Ameri. im 16
Jahrhundert; mit besonderer Berücksichtigung der
Konzilien und Synoden. Schöneck-Beckenried, Schweiz,
Administration der Neuen Zeitschrift für Mission-
swissenschaft, 1953. xxi, 247 p. -- Analysis of the
problems faced by the Roman Catholic church in Latin
America at the beginning of the colonial period.
Detailed descriptions of the early church councils,
syncretism, evangelistic methods and church discipline.

125. Varetto, Juan C. Hostilidad del clero a la independencia
americana. Buenos Aires, Imprenta Metodista, 1922.
164 p. -- A Protestant interpretation.

126. Vicuña, Benjamín Mackenna. Francisco Moyen: or, the
inquisition as it was in South America. London,
Henry Sothern, 1869. vi, 225 p. -- Trans. from the
Spanish original by James W. Duffy, M.D.

127. Vollmar, Edward R. The Catholic church in America: an
historical bibliography. 2. ed. New York, Scarecrow
Press, 1963. 399 p.

*The Roman Catholic Church in Portuguese America**

(No adequate history has been written of the Roman Catholic
church in Brazil, but a bibliography which proves helpful is
to be found in *Revista do Instituto Histórico e Geográfico-
Brasileiro* (Rio de Janeiro) 220:338 July-September 1953.)

128. Azevedo, Thales de. Catholicism in Brazil: a personal
evaluation. *Thought* (Fordham University) 70 p.
summer 1953.

129. _____, O catolicismo no Brasil, um campo para a pesquisa
social. Rio de Janeiro, Ministério da Educacão e
Cultura, Servico de Documentacão, 1955. 70 p. --
Mainly factual. Well documented. Good on Spiritism.
(See also *his* Religious problems and the Church in
Brazil. Salvador, Universidade de Bahia, 1962.)

130. Bastide, Roger. La religion et l'Eglise au Brasil.
Nashville, University of Vanderbilt, 1953.

131. Burks, Arthur J. Bells above the Amazon. New York,

* In 1973 new publications in this section are included in
Section on "BRAZIL - General Background."

McKay, 1951. illus. 241 p. -- An account of the
life and labors of a Franciscan missionary in the Rio
Cururu in Bronce.

132. J. C. de Moraes. O Catolicismo no Brasil. Rio de
Janeiro, Agir, 1950. 213 p. -- Memoirs.

133. Dornas Filho, João. O padroade e a igreja brasileira.
São Paulo, Companhia Editôra Nacional, 1939. (Ser.
5a Brasiliana, v. 125). -- An excellent account of
Church-state relations in Brazil from colonial times
to 1890.

134. Espey, Cletus. Festschrift zum silberjubilaüm der
wiedererrichtung der provnz von der unbefleckten
emfängnis im suden Brasilians, 1901-26. Werl, W.
Franzishus-Grukeree, 1929. 175 p.

135. Guerra, Aloysius. A igreja, está com o povo? Rio de
Janeiro, Cadernos do Povo Brasileiro (n.d.).

136. Guerra, Flávio. A questão religiosa do segundo império
brasileiro; fundamentos históricos. Rio de Janeiro,
Irmãos Pongetti, 1952. xix, 265 p. (Coleccão
'Pensamento e vida', 1).

137. Lacroix, Padre Pascoal. A mais urgente problema do
Brasil o problema sacerdotal e sua soluc~o. Rio de
Janeiro, S.C.J. dos Padres de Sagrado Coracão, 1936.
409 p.

138. Leite, Serafim. História da campanhia de Jesus no
Brasil. Rio de Janeiro, Civilizacão Brasileira,
1938-43. 10 v. -- A history painstakingly narrated
from 1549-1762.

139. Matchler, David E., S.J. Roman Catholicism in Brazil.
St. Louis, Washington University, 1965. (Studies in
comparative international development, v. 1, no. 80).
monograph.

140. Mecham, John Lloyd. Church and state in Latin America;
a history of politico-ecclesiastical relations. rev.
ed. Chapel Hill, University of North Carolina Press,
1966. viii, 465 p. (Cf. no. 118).

141. O catolicismo romano; um simpósio protestante. São
Paulo, ASTE, 1962. 207 p. -- Excellent essays by
Brazilian theological professors, mostly Protestants,

on current subjects and the interpretation of Roman
Catholicism in current Protestant thinking.

142. O'Neill, M. Ancilla. Tristão de Atahyde and the Catholic
social movement in Brazil. Ph. D. thesis, Catholic
University of America, Washington, D.C., 1939. x,
156 p.

143. Revista eclesiástica brasileira. Petrópolis, Est. do
Rio, Editôra Vozes, 1940-. -- Published annually by
Franciscan fathers. US$6.00.

144. Silva, Ismael da, Jr. Notas Históricas sôbre a missão
evangelizadora do Brasil e Portugal. Rio de Janeiro,
Sociedade de Evangelizacão, 1961, 3 v.

145. Strömer, Chrysostomus. Von Bahia zum amazonanstrum: das
arbeitsfeld der deutschen franziskaner in nordbras-
iliers. Berlin, Burchverlag Germania, 1931. 131 p.
On German Franciscans.

146. Tarsier, Pedro. História das perseguicões religiosas no
Brasil. São Paulo, Cultura Moderna, 1936. 2 v. --
Confirms that open persecution has never been sanc-
tioned by government, however documents persecution
at local level.

147. Thornton, Mary Crescentia. The church and freemasonry in
Brazil, 1867-75; a study of regalism. Washington,
D.C., Catholic University of America Press, 1948.
viii, 287 p. -- Select bibliography p. 266-76.

148. Willeke, Vanancio. Three centuries of mission work in
North Brazil. *The Americas* 11:2 October 1958.

149. Wiznitzer, Arnold. Jews in colonial Brazil. New York,
Columbia University Press, 1960. maps. x, 227 p.
-- Relates the activities of the Inquisition in
Brazil against those suspected of practicing the
Jewish faith.

Contemporary Roman Catholicism
See also p. 255.

General Literature

150. Abbott, Walter M., S.J., ed. The documents of Vatican II.
New York, Herder and Herder, 1966. xxvii, 792 p. --

The official texts of the II Vatican Council. An
official Protestant observer at the Council comments
on each text. Angelus book, US$.95.

151. Bates, Margaret. The lay apostolate in Latin America
      today. Washington, D.C., Catholic University of
      America Press, 1966. iv, 66 p. -- Proceedings of
      the 1959 Symposium under auspices of the Institute of
      Iber-American Studies.

152. Beguin, Oliver. Roman Catholicism and the Bible. New
      York, Association Press, 1963. 95 p. -- Detailed
      information on the use of the Bible by Roman
      Catholics in the many parts of the world.

153. Capovilla, Dona Loris, comp. Journey of the soul; Pope
      John XXIII. London, Chapman, 1965. 453 p. -- Trans.
      from Italian by Dorothy White. The writings of the
      late Pope, 1895-1962.

154. Carillo de Albornoz, Angel F. Religious Liberty; a
      general review of the present situation of the world.
      Geneva, WCC, 1964. -- (See also *his* Roman Catholi-
      cism and religious liberty. Geneva, WCC, 1959.
      95 p.).

155. The Christian challenge in Latin America. Maryknoll,
      N.Y., Maryknoll Publishing. -- Hubert Humphrey,
      Frank Tannenbaum, Douglas Hyde, Jos. Gremillion and
      others present their views on the church's opportunity
      to react to political and social revolutions.

156. Clancy, John G. Apostle for our time: Pope Paul VI.
      New York, P. J. Kenedy, 1963. illus. xiv, 238 p.
      -- A popular biography. Bibliographical footnotes.

157. Coleman, William J. Latin American Catholicism; a self-
      evaluation. A study of the Chimbote report. Mary-
      knoll, New York, Maryknoll Publications, 1958. 105
      p. -- To acquaint Catholics in the U.S. with what
      Latin Americans say and think about their own
      Catholicism. See "Notes" p. 88-94.

158. Considine, John J., M. M. A call for forty thousand.
      Toronto, Longsmans-Green, 1946. vi, 319 p. --
      Considered by many to be the book which served most
      effectively to awaken North American Ronam Catholic
      interest in Latin American Catholicism.

159. _____, The Church in new Latin America. Notre Dame, Ind., Fides Press, 1964. maps. xv, 240 p. -- Addresses at the 1964 Catholic Inter-American Cooperation meetings.

160. _____. The missionary's role in socio-economic development. Westminster, Md., Newman Press, 1960. xi, 330 p. -- Includes bibliographies. Result of the Fordham-Rural Life Socio-economic Conference, Maryknoll, N.Y., 1958.

161. _____. New Horizons in Latin America. New York, Dod and Mead, 1958. illus. 379 p. -- Includes presentation by a Catholic mission leader of the current Protestant missionary effort in Latin America.

162. _____. The religious dimension in the new Latin America. Notre Dame, Ind., Fides, 1966. 238 p.

163. _____. ed., Social revolution in the new Latin America: a Catholic approach. Notre Dame, Ind., Fides, 1967. 245 p. -- Eighteen addresses of 1965 Catholic Inter-American Cooperation meetings.

164. D'Antonio, William F. *and* Frederick B. Pike, ed. Religion, revolution and reform: new forces of change in Latin America. New York, Praeger, 1964. 276 p. -- A major book on the role of religion in the cultural change in Latin America. Spanish edition by Editorial Herder, Barcelona, 1967.

165. Dewart, Leslie. Christianity and revolution; the lesson of Cuba. New York, Herder and Herder, 1964. 320 p. -- By a Catholic journalist, a critique of the role of the Roman Catholic Church in Cuba and its inability to cope with revolution.

166. Dunne, Peter Marsten, S.J. A padre views South America. Milwaukee, Bruce, 1945. xiii, 290 p.

167. Fonseca, Jaime. Latin America -- a challenge to Catholics, Washington, NCWC, 1960.

168. Fremantle, Anne. The papal encyclicals in their historical context. 4 ed. New York, Mentor Book, no. 256, 1960. 317 p. -- Introduction by Gustave Weigel, S.J. on the significance of the papal encyclical.

169. Gibbons, William J., M.M., comp. Basic ecclesiastical

statistics for Latin America. Maryknoll, N.Y., Maryknoll Publications, 1956. 86 p. (World horizon
reports). -- Some categories are admittedly incomplete and inaccurate.

170. Grabowski, Stanley M. The center of intercultural information at Cuernavaca. Occasional bulletin (New York,
MRL) 18:4, 1966.

171. Gremillion, Jos. The other dialogue. Garden City, L.I.,
N.Y., Doubleday, 1965. 308 p. -- A study in depth
of Catholic commitment in the social problems of the
contemporary world.

172. Hillman, Eugene, C.S., Sp. The church as mission. New
York, Herder and Herder, 1965. 144 p.

173. Houtart, Francois *and* Emile Pin. The church and the
Latin American revolution. New York, Sheed and Ward,
1965. viii, 264 p. -- Translated from French original by Gilbert Barth. An able appraisal of the
demands placed by the revolutionary situation of
Latin America on the Roman Catholic Church to develop a relevant apostolate.

174. Iberoamérica: La iglesia ante sus problemas. Burgos,
Instituto Español para Misiones Extranjeras, 1963.
-- Good survey.

175. Lee, James M., ed. *and* Louis J. Putz, C.S.C. Seminary
education in a time of change. Notre Dame, Ind.,
Fides, 1965. 590 p. -- Essays on contemporary
seminary education in the U.S.A. Increasing numbers
of U.S. clergy are going to Latin America hence
volume indicative of trends in U.S. which will exert
influences in Latin America across coming decades.

176. Michael, J. B. Cristianos en busca de una iglesia; el
movimiento ecuménico y Roma, con documentos y
adiciones sociográficas. México, Editorial Jus,
1962. -- Trad. del inglés original por Efraín
González L. Morfín. Introd. por el Card. Augustín
Bea.

177. Míguez-Bonino, José. The impact of the Vatican Council
on Latin American Roman Catholicism and Protestantism.
1964. mimeographed. -- By the only Latin American
Protestant observer at the II Vatican Council.

178. _____. Vatican II and Latin America. *Christian century*
     30 December 1964.

179. Pattee, Richard. The Catholic revival in Mexico.
     Washington, D.C., Catholic Association for Interna-
     tional Peace, 1944. 60 p. -- Written with the
     Inter-American Committee.

180. _____. El catolicismo contemporáneo en hispanoamérica.
     Buenos Aires, Editorial Fides, 1951. 481 p. --
     Bibliography p. 472-74.

181. Pike, Frederick B., ed. The conflict between church and
     state in Latin America. New York, Knopf, 1964.
     ix, 239 p. -- A Borzoi book.

182. Prompeor, Werner. Priesternot in Lateinamerika. Louvain,
     Collegium pro America Latina, 1965. 317 p. -- Des-
     criptive of shortage of priests and suggested way of
     relieving shortage. See also Antoine Tibesar's
     article in *The Americas* April 1966 on the same sub-
     ject.

183. Rivera R., Pedro. La sagrada biblia y el protestantismo.
     México, Editorial Jus, 1962. 67 p. -- The best known
     Roman Catholic interpreter of Protestantism in Mexico
     analyzes for non-Protestants the centrality of the
     Bible in Protestant faith and practices.

184. Sondeos: una edición de estudios sobre el fenómeno
     religioso en América Latina. México, CIDOC, 1966-.
     -- See no. 237. Also see CIF monographs, 1962-.

185. Vallier, Ivan A. Roman Catholicism and social change in
     Latin America: from the church to sect. Paper
     delivered at 58th Annual meeting of the American
     Sociological Association. Los Angeles, Calif.,
     August 1963.

186. Vekemans, Roger, S.J. Is the church losing Latin
     America? *Ave-Maria* 9 January 1966. -- Outspoken
     presentation by a Belgian Jesuit sociologist, a lead-
     ing strategist among Roman Catholic socio-economic
     planners in Latin America. Disturbing conclusions
     but offers hopeful solutions. In *America Latina*,
     vol. 8, no. 4.

187. Wood, Brother Robert. Missionary crisis and challenge in
     Latin America. St. Louis, Herder, 1964. 94 p. --

46 PROTESTANTISM IN LATIN AMERICA

A simple presentation of some historical facts and
possible methods of missionary work today.

Documents of Regional Conferences and Consultations
                    See also p. 261.
188. Latin American Councils, held in 1889 and 1900 in Rome
      marked the beginning of improved education for the
      clergy and increased social activity. Since the turn
      of the century there have been others, but since
      Chimbote in 1963 the number of conferences is
      impressive. These are summarized in Patterns for
      Progress, Davenport, Iowa, Latin America Bureau of
      NCWC, 1966. 26 p.

189. Chapter chronicle of the Maryknoll general chapter,
      Aug.-Oct. 1966.

190. Conference on religious and social change in Latin
      America. Notre Dame, Ind., Fides, 1963. Papers by
      R. J. Alexander, Eduardo Frei, Roger Vekemans,
      Emilio Willems and others.

191. Ewing, J. Franklin. The global mission of the church.
      New York, Fordham University, Institute of Missions
      Studies, 1962. mimeographed. Proceedings of the
      Fordham University Conference of Mission Specialists.

192. Proceedings of the Lima methods conference of the Mary-
      knoll fathers. Maryknoll, N.Y., Maryknoll Fathers,
      1954. 304 p. Lima, August, 1954. -- Background
      studies and surveys of Maryknoll mission fields in
      Latin America.

193. Tercera semana interamericana de acción católica docu-
      mentos. Lima y Chimbote, 1953.

193a. Conference of Ninety Latin American bishops. Mar del Plata,
      Argentina. October 1966. Subject: "The Role of
      the Church in the Socio-economic Development and the
      Integration of Latin America."

FERES Series: Friburgo, Suiza,
Oficina Internacional de Investigaciones Sociales de FERES

Estudios Sociológicos Latino-Americanos

194. Arcos, Juan. El sindicalismo en América Latina. 1964. 192 p. no. 12.

195. Calderón Alvarado, Luís, Arturo Calle y Jaime Dorselaer. Problemas de urbanización en América Latina. 1963. 240 p. no. 13.

196. de Camargo, Cándido Procópio. Aspectos sociológicos do espiritismo en São Paulo. 1961. 125 p. no. 17.

197. Corredor, Berta. La Familia en América Latina. 1962. 141 p. no. 4.

198. Debuyst, Federico. La población en América Latina. 1961. 154 p. Charts. no. 1.

199. Díaz, Demetrio. La educación en Brasil. 1961. 114 p. no. 7.

200. Dorselaer, Jaime *y* Alfonso Gregory. La urbanización en América Latina. 1962. 167, 99 p. (2 v.) no. 2 and 3.

201. Houtart, Francisco. América Latina en cambio social. 1964. 187 p. no. 18.

202. Lannoy, Juan Luís de *y* Gustavo Pérez. Estructuras demográficas y sociales de Colombia. 1961. 199 p. no. 14.

203. _____, Los niveles de vida en América Latina. 1963. 235 p. no. 6.

204. Mencias, Jorge. Riobamba (Ecuador): estudio de elevación socio-cultural del Indio. 1962. 154 p. no. 16.

205. Pineda, Virginia Gutiérrez de. La familia en Colombia. 1962. 86 p. no. 15.

206. Torres, Camilo *y* Berta Corredor. Las escuelas radiofónicas de Sutatenza. 1961. 75 p. no. 5.

Documentos Latino-Americanos: Bogotá,
Oficina Internacional de Investigaciones Sociales de FERES

207. Cereceda, Raúl. Las instituciones políticas en América Latina. 1961. 256 p. no. 1.

208. Corredor, Berta *y* Sergio Torres. Transformación en el
     mundo rural latinoamericano. 1961. 143 p. no. 2.

209. Debuyst, Federico. Las Clases sociales en América Latina.
     1962. 217 p. no. 3.

Estudios Socio-Religiosos Latino-Americanos

210. Alonso, Isidoro, Renato Poblete *y* Ginés Garrido. La
     iglesia en Chile. 1962. 223 p. no. 6.

211. Damboriena, Prudencio, S. El protestantismo en América
     Latina. 138, 287 p. 1962-63. (2 v.) no. 12 and 13.

212. Pérez, Gustavo and Issac Wust. La iglesia en Colombia.
     1961. 195 p. no. 1.

213. _____. El problema sacerdotal en América Latina. 1962.
     (2 v.) no. 16 and 17.

214. Ramos, Rutilio, Isidoro Alonso *y* Domingo Garre. La
     iglesia en Méjico. 1963. 119 p. no. 7.

215. Tormo, Leandro. La historia de la iglesia en América
     Latina. 1962. 184 p. no. 10.

Fuera de colección

216. Alonso, Isidoro *y* Ginés Garrido. La iglesia en América
     Central y el Caribe. no. 4.

217. _____. La iglesia en América Latina: estructuras
     eclesiásticas. 1964. 223 p. no. 21.

218. _____ *y* Julio Trumir. La iglesia en Perú y Bolivia.

219. _____ et al. La iglesia en Venezuela y Ecuador. no. 3.

220. Amato, Enrique. La iglesia en Argentina. no. 5.

221. Domínguez, Oscar. El campesino chileno y la acción
     católica. no. 15.

222. Houtart, F. La iglesia latinoamericana en la hora del
     Concilio.

223. Pin, Emilio, S.J. Elementos para una sociología del
catolicismo latinoamericano. no. 20.

Periodicals and Journals
See also p. 263.

224. A.I.D. dialogue. Paterson, New Jersey.

225. America. Thurston Davis, ed., 106 W. 56th Street, New
York, N.Y.

226. C.I.F. report. Apartado 479, Cuernavaca, Morelos,
Mexico.

227. Commonweal. Edward Skillin, ed., 232 Madison Avenue,
New York, N.Y.

228. Concilium. Paulist Press, Glen Rock, New Jersey.

229. Criterio. Alsina 840, Buenos Aires, Argentina. 1928-.,
fortnightly, annually. (Cf. no. 917).

230. The criterion. 124 W. Georgia Street, Indianapolis, Ind.

231. The ecumenist. Paulist Press, Glen Rock, N.J.

232. Fede e civiltá. Yarma, Italia.

233. The Herder correspondence. Herder and Herder, Inc.,
232 Madison Avenue, New York, N.Y. 10016.

234. Jubilee. 168 E. 91st Street, New York, N.Y. monthly.

235. Mensaje. Casilla 10445, Santiago, Chile.

236. Paz e terra. Editoriais Civilizacão, Rio de Janeiro,
Brasil.

Contemporary Religious Phenomena and Secular Movements
See also p. 266.

Religious Phenomena

237. Bajeux, Jean-Claude. Pastoral considerations on Haitian
voodoo cults. Colección Sondeos no. 2. Cuernavaca
CIDOC, Morelos, Mexico, 1967.

238.   Braun, Jos.   Spirits, mediums and believers in contempor-
       ary Puerto Rico.   Transactions of the New York
       Academy of Sciences 20:340-47.

239.   Camargo, C. P. de.   (Cf. no. 196).

240.   _____.   (Cf. no. 309).

241.   Castellan, Yvonne.   El espiritismo.   Buenos Aires, Los
       Libros de Mirasol, 1962.   157 p.   -- Translated from
       French original.

242.   Kardac, Allen and Gabriel Delanne.   Los fundamentos del
       espiritismo.   México, 1954.

243.   _____.   El libro de los espíritus.   México, 1951.   --
       English translation, The spirit's book.   Sao Paulo
       (n.d.).

244.   Kelly, Isabel.   Mexican spiritualism.   *Kroeber anthropo-
       logical papers* (Mexico) 35:191-206, 1961.

245.   Kloppenburg, Boaventura.   O espiritismo no Brasil;
       orientacão para os católicos.   Petrópolis, Editôra
       Vozes, 1960.   455 p.

246.   Major, Alfred R.   (Cf. no. 1299).

247.   Metraux, Alfred.   Vodú.   Buenos Aires, Editorial Sur,
       1963.   341 p.   -- Last chapter considers relations
       between Vodú and pentecostal manifestations.   See
       also *his* Haiti: black peasants and voodoo.   New York,
       Universe, 1960.   Translated from original French by
       Peter Lengyel.

248.   Pollard, Angelina.   El culto de María Leonza.   América
       Latina 9:1:95-115 January-March 1966.   See also *Look*,
       May, 1967 for related article.

249.   Renshaw, Parke.   (Cf. no. 1301).

Communism in Latin America
See also p. 266, 267.

250.   Alexander, Robert Jackson.   Communism in Latin America.
       New Brunswick, N.J., Rutgers University Press, 1957.
       449 p.

251. Croan, Melvin. The reception of Marxism in Latin America. U.S.-L.A. Faculty Interchange Program, 1966, research in progress.

252. Halperin, Ernst. Nationalism and communism in Chile. Cambridge, Mass., M.I.T. Press, 1965. 267 p. -- Author is research associate in Communist Affairs at M.I.T.

253. Hunt, R.N.C. The theory and practice of communism. New York, Macmillan, 1961. 280 p. -- Thorough bibliography.

254. Lauerhass, Ludwig. Communism in Latin America, a bibliography; the post-war years, 1945-60. Los Angeles, Center of Latin American Studies, University of California, 1962. x 78 p. (Cf. no. 26).

255. Poppino, Rollie. International communism in Latin America; 1917-63. London, Free Press, 1964. 247 p. -- Succint survey concluding with some approaches to a problem which the author does not present as insoluble.

256. Problems of communism. Washington, D.C., Documentary Studies Section, International Association, 1954-. -- bimonthly, $2.50 annually.

257. Ravines, Eudocio. The Yenan way. New York, Scribners, 1951. 319 p. -- Written by a former top Communist organizer in South America.

258. Religion in communist-dominated areas. New York, NCCC, semi-monthly. -- Includes publications on Cuba. $10.00 annually.

259. Schmitt, Karl M. Communism in Mexico: a study in political frustration. Austin, University of Texas Press, 1965. 250 p. -- A well-researched study by a former State Department official documenting the growing weakness of the movement through internal fragmentation and incapacity to relate to a dynamic society.

PERIODICALS AND JOURNALS

See also p. 272.

260. Index to Latin American periodical literature: 1929-60.

Arthur P. Gropp, comp. Boston, Hall, 1962. xv, 6030
p. (8 v.). A supplement for 1961-65 published by the
new publisher, 1968, 2 v. Prepared from indexing done
by the Columbus Memorial Library of the Pan American
Union. (Indice general de publicaciones; periódicos
latinoamericanos. 1961-. Annual accumulations will
be found under this title.) The Serial Division of
the Library of Congress is preparing reports of Latin
American newspaper holdings from 74 research libraries. The long-term goal is to have for each Latin
American country a set of the important newspaper
files spanning the years about 1825-1938.

261. Zimmerman, Irene. Guide to current Latin American
      periodicals; humanities and social sciences.
      Gainesville, Fla., 1961. -- Classifies by country
      and by subject. Valuable annotations.

                        * * * * * *

262. América latina. Centro Latino-americano de Pesquisas em
      Ciencias Sociais, Av. Pasteur 431, Rio de Janeiro.
      -- Quarterly bulletin.

263. American anthropologist. (American anthropological
      Association) S. T. Boggs, 1530 P. Street, N.W.,
      Washington, D.C., 20005, 1888-. Bimonthly. -- v.
      57 is a special issue on Latin America. $12.00
      annually.

264. Américas. Dept. of Public Information, Pan American
      Union, Washington, D.C., 20006, 1949-. Monthly.
      Text in English, Spanish, Portuguese.

265. Americas. (Academy of Franciscan History.) Box 5850,
      Washington, D.C., 20014, 1944-. Quarterly, $6.00
      annually. -- A review of inter-American cultural
      history.

266. Anthropological quarterly. (Catholic Anthropological
      Association) Catholic University of America Press,
      620 Michigan Avenue, N.E., Washington, D.C., 20017,
      1928-.

267. Anuario de estudios americanos. Escuela de Estudios
      Hispano-Americanos, Sevilla, España, 1944-. (See
      also, Historiografía y bibliografía americanista by
      the same institution.)

268. Books abroad: an international literary quarterly.
     University of Oklahoma Press, Norman, Oklahoma 73069.
     1927-.

269. Caribbean studies. University of Puerto Rico, Box BM,
     University Station, Institute of Caribbean Studies,
     Río Piedras, 1960-. -- Text in English, French,
     Spanish. Quarterly. Devoted to social sciences, arts
     and humanities relevant to the Caribbean and circum
     Caribbean areas.

270. Cuadernos. Revista mensual de América Latina. Germán
     Arciniegas, Dir. 23 rue de la Pepiniére, Paris, 1953-.
     -- Sophisticated, scholarly and timely.

271. Cuadernos americanos: revista del nuevo mundo. Avenida
     Coyoacán, No. 1035, Apartado Postal 965, México, D.F.,
     1942-. Bi-monthly, US$9.00 annually.

272. Cuadernos hispano americanos: revista mensual de cultura
     Hispánica. Instituto de Cultura Hispánica, Avenida
     de los Reyes Católicos, Madrid 13, España, 1948-.
     Monthly. -- Review of literature on Latin America
     published by the Spanish government.

273. Desarrollo. Apartado Aéreo 2234, Barranquilla, Colombia.

274. Encounter. 25 Haymarket, London, S.W.1, England, 1953-.
     Monthly, US$8.50 annually. -- See special issue on
     Latin America, 25:3 September 1965.

275. Foreign affairs: an American quarterly review. Council
     on Foreign Relations, Inc., 58 E. 68th Street, New
     York, N.Y. 10021, 1922-. Quarterly, US$6.00 annually.

276. Fundamental and adult education. UNESCO, Place de
     Fontenoy, Paris, 1949-1960. Quarterly. -- Super-
     seded by International journal of adult and youth
     education in 1961. Title varies.

277. Hispanic American historical review. Duke University
     Press, Box 6697, College Station, Durham, N.C.,
     27708, 1918-. Quarterly, US$6.00 annually. -- Two
     valuable guides to this journal are the following:
     Guide to the Hispanic American historical review,
     1918-45. Ruth B. Butler, ed., 1950; or, Guide to
     the Hispanic American historical review, 1946-55.
     Charles Gibson, ed., 1958.

278. Hispanic American report. Stanford University Press,
     Palo Alto, Calif., 1948-64. -- Useful reference

country by country on current events of that period.

279. Hispanic American studies. University of Miami Press,
Coral Gables, Fla., 1938-. Annual.

280. Inter-American labor institute bulletin. Inter-American
Regional Organization, ICFTU, 815 Sixteenth Street,
N.W., Washington, D.C., 20006. 1951-. Monthly.

281. International student. 2627 Connecticut Avenue, Washington, D.C., 1955-.

282. Journal of Inter-American Studies and World Affairs. 1959-.
Quarterly. U.S.$10.00; students $8.00. Sage Publications, Inc., Box 776, Beverly Hills, Ca. 90210. Text
in English, French, Portuguese, Spanish, according to
the author's preference. Includes a quarterly review
of recent books and pamphlets.

283. Journal of international affairs. Capital City Press,
Montpelier, Vt., 05601, 1947-. Semi-annually. --
See special issue on "Political development on Latin
America" 20:2 1966.

284. Latin American business highlights. 1 Chase Manhattan
Plaza, Chase Manhattan Bank, New York 10015, 1950-.
Quarterly. Free. -- The "business as usual" point
of view reflected.

285. Latin America in periodical literature. Center of Latin
American Studies, University of California, Los
Angeles, 1962-. -- Abstracts arranged topically.

286. Latin American research review. Latin American Research
Review Board, University of Texas Press, Austin 78712,
1965-. -- Text in English and Spanish. Published
three times/year. Supplement, Spring 1966 reviews
research projects under way in Latin America. (Inst.
US$20.00 annually, indiv. US$13.00 annually, students
US$8.00 annually, single copy US$3.00).

287. Luso-Brazilian review. University of Wisconsin Press,
430 Sterling Court, Madison 53706. Text in English,
Portuguese, Spanish. US$3.75 annually. -- The only
American journal dealing exclusively with the
Portuguese-speaking world. Invaluable for scholars
and professors, teachers and students in the area of

Portuguese, Spanish and South American studies.

288. The OAS chronicle. Organization of American States, Pan
      American Union, Washington, D.C., 1965-. Bi-monthly.
      Text in English, Portuguese, Spanish.

289. Revista de Indias. Consejo Superior de Investigaciones
      Científicas Instituto Gonzalo Fernández de Oviedo,
      Duque de Medinaceli 4, Madrid 14, España, 1940-.
      Quarterly.

290. Revista interamericana de psicología. Carl F. Hereford,
      dir. 2014 Meadowbrook Drive, Austin, Texas. Quarterly.
      US$8.00 annually. Articles in Spanish, Portuguese,
      English.

291. Soviet periodical abstracts; Asia, Africa and Latin
      America. Slavic Languages Research Institute, Inc.,
      1 Seymour Place, White Plains, N.Y., 10605, 1961-.
      -- Two sections; the second dealing with Asis, Africa,
      Latin America.

292. The UNESCO courier. 317 E. 34th Street, New York, N.Y.
      Bi-monthly.

293. United Nations review. U.N. Sales Section, New York,
      N.Y., 10017, 1964-. Monthly. Text in English, French,
      Spanish. -- Supersedes U.N. monthly chronicle,
      1954-64.

Borzoi Books on Latin America
See also p. 275.

Under the general editorship of Lewis Hanke. Published by Alfred
Knopf, New York in paperback editions.

294. Bernstein, Marvin, ed. Foreign investment in Latin Amer-
      ica, 1965.

295. Burns, E. Bradford, ed. A documentary history of Brazil.
      1966. xii, 398 p.

296. Dozer, Donald M., ed. The Monroe doctrine: Its modern
      significance. 1965. xiv, 208 p.

297. Freyre, Gilberto. The masters and the slaves (casa grande
      e senzala); a study in the development of Brazilian
      civilization. Trans. from the Portuguese by Samuel

Putnam. Abridged from the 2. English-language ed.,
rev. 1964. 432 p.

298. Hamill, Hugh M., Jr., ed. Dictatorship in Spanish
America. 1965. x, 242 p.

299. Hanke, Lewis, ed. Do the Americans have a common history?
A critique of the Bolton theory. 1964. x, 269 p.

300. Humphreys, Robin A. *and* John Lynch, ed. The origins of
the Latin American revolutions, 1808-1826. 1965. ix,
308 p.

301. Mörner, Magnus, ed. The expulsion of the Jesuits from
Latin America. 1965. 207 p.

302. Morse, Richard M. The bandeirantes; the historical role
of the Brazilian pathfinders. 1965. viii, 215 p.

303. Pike, Frederick B., ed. The conflict between church and
state in Latin America. 1964. ix, 239 p.

304. Ross, Stanley R., ed. Is the Mexican Revolution dead?
1966. ix, 255 p.

305. Smith, Robert F., ed. Background to revolution; the
development of modern Cuba. 1966. xi, 224 p.

306. Smith, T. Lynn, ed. Agrarian reform in Latin America.
1965. ix, 206 p.

307. Ulloa, Antonio de *and* Jorge Juan. A voyage to South
America. The John Adams translation abridged. -- A
translation of Ulloa's Relación histórica del viaje a
la América meridional... Madrid, 1748. The account
of the scientific work of the expedition, written, by
Jorge Juan y Santacilla was published separately,
Madrid, 1748. It is not included in this translation.

308. Wagley, Charles. Amazon town; a study of man in the
tropics. 1964. xi, 1964 p. -- With a new epilogue
by the author.

Chapter 2.
Protestantism in Latin America, General

BIBLIOGRAPHIES AND INDICES
See also p. 277.

309. Báez Camargo, Gonzalo, ed. Indice general anotado de
     literatura evangélica. México, CUPSA, 1958. 185 p.
     -- Includes list of publishing and distribution
     houses in Latin America and some addresses. Names
     of evangelical periodicals in circulation in 1958.
     Cf. no. 16.

310. Bibliografía sobre el protestantismo en las antillas
     españolas. Guillermo Cabrera Leiva, comp. Washing-
     ton, D.C., 1954. 11 p.

311. Christian missions in Latin American countries. New York,
     UPL, 1961. 28 p. mimeographed.

312. Crow, Paul A., Jr. The ecumenical movement in biblio-
     graphical outline, New York, Dept. of Faith and
     Order, NCCC, 1965. 79 p. -- Complements two earlier
     ecumenical bibliographies: Senaud Augusto. Christian
     unity: a bibliography. 1937; also, Henry R. T.
     Brandreth. Unity and reunion: a bibliography. 2
     ed. 1948. Updated by a nine page mimeographed study.
     NCCC, 1969.

313. Damboriena, Prodencio, S. J.   El protestantismo en la
     América Latina. *En* Bibliografía sobre el
     protestantismo en la América Latina, v. 2, p. 263-73.

314. Gattinoni, Carlos F., ed. Una lista de libros útiles
     para la enseñanza teológica. s.l., Fondo de Educación
     Teológica, 1963.   -- Section on Latin America, S.591-
     S.663. A carefully selected list for seminary lib-
     raries.

315. Jacquet, Constant H.   Our neighbors to the south...New
     York, MRL, 1954. 47 p.   -- A selected, annotated
     bibliography of English titles on Central America,
     South America and the Caribbean.

316. Latin America Department, NCCC, 475 Riverside Drive, New
     York.   -- Mimeographed bibliography with listing of
     miscellaneous books, reports, pamphlets on file in
     the library of that department.

317. Latourette, Kenneth S. A bibliography of missionary
     biography. In preparation for 1968 publication.
     This work was left unfinished at the time of Dr.
     Latourette's death.

318. Morris, Raymond P., ed.   A theological book list. New
     York, Theological Education Fund, 1960. xiv, 242 p.

319. Occasional bulletin, 1950-June 1966. New York, MRL.   --
     List available of contents of all publications in
     this period on Protestant missions.

320. Reisner, Sherwood H.   A preliminary bibliography of
     Protestant missions in Latin America. Kingsville,
     Texas, Presbyterian Panamerican School, 1957. 49 p.
     mimeographed.

321. Rycroft, W. Stanley *and* Myrtle M. Clemmer. Bibliography
     for Latin American studies. New York, COEMAR, 1963.
     19 p.   -- Includes some United Nations government
     publications and many key articles published in 1962-
     63.

322. Smith, Willard H. Mennonites in Latin America. Goshen,
     Ind., Goshen College, Mennonite Historical Society.
     -- Reprint from the *Mennonite quarterly review*,
     October 1952. An annotated bibliography.

Quarterlies With Regular Reviews

323. Het messiewerk, Mgr. Dr. Alph. Mulders, comp. Nederlands
     Tijdschrift voor Missiewetenschap. Laan Copes von
     Cattenburch 127, 's-Gravenhage, Nederlands. -- The
     fourth quarterly issue every year has a bibliographi-
     cal survey of mission literature, with primary atten-
     tion to Roman Catholic publications.

324. International review of missions. Geneva, WCC. -- Each
     issue contains "Bibliography of world mission and
     evangelism." A good source of current mission liter-
     ature for non-Roman Catholics.

GENERAL LITERATURE
See also p. 278.

325. Amundsen, Wesley. The advent message in Inter-America.
     Takoma Park, Washington, D.C., Review and Herald,
     1947. -- A general review of Adventist work.

326. Andress, Paul. An educational approach to the work of
     the Protestant church in Latin America. Ph. D.
     thesis, Columbia University, New York, 1951.

327. Arms, Goodsil F. History of the William Taylor self-
     supporting missions in South America. New York,
     Methodist Book Concern, 1921. 263 p. (Duplicated
     in no. 1381).

328. _____. Origen del metodismo y su implementación en la
     costa occidental de Sudamérica. Santiago, Imprenta
     Universitaria, 1923. 68 p. Largely a chronicle
     review, including beginnings in Chile.

329. Báez Camargo, Gonzalo. The earliest Protestant missionary
     venture in Latin America. *Church history* 21:2 June
     1952. -- The 1555 French Calvinist project in
     Brazil.

330. _____. Evangelical faith and Latin American culture. *In*
     The ecumenical era in church and society: A symposium
     in honor of John A. Mackay. New York, Macmillan,
     1959. -- Statement on the contribution of Evangelical
     Christianity to Latin America and its relations to
     Roman Catholic renewal.

331. _____, ed. Obras inéditas o muy raras para la historia
del protestantismo en la América Latina. -- Diario
de Ricardo Williams. New York, CUPSA, 1959. 96 p.
maps. Los Mártires de Rio de Janeiro, México, CUPSA,
1955. 121 p. Title and text in French, Protuguese
and Spanish. Protestantes enjuiciados por la
Inquisición en Iberoamérica. México, CUPSA, 1960.
141 p. -- A remarkable piece of work. Author gleaned
data largely from the ponderous works of José Toribio
Medina on the Inquisition in Latin America. Ultimos
documentos del Capitán Allen F. Gardiner. México,
CUPSA, 1959. 110 p. maps.

332. _____, Protestantism: a symposium. W. K. Anderson, ed.
Nashville, Methodist Church, 1944. 282 p. -- See
part III on Protestantism in Latin America.

333. _____. El protestantismo en Iberoamérica. México, La
Aurora, 1945. 21 p. -- Well-written, brief statement.

334. Barbieri, Santo Uberto. The land of El Dorado. New York,
Friendship Press, 1961. 161 p. -- Trans. from Spanish original. Describes the coming of Protestantism
to Latin America, its growth, contributions, failures
and future role.

335. _____. Spiritual currents in Spanish America. Buenos
Aires, La Aurora, 1951. -- Analysis of failures of
Protestantism in Latin America as well as its contri-
butions. Emphasizes need to overcome "foreign-ness."

336. Barchwitz-Krauser, O. von. Six years with William Taylor.
Boston, McDonald and Gill, 1885. 332 p. -- Includes
story of a German colonization effort in Contulmo,
Chile, led by the author in 1884.

337. Barclay, Wade C. Greater good neighbor policy. Chicago,
Willet and Clark, 1945. viii, 257 p.

338. Beaver, R. Pierce. The Genevan mission in Brazil. *The
reformed journal*, Spring, 1967.

339. Braga, Erasmo. Pan Americanismo: aspecto religioso e
relatório e interprectacão do congresso de accão
crista na América Latina reunido no Panamá. New York,
Sociedade de preparo missionário funcionando nos
Estados Unidos e Canadá, 1916. vi, 205 p. Also
English edition, New York, Missionary Education

Movement, USA and Canada, 1917. A classic by a great
Brazilian leader.

340. Brown, Hubert W. Latin America: the pagan, the papists
and patriots, the Protestants and the present problem. New York, Revell, 1901. 308 p. -- Dated, yet
representative of Protestant views on Latin America
at the turn of the century. Lectures delivered to
students at Princeton, Auburn and Western Seminaries
are probably the first lectures on the Latin American
area in an institution of higher learning in the
U.S.A.

341. Brown, Walton J. The foundation of the Seventh-day
Adventist church in austral South America, 1785-1912.
Ph. D. thesis, Southern California, 1954.

342. Browning, Webster E. El alma americana. Montevideo,
Talleres Gráficos A. Barreiro y Ramos, 1920. 31 p.
-- Tesis para incorporarse al grado de doctor en
filosofía y letras en la Universidad de San Marcos
de Lima.

343. _____. Joseph Lancaster, James Thomson, and the Lancas-
terian system. *Hispanic American historical review*
4:1 February 1921. -- Depends heavily on Thomson
letters.

344. _____. Latin America: the land, the people and problems.
New York, 1913. -- a general review.

345. _____ and W. R. Wheeler. Modern missions on the Spanish
Main. Philadelphia, Westminster Press, 1925. 334 p.
-- Review of work in Colombia and Venezuela.

346. _____. New days in Latin America. New York, Missionary
Education Movement of the USA and Canada, 1925.
226 p. -- A study of Latin America in 1925. A brief
statement of Evangelical work and an exposition of the
character that this work should attempt to develop.

347. _____. Roman Christianity in Latin America. New York,
Revell, 1924. 80 p. -- Maintains missionaries should
emphasize social aspect of Gospel over against "other-
worldliness" of Roman Catholicism.

348. _____. The romance of the founding of evangelical missions in Latin America. Buenos Aires, 1933. mss.
-- Copies in MRL, UPL, FET. Writer had access to

unique sources and drew upon conversations with personalities involved. Work is accurate, although
there is relatively little documentation.

349. Canclini, Augustina Varetto de. Juan C. Varetto,
embajador de Cristo. Buenos Aires, 1955.

350. Canclini, Santiago. Pablo Besson, un heraldo de la
liberatad cristiana. Buenos Aires, 1933. -- An
important study of a leader in the struggle for lay
cemeteries and civil registry.

351. Castillo Cárdenas, Gonzalo. El cristianismo evangélico
en la América Latina. *Cristianismo y sociedad*
2:61-65, 1964.

352. _____. Life and mission of the church in Latin America.
Information catholique international 14 September
1963.

353. Castro, Emilio. Evangelism and ecumenism in Latin
America. *The student world* 49:4:313-13. -- Very
general discussion of a complex theme.

354. _____. Misión: presencia y diálogo. Buenos Aires,
Methopres, 1964. 61 p. -- Summary of DWME assembly
in Mexico. Foreword by Gonzalo Báez Camargo. Chap.
7 on Latin America.

355. Castro, Vincent R. Protestant attitudes toward missionary
work in Latin America. S.T.M. thesis, San Francisco
Theological Seminary, San Anselmo, Calif., 1958.

356. Celada, Claudio. Un apóstol contemporáneo. Buenos Aires,
La Aurora, 1945. 326 p. -- The life of Francisco
Penzotti. Written with pious overtones. This great
Christian was probably more masculine than the deli-
cate fancy of the author's indication.

357. Chain, Beverly. Days of decision. New York, Friendship
Press, 1961. 214 p. -- A collection of short
stories about Protestant youth in Latin America.

358. Cherry, Thomas J. A review of indigenous church principles in Latin America in the light of changing world
conditions. M.R.E. thesis, Fuller Theological
Seminary, Pasadena, Calif., 1957. 69 p.

359. Church of God in the Americas. Cleveland, Tenn., Board

of Foreign Missions, Church of God, 1954. 54 p. --
Description of the Latin American work of this denomination.

360. Coble, Aulden D. The justification of Protestant missionary work in South America. B.D. thesis, Presbyterian
Theological Seminary, Chicago, 1940. -- Refers also
to the decadence of Roman Catholic church in its
clergy and theology, reactions to Protestantism and
effects of missionary endeavors.

361. Converse, Hyla S., comp. Raise a signal: God's action
and the church's task in Latin America today. New
York, Friendship Press, 1961. 126 p. -- One of the
best popular presentations available.

362. Cristobal, Ariel D. An Apostle of Christ. San Pablo 1:
9 September 1954. -- An article on William C. Morris.

363. Daniels, Margarette. Makers of South America. New York,
Missionary Education Movement; USA and Canada, 1916.
247 p. -- Interesting biographies including David
Trumbull, Allen Gardiner, W. Barbook Grubb, Francisco
Penzotti, as well as Pizarro, José de Anchieta, San
Martín, Bolívar, Juan M. Rosas, Sarmiento and Don
Pedro II. A bibliography on each personality.

364. Darby, Marion *and* James E. Ellis. Latin America lands in
focus. New York, Editorial Dept. of Methodist Church,
1961. 147 p. -- Brief history and description of
Methodist work in Latin America.

365. Eudaly, Nathan H. A critical evaluation of leadership for
Baptist churches in Spanish America. D.R.E. thesis,
Southwestern Baptist Seminary, Dallas, 1959.

366. Evangelism in depth. Chicago, Moody Press, 1961. 126 p.
-- Introduction by R. Kenneth Strachan. Report by
team members of the Latin American Missions experi-
ments in new evangelistic techniques involving every
church member and directed toward the entire community.

367. Gibson, Delbert L. Protestantism in Latin American acculturation. Ph. D. thesis, University of Texas, Austin,
1959. microfilmed. --Discusses Latin Americans in
Texas. Has very significant discussion on reasons
Catholics become Protestants, motivation for conversion and factors which lead Protestants to chose certain churches. Important since the author does not

write from a "religious" point of view.

368. Gingrich, Melvin. North American Mennonite overseas out-
      reach in perspective, 1890-1965. *Mennonite quarterly
      review* 39:262-79 October 1965.

369. González, Arrili, Bernardo. Vida y milagros de Mr. Morris.
      Buenos Aires, 1955. -- Does not emphasize the evan-
      gelical nature of his work. Author was a personal
      acquaintance of W. P. Morris.

370. Goslin, Thomas S. Los evangélicos en la América Latina,
      siglo XIX; los comienzos. Buenos Aires, La Aurora,
      1956. 127 p. -- An important contribution to Evan-
      gelical history which brings together in panoramic
      fashion the principal data from the first stages of
      national church development through the 19th century.

371. Graber, Jos. D. The church apostolic; a discussion of
      modern missions: changes in misison policy and
      practice adjusted to cultural change in Latin America.
      M.A. thesis, Hartford Seminary Foundation, Hartford,
      Conn., 1957. 137 p. -- Related primarily to the
      missionary practice of the Mennonite church.

372. Green, Dana S. Ecumenical dimensions of U.S. missions in
      Latin America. June 1964. -- Mimeographed statement
      to LAD-NCCC. Refers to the prophetic role of Protes-
      tant churches and the factor of nationalism in church
      development.

373. Grubb, Kenneth G. An advancing church in Latin America.
      London, World Dominion Press, 1936. 81 p. --Descriptive.

374. _____. Amazon and Andes, London, Methuen, 1930. xii,
      296 p.

375. _____. From Pacific to Atlantic: South American studies.
      London, Methuen, 1933. x, 159 p. illus., maps.

376. _____. The lowland Indians of Amazonia. London, World
      Dominion Press, 1927. 159 p. -- Nine countries sur-
      veyed. Maps, tables on linguistic families. Important
      work. (Duplicated as no. 1194). In 1939 an eight
      page tract 'A review of ten years of Evangelical pro-
      gress to 1938' was published by the same publisher and
      reviews the 1928-1938 period.

377. _____. The Norhern republics of South America: Ecuador,

Colombia and Venezuela. London, World Dominion Press. 1931. vi, 151 p. (Cf. no. 1544).

378. _____. The northern republics of South America: a review of ten years of Evangelical progress to 1938. London, World Dominion Press, 1939. -- A supplement to his 1931 publication on this same subject.

379. _____. Parables from South America. London, World Dominion Press, 1937. 147 p. -- Interpretative.

380. _____. South America, the land of the future. London, World Dominion Press, 1931. iv, 71 p. -- A review of missionary work.

381. Guiness, Harry G. Not unto us. London, Regions Beyond Mission, 1938. 191 p. -- Review of twenty-one years of missionary service of the Regions Beyond Mission.

382. Hallock, Constance M. Looking south. New York, Friendship Press, 1951. 120 p. -- A good overall view of missionary work in Latin America.

383. Hampares, Katherine. The North American as viewed in the contemporary Spanish-American novel, 1900-60. Ph. D. thesis, Columbia University, New York, in preparation. -- Contains a chapter with a bibliography on the image of the missionary.

384. Hargrove, Berrie V. Evangelical social work in Latin America. Ph. D. thesis, Trinity University, San Antonio, 1951. Emphasis on the Methodist social work in Chile.

385. Hennig, Martin. Sie gingen übers meer: die evangelischen kirchen deutscher herkunft in ubersee, ihre eigenart, ihre probleme und ihre arbeit. Hamburg, Agentur des Rauhen Hauses (n.d.). 232 p. -- Short articles of general information about the Lutheran churches of German origin in Latin America. Articles of different value.

386. Hollenweger, Walter J. The Pentecostal movement and the World Council of Churches. *Ecumenical review* 18:6 July 1966.

387. Housley, John B. Protestant political ethics in the context of Latin America. Th. D. thesis, Union Theological Seminary, New York, 1964. -- Excellent.

388. Howard, George P. La otra conquista de América. Buenos Aires, La Aurora, 1951. 167 p. -- A rationale for Evangelical mission endeavor in Latin America.

389. _____. Nuestra civilización apóstata frente al cristianismo: diagnosis de la enfermedad espiritual de nuestro siglo. Buenos Aires, Círculo de Estudios Cristianos, 1935. 125 p.

390. _____. Religious liberty in Latin America? Philadelphia, Westminster Press, 1944. xxii, 170 p. -- Spanish translation available as ¿Libertad religiosa en la América Latina? Buenos Aires, La Aurora, 1945. 249 p. Foreword by John A. Mackay. Level-headed discussion of Catholic-Protestant relations in Latin America which avoids name-calling. Clearly a Protestant point of view. See also Religious liberty in Latin America: documents related to a campaign to oppose Protestant missions in Latin America. New York, CCLA, 1943. 32 p.

391. _____. A spiritual adventure in South America. New York, CCLA, 1943. 68 p. -- On efforts to reach intellectuals in the 1940's.

392. _____. We Americans: north and south. New York, Friendship Press, 1951. c, 148 p. -- Some essential information on cultural and religious conditions.

393. Hulbert, Winifred. Latin American backgrounds. New York, Friendship Press, 1935. xii, 209 p. -- Characteristics of Latin American culture and missionary endeavors.

394. Inman, Samuel Guy. Latin America: its place in world life. new rev. ed. New York, Harcourt, Brace, 1947. -- Original English ed., 1937. Spanish translation as El destino de América Latina. Santiago, Ediciones Ercilla, 1941. 393 p. Trad. por R. Elizalde. Available in Portuguese as América Latina, sua importância mundial. São Paulo, Editôra Atlas s.a., 1945. 545 p. Trad. do Dr. Guilherme Boeing. One of the many thoughtful appraisals of Latin America by the scholarly long-time secretary of the Committee on Cooperation in Latin America.

395. _____. América revolucionaria: conferencias y ensayos. Madrid, J. Morata, 1933. 340 p.

396. _____. Christian cooperation in Latin America. New York,
     CCLA, 1917. 186 p. -- A report of visits to Mexico,
     Cuba, South America, March-October 1917.

397. _____. Conferencias dadas en la universidad nacional de
     México. México, Talleres Gráficos de la Nación, 1929.
     300 p. -- Lectures given in the summer of 1927.

398. _____. Evangelicals at Havana; being an account of the
     Hispanic American Evangelical Congress at Havana,
     Cuba, June 20-30, 1929. New York, CCLA, 1929. 174 p.

399. _____. Hacia la solidaridad americana. Madrid, D. Jorro,
     1924. 448 p.

400. _____. Intervention in Mexico. New York, Association,
     1919. xi, 248 p. -- Foreward by Prof. William R.
     Shepherd.

401. _____. Inter-American conference for the maintenance of
     peace. Philadelphia, Friends' Peace Committee, 1936.
     40 p.

402. _____. Problems in Pan Americanism. New York, Doran,
     1935. xii, 439 p.

403. _____. The religious approach to the Latin American
     mind. *Journal of religion* September, 1922.

404. _____. South America today: social and religious move-
     ments as observed on a trip to the southern continent
     in 1921. New York, CCLA, 1921. 116 p.

405. _____. Trailing the conquistadores. New York, Friendship
     Press, 1930. 236 p. -- On the Spanish-speaking
     islands. Bibliographical notes.

406. Isais, Juan. The other side of the coin. Grand Rapids,
     Erdmans, 1966. 104 p. -- An analysis in fictional
     form of the tensions between foreign missionaries and
     Latin American Christians.

407. Jacobs, Manfred. Die kirchengeschichte sudamerikas
     spanischer zunge. *In* Die kirche in inher geschichte.
     Kurt D. Schmidt *und* Ernst Wolf, ed. Götteningen,
     Vanderhoeds and Ruprecht, 1963. -- First comprehen-
     sive church history of Latin America in German, with
     many bibliographical notes. History of Latin American
     Protestantism, p. 56-63, is all too short and general.

408. Knowles, James P. Samuel A. Purdie, his life and letters,
     his work as a missionary and Spanish writer and
     publisher in Mexico and Central America. Plainfield,
     Association of Friends, 1908.

409. Krabel, Alf M. Lutherans at work on continental frontiers.
     Chicago, National Lutheran Council. 47 p. -- Brief
     summary of work of American Lutherans in some Latin
     American countries.

410. Lara Braud, Jorge. The justification given by some United
     States Protestant mission boards for the establishment
     of Protestant missions in Latin America in the 19th
     century. Th. D. thesis, Princeton Theological Semin-
     ary, Princeton, N.J. in preparation.

411. Latourette, Kenneth S. Desafío a los Protestantes.
     Buenos Aires, La Aurora, 1956. 158 p. -- The
     Carnahan Lectures by a great church historian. No
     English edition.

412. Lee, Elizabeth M. *and* Alfred W. Wasson. He wears
     orchids and other Latin American stories. New York,
     Friendship Press, 1951. x, 181 p. -- Spanish trans-
     lation as El hombre de la orquídeas. Buenos Aires,
     La Aurora, 1951. Ten portraits of a cross-section of
     Latin American Protestants.

413. _____. The Latin American circuit. New York, Joint
     Division of Education and Cultivation, Board of
     Missions and Church Extension, Methodist Church,
     1942. 190 p. -- Travel chronicle.

414. _____. World War II and the younger churches of Latin
     America. In Christian world mission. Nashville,
     Abingdon, 1946. -- See chap. 12.

415. Lee, John. Religious liberty in South America. New York,
     Eaton and Mains, 1907. -- Special reference to legis-
     lation in Peru, Ecuador and Bolivia of that period.

416. Liggett, Thomas J. Latin America -- a challenge to
     Protestantism. Río Piedras, Evangelical Seminary of
     Puerto Rico, 1949. 11 p. -- A reprint from the
     College of the Bible quarterly.

417. _____. Dilemas evangélicos en la América Latina. El
     boletín (Río Piedras, Seminario Evangélico de Puerto
     Rico) 29: 3 1964.

John A. Mackay

Addresses:

418. Mackay, John A. Adventures in the mind of Latin America. Address to the Tenth Quadrennial Convention of the SVM, Detroit, Mich., 1927. New York, SVM, 1928. 167-172 p.

419. _____. Cultural peaks in contemporary South America. Address to CCLA, 1928 New York, UPL, 1928.

420. _____. God's springtime in Latin America. Address to the Eleventh Quadrennial Convention of the SVM, Buffalo, New York, 1931. New York, SVM, 1932. 51-59 p.

421. _____. The power of evangelism in South America. Address at the Jerusalem Conference, 1928. New York, IMC, 1928. v. 8, p. 90-93.

Articles:

422. _____. Contemporary life and thought in Latin America in their relation to evangelical Christianity. New York, Foreign Missions Conference of North America, 1928. 135-142 p.

423. _____. The evangelistic duty of Christianity. Supplementary paper written for the Jerusalem Conference of 1928. New York, IMC, 1928. v. 1, p. 383-96.

424. _____. An introduction to Christian work among South American students. *IRM*, 17:278-90, 1928.

425. _____. Report of a tour of missionary investigation in South America. *The instructor of the Free Church of Scotland* (Edinburgh) v. 9-11, 1915-1917.

426. _____. Special religious problems in South America. Report of Commission Eleven of the Congress on Christian Work in South America, Montevideo, 1925. Prepared by the Chairman of the Commission, John A. Mackay. v. 2, 289-377.

427. _____. Student life in a South American university. *Student world* 13:3:89-97, 1920.

428. _____. Student renaissance in South America. *Student world* 17:2:62-66, 1924.

429. _____. The unfulfilled dream of Columbus. New York, Presbyterian Board of Foreign Missions, UPL, 1926. p. 84-93.

Chapters In Surveys:

430. _____. Christianity on the frontier. New York, Macmillan, 1950. -- A theological meditation on Latin America, p. 153-168; and, Mexican musings, p. 169-76.

431. _____. A new chapter in church history. Geneva, Alliance of Reformed Churches, 1959. p. 9-12. -- Foreward to the Sao Paulo story. Proceedings of the Eighteenth General Council of the Alliance of Reformed Churches, Sao Paulo, 1959.

Books:

432. _____. That other America. New York, Friendship Press, 1935. x, 214 p. -- A character study of the traditional Latin American and of the new trends as seen emerging in 1935.

433. _____. The other Spanish Christ: a study in the spiritual history of Spain and South America. London, Student Christian Movement Press, 1932. xv, 228 p. -- Translated by Gonzalo Báez Camargo in Colección renovación IV. México, CUPSA, 1952. 283 p. This volume stands alone as a classical interpretation of the spiritual depths and heights of Hispanic culture. Reprinted by University of Michigan Press, 1967.

434. Maddox, James G. Technical assistance by religious agencies in Latin America. Chicago, University of Chicago Press, 1956. 130 p. -- An analysis and critical appraisal of technical aid promoted by religious organizations in Bolivia, Brazil, Chile, Ecuador, Mexico, Nicaragua and Paraguay. See also A. T. Mosher. Technical cooperation in Latin America - agriculture. Chicago, University of Chicago Press, 1956. 449 p.

435. Marsh, John William. Narrative of the origin and progress of the South American mission. First fruits, enl. London, South American Missionary Society, 1883. 160 p.

436.   _____. Rays of sunlight in darkest South America; or,
        God's wondrous working on southern shores and seas.
        3. ed. London, W. Gardner Darton, 1890. 79 p.

437.   _____ *and* Waite H. Stirling. The story of commander
        Allen Gardiner, R.N., with sketches of missionary
        work in South America. 3. ed. London, J. Nisbet,
        1874. xiii, 172 p.

438.   McConnell, Harry C. The development of the hymn among
        Spanish-speaking evangelicals. Th. D. thesis,
        Southern Baptist Theological Seminary, Louisville,
        Ky., 1953.

439.   McCorkel, Henry L. The quiet crusaders. New York,
        Friendship Press, 1961. 175 p. -- Biographical
        sketches of twelve contemporary Latin American evan-
        gelicals, both leaders and followers.

440.   McLean, James H. The living Christ in Latin America.
        Philadelphia, Presbyterian Board of Publications,
        1917. 198 p. -- General description of Evangelical
        work in Latin America with emphasis on Presbyterian
        work.

441.   McNairn, Stuart A. Why South America? London, Marshall,
        Morgan and Scott, 1936. 144 p. -- Attempts to
        interpret background and atmosphere for Evangelical
        work. Somewhat polemical.

442.   Míguez Bonino, José. The prospects of Christianity
        throughout the world. M. Searle Bates, ed. New
        York, Scribners, 1964. -- Latin America, chap. 10.

443.   Millard, E. C. *and* Lucy E. Guiness. South America: the
        neglected continent. London, E. Marlborough, 1893.
        182 p. -- An account of an exploration trip of the
        Rev. G. C. Grubb and party in 1893. Historical
        sketches and a summary of the missionary enterprise
        of that period.

444.   Miller, George A. Adventures with Christ in Latin America.
        New York, Abingdon, 1927. 198 p. -- Reveals a sensi-
        tivity to similar problems which North American
        missionaries still must face. See also *his* Prowling
        about Panama. (Cf. no. 1716).

445.   Millham, William T. T. Heroes of the cross of South
        America. London, Mildmay Press, 1947. -- Life

stories of Allen Gardiner, David Trumbull, Francisco
Penzotti, John Jarrett, Kalley of Brazil and Morrison
of Argentina. By a careful writer who had the advan-
tage of knowing some of the people personally and
having had long contact with others who had known
those about whom he wrote. (Duplicated in no. 1467.)

446. _____, ed. Latin America, expanding horizons. London,
World Dominion Press, 1951. 124 p. -- Valuable but
brief survey of several countries.

447. Milne, Inés. Desde el cabo de hornos hasta Quito con la
Bíblia. Buenos Aires, La Aurora, 1944. -- Based on
Andrew Walker's From Cape Horn to Quito with the
Bible. Buenos Aires, Rosario, 1942. A very incom-
plete review of his extensive travels as colporteur
from 1864-1907.

448. Mitchell, Donald. James Thomson. Ph. D. thesis, 1972,
Princeton Theological Seminary, Princeton, N.J. --
Draws from extensive research in several national
libraries in Latin America.

449. Moore, C. R. Los evangélicos en marcha en América Latina.
Buenos Aires, Casa Bautista de Publicaciones, 1959.
176 p.

450. Moses, Jasper Turney. Survey of evangelical education in
Latin America. M.A. thesis, University of Chicago,
Ill., 1915. 63 p.

451. Mott, John R. Advanced steps for the evangelical forces
in Latin America. October 1941.

452. Navarro Monzó, Julio. The religious problem in Latin
American culture. New York, Association Press, 1925.
Title and text in Spanish. -- Reflects the position
of the YMCA in the first decades of the century in
Latin America.

453. _____. South America: a mission field. Cincinnati,
Jennings and Graham, 1906. 107 p. -- A defense of
Protestant missionary efforts in Latin America.

454. Nida, Eugene A. African influence in the religious life
of Latin America. *Practical anthropology* 56:3:173-87.

455. _____. La comunicación del evangélico en la América
Latina. Noticiero audio-visual evangélico (México)

special supplement no. 1, 1963. (Cf. no. 728).

456. _____. The relationship of social structure to the problems of evangelism in Latin America. *Practical
anthropology* 5:3 May-June 1958.

457. _____. The Roman Catholic, Communist and Protestant
approach to social structures. *Practical anthropology*
4:6 November-December 1957.

458. Nollenburg, W. *und* H. Stubbe. Wo die erdee aufhört:
Protestentische impressionen aus Sudamerika. Gerd
Mohn, Gütersloher Verlagshaus, 1964. 131 p.

459. Obermüller, Rudolf. Das Evangelium en Latinamerika.
Die evangelische diaspora, A reprint, no. 922.

360. _____. Evangelism in Latin America: an ecumenical survey. London, IMC, 1957. 32 p. -- Excellent
summary.

461. Odell, Edward Albert. It came to pass. New York, BNM,
PCUSA, 1952. 174 p. -- A review of Protestant work
in the Caribbean.

462. Oliphant, J. Orin. The Parvin-Brigham mission to Latin
America, 1823-26. *Church history* 14:2:85-103. June
1945. -- A report of two representatives of the
American Board after an extended South American trip.
Brigham reported that the time did not yet seem
propitious for Protestant missions in South America,
yet reflects some quickening of interest in Latin
America among North Americans in early 19th century,
especially among Presbyterians.

463. Ortis, González Juan. El destino de los pueblos ibéricos.
Madrid, Libería Nacional Extranjera, 1932. -- One of
the great interpreters of Latin American culture and
of the role of Protestantism in this culture.

464. Pearson, Benjamin H. The monk who lived again; a tale of
South America. Winona Lake, Ind., Light and Life,
1940. 185 p. Title and text in Spanish and Portuguese. -- The life of Walter Montaño, a former
Capuchin monk.

465. Peña, Washington de la. Un héroe del porvenir -- William
C. Morris. Buenos Aires, Asociación, 1940. 175 p.

-- Author ignores Morris' evangelical ideology and
relationships.

466. Penzotti, Francisco. Spiritual victories in South
     America. New York, American Bible Society, 1916.
     Original text in Spanish. -- Brief autobiography.

467. Pifer, Marjorie. An introduction to South America with
     emphasis on the history, influence and trends of
     Roman Catholicism. M.A. thesis, Graduate School of
     Missions, Columbia Bible School, S.C., 1956.

468. Protestantism in Latin America. *Religion in life*,
     winter 1958-59. -- Series of articles by leading
     writers.

469. Read, William R., Harmon Johnson *and* Victor Monterroso.
     Church growth research in Latin America reports.
     Pasadena, Calif., Institute of Church Growth, in
     preparation for publication in 1967-68. 3 v. --
     Promises to be first major contribution to the docu-
     mentation and interpretation of present patterns of
     church growth.

470. Reisner, Sherwood H. The attitudes of Protestant mis-
     sionaries toward Latin American culture to 1916.
     Ph. D. thesis, University of Texas, Austin, in
     preparation.

471. Rembao, Alberto. Democracia trascendente. Buenos Aires,
     La Aurora, 1945. 266 p. -- A distinguished Mexican
     Protestant author and journalist.

472. _____. Discurso a la nación evangélica: aportaciones
     para un estudio de la transculturación religiosa en
     el Mundo de habla española. Buenos Aires, La Aurora,
     1949. 96 p. -- The relation of the Gospel and the
     Evangelical community to Latin American culture.

473. _____. Lecciones de filosofía de la religión. Matanzas,
     Cuba, Seminario Evangélico (n.d.). -- Lectures at
     Matanzas Union Seminary, 1955-56.

474. _____. Lupita. Santiago, Ediciones Ercilla, 1941. 146
     p. -- A novel of the Mexican Revolution. Prologue
     by John A. Mackay, epilogue by Carlton Beals.

475. _____. Meditaciones neoyorquinas. Buenos Aires, La
     Aurora, 1939. 236 p.

476.   _____. Mensaje, movimiento y masa. Buenos Aires, La
        Aurora, 1939. 108 p.

477.   _____. Pneuma; los fundamentos teológicos de la cultura:
        la realidad protestante en la América hispana.
        México, CUPSA, 1957.

478.   Riffel, Jakob, ed. Die russlanddeutschen insbesondere
        die wolgadeutschen am La Plata (Argentinien, Uruguay,
        und Paraguay). 2. ed. Buenos Aires, (n.d.). 128 p.
        -- Contains a prehistory, the history and the expan-
        sion of the immigration of the Germans who came from
        Russia to South America. Only source concerning this
        Protestant immigration, although written by "non-
        professionals."

479.   Roberts, Dayton. Latin America: a challenge of a new
        day. *Christianity today* 7:21 July 1963. -- A good
        survey article by a leader of the Latin American
        Mission, himself a United Presbyterian minister.

480.   Rycroft, W. Stanley, ed. Indians of the high Andes. New
        York, CCLA, 1946. 330 p. illus. -- Sociological
        study of Indians of Perú, Ecuador and Bolivia which
        led to the organization of the United Andean Mission
        in Ecuador. (Cf. no. 687).

481.   _____. Latin America. *In* Christianity today. New York,
        Morehouse-Goreham, 1947. -- Chap. 2.

482.   _____. Latin America. *In* World faith in action. Charles
        T. Leber, ed. New York, Bobbs-Merrill, 1951.

483.   _____. Latin America: its place and its problems as a
        mission field. New York, IRM, 1941.

484.   _____. Latin America's open doors. New York, CCLA,
        1940. 55 p. -- Based on a series of visits of the
        author with John R. Mott to Latin America, 1940-41.

485.   _____. On this foundation, the evangelical witness in
        Latin America. New York, Missionary Education Move-
        ment, 1942. 210 p.

486.   _____. The Protestant churches and religious freedom in
        Latin America. *Journal of church and state*, Spring
        1966.

487.   _____. Religion and faith in Latin America. Philadelphia,

Westminster Press, 1958. 208 p. -- Available also in
Spanish; Buenos Aires, La Aurora, 1951. 185 p.
Excellent review of Latin American religious history
and principal ideological currents.

488. _____. Roman Catholic clericalism. *Journal of church and
state*, Spring, 1966.

489. _____. Sobre este fundamento. Buenos Aires, La Aurora,
1944. 223 p. -- Trans. by Adam F. Sosa into Spanish
from English original. Achievements of and opportunities for evangelical work in Latin America.

490. Salem, Luis D. pseu. Francisco G. Penzotti: apóstol de la
libertad y de la verdad. México, Sociedades Bíblicas
en la América Latina, 1963. 46 p.

491. Scanlon, A. Clark. A program of Baptist minister training
in Spanish America. Th. D. thesis, Southwestern
Baptist Seminary, Dallas, 1964.

492. Shank, J. W. Mennonitism in Latin American background.
Mennonite quarterly review 2:192-97 July 1928.

493. Shaull, M. Richard. Encounter with revolution. New York,
Association, 1955. 145 p. -- Contains keen and
prophetic insights into the events of the past decade.

494. _____. Evangelism and proselytism in Latin America.
Student world 46:14-20, 1953.

495. _____. A study of contemporary Latin American political
ideologies. Guggenheim Foundation grant, begun 1965.

496. Smith, Donald P. Some preaching values of the books of
the Romans for evangelicals in Spanish Catholic
countries. S.T.M. thesis, Union Theological Seminary,
New York, 1956. 153 p.

497. Speer, Robert E. The case for missions in Latin America.
New York, BFM, UPCUSA, 1912. 24 p.

498. _____. Missions in South America. New York, BFM,
UPCUSA, 1909. 178 p.

499. _____. South American problems. New York, Student
Volunteer Missions for Foreign Missions, 1919. 270 p.

500. _____. The unity of the Americas. New York, Laymen's

Missionary Movement, 1916. 115 p. -- A discussion of
the political, commercial, educational, religious
relationships of Anglo-America and Latin America.
Prophetic in parts, however, echoes concept of Pan
Americanism of that epoch. Comments on reports of
commissions of Panama Conference of 1916.

501. Stauffer, Milton, ed. As Protestant Latin America sees
it. New York, Student Volunteer Movement and Missionary Education Movement, 1927. 170 p. -- Seven Latin
American leaders speak.

502. Stone, Barbara W. Home and family life in Latin America;
influence of the Evangelical church on standards of
living and family stability. M.A. thesis, Kennedy
School of Missions and the Hartford Seminary Foundation, Conn., 1953. 99 p. -- Deals with the changing
status of women and parental authority.

503. Stone, L. Paul. Agricultural missions in Latin America;
their correlation with technical assistance program.
M. A. thesis, Kennedy School of Missions, Hartford
Seminary Foundation, Conn., 1953. 113 p.

504. Stuntz, Homer C. Outlook in the River Plate. New York,
Friendship Press, 1942. 64 p.

505. _____. South American neighbors, New York, Missionary
Education Movement of the USA and Canada, 1916. c,
217 p. -- Draws on reports of Panama Congress and
publications of the P.A.U. Text contains many
inaccuracies and unsupported generalizations.

506. Sumrall, Lester F. Through blood and fire in Latin
America. Grand Rapids, Zondervan, 1944. -- Biograph-
ies of Walter Montaño from Perú, Manuel G. Aldama in
Perú and Ecuador, Robert Elphick of Chile and others.

507. Taylor, William. Our South American cousins. New York,
Nelsons and Phillips, 1879. 366 p.

508. _____. Story of my life; and account of what I have
thought and said and done in my ministry of more than
fifty-three years in Christian lands and among the
heathen. John Clark Ridpath, ed. New York, Hunt and
Eaton, 1895. 750 p. -- Copiously embellished with
original engravings and sketchings.

509. Testa, Michael P. O apóstol de Madeira. Lisboa, Igreja

Evangélica Presbiteriana do Portugal, 1963. 154 p.
Text also in English. -- The life and work of Robert
R. Kalley, M.D. in Madeira, the U.S. and Brazil.

510. Thomas, James. Letters on the moral and religious state
of South America. London, Nesbitt, 1827. 296 p. --
Letters of one of the most important missionary jour-
neys in the history of the Christian church by a
Bible colporteur and pioneer educator. Valuable perspective on the religious and cultural life of the
newly independent republics. Copies in MRL, PTSL,
UPL, Museo Mitre and Biblioteca Nacional, Buenos
Aires.

511. True stories from South America. London, Evangelical
Union of South America (n.d.). 47 p. -- Stories of
individual conversions in Brazil, Argentina and Perú.
Illustrates the strengths and weaknesses of Protestantism in the application of the Gospel.

512. Tschuy, Theo. Latin American Protestantism, the coming
crisis. *The Christian century* 26 December 1962. --
A perceptive study by a Swiss Protestant.

513. Turner, Charles W. La Biblia en América Latina. Buenos
Aires, La Aurora, 1951. 155 p. -- The story of the
Bible societies' work in Latin America in terms of
effect on people and the ministry of the church. See
also *his* La Biblia construye en América Latina.
Buenos Aires, La Aurora, 1954. 108 p.

514. Twentyman, John H. James Thomson, M.D.: intrepid agent
of the Bible society. mss, Hartford Seminary Foundation, Hartford, Conn., 1957. 22 p.

515. Unforgettable disciples. New York, BFM, PCUSA, 1942.
247 p. -- Chap. on Dr. Peña of Chila, Doña Martina
de Chile and Col. Rodolfo Curti of Mexico. Of
special interest is the story of Marcelino Vásquez,
a converted Guatemalan witch doctor.

516. Vago, Ismael A. Morris, una vida consagrada a la niñez.
Buenos Aires, La Aurora, 1947. -- A simple book with
emphasis on his evangelical work.

517. Varetto, Juan C. El apóstol de la Plata. Buenos Aires,
La Aurora, 1943. -- The life of Juan Francisco
Thomson, a pioneer of the Spanish work of Methodism

in Uruguay, who was strongly influenced by James
Thomson.

518.   _____. Diego Thomson, apóstol de la instrucción pública
e iniciador de la obra evangélica en América Latina.
Buenos Aires, Imprenta Evangélica, 1918. 183 p. --
Varetto writes well, however, it would have been pro-
fitable if he had spent more time in evaluating the
work of Thomson. Published to commemorate the centenary of his arrival in Argentina. Author introduces
a polemical attitude notably absent from James
Thomson's ministry. Narrative includes some valuable
primary material (government decrees, etc.).

519.   _____, ed. Don Prudencio y sus muchachos. Buenos Aires,
1944. -- Biographical.

520. Webster, Douglas. Patterns of part-time ministry in some
churches in Latin America. London, World Dominion
Press, 1963. -- A general review of new patterns of
the ministry in Brazil, Uruguay and Chile.

521. Wenger, A. Grace. God builds the church in Latin America.
(s.l.), 1961.

522. Whitfield, Ray G. Through five republics on horseback.
16. ed. Cleveland, Evangelical Publishing House, 1920.
277 p. -- An account of many wanderings in South
America.

523. Will, John H. Exploring evangelical effort toward a united
witness in Latin America. B.D. thesis, Eden Theological Seminary, 1962. 184 p.

524. Wilson, Stanton R. Studies in the life and work of an
ecumenical churchman, John A. Mackay. Th. M. thesis,
Princeton Theological Seminary, Princeton, N.J., 1958.
-- See also Clemente, Abel. The Understanding of the
Church in the Writings of John A. Mackay. M. Th.
thesis. New College, Edinburgh, 1967.

525. World missionary conference, 1910: Edinburgh. Edinburgh,
Oliphant, Anderson and Ferrier, 1910. (Edinburgh conference series, v. 1, p. 246-52). -- Only reference
in records of this historic missionary conference to
needs for missionary work in Latin America.

526. Yoder, Howard W. This is Latin America. New York,

Friendship Press, 1961. 36 p. -- A popular, accurate
primer of Protestant work in Latin America.

BASIC RESOURCES AND STUDY TOOLS
See also p. 284.

Atlases

527. Beach, Harlan P. A geography and atlas of Protestant
      missions. New York, Student Volunteer Movement for
      Foreign Missions, 1903. 2 v. -- v. 1, "Geography"
      is now of little value, but v. 2, "Atlas and Statis-
      tics" is of permanent value.

528. _____ *and* Charles H. Fahs. World missions atlas. New
      York, Institute of Social Religious Research, 1925.
      178 p.

529. _____ *and* Burton St. John. World statistics of Christian
      missions. New York, Commission of Reference and
      Counsel of the Foreign Missions Conference of North
      America, 1916. 148 p. -- Authoritative.

530. A bird's eye view of Latin America. London, World
      Dominion Press, 1925. 40 p. maps, tables. (World
      Dominion Press survey series). -- Fairly complete
      statistical survey of Latin America.

531. Dennis, James D., Harlan P. Beach *and* Charles Fahs. World
      atlas of Christian mission. New York, Student
      Volunteer Movement for Foreign Missions, 1911. 172
      p. -- A standard reference.

532. Evangelical handbook of Latin America. London, World
      Dominion Press, 1937. 119 p. Also 1939 edition.
      121 p. LAWG. -- Valuable statistics. Published for
      the Committee on Cooperation in Latin America.

533. Missionary atlas: a manual of foreign mission work of
      the Christian and missionary atlas. A. C. Snead, ed.
      Harrisburg, pa., Christian Publications, 1964. vi,
      207 p. -- Exceedingly useful and well done. Emphasis
      on C.M.A. work, but includes general information on
      other missions. Also 1924, 1936 and 1950 editions.

534. Parker, Jos. I., ed. Interpretative statistical survey
      of the world mission of the Christian church. New

York, IMC, 1938. 323 p.

535. Protestant missions in Latin America, a statistical sur-
      vey. Clyde W. Taylor *and* Wade T. Coggins, ed. Wash-
      ington, D.C., EFA, 1045 "G" St., N.W., 1961. 314 p.
      maps, tables. -- 23 separate maps on all Latin
      American countries. Also maps and statistics on the
      Guyanas, Jamaica, British Honduras, the Bahamas,
      Puerto Rico, Windward and Leeward Islands, and Nether-
      land Indies. Best available coverage of conservative
      evangelical missions in Latin America. Unfortunately
      is weak on traditional denominations in some areas.
      Fair listing of missionary bodies and addresses of
      some national churches. Provides comparison with
      figures to 1937 edition of Evangelical handbook of
      Latin America.

536. World Christian handbook, 1962. H. Wakelin Coxill *and*
      Kenneth Grubb, ed. London, World Dominion Press,
      1962. xxiii, 400 p. -- Earlier editions for 1949,
      1952, and 1957 contain much valuable information.
      Unfortunately some of the statistics in the 1962 v.
      are not only unreliable but often misleading. 1968
      edition, London, Lutterworth Press. 1973 edition,
      Macmillian, which adds polygot glossary, extensive
      indices and tables and foldout map. MARC has a
      microfilm version in hard cover.

          Surveys, Histories of Missions
        and Comprehensive Mission Studies
              See also p. 284.

There is no attempt here to include all the histories of the
great missionary boards and societies that have worked in Latin
America. For a partial list see the bibliography in Neill's
History of Christian Missions (p. 582-83) and Glover and Kane's
The progress of world-wide missions (p. 464-66). The annual
conference and assembly proceedings and reports of various
church bodies and missionary societies at work in each country
are important sources of information, but they are not listed
here in this *Guide*.

537. An advisory study. New York, COEMAR, 1961. 94 p. -- An
      important working paper on relations between older
      and younger churches which work together in mission
      and fellowship. (Cf. no. 662).

538. Albrecht, Paul. The churches and rapid social change.

Garden City, L. I., N. Y., Doubleday, 1961. -- Prepared by WCC staff members with extended acquaintance with Latin American problems.

539. Alter, James P. Christian study and lay training centers
      in Asia, Africa, Latin America. New York, COEMAR,
      1964. mimeographed. -- A survey made in 1963-64.

540. Anderson, Gerald H. The theology of the Christian mission.
      New York, McGraw-Hill, 1961.

541. Barclay, Wade C. History of Methodist missions. New York,
      Methodist Board of Missions, 1949-57. 3 v. -- v. 1,
      1769-1844; p. 344-57 has a brief but valuable state-
      ment on Methodist beginnings from U.S. initiative in
      1825. v. 3 1845-95; p. 758-68 provides a concise
      review of Methodism in Latin America in that period.
      The remaining three volumes are in preparation by
      J. Tremayne Copplestone.

542. Beach, Harlan P., et al. Protestant missions in South
      America. Chicago, Missionary Campaign Library, 1900.
      vii, 239 p. -- Earliest comprehensive sketches pre-
      pared for students. Bibliography.

543. Beaver, R. Pierce. Ecumenical beginnings in Protestant
      world missions: a history of comity work. New York,
      Nelson, 1962. 356 p. -- A definitive study.

544. Brown, Arthur J. One hundred years, 1837-1936: a history
      of the foreign mission work of the Presbyterian Church,
      USA, New York, Revell, 1936. 1140 p.

545. Canton, William. History of the British and foreign Bible
      society. London, Murray, 1910. 5 v.

546. Davis, J. Merle. New buildings on old foundations. New
      York, IMC, 1947. 320 p. (Studies in the world mis-
      sion of Christianity, no. 4). Spanish edition.
      Construyendo sobre Cimientos Antiguos. -- Good bib-
      liography. Some references, though dated, to younger
      churches in Latin America.

547. DuPlessis, David J., ed. A brief history of the Pente-
      costal assemblies. mss, 1957. -- Written by several
      authors. Available from the editor.

548. _____. The spirit bade me go. Dallas, privately publish-
      ed by the author, 2129 E. Illinois (1960). 96 p. --

"A survey of the work of the Holy Spirit in the ecumenical movement during the decade 1951-61." More precisely, a record of the experiences, lectures and addresses of the writer. Spanish translation by Gerardo Valdivia. El Espiritu me ordenó que fuera. Plainfield, N.J., Logos International, 1970. 144 p.

549. Dwight, Henry O. The centennial history of the American Bible Society. New York, Macmillan, 1916. 2 v.

550. Fife, Eric S. *and* Arthur F. Glasser. Mission in crisis; rethinking mission strategy. Chicago, Intervarsity Press, 1961. 269 p.

551. Fleming, Daniel J., chrmn. International survey of the YMCA and YWCA. New York, International Survey Committee, 1932. 421 p.

552. Food with dignity. Ketherine P. Riddle *and* R. D. Gatewood, comp. New York, NCCC, 1966. 67 p. -- A survey presentation of major Protestant efforts to combat world hunger. Includes selected list of books, periodicals and other materials concerning world hunger.

553. Glover, Robert H. The progress of world-wide missions. New York, Harper, 1960.

554. Goddard, Burton L., ed. Encyclopedia of modern Christian missions: the agencies. Camden, N.J. and Toronto, Thomas Nelson and Sons, 1967. x. 743 p. Since publication of Bliss' *Encyclopedia of Missions* in 1891 (revised, 1964) no similar work has appeared. Largely limited to Protestant agencies and statistics are of mid-1960's. A comprehensive directory which gives a picture of the extent and variety of the operations of the organizations.

555. González, Justo L. Historia de las misiones. New York, TEF, 1967. (TEF series). -- Chap. 9 on Latin America.

556. Hogg, W. Richey. Un mundo, una misión. Buenos Aires, La Aurora, 1961. -- Trans. from English original. See reference to Latin America in *his* Ecumenical foundations. New York, Harper, 1952.

557. Hollenweger, Walter J. Handbuch der pfingstbewegung. Ph. D. thesis, University of Zürich, 1965. 8 v. -- A member of the Reformed Church, from a Pentecostal

background, has prepared 10 volumes on the Pentecostal
movements in the world. v. 1:   Introduction to
Pentecostal experience, history and doctrine; v. 2-7;
Descriptive listing of Pentecostal movements in catalogue form: v. 8; Who's who in Pentecostalism. v. 1
is of greatest value. Ten volumes now available on
xerox or microfilm DMC, Yale Divinity School. 1972.

558. Horner, Norman A. Cross and crucifix in mission: a comparison of Protestant and Roman Catholic missionary
strategy. New York, Abingdon, 1965. 223 p. -- The
first truly comprehensive and objective comparison of
both Roman Catholic and Protestant missionary methods.
Sympathetically written by a former Protestant
missionary who worked in close proximity to Roman
Catholic missions in the Cameroons.

559. Hymer, Esther W. Education, women and church in the
Americas. New York, NCCC, 1961. 40 p. -- One of
the few surveys of the new role of women in the
Americas.

560. Issues in theological education: Asia, Africa and Latin
America. New York, TEF, 1966. -- A report of the
Theological Education Fund.

561. Latourette, Kenneth Scott. Christianity in a revolutionary age. New York, Harper, 1961. 5 v. -- The same
thoroughness as the earlier work. V. 3 and 5 include
sections on Latin America: v. 3, p. 284-352; v. 5,
p. 158-240.

562. _____. History of the American Bible Society. (Left
unfinished at the time of his death).

563. _____. A history of the expansion of Christianity. New
York, Harper, 1945. 7 v. -- The most important work
in the field. Comprehensive and definitive. Valuable
bibliography on Latin American countries.

564. _____. World service: a history of the foreign work and
world service of the YMCA. New York, Association,
1957. 489 p. Includes chapters on the history of
the YMCA in Latin American countries.

565. Lindsell, Harold, ed. The church's world wide mission.
Waco, Texas, World Books, 1966. -- The basic documents of the Congress on the church's world-wide
mission, held in Wheaton, Ill., 1966. Cf. also his

"Barriers to Church Growth", Erdmans, 1966. The
1966 Lectures on Church Growth.

566. McGavran, Donald A., et al. Church growth and Christian
mission. New York, Harper and Row, 1965. --
Translated into Portuguese, 1967. See also *his* How
churches grow and the bridges of God. 1963 Lectures
on Church Growth after date of English publication.

567. Mitchell, P. D. Misión y comisión del metodismo. México,
1949. -- Brief review of Methodist work in Latin
America.

568. Moomaw, I. W. Deep furrows. New York, Agricultural
Missions, 156 Fifth Avenue, 1957. -- Survey of
experiences with village people including Latin
American.

569. Müller, Karl *und* Adolf Schulze. 200 jahre brüdermission.
Herrnhut, Verlag der Missionbuchhandlung, 1932. 2 v.
-- Best available on Moravian mission history. V. 2
reviews work in Nicaragua and Santo Domingo.

570. Neill, Stephen. Colonialism and Christian mission. New
York, McGraw-Hill, 1966. -- A much-needed, critical
inquiry by an eminent mission historian.

571. _____, ed. Concise dictionary of Christian missions.
In preparation. -- Chapter on Latin America by Jorge
Lara Braud.

572. _____. A history of Christian missions. Grand Rapids,
Erdmans, 1964. 622 p. -- Also a Penguin book. This
is the most important work on the Protestant side,
next to Latourette's history.

573. Nicol, John T. Pentecostalism: a study of the growth and
development of a vital new force in American Protestantism. New York, Harper and Row, 1966. 264 p.

574. Norton, H. Wilbert. European background and history of
the Evangelical Free Church foreign mission. Moline,
Ill., Christian Service Foundation, 1964.

575. Olsen, M. Ellsworth. A history of the origin and progress
of the Seventy-day Adventists. 3. ed. Washington,
.D.C., Herald and Review, 1932.

576. Pascoe, C. F. Two hundred years of the S.P.G., 1701-1900.

London, 1901. 2 v. -- Brief but important survey of
early Anglican work in the Caribbean and Central
America.

577. Prescott, Lyle. Luz en la América Latina. Kansas City,
Nazarene (n.d.). 192 p.

578. Protestant churches of Asia, Middle East, Africa, Latin
America and the Pacific area. New York, MRL, 1959.
75 p. -- A revision of The Younger churches: some
facts and observations. Very cursory.

579. Rouse, Ruth, ed. *and* Stephen C. Neil. A history of the
ecumenical movement, 1517-1948. Philadelphia, Westminster Press, 1954. 822 p.

580. Rycroft, W. Stanley. The ecumenical witness of the
United Presbyterian church. New York, Commission on
Ecumenical Missions and Relations, 1968. Grand
Rapids, 1967. -- Historical and interpretative.
Traces the development of a missionary church and
the emergence of mission in unity.

581. _____. Latin America and the United Presbyterians. New
York, COEMAR, 1961.

582. Scopes, Wilfred E., ed. The Christian ministry in Latin
America and the Caribbean. New York, DWME-WCC, 1962.
264 p. -- Report of a survey of the Evangelical
seminaries undertaken in 1961.

583. Shedd, Clarence P. History of the world alliance of the
YMCA. London, SPCK, 1955. xvii, 746 p. -- Published
for the World's Committee of YMCA.

584. _____. Two centuries of student Christian movements:
their origin and intercollegiate life. New York,
Association, 1934. xxii, 466 p.

585. Taylor, Delong *and* Mendell Taylor. Fifty years of Nazarene missions. Kansas City, Nazarene. 3 v.

586. Thiessen, John C. A survey of world missions. 3. rev.
ed. Chicago, Moody Press, 1961. xiii, 544 p. --
General survey from a conservative evangelical point
of view. Revised edition is more accurate than previous editions.

587. Thompson, Henry P. Into all lands; the history of the

society for the propagation of the gospel in foreign
parts, 1701-1950. London, SPCK, 1951. xv, 760 p.

588. Ure, Ruth. The highway of print: a world-wide study of
the production and distribution of Christian literature. New York, Friendship Press, 1946. (Studies of
the world mission of Christianity, v. 7). -- Section
on literature production in Latin America. One of
the few sources of this information in survey form.

589. Vallier, Ivan. Anglican opportunities in Latin America.
New York, Bureau of Applied Social Research, 1963.
-- Solid study of Argentina, Bolivia, Chile and Peru,
on current religious belief and practice, based on
sociological data.

590. Wallis, Ethel. 2000 tongues to go. New York, Harper and
Row, 1959. -- Survey of work of Wycliffe Bible
translators.

591. Wenger, J. C. Compendio de historia y doctrina menonita·
Scottsdale, Pa., Herald Press. 284 p. -- Trans. by
Ernesto Suárez. Although a translation, the final
chapter, added by the translator, carries a valuable
resumé of the history and program of the Mennonites
in South America.

592. Wheeler, W. Reginald, ed. The crisis decade, 1936-47.
New York, BFM, UPC, 1951. 369 p. -- A supplement to
the centenary volume of Arthur J. Brown. Chapters on
Brazil, Chile, Colombia, Guatemala, Mexico and
Venezuela.

593. White, Charles L. A century of faith. Philadelphia,
Judson Press, 1932. 320 p. -- Centenary volume of
American Baptist Home Mission Society.

594. Yorke, Allen. A seminary survey. New York, Harper, 1960.
xxvi, 640 p. -- A comprehensive, detailed survey of
Protestant, Roman Catholic and Orthodox seminaries in
Africa, Asia and Latin America.

Directories
See also p. 288.

595. Directories of Christian councils. London, IMC, 1959.
-- 1960 supplement.

596. Directorio protestante de la América Latina. Camilio
     Crivelli, S. J., ed. Isola dei Liri, Roma, Italia,
     Soc. Tipografia A Maciore, 1933. 714 p.

597. Directory of evangelical missions in Latin America. New
     York, CCLA, 1922.

598. Directory of Protestant church-related hospitals outside
     Europe and North America. New York, MRL, 1963. vii,
     159 p. -- Information on 1228 hospitals in 85 coun-
     tries.

599. Lutheran directory. Geneva, World Lutheran Foundation,
     1966. 69 p.

600. North American Protestant missionary agencies. 6. ed.
     New York, MRL, 1964. xvi, 80 p. -- Includes infor-
     mation on most of the Protestant agencies from North
     America working in Latin America. 1968 ed. Word
     Press, Waco, Texas.

601. Pequeño diccionario de las sectas protestantes. Camilio
     Crivelli, S. J., ed. México, Editorial Buena Prensa,
     1948. 308 p. Title and text in Italian.

602. Protestant theological seminaries and Bible schools in
     Asia, Africa, Middle East, Latin America, the Caribbean
     and Pacific areas. Frank W. Pierce, ed. New York,
     MRL, 1960. (MRL directory series, no. 12).

REPORTS OF CONTINENTAL AND REGIONAL CONFERENCES

Interdenominational
See also p. 288.

General

603. 1900 Ecumenical missionary conference on foreign missions.
     New York, American Tract Society, 1902. 2 v. State-
     ments on work in Latin America.

604. 1913 Conference on missions in Latin America, 1913. New
     York, International Missionary Committee, 1933. 192
     p. -- Under the auspices of the Foreign Missions
     Conference of North America. Records discussion as
     well as addresses and statements adopted.

605. 1916 Beach, Harlan P. Renaissant Latin America: Panama
      1916. New York, Missionary Education Movement, CCLA,
      1916. 258 p. -- An interpretation of the Panama
      Congress.

606. Congress on Christian work in Latin America, Panama, 1916.
      New York, Missionary Education Movement, CCLA, 1917.
      3 v. tables. -- Useful for reference. A bound
      volume of bulletins, minutes and other documents on
      this conference is on file in the LAD-NCC.

607. Fox, John. Christian unity, church unity and the Panama
      Congress. *Princeton theological review*, p. 545-78.
      1917.

608. Inman, Samuel G. Christian cooperation in Latin America.
      New York, CCLA, 1917. 186 p. -- Report of a contin-
      ental visit the year after the Panama Congress.

609. Regional conferences in Latin America. New York, MEM,
      1917. 452 p. -- Reports of seven conferences follow-
      ing the Panama Congress; Lima, Santiago, Buenos Aires,
      Rio de Janeiro, Havana, San Juan, Barranquilla.

610. 1925 Christian work in South America: Montevideo, 1925.
      New York, CCLA, 1925. 2 v. -- Spanish translation
      of original available. Is the official report of the
      Congress on Christian work in Latin America. A land-
      mark of Protestantism in Latin America.

611. 1929 Hacia la renovación religiosa en Hispano-América.
      México, CUPSA, 1930. 213 p. -- Report of the Con-
      greso Evangélico Hispanoamericano, Havana, 1929 by
      Gonzalo Báez Camargo.

612. 1941 Informe oficial del congreso evangélico centro-
      americano. Guatemala City, Imprenta El Mensajero,
      1941. 233 p. -- Report on conference held in Guate-
      mala City, May 1941 on occasion of visit of John R.
      Mott.

613. 1949 El cristianismo en la América Latina. Buenos Aires,
      La Aurora, 1949. 103 p. -- Report of the First
      Latin American Evangelical Conference.

614. Presencia y mensaje. -- Four addresses given at the
      above conference. 23 p.

615. 1955 Consultation on religious liberty in Latin America.

New York, CCLA, 1955. 100 p. -- Held in Buck Hill
Falls, Pa., November 1955.

616. 1957 The listening isles. New York, IMC, 1957. 92 p.
-- Report of the Caribbean consultation held in San
Germán, Puerto Rico, 1957. See also Cuba to Surinam.
An IMC report of a journey in the Caribbean by E. J.
Bingle. 46 p.: preparatory for this consultation.

617. 1961 Cristo, la esperanza para la América Latina. Buenos
Aires, Confederación Evangélica del Río de la Plata,
1963. -- Ponencias, informes y comentarios de la
Segunda Conferencia Evangélica Latinoamericana, Lima,
1961.

618. 1963 Witness in six continents. Geneva, DWME, 1964. --
First meeting of the DWME-WCC, Mexico City. Addresses
by Alfonso Lloreda, Emilio Castro, Gonzalo Castillo
and others.

Special Concerns

Christian Education
(Many other publications available through Sec. General,
CELEDEC, Apartado 3994, Lima, Peru).

619. 1949 El cristianismo evangélico en la América Latina.
Informe de la Primera Conferencia Evangélica Latinoamericana, Buenos Aires, 1949. -- One of the chapters
deals with Christian education. Chap. 2. of the Plan
of Action deals with education of the Christian
community.

620. 1953 Preparación para el servicio en la educación cristiana. Chile, Informe del Instituto de Santiago,
1953. -- Under the auspices of CCLA and WCCE in
collaboration with the Evangelical Council of Chile
and the Confederation of Churches of the Río de la
Plata.

621. 1961 Consulta de educación cristiana. Huampaní, Perú,
1961. -- Preparatory to the II Latin American
Evangelical Conference, Peru, 1961.

622. 1962 Organización de la comisión evangélica Latinoamericana de educación cristiana (CELADEC). Huampaní,
Perú, 1962. -- Addresses, reports, resolutions and
resume of acts.

623.   1963 Informe interpretativo de la conferencia-taller para
       el curso nueva vida en Cristo. Lima, Peru, julio-
       agosto 1963. -- Course for persons of low academic
       level.

624.   1964 Memoria de la consulta sobre preparación de líderes
       cristianos. Alajuela, Costa Rica, agosto 1964. --
       Reports, addresses, conclusions.

625.   1966 Primer congreso rioplatense de educación cristiana.
       Buenos Aires, Informes, 1966.

Christian Literature

626.   1941 Christian literature program for Latin America.
       México, CCLA, 1941. Title and text in Spanish. --
       Report of 1941 Conference on Christian literature.

627.   1956 Panorama de la asamblea constituyente. San José,
       Costa Rica, 1956. -- Report of the organizing
       assembly of the L.E.A.L.

The Christian Mission in Latin American Culture

628.   1955 Toward an understanding of Latin America: an
       inquiry. Hartford, Impre. Leempoel (n.d.). --
       Reports of study conference on the relevance of the
       Christian message to the culture of Latin America.
       Papers by John Gillen, Sol Tax, José John Arrom,
       S. G. Inman, W. S. Rycroft and others. Published in
       French and English, titled Civilizations. Available
       in MRL.

629.   1959 El coloquio de Hartford. -- Addresses published as
       a special number in *La nueva democracia*, July 1960.
       p. 128.

Church and Society

630.   1961 Primera consulta latinoamericana de iglesia y
       sociedad: Huampaní, Perú, 1961. México, CUPSA,
       1961. 70 p. -- Report published under title
       Encuentro y desafío. Preface by José Míguez Bonino.

631.   1963 Informe de la consulta celebrada en Río de Janeiro.
       Montevideo. (Strategy and Methodology), 1963. 20 p.

632.   1966 Consulta sobre misión urbana industrial de la
          iglesia. Buenos Aires. mimeographed. -- Available
          PIIR, 8000 W. Belden Avenue, Chicago, Ill.

633.   Segunda consulta latinoamericana de iglesia y sociedad.
          El Tabo, Chile, 1966. Montevideo, LEL, Paysandú 839,
          1° Piso, núm. 1930. 132 p. -- Report published
          under title América hoy.

634.   II Consulta andina de iglesia y sociedad. 1:1 December
          1966.

Mass Communication

635.   1959 I Latin American congress on evangelical communica-
          tions, Cali, Colombia. -- Report of meetings.

636.   1962 II Latin American congress on evangelical communica-
          tions, Huampaní, Perú. -- Report of meetings.

Rural Work

637.   1956 Informe de la primera asamblea evangélica inter-
          americana de obra rural. México, CCLA y Comité
          Cooperativo de Misiones Rurales, 1956. 118 p.

638.   1963 Comité de obra rural de la alianza evangélica
          costarricense. San José, C.R., Editorial Caribe,
          1963. 145 p. -- Report of the II Inter-American
          Evangelical Assembly of Rural Work.

University Students

639.   1952 São Paulo conference. Geneva, WSCF, 1952. 84 p.
          -- Report on leadership training conference for
          Latin America.

640.   1966 Conferencia vida y misión de la iglesia, Embalse,
          Argentina. -- See *Testimonium* 10:3 and 4. Also
          three mimeographed documents including "Cuadernos de
          Embalse" and "Presencia cristiana en la revolución
          en América Latina."

641.   Informes de conferencias de los MECs centroamericanos,
          Las Nubes, Nicaragua; de los MECs de los países
          andinos. La Paz, Bolivia; de los MECs del Caribe,

Kingston, Jamaica. Buenos Aires, FUMEC, Cangallo
1644, 1966.

642. Hacia una estrategia ecuménica para la tarea universitaria en la América Latina. Buenos Aires, FUMEC,
Cangallo 1644, 1966. 31 p. -- Report of the study
conference of UNELAM and FUMEC held in El Tabo, Chile.

Youth

643. 1941 Con Cristo un mundo nuevo. Rosario, Argentina,
ULAJE, 1941. 160 p. -- Complete report of the 1941
Lima Conference.

644. 1951 Edmeston, Rhoda C. The Protestant youth movement in
Latin America. New York, CCLA, 1954. 128 p. -- A
general history and collection of principal statements
of the FALJE and ULAJE until 1951. Continental
conferences were held in Lima, 1941; Havana, 1946;
Buenos Aires, 1951; Mexico, 1961; and San Germán,
P.R., 1966. A review of the developments of FALJE
(federación de América Latina de juventudes evangélicas) from 1927-53 is found in this volume.

Denominational
See also p. 289.

Lutheran

645. Committee on Latin America. Geneva, LWF, 1963. 28 p. --
Reports covering 1957-63 to the 4th Assembly of the
Lutheran World Federation, 1963. (Cf. no. 599).

646. IV congreso luterano latinoamericano. *Ekklesia* 9:20-21
December 1965. -- Report and major addresses. Note
especially D. Rodolfo Obermüller's Integración de
iglesia y misión en América Latina, and appended
bibliography. See also extensive listing of related
articles on Indice General, *Ekklesia* 1961-64.

647. Fülling, Erich. Cristus im sechsten kontinent. Stuttgart,
Evang. Missionsverlag, GMCH, 1966. 96 p. -- Selected
reading list largely in German. Excellent survey.

648. Herman, S. W. Lutheranism in Latin America. *In* Lutheran

churches in the Latin American World. Minneapolis,
Augsburg, 1957.

649. Lutheran world 8:4 December 1961. -- Special issues
dedicated to Latin America. (Cf. no. 409).

650. Statement by Missouri Synod Conference of the Caribbean.
SEL, November 1966. -- Basis of ecumenical participation in Latin America. A significant declaration.

Methodist
See also p. 289.

651. Gattinoni, Carlos. ed. Vida y misión de la iglesia
metodista. Buenos Aires, Consulta Latinoamericana,
1962. -- Study papers, four essays on the church and
revolution and findings and recommendations. Of
special value is Emilio Castro's study on religion
and morality in the Methodist church in Latin
America.

652. Mensaje del congreso sudamericano de la iglesia evangélica
metodista... Buenos Aires, Imprenta Metodista, 1945.
16 p.

653. Objectivos de las escuelas metodistas. Buenos Aires, La
Aurora, 1952. -- Reports and addresses.

Presbyterian and Reformed
See also p. 289.

654. Manual de la conferencia de las iglesias presbiterianas
de la América Latina. 58 p. mimeographed. --
Reports of the 2ª Conferencia (México, 1958) and the
3ª Conferencia (El Tabo, Chile, 1961) are available
from the file of the former CCPAL (Comisión de
cooperación presbiteriana en la América Latina) now
AIPRAL (Asociación de iglesias presbiterianas y
reformadas de la América Latina).

Study papers, recommendations and related publications of the
Special Study Conference of the CCPAL (Bogotá, 1963) are the
following:

655. Castillo Cárdenas, Gonzalo. La congregación como
comunidad misionera. Bogotá, CCPAL, 1964.

656. _____. El Desafío de la América Latina a las iglesias
     evangélicas; una interpretación. Bogotá, CCPAL
     (n.d.). 11 p.

657. _____. Guía de estudios bíblicos para la congregación de
     la iglesia local. Bogotá, CCPAL, 1963. 53 p.

658. _____, ed. La naturaleza de la iglesia y su misión en
     latinoamérica. Bogotá, CCPAL, 1963. 226 p. -- Major
     addresses and recommendations of the Bogotá study
     conference.

659. _____. La renovación de la congregación local. Bogotá,
     CCPAL, 1964.

660. Congreso especial de restructuración. México, 1966. 92 p.
     -- Record of the congress in which the former CCPAL
     became the Association of Presbyterian and Reformed
     Churches in Latin America.

661. Consulta mundial sobre misiones, recomendaciones. s.l.
     (n.d.). 24 p. -- Translation of report of Confer-
     ence on World Mission of the Presbyterian Church,
     U.S.

662. La misión de la iglesia -- un estudio asesor. July 1962.
     -- Translation of an Advisory Study, 1961. 84 p.
     Report of the committee of fifteen church leaders to
     the COEMAR. (Cf. no. 537).

Reports of Regional Consultative and Cooperative Bodies

663. Comisión provisional de unidad evangélica en la América
     Latina. Montevideo, UNELAM, 1965. -- Reports.

664. Committee on cooperation in Latin America (CCLA), 1916-65.
     -- Annual reports to be found in MRL. SML has 1923,
     1925-300, 1935 reports.

665. Latin America Department of the National Council of
     Churches of Christ, U.S.A., 1964. -- Annual reports
     in mimeographed form available through LAD-NCCC,
     475 Riverside Drive, New York.

LITERATURE ON THE SPECIAL CONCERNS
OF PROTESTANTISM IN LATIN AMERICA
See also p. 289.

Work Among Indigenous Groups

Articles
See also p. 291.

666. Hamilton, Keith E.   Consultation on Andean Indian work.
     Practical anthropology 2:1.

667. Loewen, Jacob A.   The church: indigenous and ecumenical.
     Practical anthropology 2:6.

668. Nida, E. W.   Christo-paganism.   *Practical anthropology*
     8:1-15.

669. _____. Drunkenness in indigenous religious rites.
     Practical anthropology 6:20-3.

670. _____. The indigenous churches in Latin America.
     Practical anthropology 8:97-105.

671. _____. *and* William L. Wonderly.   Selection, preparation
     and function of leaders in Indian fields. *Practical
     anthropology* 10:6-11.

672. Robinson, Dow F.   The Indian church in a sponsor-oriented
     society. *Practical anthropology* 9:90-3.

673. Turner, Glen D.   Indian assimilation and bi-lingual
     schools. *Practical anthropology* 11:5.

674. Winter, Ralph D.   The first evangelical Indian congress.
     Practical anthropology 9:85-90.

Books, Essays and Pamphlets
See also p. 289.

675. Collier, John.   The Indians of the Americas.   abridged ed.
     New York, New American Library, 1948.   191 p.   --
     Mentor book MP494.

676. Cowell, Adrian.   The heart of the forest.   New York,
     Knopf, 1961.   283 p.   -- Deals with Brazil's effort
     to save the remnants of the tribes.   Main theme is

that the Indian of the Amazon is doomed to extinction.

677. Hanke, Lewis. The dawn of conscience in America: Spanish
     experiments and experiences with Indians in the New
     World. *Proceedings of the American philosophical
     society* 107:2 April 1963.

678. Hay, Alexander R. The Indians of South America and the
     Gospel. New York, Revell, 1928.

679. Indian languages of Mexico and Central America and their
     geographical distribution. Washington, D.C., U.S.
     Government Printing Office, 1911. 108 p. maps.

680. Indians in Latin America. New York, CCLA, 1924. -- A
     plea, survey, program and bibliography. One of the
     first appeals to the Protestant conscience in North
     America.

681. Jordan, W. F. Central American Indians and the Bible.
     New York, Revell, 1926. 91 p. -- American Bible
     Society representative reports on Indian work prin-
     cipally in Guatemala and Panama.

682. _____. Glimpses of Indian America. New York, Revell,
     1923.

683. Metraux, Alfred. The social and economic structure of
     the Indian communities of the Andean region.
     International labor review 89:3 March 1959.

684. Nida, Eugene W. Customs and cultures -- anthropology for
     the Christian mission. New York, Harpers, 1954.

685. Radin, Paul. Indians of South America. Garden City,
     N.J., Doubleday, 1942. 324 p. (The American museum
     of national history science series).

686. Redfield, Robert. The primitive world and its transfor-
     mations. Ithaca, N.Y., Cornell University Press,
     1958. xiii, 185 p. (Great seal books).

687. Rycroft, W. Stanley, ed. Indians of the high Andes. New
     York, CCLA, 1946. 330 p. -- Report of a commission
     of the CCLA on possibilities of establishing a
     cooperative Christian enterprise in the Andean high-
     lands. (Cf. no. 480).

688. Sáenz, Moisés. (Cf. no. 1452).

689.   Steward, Julian H., ed. Handbook of South American
       Indians. (Cf. no. 73).

690.   _____ *and* Louis C. Faron. Native peoples of South
       America. New York, McGraw-Hill, 1959. 481 p. --
       Vivid reconstruction of their cultural history show-
       ing presistence of traditional forms.

691.   Van Haagen, Victor W. The Aztec, man and tribe. (MP264);
       Realm of the Incas. (MP355); World of the Maya.
       (394). -- All three are Mentor paperbacks. $0.65.

692.   Vela, David, ed. Orientaciones y recomendaciones del
       primer congreso indigenista interamericano, April
       1940. Guatemala, Comité Organizador del IV Congreso,
       1959. 231 p. -- Compilation of a series of articles
       in *El imparcial* after the Pátzcuaro congress.

                    Unpublished Doctoral Dissertations

(For example, over 30 Ph. D. theses are listed in the Columbus
Memorial Library.)

                            Other Resources

693.   Baldus, Herbert. Bibliografia comentada de etnologia
       brasileira, 1943-50. Río de Janeiro, Editora Souza,
       1954. 142 p. -- Many valuable references among the
       354 listings.

694.   Bulletins of Bureau of American Ethnology. Washington,
       D.C., Smithsonian Institute. -- e.g., no. 63 on
       Tribes of Tierra del Fuego; no. 64 on Mayan Indians
       of southern Yucatán and northern British Honduras;
       no. 79 on Jíbaro Indians of eastern Ecuador.

695.   Murdoch, George P., et al. Human relations area files.
       New Haven, Conn., Yale University, Dept. of Anthro-
       pology. -- Extensive files now in twenty centers in
       universities in the United States. Section on Central
       and South America.

Youth and University Students
See also p. 291.

696. Galland, Valdo. Review of the present situation of the
Christian student work in Latin America. New York,
CCLA, 1957. 7 p. -- Cursory review.

Youth (Non-University)
See also p. 291.

Among the mimeographed publications of ULAJE, Montevideo, are
the following:

697. Campamentos de trabajo. 43 p.

698. Etica cristiana para el joven contemporáneo. 29 p.

699. La iglesia y la crisis latinoamericana. Address by Emilio
Castro at ULAJE-FUMEC conference, 1961.

700. La juventud evangélica y la iglesia; estudio sobre Cuba.
29 p.

701. Material ocasional para la juventud y sus líderes. 23 p.

702. Palabra viva; estudios bíblicos. Lautaro 245, Buenos
Aires. Quarterly.

703. Viviendo en estos tiempos.

University Student Work
See also p. 292.

704. AGEUP: la evangelización en la universidad. Lima,
Editorial La Antártida (ca. 1967). 90 p. -- Used by
the Asociación de Grupos Evangélicos Universitarios
del Perú.

Among the publications of the FUMEC are the followingÑ

705. Noticias de los movimientos estudiantes cristianos en
América Latina. Leonardo Franco, ed. Buenos Aires,
Cangallo 1644. -- A review of activities.

706. Vida y misión de la iglesia. México, ULAJE y FUMEC, 1962.
3 v.

Literature and Literacy
See also p. 292.

707. Biblioteca de ALFALIT (Alfabetización y literatura para la
      América Latina). Alajuela, Costa Rica (n.d.). 104 p.
      -- Extensive mimeographed bibliography of literature
      in areas of mass communications, with emphasis on
      literacy.

708. Dailey, Dorothy T. Communicating to Spanish-speaking new
      literates through written materials on Christian family
      relations, with special reference to the Caribbean
      area. M.A. thesis, Kennedy School of Missions, Hart-
      ford, Conn., 1959.

709. Rycroft W. Stanley *and* Myrtle M. Clemmer. The struggle
      against illiteracy. New York, COEMAR, 1964. 50 p.
      -- A survey of facts, based on U.S. statistics and a
      review of programs under way in the "decade of
      literacy."

Christian Healing

710. Hasselblad, O. W., M.D. Leprosy missions in South America.
      April 1964. American Leprosy Missions, 1964. Mimeo-
      graphed.

Church and Society
See also p. 292.

711. Castillo Cárdenas, Gonzalo. Christians and the struggle
      for a new social order in Latin America. *Cristianismo
      y sociedad*, no. 9 and 10, 1965. -- Special issue on
      the religious problem in Latin America by several
      authors. A rich source of articles on many of the
      concerns of Protestantism throughout the continent.

712. Christian non-violence in the Latin American social revolu-
      tion. Montevideo, 1966. mimeographed. -- Report of
      the consultation of this subject. Organized by the
      Fellowship of Reconciliation.

713. Desafío y respuesta. Buenos Aires, Centro Urbano,
      Biamonte 3445, Valentía Alsina Lanús. -- Bulletin
      on missions in urban induatrial zones in Buenos Aires.

714. Fé cristiana y marxismo. Montevideo, ISAL, 1964. 78 p.
-- Carlos Lenkersdorf, Julio Barreiro, Andres Dumas
and Jos. L. Hromdka analyze objectively the thought
of Karl Marx as this confronts the fundamental
affirmations of Christianity.

715. González, Justo L. Revolución y encarnación. Río Piedras,
Puerto Rico, La Reforma, 1965. (Colección universitario, no. 1).

716. Mackay, John A. Latin America and revolution; the new
mood in the churches. Christian century 24 November
1965.

717. Maury, Phillipe. Cristianismo y política. Buenos Aires,
Methopress, 1964. 140 p. -- Original text in English
and trans. by Adam F. Sosa.

718. Míguez Bonino, José. Christians and the political revolution. *Motive* December 1966. -- A mature view by a
competent theologian and able church leader.

719. Polémica, diálogo y misión. Montevideo, ISAL, 1965. 86
p. -- A team of experts under direction of Dr. José
Míguez Bonino analyze situations of Roman Catholicism
and Protestantism in Latin America.

720. Realidad social de América Latina. Montevideo, ISAL,
1965. 100 p. -- Five studies on important social
problems.

721. La responsibilidad social del cristiano; guía de estudios.
Montevideo, ISAL, 1964. 140 p. -- Prepared by leading Latin American theologians and social thinkers
with an excellent appendix on "Vocabulario de los
aspectos social, político y económico de América
Latina."

722. de Santa Ana, Julio, ed. Aspectos religiosos de la
sociedad uruguaya. Montevideo, LEL, 1966. 143 p.
-- Based on careful survey, together with a final
chapter by Don Romeo Diore on "Los supersticiones y
creencias en el Uruguay." Glossary of popular
religious terminology.

723. _____, ed. Hombre, ideologia y revolución en América
Latina. Montevideo, LEL, 1965. 133 p. -- Essays by
' Latin American leaders on the place of man in the

revolutionary situation in Latin America. Written
from several points of view in Christian thought.

724. Shaull, M. Ricardo. Cristianismo y revolución social.
Buenos Aires, La Aurora (n.d.). 121 p. -- Attitudes
which Christian should adopt in relation to Communism.
See also *his* An examination of some of the implications of recent developments in the world situation
and in the theology of mission for the form and
structure of the Church's life and mission. Ph. D.
thesis, Princeton Theological Seminary, Princeton,
N.J., 1959.

725. Smith, John C. How the church addresses the world. New
York, COEMAR, 1966. 8 p. -- A published address on
a subject in every age facing the churches everywhere.

Mass Communications
See also p. 296.

726. Conference on the communication and interpretation of the
world mission of the church. New York, WCC-NCCC,
September 1965. 97 p. -- Addresses and recommendations. First conference which addressed itself to
realities of mass media in the context of Christian
mission.

727. DIA informe: boletín de difusiones evangélicas inter-
americanas. San José, Costa Rica. -- Occasional
publication of Difusiones Inter-Americanas.

728. Nida, Eugene W. Message and missions; the communication
of the Christian faith. New York, Harpers, 1960.
253 p. -- The principle and procedure of communication, with particular reference to religion. See
also *his* God's word in man's language, 1952; and,
his Bible translation and customs and culture, 1954.
Reprint, William Carey Library, 1973, of 1960 and
1952 volumes.

729. Noticias CAVE: boletín del centro audio-visual evangél-
ical en Brazil. 1954-. -- Articles and information.
Cf. no. 730 for complete listing of radio stations
and audio-visual centers in Latin America.

730. Noticiero. Centro Audio-visual Evangélico (CAVE), Aptdo.
Postal M-9223, México 1, D.F., 1963-. -- An informa-
tional bulletin on materials and methods for mass

communications in Latin America. Special attention is called to the following articles:
no. 1.: Nida, Eugene W. La comunicación del evangélico en América Latina. Supplement. Cf. *Practical anthropology* 8:145-56.
no. 2.: Wonderly, William L. Algunas investigaciones necesarias para el progreso de la obra evangélica en América Latina.

731. Wilson, Frederick *and* Abbey Jacobs. Without communication man stands alone. New York, COEMAR, 1964. 80 p. -- Describes how, why and by whom the Gospel can be shared through mass media.

Sociology of Protestantism

See also p. 298.

732. Lalive, Christian D'Epinay. (Cf. no. 1386).

733. Lara Braud, Jorge *and* William L. Wonderly. (Cf. no. 1824).

734. Minnich, R. Herbert, Jr. A sociological study of the Mennonite immigrant communities in Paraná, Brazil. Ph. D. thesis, University of Florida, Gainesville, 1966. 358 p. -- A sociological analysis of communities in four states in northern Brazil. Data includes comparisons with situations which prevailed in Mennonite communities in Russia from which immigrants came and attitude measurement of students attending non-Mennonite educational institutions. See also *his* A synthesis of applied social science material for agents of change, with special application to missionaries. M.S. thesis, Cornell University, Ithaca, N.Y., 1958. 76 p.

735. de Santa Ana, Julio, ed. (Cf. no. 1018).

736. _____. Id por el mundo: estructuras para la misión. Buenos Aires, Methopress, 1966. 103 p. -- A study of some River Plate congregations from historical and sociological perspectives, including analysis of the complexity of their structures and plan of work which impede fulfillment of their mission. Suggestions for renewal of structures in last chapter. (Cf. no. 722).

Additional notes:

A study is projected in Colombia by the Episcopal Church to
study the attitudes of the middle class Protestant community.
No further details are available at this time.

The Junta Latinoamericana de Iglesia y Sociedad has initiated
a four-year project under Christian Lalive D'Epinay to study
the impact of the Evangelical faith in certain Latin American
groups, the level of participation by evangelicals in society,
the relations of evangelicals in indigenous culture, new lines
of thought and action which respond to the Latin American situation and the needs to prepare leadership in theology and the
social sciences for the Church in the fulfillment of its mission. (Cf. SEI, no. 8, 1966).

The Association of Evangelical Theological Seminaries (ASTE) in
Brazil has recently established an *Instituto Evangelico de
Pesquias* to pursue research related to Protestantism in Brazil.

For social researchers who wish to find further study aids, it
is suggested that the following works be consulted:

737. Arensberg *and* Nichoff. Introducing social change: manual
        for overseas Americans. s.l. (n.d.).

738. Barzun, Jacques *and* Henry F. Graff. The modern researcher.
        New York, Harcourt, Brace, 1957. 386 p.

739. Fals Borda, Orlando. The ideological biases of North
        Americans studying Latin America. New York, LAD-NCCC,
        1966. -- An address on December 2, 1966 at Columbia
        University, New York.

740. Hauser, Philip M., ed. Handbook for social research in
        urban areas. Paris, UNESCO, 1964. 214 p. --
        Bibliography at end of chapters.

741. Heath, Dwight B. *and* Richard N. Adams. Contemporary
        cultures and societies in Latin America: a reader
        in social anthropology of Middle and South America
        and the Caribbean. New York, Random House, 1965.
        586 p.

742. International social science journal. New York, UNESCO
        (n.d.). -- Cf. special issue, Sociology of develop-
        ment in Latin America 15:4, 1963. US$6.50/annually.

743. Lambert, Jacques. América Latina: estructuras sociales

e instituciones políticas. Barcelona, Ediciones
Ariel, 1964. 552 p.

744. Lewin, Kurt. Field theory in social science: selected
theoretical papers. Dorwin Cartwright, ed. New York,
Harpers, 1951. xx, 346 p.

745. Miller, D. C. Handbook of research design and social
measurement. New York, David Mckay, 1964. 332 p.

746. Sellitiz, Claire, et al. Research methods in social
relations. New York, Holt, 1960. 622 p.

747. Three preliminary bibliographies of works related to the
social sciences in Latin America. San José, C.R.,
Programa Interamericano de Información Popular, 1962.
144 p. -- 1. Studies about Latin America by North
Americans; 2. Studies about Latin America by Latin
Americans; and, 3. Studies published by various
institutions in Latin America.

748. Vries, Egbert *and* José Medina Echavarría. Social aspects
of economic development in Latin America. Paris,
UNESCO, 1963. 2 v.

749. Wagley, Charles, ed. Social science research on Latin
America. New York, Columbia University Press, 1964.
338 p. -- Report and papers of a seminary on Latin
American studies, July-August 1963.

750. _____ *and* Marvin Harris. A typology of Latin American
subcultures. *American anthropologist* 57:428-51
June 1955.

Christian Education (See Page 90)
See also p. 299.

751. Borrie, W. D. The cultural integration of immigrants.
Paris, UNESCO, 1959. -- A survey based upon the
papers and proceedings of the UNESCO Conferences,
Havana, 1956, together with case studies by M.
Diegues, Jr., J. Isaac, A. H. Neiva, C. A. Price and
J. Zubrzycki. (This entry belongs properly under
previous section, Sociology of Protestantism.)

Theological Education
See also p. 300.

752. Barnett, Das Kelly, ed. Misión de la comunión anglicana en México y Centro América. Austin, Centro de Investigación en la Teología Cristiana y en la Cultura (n.d.). 47 p. -- Review of post graduate courses with practical and theological conclusions.

753. Liggett, Tomás j. Hacia una educación teológica superior en la América Latina. *El boletín*, núm. 1, enero-marzo 1967. -- Published in the Seminario Evangélico de Puerto Rico, Río Piedras, 00928.

754. New challenge to seminary teachers in a rapidly changing world. New York, NCCC, 1966. 79 p. -- Report of a consultation on theological education. See brief summary on Latin America.

755. Scopes, Wilfred E. (Cf. no. 582).

Church and State; Religious Liberty
See also p. 301.

756. Barclay, Wade C. (Cf. no. 337).

757. Castillo Cárdenas, Gonzalo. (Cf. no. 1513 in Colombia).

758. Childs, Harwood L. The constitutions of Latin American republics. New York, CCLA, 1955. 32 p. -- Statement on historical setting and provisions for religious liberty.

759. Goff, James E. The persecution of Protestant Christians in Colombia. (Cf. nos. 1539-43).

760. Murray, John C., S.J., ed. Religious liberty: an end and a beginning. New York, Macmillan, 1966. -- Nine pages of a symposium at Loyola University in 1966. Appendix and text in Vatican II declaration on religious liberty.

761. Pike, Frederick B. (Cf. no. 303).

762. Rycroft, W. Stanley. The bitter struggle in Colombia. *Christian century* 1 February 1960. -- One of the first articles written on religious liberty in Colombia.

763. Yoder, Howard W. Present limitations on religious liberty
      in Latin America. New York, CCLA, 1955. 33 p. --
      Statement prepared for 1955 conference in Buck Hill
      Falls.

764. Zavala, Silvio. The defense of human rights in Latin
      America: 16th to 18th centuries. Paris, UNESCO, 1964.

                    Interconfessional Studies

None available for present listing.

        INTERPRETATION OF PROTESTANTISM IN HISPANIC CULTURE

                          By Protestants
                       See also p. 305.

        *Study Papers and Addresses Published by the Committee
           on Cooperation in Latin America and the Latin
        America Department of the National Council of Churches
           of Christ, 475 Riverside Drive, New York, 1957-67*

*765. Arrastía, Cecilio. How shall the people hear the word of
       God?

*766. Chamberlain, J. Gordon. Using the Bible in Christian
       education in Latin America.

 767. Davis, Thomas B., Jr. On being intellectually respectful.
       -- An open letter to missionaries in Latin America by
       a New York university professor.

 768. Derby, Marian. Latin American churches and North American
       organizations.

 769. Dickson, Murray. Latin American youth in a world of
       ferment.

 770. Goslin, Thomas S., II. The evangelical message in Latin
       America.

---

*   Addresses on the general theme "The Role of the Scriptures
       in Latin America"

*771. Holmgren, Latham E.   The Living Word in the living language
        of Latin America.

772. Jones, Henry D.   Christian responsibility in Latin America's
        emerging industrial society.

773. Liggett, T. J.   The Latin American evangelical church in
        inter-church relationships.

774. _____.   The role of the missionary in Latin America today.

775. Mackay, John A.   The Latin American churches and the
        ecumenical movement.   Available also in Spanish and
        Portuguese.

776. _____.   The spiritual spectrum of Latin America.

777. Mathews, James K.   The mission concept of the North Ameri-
        can churches.

*778. McCoy, Lewistine M.   The church's obedience to the Scrip-
        tures in Latin America.

779. Means, Frank K.   The mission boards and evangelical
        churches in Latin America.

780. Nida, Eugene W.   The Latin American indigenous church.

781. Pike, Frederick B.   Church and state in mid-century Latin
        America: a Catholic's view.

782. Rembao, Alberto.   The growing church and its changing
        environment in Latin America.

783. Ruoss, Meryl.   New factors in the expanding urban situation.

784. Rycroft, W. Stanley.   The national councils and federations
        of churches in Latin America.

*785. Sánchez, Gildo.   Meeting the man without the scriptures in
        Latin America

786. Sinclair, John H.   Conversations with Roman Catholics and
        the Latin American churches.

*787. _____.   The scriptures speak in Latin America.

_____

*   Addresses on the general theme "The Role of the Scriptures
      in Latin America"

788. Shaull, M. Richard. The new revolutionary mood in Latin America.

789. Strachan, Kenneth. The missionary movement of the non-historical groups in Latin America.

790. Tornquist, Guido. The role of confessionalism in the ecumenical movement in Latin America.

Protestants and the Second Vatican Council
See also p. 305.

791. Los protestantes y el segundo concilio vaticano. México, CUPSA, 1964. 101 p. -- Report of a consultation on the actual relations and attitudes between Roman Catholics and Evangelicals. Chapters by José Míguez Bonino, Protestant observer from Latin America; others by Gonzalo Báez Camargo, Jorge Lara Braud, F. J. Huegel and T. H. Patrick.

Protestant Influence in Literary and Political Life

792. López Michaelson, Alfonso. Cuestiones colombianas (ensayos). México, Impresiones Modernas, 1955. 400 p. -- See essay on "La estirpe calvinista de nuestras instituciones políticas", p. 136-201, which appeared first in 1947. Separately published by the Universidad Nacional de Colombia, Bogotá in 1966 by Ediciones Tercer Mundo, Bogotá, 1966. 90 p.

793. Monti, Daniel P. La preocupación religiosa en los hombres de Mayo. Buenos Aires, La Aurora, 1966. 110 p. -- Series of loosely related essays demonstrating the spiritual and cultural values quickened by the Scriptures in men and events during the independence period in the River Plate area.

794. Salem, Luis D. pseu. La Biblia y la lira. México, Ediciones ESLA, 1964. 69 p. -- The influence of the Holy Scriptures in the lives of outstanding men of letters of Spain and Latin America. Three other pamphlets by the same author are also available on similar subjects.

Spanish Mystics, the Reformation
in Spain and Related Subjects
See also p. 305.

795. Arce, Sergio S. La lucha y la paz de Miguel de Unamuno.
      Th. M. Thesis, Princeton Theological Seminary, Prince-
      ton, N.J. (n.d.). iv, 119 p.

796. Bainton, R. H. El alma hispana y el alma sajona. Buenos
      Aires, La Aurora, 1961. 142 p. -- Carnahan lectures
      of 1960.

797. Barra, Arturo. Unamuno. New Haven, Conn., Yale Univer-
      sity Press, 1952. 161 p. -- A guide through the
      world of Unamuno's ideas and their relation to modern
      Spain.

798. Bollman, Benjamin E. The significance of the sacraments
      in a strategy for evangelical missions in countries
      of Hispanic culture, with special reference to the
      Philippine Islands. Th. M. thesis, Princeton Theo-
      logical Seminary, Princeton, N.J., 1938. 123 p.

799. Gutiérrez Marín, Claudio. Historia de la reforma en
      España. México, CUPSA, 1942. 445 p.

800. _____. Los místicos españoles del siglo XVI. México,
      CUPSA (n.d.).

801. Haselden, Kyle. Death of a myth; new locus for Spanish
      American faith. New York, Friendship Press, 1964.
      175 p. -- Excellent critique of the concept that
      people of Spanish American culture are congenitally
      averse to Protestant Christianity.

802. Hauck, Allan. Juan and Alfonso de Valdés: a study of
      the 16th century movement for religious reform. Th.
      D. thesis, Hartford Seminary Foundation, Hartford,
      Conn., 1950.

803. Mackay, John A. Don Miguel de Unamuno: su personalidad,
      obra e influencia. Ph. D. thesis, Universidad de San
      Marcos, Lima, Perú, 1918.

804. Maysonet Marrero, Pablo. Cristo en la agonía de Miguel
      de Unamuno. B.D. thesis, Seminario Evangélico de
      Puerto Rico, Río Piedras, 1965. 93 p.

805. McCrie, Thomas. Historia de la reforma en España en el
     siglo XVI. México, CUPSA, 1942. 271 p.

806. Mergel, Angel M. Reformismo cristiano y el alma española.
     México, CUPSA (n.d.).

807. Metzidakis, Philip. Unamuno y Hispanoamérica. Ph. D.
     thesis, Yale University, New Haven, Conn., 1960.

808. Moros Ruano, Edger R. Faith and reason in Miguel de
     Unamuno. Th. M. thesis, Princeton Theological Semin-
     ary, Princeton, N.J., 1965. 144 p.

809. Navarro Monzó, Julio. Los conceptos que de Cristo tiene
     la América Latina. *La reforma* (Buenos Aires) abril
     1930.

810. Peters, Harry. The theology of the great Spanish mystics
     with special reference to their evangelical concep-
     tions. Th. M. thesis, Princeton Theological Seminary,
     Princeton, N.J. (n.d.).

811. Rojas, Ricardo. The invisible Christ. Nashville, Abing-
     don, 1931. -- Trans. by Webster Browning from Spanish
     original, El Cristo invisible. 3. ed. Buenos Aires,
     Librería La Facultad, J. Roldán, 1928. 378 p.

812. Sánchez Figueroa, Gildo. Aspectos de pensamiento religioso
     en Don Miguel de Unamuno. B. D. thesis, Seminario
     Evangélico de Puerto Rico, Río Piedras, 1945. 75 p.

813. Serrano, Antonio. The Spanish endeavor to harmonize the
     Renaissance with the Reformation. Th. M. thesis,
     Princeton Theological Seminary, Princeton, N.J., 1942.
     ii, 54 p.

814. Smith, LeGrand III. Analytical study of the Christology
     of Miguel de Unamuno. M. A. thesis, Northwestern
     University and Garrett Biblical Institute, Evanston,
     Ill., 1931.

815. Strachan, R. Kenneth. Religion in Spain in the 16th
     century; an interpretation of the Spanish reformation.
     Th. M. thesis, Princeton Theological Seminary,
     Princeton, N.J., 1942. i, 130 p.

See addresses and discussion of Sixth Carnegie Study Conference,
"Interrelations of philosophy and theology and their relevance
to the cultures of Latin America." The Kennedy School of

Missions, Hartford, Conn., 1959. Also, Raymond Valenzuela's
thesis, "The emerging concern for transcendental value in
Spanish American philosophy." Drew Theological Seminary, 1955.

See extensive literature on interpretation of the essence of
Hispanic-American culture in S. de Madariaga's Presente y porvenir
de Hispanoamérica, otros ensayos; Barohona's El ser Hispanoamericano; Cosío Villegas' American extremes; L. Zea's The Latin
American mind; A. Del Rio's El mundo hispánico y el mundo Anglo-
sajón en América: choque y atracción de dos culturas; R. Rojas'
Eurindia.

                        By Roman Catholics

816.   Alvarez Herrera, Felix María. Las misiones protestantes
       en América. Lima, Ediciones Renovabis, 1959. 98 p.

817.   Armas Medina, Fernando de. Misiones protestantes. *Revista
       de estudios americanos* (Sevilla) 10:50-1 noviembre-
       diciembre 1955.

818.   Crivelli, Camilo, S.J. Los protestantes y la América
       Latina: conferencias, acusaciones, respuestas. Roma,
       Isola de Liri, Soc. Tip. A. Maciore y Pisani, 1931.
       314 p. -- CET. Polemical work intended to be useful
       to Catholic priests and writers who wish to combat
       Protestant propaganda. Very selective quotations
       involving some distortion, but also revealing some
       Protestant contradictions. See also *his* Directories,
       no. 596, 601.

819.   Damboriena, Prudencio J. El protestantismo en América
       Latina. Bogotá, FERES, 1962. 2 v. -- Highly detail-
       ed yet summary presentation of the history of Protes-
       tantism in Latin America. Written by a Jesuit, notably
       objective in his presentation. Extensive bibliography.
       See also an extended study of Protestant groups in *his*
       Fé católica e iglesias y sectas de la reforma. Madrid,
       Editorial Razón y Fé, 1961.

820.   Hardon, John A., S.J. Las iglesias protestantes de
       América. México, Buena Prensa, 1959. 420 p. --
       Translation of English original.

821.   Papiol, Remigio de. El protestantismo ante la Biblia. 6.
       ed. Cartago, Costa Rica, Imprenta El Heraldo, 1958.

822. Planchet, Regis. La intervención protestante en México y
      sud América. El Paso, Revista Católica, 1928. 199 p.

823. Soler, Mariano. Catolicismo y protestantismo. Montevideo,
      1902. -- A document from the period of controversy
      between Catholics and Protestants as Protestantism
      sought acceptance in the Latin American world. Written
      by the Archbishop of Montevideo.

      PERIODICALS AND JOURNALS, MAINLY PROTESTANT
      (With reference to two or more countries)
      See also p. 305.

824. Ma, John T. Current periodicals in the Missionary Research
      Library. 2. rev. ed. New York, MRL, 1961. 38 p. --
      An alphabetical list of 77 current periodicals received
      by the Missionary Research Library. Gives title, sub-
      scription address, main subject matter, place of publi-
      cation, language, religion or denomination represented,
      frequency and beginning year of publication and collec-
      tion in the MRL. Three indices.

      Past Publications

825. British and foreign Bible society reports.

826. Evangelical Christendom: the Evangelical Alliance. SML,
      1847-96. -- Seven articles by James Thomson, 1847.
      See also Francisco Penzotti on Chile and Peru.

827. Forth. 1941-60.

828. The Moravian missionary reporter. 1879-1902.

829. Moravian missions. 1903-57.

890. The neglected continent. Evangelical Union of South
      America, 1910-21.

891. La nueva democracia. New York, CCLA, 1921-63.

892. South American messanger. South American Missionary
      Society, 1937-65.

893. South American missionary magazine. 1867-1936.

894. The spirit of the mission. Protestant Episcopal Church, 1840-1940.

895. Women and missions. Presbyterian Church in the U.S.A. 1924-1946.

896. World dominion. -- Articles by Roland Allen, R. B. Clark, J. A. Ritchie, J. A. Mackay, S. A. McNairn, J. Savage, K. C. Grubb and others.

Current Publications, Protestant and Roman Catholic
(With Publishing Addresses)
(see also page 41, Contemporary Roman Catholicism)
See also p. 306.

897. Advent review and sabbath herald. Takoma Park, Washington, D.C., 1910-. Weekly.

898. Alliance witness. Third and Reilly Streets, Harrisburg, Pa., 1957-. Weekly.

899. Amazon valley Indian. South American Indian Mission. 1404 Forsythe Street, West Palm Beach, Fla., 1905-.

900. Bible society record. American Bible Society, Broadway and 61st Streets, New York, 1849-. Monthly.

901. La Biblia en América Latina. Apartado 6-775, Mexico, 6, D.F., 1951-. Quarterly. -- For Evangelical pastors and missionaries. No charge.

902. A Biblia no Brasil. Rua Buenos Aires 135, Rio de Janeiro, 1956-. Quarterly.

903. Carta latinoamericana. Published by ISAL, MEC, CEC, and ULAJE, Casilla 179, Montevideo, 1965-. 8/year, US$2.00/ annually.

904. C.E.I. Centro Ecuménico da Informacão, Praia da Botafogo, 439 Sobreloja, 2c-02, Rio de Janeiro. -- Analysis of contemporary events.

905. The Christian broadcaster. 475 Riverside Drive, room 1930, New York, 10027. 1954-. -- 4/uear, US$3.00/annually.

906. Christian century. 407 S. Dearborn St., Chicago, Illinois. -- Partial coverage of news in Protestant world of Latin America.

907. Christian heritage. Christ's Mission, 369 Carpenter Avenue, Sea Cliff, New York, 1884-. Monthly.

908. Christian rural fellowship bulletin. Agricultural Missions, 475 Riverside Drive, New York, 10027, 1935-. Monthly.

909. Christianity today. 1014 Washington Bldg., Washington 5, D.C., 1956-. Fortnightly. -- See 7:21 for review article on missionary situation in Latin America.

910. Church growth bulletin. Institute of Church Growth, 135 N. Oakland, Pasadena, Calif., 91101, 1965-. Bi-monthly. US$1.00/annually.

911. The churchman. 1074 23rd Avenue, No., St. Petersburg, Fla., 33704, 1831-.

912. The church woman. Church Women United, 475 Riverside Drive, New York, 10027. Monthly.

913. C.I.F. reports. Center of Intercultural Formation, Aptdo. 479, Cuernavaca, Mor., Mexico. Title and text in Spanish, Portuguese and French. Bi-weekly. US$5.00/ annually. -- Spanish entitled CIDOC INFORMA. Reports on events relevant to socio-economic change and the church in Latin America.

914. C.M.S. newsletter. Church Missionary Society, 6 Salisbury Square, London, E.C., 4. Monthly.

915. Concern. UPCUSA, 475 Riverside Drive, New York, 10027, 1959-. Monthly. -- Special issue on Latin America, October 1965. 10/year. US$2.00/annually.

916. Cristianismo y sociedad. Casilla 179, Montevideo, 1962-. Quarterly. US$1.00/annually.

917. Criterio. Alsina 840, Buenos Aires. -- A Roman Catholic publication.

918. Cuadernos teológicos. La Aurora, Corrientes 728, Buenos Aires, 1951-. Quarterly. US$1.50/annually. Dr. José Míguez Bonino, dir.

919. Das wort in der welt. Beutsche Evangelische Missions, Hilfe, Hamburg 13, Mittelweg 143. Bi-monthly.

920. Decisión. Asociación Billy Graham en América Latina, Casilla 5055, Buenos Aires.

921. Diálogo. Asociación de Pastores Presbiterianos, 242 E.
      14th Street, New York, 10003. 11/year.

922. Die evangelische diaspora. Zeitschrift des Gustav-Adolf-
      Werkes, Leipzig, 1919-. D. Franz Lau, ed. --
      Beginning in 1967 will be published as a yearbook.
      Reviews German evangelical *diaspora* in all the world.

923. Ecumenical press service. WCC, Geneva, 1933-. Weekly.

924. The ecumenical review. WCC, Geneva, 1948-. Quarterly.

925. The ecumenist. Glen Rock, N.J., 1963-. Bi-monthly.

926. Educación cristiana. Lautaro 245, Buenos Aires, 1945-.
      US$1.50/annually.

927. Ekklesia. Gaspar Campos 6151, José C. Paz, FCGSM, Prov.
      de Buenos Aires, 1959-. Quarterly. US$2.00/annually.

928. The Episcopalian. 1930 Chestnut Street, Philadelphia,
      Pa., 19103.

929. Evangelical Christendom. 30 Bedford Square, London, 1847-.

930. Evangelical foreign missionary association missionary news
      service. 1405 "G" Street, Washington, D.C., 1956-.
      Semi-monthly.

931. Evangelical missions quarterly. 1405 "G" Street, Washing-
      ton, D.C., Quarterly.

932. The Evangelical quarterly. Paternoster Press, Exeter,
      England. US$3.00/annually. F. F. Bruce, ed.

933. Foreign affairs. Council on Foreign Relations, Inc., Pub.,
      58 E. 68th Street, New York, 10021. Quarterly.
      US$6.00/annually.

934. Foreign missionary radio. World Conference on Missionary
      Radio, Talcottville, Conn., 1955-. Monthly.

935. From the frontiers. Free Church of Scotland, The Mound,
      Edinburgh, 1964-.

936. Frontier. 34 Brook Street, London, W-1, 1958-. Quarterly.

937. Herder's correspondence. 232 Madison Avenue, New York,
      10016, 1956-.

938. HIS. Inter-varsity Christian Fellowship, 1519 N. Astor, Chicago 10, Ill., 1957-.

939. In alle welt. Evangelische Lutherein Mission, Freimund-Verlaag, Neuendettelsau, Germany, 1949-. Monthly.

940. International review of missions. WCC, 150 route de Ferney, 1211, Geneva 20, 1949-. Quarterly.

941. Journal of ecumenical studies. 1936 N. Broad Street, Temple University, Philadelphia, Pa., 19122, 1964-. Quarterly. US$8.00/annually.

942. Latin America calls. Box 6066, United States Catholic Conference, Washington, D.C. 20005, Latin American Bureau, National Catholic Welfare Conference, Washington, D.C.

943. The Latin American evangelist. Box 1307, San José, C.R., 1929-. 5/year. US$1.00/annually. -- Primarily on work of Latin American mission. Also reports of Evangelism-in-depth movement in all Latin America.

944. Latin American news letter. Latin American Dept., NCCC, 475 Riverside Drive, New York, 1941-. Occasional.

945. L'etoile du matin (pro Hispania). 47 Clairac, France. Quarterly. J. Delpech, dir.

946. The living church. 407 E. Michigan Street, Milwaukee 2, Wisc., 1869-.

947. Macaoyoc. Boletín del Seminario Teológico Presbiteriano, Aptdo. Postal 21-939, Coyoacán, México 21, D.F. 3/year.

948. Maryknoll. Catholic Foreign Mission Society of America, Maryknoll, New York, 1949-. Monthly.

950. Mensaje. Casilla 10445, Santiago de Chile.

951. The Mexican Indian. 325 No. 13th Street, Philadlephia 7, Pa., 1957-. 5/year.

952. Missionalia hispánica. Depto. de Misionologia Española, Consejo Superior de Investigaciones Científicas, Patronato Menédez Pelayo Serrano 123, Madrid 6. Quarterly.

953. Misiones extranjeras. Revista de Misionología, Seminario
     Nacional de Misiones Extranjeras, Aptdo 264, Burgos,
     España. Quarterly.

954. Missiewerk, het. Laan Copes van Cattenbruch 127, 's-
     Gravenhedge, Hederlands, 1951-. Quarterly.

955. Mission. Society for Propagation of the Faith, 366 Fifth
     Avenue, New York, 1924-. Monthly.

956. Missionary aviation. Box 32, Fullerton, Calif., 1949-.

958. The missionary tidings. Women's Missionary Society of
     the Free Methodist Church, Winona Lake, Ind. Monthly.

959. Missions quarterly. 6840 Eastern Avenue, N.W., Washington,
     D.C.

960. The Moravian. 79 W. Church Street, Bethlehem, Pa., 1822-.
     Monthly.

961. The Moravian messenger. 5-7 Muswell Hall, London, N. 10,
     1957-. Monthly.

962. Niñez. Santa Rosa 367, Of. 15, Córdoba, Argentina. US
     $2.00/annually. -- Organ of the Alliance for the
     Evangelization of the Latin American child.

963. Occasional bulletin. Division of Overseas Ministries,
     NCCC, 475 Riverside Drive, New York, 1950-. Monthly.
     -- Formerly a publication of the MRL.

964. Other sheep. 2329 Troost Avenue, Kansas City, Mo. 1913-.
     Monthly.

965. Pensamiento cristiano. Casilla 165, Córdoba, Argentina.
     US$1.50/annually. -- Conservative evangelical journal
     on problems of theology and the mission of the church.

966. Pentecostal evangelical. 434 W. Pacific Street, Springfield
     1,, Mo., 1953-. US$2.00. Weekly.

967. Practical anthropology, continuing as "Missiology, an
     international review." 1973-. Quarterly. $8.00/annual.
     P. O. Box 1041, New Canaan, Conn. 06840. -- Devoted to
     more effective worldwide Christianity by the investiga-
     tion, interpretation and dissemination of the practical
     implications of anthropology and other culturally
     oriented subjects. Ten year index 1953-63 available.

968. El predicador evangélico. La Aurora, Corrientes 728, Buenos Aires, 1950-. Quarterly. US$1.50/ annually.

969. Reconciliación. Movimiento de Reconciliación, 25 de May 171, Of. 28, Buenos Aires. D. D. Lura Villanueva, dir.

970. The Reformed and Presbyterian world. 17 route de Malagnau, Geneva, 1956-. Annual. -- Periodic news from Reformed and Presbyterian churches in Latin America.

971. Regions beyond. Harley House, 99 Thurleigh Road, London, S.W. 12, 1880-. Quarterly.

972. Revista teológica presbiteriana. Caixa Postal 133, Campinas, São Paulo, 1959-.

973. Rural missions. Agricultural Missions, 475 Riverside Drive, New York, 1932-. Quarterly.

974. S.E.I. Servicio Evangélico de Información, Casilla 1773 and 2110, Montevideo, 1966-. Monthly. US$5.00/annually in Latin America. -- Monthly review of "ideas y hechos que circulan en el mundo evangélico."

975. SENDA. Servicio Evangélico de Noticias de América Latina, San José, C.R. monthly. -- Primarily focused on news of conservative evangelical churches.

976. Sight-sound. RAVEMCCO and WCCE, 475 Riverside Drive, New York, 1953-. Monthly.

977. South America. Evangelical Union of South America, 6 Novar Road, London, S.E. 9, 1907-. Quarterly.

978. South American missionary magazine. 157 Waterloo Road, London, S.E. 1, 1867-. Monthly.

979. Student world. World Student Christian Foundation, 13 Rue Calvin, Geneva, 1908-. Quarterly.

980. Studia. Centro de estudios históricos ultramarinos, Lisboa. Revista semestral.

981. Testimonium. Federación mundial cristiana de estudiantes, 13 Rua Calvin, Ginebra, Suiza. Also Cangallo 1644, Buenos Aires. Quarterly. US$1.00/annually.

982. Translation. Wycliffe Bible Translator, Box 870, Glendale,

Calif., 1943-. Quarterly.

983. United Bible societies bulletin. 146 Queen Victoria Street, London, E.C. 4, 1950-. Quarterly.

984. World communique. YMCA, 37 Quai Wilson, Geneva, 1946-. Bi-monthly.

985. World literacy news letter. World Lit-Lit, 475 Riverside Drive, New York, 1947-.

986. World mission. National office of the Society for the Propagation of the Faith, 366 Fifth Avenue, New York, 10001, 1949-.

987. World vision magazine. Box "O", Pasadena, Calif., 1957-. Bi-monthly.

988. YWCA magazine. 600 Lexington Avenue, New York, 1907-. Monthly.

Chapter 3.
Protestantism in Latin America, Country by Country

RÍO DE LA PLATA

Argentina
See also p. 308.

Bibliography
See also p. 308.

999. Carbía, Rómulo D. Historia crítica de la historiografía
argentina. (BLCU). -- A new publication was begun
in 1960 as Bibliografía argentina de historia by the
Instituto Bibliográfico del Ministerio de Educación.

1000. Levene, Ricardo. A history of Argentina. Trans. 8. ed.
by William Spence Robertson. Chapel Hill, University
of North Carolina Press, 1937. -- Also a Spanish
translation as Historia de la nación argentina. Of
special value.

General Background
See also p. 308.

1001. Alameda, Julián. Argentina católica. Buenos Aires, P. P.
Benedictinos, 1935. 1031 p. -- Largely historical.

1002. Auza, Néstor Tomás. Católicos y liberales en la genera-
       ción del ochenta. México, CIDOC (n.d.).   764 p.   --
       Bibliography p. 743-52.

1003. Boleslao, Lewin. Supresión de la Inquisición y libertad
       de cultos en la Argentina. La Plata, Universidad
       Nacional de la Plata, 1957. 69 p. -- Traces steps
       from the abolition of the Holy Office in 1513 through
       the present.

1004. Bunkley, Allison W. The life of Sarmiento. Princeton,
       N.J., Princeton University Press, 1952. xv, 566 p.
       -- See also Tristan E. Guevara. Los maestros norte-
       americanos que trajo Sarmiento. Buenos Aires,
       Servicio Cultural e Informativo de E.U.A. (n.d.).
       32 p. The origin of the idea, the teachers and their
       work.

1005. DiTella, Torcuato S., ed. Gino Germani y Jorge
       Graciarena. Argentina: solidad de masas. Buenos
       Aires, Endeba, 1965.

1006. Harrison, Margaret H. Captain of the Andes; the life of
       José de San Martín, liberatador de Argentina, Chile
       y Perú. New York, Smith, 1943. 216 p.

1007. Kennedy, John J. Catholicism, nationalism and democracy
       in Argentina. Notre Dame, Ind., Notre Dame Press,
       1958. 219 p. -- Scholarly treatment.

1008. Wright, Almon R. Church and state in the province of La
       Plata to 1861. Ph. D. thesis, Illinois, 1934.

1009. Zuretti, Juan C. Historia eclesiástica argentina. Buenos
       Aires, Editorial Huarpes, 1945. 340 p. maps.

Protestantism in General
See also p. 309.

1010. Bridges, E. Lucas. Uttermost part of the earth. London,
       Hodder and Stoughton, 1945. 558 p. -- The religious
       work in the Patagonia after the time of Capt. Allen
       Gardiner.

1011. Browning, Webster E. The River Plate republics... London,
       World Dominion Press, 1928. 139 p. appendices, maps.
       (World Dominion press series). -- Panoramic view of
       historic, social and economic factors which have

influenced Protestantism in this area. Outlines
Methodist and Baptist contribution to struggle for
religious freedom.

1012. Canclini, Arnoldo. Primer intento de evangelización en
América Latina en el Río de la Plata. *Tribuna
evangélica* 6:31 octubre-noviembre 1950.

1013. Davis, J. Merle. The evangelical church in the River
Plate republics; Argentina and Uruguay. New York,
IMC, 1943. 119 p. -- A study of the economic and
social basis of the Evangelical churches in Argentina
and Uruguay.

1014. Guía de las iglesias evangélicas. Buenos Aires, Confederación de Iglesias Evangélicas de Argentina, 1953.
109 p. -- Listing of non-Catholic churches in
Argentina, Uruguay and Paraguay.

1015. Informe oficial del congreso evangélico. Buenos Aires,
La Aurora (n.d.). 139 p. -- Report of meetings held
upon the occasion of the visit of Dr. John R. Mott.

1016. Protestantismo de inmigración en Argentina. Buenos Aires,
CEC, Cangallo 1644, 1966. 18 p. -- Bibliographical
list.

1017. Sabanes, Julio R. La república argentina como campo de
evangelización. mss, Facultad Evangélica de Teología,
Buenos Aires, 1948. -- Includes a good review of
the situation when Spanish language preaching began
in Argentina.

1018. de Santa Ana, Julio. Aproximación a la autocomprensión
de la comunidad... en el Río de la Plata. mss, Centro
Emanuel, Colonia Valdense, Uruguay (n.d.). -- A pro-
found study of the different evangelical groups;
their origins, problems and message. Includes complete bibliography.

(See biographical works on James Thomson, William C. Morris,
Pablo Besson and other outstanding Río Platenses leaders in
Chapter Two, General Literature; Books, Articles and Unpublished
Theses, Page 59.)

Denominational History
See also p. 310.

Anglican

1019. Canclini, Arnoldo. Hasta lo último de la tierra. Buenos
       Aires, La Aurora, 1951. 255 p. -- The life of
       Gardiner and documentation of missions in southern
       Argentina from 1852-1916. Appendices of great
       interest.

1020. Every, Edward F. Twenty-five years in South America.
       London, SPCK, 1929. 212 p. -- See also *his* South
       American memories of 30 years. London, SPCK, 1933.
       210 p.

1021. MacDonald, Frederick C. The Anglican church in South
       America. London, SPCK, 1915. 155 p.

1022. _____. Bishop Sterling of the Falklands. London, Seely,
       1939. 255 p. -- His life, anecdotes, photographs
       and copies of documents. Certain chapters describe
       well the solitary life of the natives.

1023. Phillips, G. W. The missionary martyr of Tierra del
       Fuego. London, Werthein, McIntosh and Hunt, 1961.
       -- Memoirs of the catechist J. Garland Phillips of
       Patagonia. By his brother.

Baptist

1024. Anderson, Justice C. Church-state problems among Baptists
       in Argentina in the light of historic Baptist perspec-
       tives. Th. D. thesis, Southwestern Baptist Theologi-
       cal Seminary, Da..as, 1965.

1025. Argentine Baptists move ahead. Richmond, Va., Foreign
       Mission Board of Southern Baptist Convention, 1954.
       86 p.

1026. Bedford, Allen B. A critique of Argentine mission work
       in light of fundamentals laid down by Christ and the
       Apostles. mss, Southwestern Baptist Theological
       Seminary, Fort Worth, 1957.

1027. Carroll, Daniel M. The development of religious educa-
       tion in the Baptist work in Argentina. Th. D. thesis,
       Southwestern Baptist Seminary, Fort Worth, 1960.

1028. Graves, William W. Southern Baptist principles in
religious education and their implementation in
Argentina. Th. D. thesis, Southern Baptist Seminary,
Dallas, 1961.

1029. Los bautistas del Río de la Plata. Buenos Aires, Convención Evangélica Bautista, 1930. 320 p. -- Large
quantity of facts about workers and congregations
from earliest times.

1030. Marotta, Orestes. Dr. Sidney MacFarland Sowell. Buenos
Aires (n.d.). -- Life of founder of Baptist work in
Argentina.

Church of Scotland Congregations

1031. Dodds, James. Records of the Scottish settlers in the
River Plate and their churches. Buenos Aires, Grant
and Sylvester, 1897. xiv, 460 p.

1032. Drysdale, J. Monteith. A hundred years in Buenos Aires,
1828-1929. Buenos Aires, 1929. 116 p. -- A record
of the Iglesia Escocesa in Argentina.

1033. Un hombre bueno: vista de Jaime Clifford. Cordoba, El
Amanecer, 1957. 116 p. -- Simple biography of a
Scottish missionary and his work in northern Argen-
tina.

Disciples of Christ

1034. Barnes, Vera F. de. Luz sobre el horizonte. Buenos
Aires, Liga Argentina de Mujeres Evangélicas, 1956.
138 p. -- Biography of a North American Disciples
missionary. Rather apologetic, but valuable for
beginnings of work in sectors of Buenos Aires.

1035. Burner, Willis J. South America; our mission in Argentina. Indianapolis, Christian Women's Board of
Missions, 1912.

1036. Montgomery, J. Dexter. Disciples of Christ in Argentina,
1906-56. St. Louis, Mo., Bethany Press, 1956. 180
p. -- A history and description of fifty years of
work of the Disciples of Argentina.

Indigenous Churches

1037. Buckwalter, Albert. A Toba anthology. *Practical anthro-pology* 4:2:92-95 March-April 1956.

1038. ____. Building the church among the Toba Indians. *Mennonite quarterly review* 29:263-75 October 1955.

1039. Loewen, Jacob A., Albert Buckwalter *and* James Kratz. Shamanism, illness and power in Toba church life. *Practical anthropology* 12:6:250-86 November-December 1965. -- A thorough study of the Toba church (Iglesia Evangélica Unida) by two career missionaries and an experienced anthropologist having also had deep personal involvement in other indigenous Indian churches in Latin America.

1040. Reyburn, William D. The Toba Indians of the Argentine Chaco: an interpretative report. Elkhart, Ind., Mennonite Board of Missions and Charities, 1954. 60 p. Third printing, 1970. 84 p. Excellent account by professional anthropologist about group with which Mennonite missionaries have served since 1943. Also ethnographic survey and an interpretative chapter to assist missionaries in role in this indigenous culture.

Lutheran

1041. Jensen, Alfredo. La congregación de immigrantes como base de la misión. *Ekklesia* 9:35-45, 1965. -- The origins of an immigrant church as seen in the Danish Lutheran congregations in Argentina.

1042. Kramer, T., S. H. Beckman *und* J. Fehlauer, ed. 50 jahre evangelisch Lutherische kirche in Argentinen. Buenos Aires, 1955. 152 p. -- Articles on Evangelical Lutheran Church-Mission Synod in Argentina. Photos and statistics. Good for general information.

1043. Ministers of the general assemblies of German evangelical la Plata synod. Buenos Aires, Archives, Emeralda 162 (n.d.). -- From pre-synod of 1899 to 1965.

1044. Ostrowski, Hans J. Das selbstverständnis einer auslandskirche. *Die evangelische diaspora* 27:3:139-54. -- Interpretation of the self-understanding of German Evangelical La Plata Synod by its late president.

1045. Schmidt, Hermann. Geutsche evangelische la Plata synode,
       1849-1949. Buenos Aires, Deutsche Evangelische la
       Plata Synode, 1949. 93 p. -- A general description
       of the development of the Synod over the century.

1046. _____. Geschichte der Deutschen evangelischen gemeinde
       Buenos Aires 1843-1943. Buenos Aires, Deutschen
       Evangelische Beneinde, 1943. 287 p.

1047. Trünon, Carl F., ed. 25 jahre sugensreichen wirkens der
       treulutherischen kirche in Argentinen. s.l., 1930.
       50 p. -- Similar information on 25th anniversary.

1048. Wohl dem, der seiner väter gern gidenkt. Buenos Aires,
       Deutsche Evangelische la Plata Synode, 1943. 165 p.
       -- A calendarium of historical data on pastors and
       congregations of German evangelical La Plata Synod.

Mennonite

1049. Klassen, Abraham. La doctrina de la no-resistencia en
       el pensamiento y la práctica de los Menonitas en
       América Latina. mss, Seminario Evangélico Menonita
       de Teologia, Montevideo, 1961. -- Brief survey of
       historical roots of non-resistance; evaluation of
       modern Mennonite South American life (German and
       Spanish-speaking) with relation to this doctrine.
       Based upon questionnaires and personal interviews.

1050. Kniper, Os. Fritz. El predominio de la Bíblia en la
       historia menonita. Montevideo, Seminario Evangélico
       Menonita de Teologia, 1965. 37 p. -- Farewell
       address by a Dutch Mennonite pastor-teacher. Insists
       that "la clave para entender el movimiento anabaptista-
       menonita se halla en su forma especial de biblicismo."

1051. Shank, J. W., ed. The gospel under the southern cross.
       Scottsdale, Pa., Mennonite Publishing, 1943. 272 p.
       -- A history of the Argentine Mennonite mission on
       its twenty-fifty anniversary, 1917-42. Detailed
       history of each church missionary and national worker.
       One chapter deals with relationship with Argentine
       government.

1052. Weber, Lewis S. Argentina from within. Scottsdale, Pa.,
       Mennonite Publishing, 1945. 174 p. -- Major emphasis
       on evangelical movement, especially work of Mennonites

since 1919 and the factors in the cultural and
historical background.

1053. Wiens, Ernesto. Investigación de la práctica actual del
bautismo, de la santa cena en las iglesias menonitas
de América del Sur. mss, Seminario Evangélico
Menonita de Teología, Montevideo, 1961. -- Based
also on questionnaires used with Mennonite leaders
in Paraguay, Brazil, Argentina and Uruguay.

1054. Yoder, Sanford C. Down South America way. Scottsdale,
Pa., Harold Press, 1943. 148 p.

Methodist

1055. Barrvetaveña, Federico A. Luces y apuntes del camino.
Buenos Aires, La Aurora, 1938. 178 p. -- Anecdotes
of outstanding Methodists of the beginning of the
20th century.

1056. Estandarte evangélico, El. 22 noviembre 1911. -- Special
issue on 75th anniversary of Methodist in South America (1836-1911). Valuable sources, including works
on Paraguay.

1057. Mezzuchelli, Juan. Ramón Blanco, infatigable obrero de
bien. Buenos Aires, La Aurora, 1942. 89 p. --
Simple biography of a Methodist pastor who worked in
the field of education.

1058. Poole, William C., comp. One hundred years of the first
Methodist Episcopal church, American Church, 1836-
1936. Buenos Aires (n.d.). 39 p.

1059. Tallon, A. G. Historia de metodismo en el Río de la
Plata. Buenos Aires, Imprenta Metodists, 1936. --
Largely a history of individual congregations with
photographs of buildings, pastors, etc. Also refers
to Methodism in other Latin American countries.

Waldensian (see also Uruguay, Waldensian)

1060. Comba, Ernesto. Historia de los Valdenses. Buenos Aires,
1926. -- Includes South American colonies.

1061. Lantaret, P. Les vaudois dans l'Uruguay. Pignerol, Jos.

Chiantare, 1870. 101 p. -- A diary of the Moderator's visit in 1869.

1062. Tourn, N. I valderi in America. Torino, Unione Tipograice Editrice, 1906. 127 p. maps.

1063. Tron, Ernesto y Emilio H. Ganz. Historia de las colonias valdenses sudamericanas, 1858-1958. Colonia Valdense, Librería Pastor Miguel Morel, 1958. 371 p. -- The pioneers, colonizations, cultural, social and religious life, industry and commerce of the Waldension immigration.

1064. Tron, Ley. Colonia Iris en sus primeros 25 años. Buenos Aires, El Faro, 1926. -- History of Waldensian colonies of southern Argentina.

Periodicals
See also p. 311.

1065. El discípulo cristiano. Casilla 126, Suc. 1., Buenos Aires, 1962-. US$1.00/annually. -- For Mennonite churches in Latin America. Successor to La voz menonita, 1931-61.

1066. El estandarte evangélico. Doblas 1753, Buenos Aires 24, 1882-. -- Organ of the Methodist church in Argentina, Bolivia, Uruguay. UML has many of past volumes.

1067. Evangelisches gemeinbeblatt der evangelischen dir he am la Plata. Esmeralda 102, Buenos Aires, 1894-. Monthly.

1068. Luz y verdad. Cuenca 3285, Buenos Aires, 1920-. Monthly. -- Organ of the Iglesia Evangélica Luterana Unida en Argentina.

Paraguay
See also p. 312.

Bibliography

1070. Bibliografía paraguaya; catálogo de la biblioteca paraguaya. s.l., Solano López, 1906. BLCU. -- The best! Some 3500 titles, 400 referring to Paraguay, are found in José Segundo Decoude in a supplement to *his* Handbook of Paraguay. 1904.

General Background

1071. Elliott, Arthur Elwood. Paraguay: its cultural heritage, social conditions and educational problems. New York, Bureau of Publications, Teachers' College, Columbia University, New York, 1931. xiv, 210 p. -- See chapters "El progreso social en el Paraguay" and "Escuelas privadas."

1072. Hicks, Frederick, Politics, power and the role of the village priest in Paraguay. *Journal of inter-American studies* (University of Miami) 9:2:273-82 April 1967. -- A sociological study of the role a politically neutral person can carry out in a hyper-politicized community.

1073. Morton, Clement M. Paraguay, the island republic. Cincinnati, Powell, White, 1926. 117 p.

1074. Raine, Philip. Paraguay. New Brunswick, N.J., Scarecrow, 1956. 443 p. -- A good account of 20th century Paraguay.

1075. Service, Elman R. *and* Helen S. Tobati: Paraguan town. Chicago, University of Chicago Press, 1954. -- A community-type study done by an anthropologist and his wife. Special attention given to supposed Indian influence on Paraguyan culture. They find very little.

Protestantism in General

1076. Guía de las iglesias evangélicas del Paraguay. Asunción, Crusadas Evangelísticas Unidas (n.d.). 20 p. -- Brief listing.

1077. Wood, Thomas B. Los matrimonios protestantes en la república del Paraguay. Asunción, Imprenta El Heraldo, 1886. xxi, 50 p.

Denominational History
See also p. 312.
Anglican

1078. Grubb, W. Barbrooke. An unknown people in an unknown

land. London, 1941. -- Anecdotes about the relationships between missionaries and natives. Description
of customs, yet, more a personal diary.

Free Methodist

1079. Thompson, William R. Factors in the establishing of a
free Methodist training school in Paraguay. M. Th.
thesis, Biblical Seminary of New York, 1950.

Mennonite (see also bibliography on "Mennonites
in Latin America", Cf. no. 322)

See articles in the Mennonite encyclopedia on their immigrant
colonies.

1080. Drause, Annemarie Elizabeth. Mennonite settlement in the
Paraguayan Chaco. Ph. D. thesis, Chicago, 1952.

1081. Durkson, Martin. Resumen de la historia menonita en
Europa. mss, Colegio Bíblico, Bragado, Argentina,
1947. 48 p. -- Written by a Russian refugee born
in the Ukraine. His own experiences provide an
insight into the background of many of the Mennonites
in the Paraguayan Chaco.

1082. Fretz, J. Winfield. Immigrant group settlements in
Paraguay. North Newton, Ka., Bethel College, 1962.
196 p. illus., maps. -- A study of the sociology
of colonization.

1083. _____. Pilgrims in Paraguay, the story of Mennonite
colonization in South America. Scottsdale, Pa.,
Herald Press, 1953. xvi, 247 p. illus., --
Critical history in the form of a sociological study.

1084. Graber, Christian L. The coming of the Moros; from
spears to pruning hooks. Scottsdale, Pa., Herald
Press, 1964. 91 p. -- Heroism and sacrifice of
Mennonite colonies in the Chaco.

1085. Janzen, R. E. Glimpses of South America. Hillsboro, Ka.,
Mennonite Brethren Publishing, 1944. 130 p. --
Account of a visitor to Mennonite colonies in Para-
guay and Brazil.

1086. Paetkau, Enrique. Métodos de regulación de conducta; la

disciplina de congregaciones menonitas. Montevideo,
Seminario Evangélico Menonita de Teología, 1961. --
A study based on both Biblical theology and Christian
experience, especially with relation to European
Mennonites. Unfortunately little is said about this
problem in the Paraguayan Mennonite colony to which
he belongs.

1087. Smith, Willard. Paraguayan interlude. Scottsdale,
Herald Press, 1950. 184 p.

Uruguay
See also p. 312.

Bibliography
See also p. 312.

1088. Ambrosi, Luis Alberto Musso. Bibliografías de bibliografías uruguayas. s.l., 1964. -- A valuable updating, especially on the history of journalism, of
the work by Estrada (below).

1089. Arredondo, Horacio. Bibliografía uruguaya; contribución.
Montevideo, El Siglo Ilustrado, 1929. 182 p. --
Supplements Estrada (below) and is arranged chrono-
logically. (BLCU).

1090. Estrada, Dardo. Historia y bibliografía de la imprenta
en Montevideo, 1810-65. Montevideo, Librería Cervantes, 1912. 318 p. -- An important source of information concerning the periodical press.

General Background

1091. Hanson, Simón G. Utopia in Uruguay; chapters on the
economic history of Uruguay. New York, Oxford
University Press, 1938. viii, 262 p.

1092. Zum Felde, Alberto. Revolución histórica del Uruguay.
Montevideo, Librería Maximino García, 1941. 235 p.

Protestantism in General

1093. Ardao, Arturo. El protestantismo en el Uruguay. *Nueva* democraca (Nueva York) 4212:84-87 abril 1962.

1094. _____. Racionalismo y liberalismo en el Uruguay. Montevideo, Universidad, 1962. 398 p. -- The contest of university classes with separate criteria for each religious and philosophic position. See also *his* Espiritualismo y positivismo en el Uruguay. México, Fondo de Cultura Económica, 1950.

1095. Aspectos religiosos de la sociedad uruguaya. Montevideo, Centro de Estudios Cristianos de la Federación de Iglesias Evangélicas del Uruguay, San José, 1547, 1965. 143 p. -- Summary of public opinion survey of religious beliefs, secularization, religious practices and superstition in Uruguay.

1096. II Congreso evangélico nacional; la presencia evangélica en Uruguay de hoy. Montevideo, 1959. 11 p. -- A good but short review of many aspects of evangelical work.

Denominational History
See also p. 313.

Methodist (See also life of Juan C. Varetto, pioneer Methodist, Cf. no. 34)

1097. Berria, Cecilia Guelfi de. Dos vidas fecundas: Antonia y Cecilia Guelfi. Buenos Aires, La Aurora, 1940. 178 p. -- Were Methodist pioneers.

1098. Howard, Jorge P. Los 80 años de la iglesia metodists en el Uruguay, 1878-1958. s.l. (n.d.). -- A chronicle.

Waldensians (See also Argentina, Page 121)

1099. Boletín de la sociedad Sudamericana de historia valdense. Colonia Valdense, 1935. -- One of the most serious historical publications on denominational history in Latin America. Over thirty publications.

1100. Bounus, F. C. *y* L. El pastor Bounus y su historia de Colonia Cosmopólita. Colonia, Iglesia Valdense, 1952. 216 p. -- Includes collection of articles from the secular and evangelical press.

1101. Collazo, Florencio. Cincuentenario de Liceo Daniel

Armanel Ugon. s.l., 1938. 96 p.

1102. Ganz E. *y* E. Rostan. Il centenario della colonizzagione
        valdese nel Río de la Plata. Colonia Valdense,
        Iglesia Valdense, 1959. 32 p. -- Historical review
        upon the occasion of the visit of the moderator from
        Italy.

1103. Watts, George B. The Waldensians in the New World.
        Durham, N.C., Duke University Press, 1941. 309 p.
        -- Excellent bibliography and appendix. LAWG.

Periodicals
See also p. 313.

Past Publications

1104. El evangelista. 1877-?. -- First evangelical periodical
        in Uruguay. Founded by Thomas B. Wood.

Current Publications

1105. El mensajero valdense. Official organ of the Sínodo de
        la Iglesia Valdense del Río de la Plata. Casilla 23,
        Paysandú, Uruguay.

1106. Renacimiento. Official organ of the Federación Juvenil
        Valdense.

BRAZIL
See also p. 313.

Bibliography
See also p. 313.

1107. Burns, E. Bradford. A working bibliography for the study
        of Brazilian history. *The Americas* 20:54-88 July
        1965. -- An attempt to compile a truly working
        bibliography of significant sources, both in English
        and in Portuguese. Extensive yet not so long as to
        discourage use.

1108. Simones de Reis, Antonio. Bibliografia das bibliografias
        brasileiras. Rio de Janeiro, 1942. 186 p. (BLCU).
        -- Dr. Rubén Borba de Morais, Director of the

Biblioteca Pública Municipal de São Paulo, has two
volumes on *Bibliografia brasiliana*, Rio de Janeiro,
1958. (BLCU). These refer to works before 1822
published by Brazilian authors and works from 1504-
1900 published about Brazil. Rodrigues' *Historio-
grafia e bibliografia do Domínio Holandes no Brasil*
is of interest in early Protestant history in Brazil
(BLCU).

1109. Topete, José M., ed. A working bibliography of Brazilian
literature. Gainesville, University of Florida
Press, 1957. -- Excellent.

1110. Amazônia, 1614-1962. Rio de Janeiro, Instituto Brasileiro
de Bibliografia e Documentacão, 1963. xxix, 842 p.
(BLCU). -- A survey of literature on Brazil of
sociological significance published to 1940 by Donald
Pierson. Is valuable for researchers in the social
sciences.

1111. Annaes de bibliotheca nacional. Rio de Janeiro (n.d.).
-- These publications are an indispensable tool for
historical and bibliographical studies.

1112. Levine, Robert M., ed. Brazil: field research guide in
the social sciences. New York, Institute of Latin
American Studies, Columbia University, 1966. vi,
298 p. -- Includes bibliographies.

1113. Manual bibliográfico de estudos brasileiros, 1949. (BLCU).
-- Published with William Berrion of Howard; an
essential tool.

1114. Pierson, Donald. Survey of the literature on Brazil of
sociological significance published up to 1940...
Cambridge, Mass., Harvard University Press, 1945.
xvi, 60 p.

General Background
See also p. 313.

1115. Anuário estatístico do Brasil. Valdemar Calvalcante, ed.
Rio de Janeiro, Conselho Nacional de Estatística
(n.d.), published annually.

1116. Araujo, Alceu Maynard. Folklore nacional. São Paulo,
Edicoes Melhoramentos, 1964. 3 v. -- Covers the
whole area of Brazilian folk culture. Author is

trained anthropologist and member of the Academia
Paulista de Letras.

1117. _____. Medicina rústica. São Paulo, Campanhia Editora
Nacional, 1961. (Brasiliana, no. 300). -- Extensive
exposition of folk world view and concepts of dis-
eases, their causes and cures. Author appeals for
a sympathetic comprehension of Northeastern Brazilian
folk world view on the part of medical doctors and
others who would work with these people. Very
practical.

1118. Azevedo, Fernando de. Brazilian culture; an introduction
to the study of culture in Brazil. New York, 1950.
562 p. -- Trans. by W. R. Crawford. A comprehensive
monograph on the history of Brazilian culture from
16th century to 1940.

1119. Bastide, Roger e Florestan Fernandes. Brancos e negros
em São Paulo; ensaio sociológico sobre aspectos da
formacão, manifestacões atuais e efeitos do procen-
cieto de cor na sociedade paulistana. 2. ed., rev.
e ampliada. São Paulo, Companhia Editora Nacional,
1959. 371 p. (Brasiliana, no. 305). -- An exposition by two sociologists of race prejudice in São
Paulo (city) in spite of prevailing Brazilian myth
of racial democracy. Originally published by Editora
Anhembi, São Paulo, 1955 under a UNESCO grant.

1120. Bello, José Maria. A history of modern Brazil, 1889-
1964. Palo Alto, Calif., Stanford University Press,
1965. 362 p. -- Trans. by James L. Taylor. First
English translation of the most comprehensive one-
volume history of Brazil now available. New concluding chapter covers 1954-64. The translator has
greatly improved the original by completing references to persons, places and incidents, and by
including a very comprehensive index.

1121. Boxer, Charles R. The Dutch in Brazil, 1624-54. Oxford,
Clarendon, 1957. 313 p. -- The story of the 30-
year Dutch occupation of Northeastern Brazil. Some
references to the establishment of the Reformed Church
in Brazil and attempts to do missionary work. See
also his Bibliography of period of Dutch occupation
in Bahia.

1122. _____. The golden age of Brazil, 1695-1750; growing
pains of a colonial society. Berkeley, University

of California Press, 1962. xiii, 443 p.

1123. Burns, E. Bradford. The unwritten alliance; the Rio
      Branco and Brazilian-American relations. New York,
      Columbia University Press, 1966. 305 p.

1124. Calmon, Pedro. História de civilizcão brasileira. São
      Paulo, Campanhia Editora Nacional, 1940. 359 p.

1125. Calógeras, João P. A history of Brazil. New York,
      Russell and Russell, 1963. 374 p. -- Trans. and ed.
      by Percy Alvin Martin from Portuguese original,
      Formacão histórica do Brasil. Rio de Janeiro,
      Pimenta de Mello, 1930; 4. ed., São Paulo, Campanhia
      Editôra Nacional, 1945; 5. ed., Rio de Janeiro, 1957.
      First English ed., 1939.

1126. Crosby, Ella Mae. Extension work in Brazil and sugges-
      tions for its further development. Ph. D. thesis,
      Cornell University, Ithaca, N.Y., 1958. microfilmed.

1127. Cruz Costa, João. Contribuicão à história das ideias no
      Brasil, o desenvolvimento da filosofia no Brasil e a
      evolucão histórica nacional. Rio de Janeiro, José
      Olympio, 1956. 484 p. -- Trans. by Suzette Moredo
      as A history of ideas in Brazil... Berkeley, Univer-
      sity of California Press, 1964. x, 427 p. Trans.
      into Spanish by Jorge López Páez as Esbozo de una
      historia de las ideas en el Brasil. México, Fondo
      de Cultura Económica, 1957. 175 p.

1128. Cunha, Euclydes da. Rebellion in the backlands. Chicago,
      University of Chicago Press, 1957. 532 p. -- Trans.
      by Samuel Putnam from Os sertões. Rio de Janeiro,
      many editions. 1. ed., 1902.

1129. Dos Passos, John. Brazil on the move. Garden City, N.Y.,
      Doubleday, 1963. ix, 205 p.

1130. Ellison, Fred P. Brazil's new novel; four Northeastern
      masters: José Lins do Rego, Jorge Amado, Graciliano
      Ramos, Rachel de Queirós. Berkeley, University of
      California Press, 1954. 191 p.

1131. Freyre, Gilberto. Brazil, an interpretation. New York,
      Knopf, 1947. 179 p. -- Stresses three ethnic ele-
      ments which have contributed to the formation of the
      Brazilian racial amalgam.

1132. _____. The mansions and the shanties, (Sobrados e
       mucambos); the making of modern Brazil. New York,
       Knopf, 1963. 431 p. -- With an introduction by
       Frank Tannenbaum. Trans. by Harriet de Onís from
       Portuguese original, Sobrados e mucambos; decadência
       do patriarcado rural e desenvolvimento do urbano.
       Rio de Janeiro, José Olympio, several editions.
       Second in Freyre's series of sociological history,
       dealing with the period of the Empire and formation
       of Brazilian urbanism.

1133. _____. The master and the slaves (Casa grande e senzala);
       a study in the development of Brazilian civilization.
       2. English ed., rev. New York, Knopf, 1956. lxxi,
       537 p. -- Trans. by Samuel Putnam from Casa-grande
       e senzala; formacão da família brasileira sob o regime
       econômico patriarcal. 5. ed. rev. Rio de Janeiro,
       José Olympio, 1946. A classic on Brazilian society;
       deals with race problems, climate, the arts, litera-
       ture, history, economics and politics. A portrayal
       of a Brazilian family during the sugar plantation
       period.

1134. _____. New world in the tropics; the culture of modern
       Brazil. New York, Vintage, 1959. 385 p. -- A study
       of the Brazil which exists today. Chapters on litera-
       ture and architecture are expecially exciting.

1135. _____. Ordem e progresso; processo de desintegracão das
       sociedades patriarcal e semipatriarcal no Brasil sob
       o regime do trabalho livre: aspectos de um quase
       meio século de transicão do trabalho escravo para o
       trabalho livre; e da monarquia para a república. Rio
       de Janeiro, José Olympio, 1959. -- Third in his
       series of sociological history of Brazil, covering
       the late Empire, first Republic and the disintegra-
       tion of the patriarchal society.

1136. Furtado, Celso. Diagnosis of the Brazilian crisis.
       Berkeley, University of California Press, 1965.
       xxiv, 168 p. -- Trans. by Suzette Moredo from
       Portuguese original, Dialética do desenvolvimento.
       Rio de Janeiro, Editora Fundo de Cultura, 1964. 173
       p. -- Part I is a theoretical discussion of Marxism
       in the light of more recent literature and experience.
       Part II is a diagnosis of the Brazilian crisis with
       special emphasis on the period preceeding the March
       31st movement of 1964. His chapter on the problems
       of the Northeast clears away much popular political

and economic mystification of that troubled area and
is essential reading for those whose knowledge of
that area is limited mainly to news releases.

1137. _____. The economic growth of Brazil, a survey from
colonial to modern times. Berkeley, University of
California Press, 1965. x, 285 p. -- Trans. by
Ricardo W. de Aguiar and Eric Chas. Drysdale from
the Portuguese original Formacão econômica do Brasil.
4. ed. Rio de Janeiro, Editora Fundo de Cultura,
1961.

1138. Galvao, Eduardo E. The religion of an Amazon community,
a study in culture change. Ph. D. thesis, Columbia
University, N.Y., 1951. 189 p. -- Outstanding work.
Also available in the book Santos e visagens, um
estudo da vida religiosa de Itá, Amazonas. São
Paulo, Companhia Editora Nacional, 1955. 202 p.

1139. Gauld, Charles A. The last Titan: Percival Farguhar,
American entrepreneur in Latin America. Ph. D.
thesis, Stanford University, Palo Alto, Calif., 1964.
427 p. maps, illus. -- Story of a Pennsylvania
Quaker, 1864-1953; a significant figure in the
economic history of Brazil in railroads, cattle and
iron.

1140. Graham, Richard. *Hispanic American historical review*
May 1966. -- Lead article on the relationship
between economics and the emancipation of the slaves
in Brazil.

1141. Harris, Marvin. Town and country in Brazil. New York,
Columbia University Press, 1956. x, 302 p. --
A study of urbanism in the mountains of eastern
Brazil.

1142. Henderson, Lawrence W. Portuguese colonial policy.
M.A. thesis, Kennedy School, Hartford Seminary
Foundation, Hartford, Conn., 1958. -- Includes
history of the colonial expansion and chief contributing factors, colonial law and the hierarchic
partnership which resulted.

1143. Hill, Lawrence W., ed. Brazil. Berkeley, University of
California Press, 1947. xxi, 394 p. (United Nations).
-- Political, diplomatic, economic phases of Brazilian
history. Gives attention to church-state relations.

1144. Hunnicutt, Benjamin H. Brazil, world frontier. New York, Van Nostrand, 1949.

1145. Kelsey, Vera. Seven keys to Brazil. New York, Funk and Wagnalls, 1945. xx, 314 p. -- First published in 1940.

1146. Kidder, D. P. e J. C. Fletchet. O Brasil e os Brasil- eiros; esboço histórico e descritivo. Rio de Janeiro, Editora Nacional, 1941. 2 v. -- Portuguese transla- tion of English original, 1857; many editions. Kidder was a Methodist missionary in Brazil, 1836-42. Still a classic on early Brazil.

1147. Jesus, Carolina Maria de. Child of the dark: the diary of Carolina... New York, Dutton, 1962. -- Trans. by David St. Clair from the Portuguese original, Quarto de despejo; diário de uma favelada. 5. ed. São Paulo, Livraria F. Alves, 1960. 182 p. A diary of the culture of poverty in the urban slums of São Paulo. See also *her* sequel, Casa de alvenaria which tells of her difficulties and disappointments after she left the slum for a middle class neighborhood.

1148. Lima, Alceu Amoroso. Psicologia do povo brasilerio. *Revista do Instituo geográfico e histórico de Bahia* 60:218-39, 1934.

1149. Moog, C. Vianna. Bandeirantes and pioneers. New York, G. Brazilles, 1964. 316 p. -- Trans. by L. L. Barrett from Portuguese original, Bandeirantes e pioneiros; paralelo entre duas culturas. 2. ed. Rio de Janeiro, Editôra Globo, 1959. Compares and contrasts North American and Brazilian sociological history, attempting to dispel many myths and reject- ed hypotheses.

1150. _____. Um rio imita o reino. 7. ed. Rio de Janeiro, Editôra Globo, 1957. 260 p. (Colecão autores brasileiros, no. 28). -- A sociological study of German colonization in the south of Brazil. English trans. to appear soon under the auspices of the Chas. Frank Publications, New York.

1151. Morse, Richard M. From community to metropolis; a biography of São Paulo. Gainesville, University of Florida Press, 1958. xxiii, 341 p.

1152. Oliveira Lima, Manoel de. The evolution of Brazil

compared with that of Spanish and Anglo-saxon America. New York, Russell, 1966. -- First published in 1914.

1153. Pierson, Donald. Negroes in Brazil, a study of race contact in Bahia. Chicago, Ill., University of Chicago Press, 1947. xxviii, 392 p. Revised edition in Portuguese *Brancos e Pretos ra Bahia*, Sao Paulo, Companhia Editora Nacional, 1971.

1154. Ramos, Arthur. Introducão à antropologia brasileira. 3. ed. Rio de Janeiro, Colecão Estudos Brasileiros, 1961, 1962. 3 v. -- The most complete work on the subject but quite dated. First published in 1943-47.

1155. Robcock, Stefan H. Brazil's developing Northeast; a study of regional planning and foreign aid. Washington, D.C., Brookings, 1963. 204 p.

1156. Rocha Pombo, José F. de. História do Brasil. Rio de Janeiro, Benjamîn de Aquila Editora, 1960. 10 v. -- First published in 1905.

1157. Rosa, João Guimarães. The devil to pay in the backlands. New York, Knopf, 1963. 449 p. -- Trans. by James L. Taylor and Harriet de Onîs from Portuguese original *Grandes sertão: veredas*. Rio de Janeiro, 1956. Several later editions in Portuguese.

1158. Schurz, William L. Brazil, the infinite country. New York, Dutton, 1961. 346 p.

1159. Seitz, George. People of the rain-forests. London, Heinemann, 1963. 208 p. -- Trans. by Arnold J. Pomerands from German original Hinter dem grünen Vorkong. Well written, informative, with exicitng moments.

1160. Sick, Helumt. Tukani. New York, Erikson-Taplinger, 1960. 240 p. -- Trans. by R. H. Stevens. Fascinating account of a dangerous but successful Indian expedition.

1161. Smith, T. Lynn. Brazil: people and institutions. rev. ed. Baton Rouge, Louisiana State University Press, 1963.

1162. _____ *and* Alexander Marchant, ed. Brazil, portrait of half a continent. New York, Dryden, 1951. viii, 466 p. -- A compilation of original articles on

Brazil, many by Brazilian specialists.

1163. Tannanbaum, Frank. Slave and citizen; the negro in the
       Americas. New York, Vintage, 1963. xi, 128 p. --
       First published by Knopf in 1947.

1164. Turner, Charles. Ruy Barbosa, Brazilian crusader for
       the essential freedoms. New York, Abingdon-Cokesbury,
       1945. 208 p. -- With a foreword by His Excellency
       Dr. Oswaldo Aranha. Excellent biography of one of
       Brazil's greatest heroes.

1165. Veríssimo, Erico. O tempo e o vento. Porto Alegre,
       Editora Globo, 1948-62. 3 v. -- A historical novel
       in three volumes (seven books) tracing the life and
       fortunes of one family from early colonial period of
       Rio Grande do Sul to 1945, accurately portraying
       historical, political and social backgrounds in their
       changing modes over a 200 year period. The author is
       a member of the Brazilian Academy of Letters and the
       second most translated writer in Brazil. This work
       has many references to early Lutheran and modern
       Methodist missionaries. V. 2, O retrato, in English
       as Time and the wind, trans. by L. L. Barrett, New
       York, Macmillan, 1951. 624 p.

1166. Vernon, Vance O. Illiteracy in Brazil. M. A. thesis,
       Southern Baptist Theological Seminary, Louisville,
       Ky., 1951.

1167. Wagley, Charles, Amazon town: a study of man in the
       tropics. New York, Knopf, 1964. 315 p. -- With a
       new epilogue by the author. First published in 1953.
       An anthropological community study. Also a Borzoi
       book, Knopf, 1965.

1168. _____. An introduction to Brazil. New York, Columbia
       University Press, 1963. 322 p. -- Columbia paper-
       back, 1965. An excellent introduction to Brazil for
       North Americans: the chapter on "Family and educa-
       tion" clarifies much confusion in North American
       minds about the Brazilian educational system; up-to-
       date "Selected bibliography on Brazil."

1169. _____. Race and class in rural Brazil. 2. ed. Paris,
       UNESCO, 1963. 158 p. -- First ed. 1952.

1170. Zweig, Stefan. Brazil, land of the future. New York,
       Viking, 1941. 282 p. -- Trans. by Andrew St. James

from German original, Brasilien, ein land der zukunft.
Stockholm, Bermann-Fischer, 1941. 293 p.

Protestantism in General
See also p. 319.

1171. A tentative bibliography of the history of Christian and
       missionary work in Brazil. Missionary Information
       Bureau, Rua da Constituicao, 14, Rio de Janeiro, 1966.
       14 p. mimeographed.

1172. Revista bibliografica da literatura evangélica. Camara
       de Literatura Evangélica do Brasil, Caixa Postal 955,
       Campinas, S. P., Brasil. 1958-.

                    * * * * * *

1173. Amaral, Epaminondas M. do., et al. Apreciacão e diretrizes.
       Rio de Janeiro, Centro Brasileiro de Publicidade, 1937.
       207 p. -- Considers problems of Brazilian Protestan-
       tism related to the 50 Congresso Evangélico do Brasil.
       See also *his* O Protestantismo e a reforma. São Paulo,
       Livraria Saleluz, 1962. 199 p.; and, *his* O magno
       problema. Rio de Janeiro, Centro Brasileiro de Publi-
       cadade, 1934. 194 p. Both discuss problems of the
       unity of the churches.

1174. Baez Camargo, Gonzalo. Earliest Protestant missionary
       venture in South America. *Church history* 21:2 June
       1952. -- A good brief resumé of the Huguenot colony
       in Rio.

1175. Begrich, Martin. Kirchengeschichte brasiliers im abiss.
       Göttenger, Vanderhoech and Ruprecht, 1963. 63 p.
       (Die kirche in inher geschichte, ein handbuch,
       Schmidt und Wolf, ed., v. 4, S.22-S.34).

1176. The Bible in Brazil: colporteur experience. New York,
       Young People's Missionary Movement, 1902. 293 p.
       illus. -- Picture of Brazil in the latter part of
       the 19th century and the experiences of a colporteur
       in that period. References to European Protestant
       immigrants.

1177. Bittencourt, Bendito de Paula. The Portuguese New
       Testament in the light of modern research; its

translations and text. Ph. D. thesis, Boston University, Mass., 1956. microfilmed.

1178. Braga, Erasmo *and* Kenneth G. Grubb. The republic of Brazil: a survey of the religious situation. London, World Dominion Press, 1932. 184 p. maps. - A thorough study of evangelical movement in Brazil from the early beginnings of the first quarter of this century. To be translated soon in Portuguese.

1179. Burckhardt, G. E. *e* R. Gruendemann. Les missions evangéliques. Lausanne, George Bridel Editeur, 1884. 4 v. -- References to early missionary ventures in Brazil.

1180. Caldeira de Andrada, Laercio. A igreja dos fiéis; Coligny, no feudo do Villegagnon. Rio de Janeiro, Centro Brasileiro, 1947. illus., tables. 149 p. -- Story of the ill-fated Huguenot colony in Rio.

1181. Chamberlain, Henriqueta. Where the sabiá sings. New York, Macmillan, 1947. 246 p. -- About a mulotto fishing village near Recife.

1182. Chaves, Maria de Melo. Bandeirantes da fé. Belo Horizonte, 1947. 195 p. -- Biographies of Protestant leaders.

1183. Crespin, Jean. A tragédia da Guanabara ou história dos protomártyres do christianismo no Brasil. Rio de Janeiro, Pimenta de Mello, 1916. 155 p. -- Original text in French and trans. by Domingos Ribeiro.

1184. Dauphinee, Bede A. Church and parliament in Brazil during the First Empire: 1823-31. Ph. D. thesis, Georgetown University, Washington, D.C., 1965.

1185. Davis, J. Merle. How the church grows in Brazil. New York, IMC, 1943. 167 p. -- A study of the economic and social basis of the Evangelical Church in Brazil.

1186. Delery, Jean. Le voyage du Brésil. Paris, Payot, 1927. 319 p. illus., maps. -- The story of the ill-fated Huguenot colony as told by one of the members of the colony.

1187. Estatística do culto protestante do Brasil, 1960-64. Rio de Janeiro, Depto. do Imprensa Nacional, anual. -- Servco gráfico do Instituo Brasileiro de Geografia e Estatística. Official government statistics based on national census figures.

1188. Farra, Robert M. Protestantism in Brazil: a study of the activities and results of the Protestant foreign missionary movement in the U.S. of Brazil. Thesis, University of Nebraska, Lincoln, 1960.

1189. Ferreira, Júlio Andrade. Galeria evangélica. São Paulo, Casa Editora Presbiteriana, 1952. 228 p. -- Biographies of outstanding evangelical pioneers in Brazil.

1190. _____. Realidade brasileira, desafío ao evangelismo. *Revista teológica* 24:31 July 1963. -- English trans. by Chalmers Brown.

1191. Gammon, Samuel R. The evangelical invasion of Brazil: or, a half-century of evangelical missions in the land of the southern cross. Richmond, Presbyterian Committee of Publication, 1910. 179 p. -- Little documentation, but interpretative of the period at the turn of the century.

1192. Ginsburg, Solomon L. A wandering Jew in Brazil: an autobiography. Nashville, Tenn., Sunday School Board, Southern Baptist Convention, 1922. 265 p.

1193. Glass, Frederick C. Through the heart of Brazil. London, Evangelical Union of South America (ca. 1906). -- A colporteur's experiences. See also *his* Adventures with the Bible in Brazil. New York, Laizeux Bros., Bible Truth Dept., 1943.

1194. Grubb, Kenneth G. The lowland Indians of Amazonia. London, World Dominion Press, 1927. 159 p. maps. -- Description of the location and religious conditions of the Indians of Colombia, Venezuela, the Guyanas, Ecuador, Peru, Brazil and Bolivia in the 1920's.

1195. Higgins, P. O., ed. Almanack evangélico brasileiro. Rio de Janeiro, 1922.

1196. Léonard, Emile G. L'illumisme dans un protestantisme de constitution recénte Brésil. Paris, Presses Universitaires de France, 1953. 114 p. -- Study of the Pentecostal phenomena in Brazil from its beginnings until 1950.

1197. _____. O protestantismo brasileiro; estudo de eclesiologia e história social. São Paulo, Associacão de Seminários Teológicos Evangélicos, 1963. 354 p. -- Original text

in French and trans. by Linneu de Camargo Schutzer.
It is the most complete work about Protestantism in
Brazil. Researched 1949-50. Originally published in
eight articles, 1951-52. See also *his* three volume
work on Protestantism in French. Two volumes now
available in English.

1198. Lodwick, Robert Eugene. The significance of the church-
state relationship to an evangelical program in
Brazil. M. A. thesis, Oberlin Graduate School of
Theology, Oberlin, Ohio, 1945.

1199. Mattos, Domício P. do. Posição social de igreja. 2. ed.
Rio de Janeiro, Editora Praia, 1965.

1200. Morris, C. H. The Bible in Brazil. London, British and
Foreign Bible Society (n.d.). 35 p. -- A Bible
society publication about the distribution of the
Bible in Brazil.

1201. Pannier *e* Mondain, éd. L'expansion francais antie-mer
et protestantes francais. Paris, Societé de Missions
Evangelique, 1931. -- Story of the ill-fated Huguenot
colony in Rio de Janeiro.

1202. Pereira, E. Carlos. O problema religioso da América
Latina; estudo dogmático-histórico. São Paulo,
Empresa Editora Brasileira, 1920. 442 p. -- Analy-
zes the problem faced by the Protestant churches in
Brazil.

1203. Perkins, Rodger W. Protestant beginnings in the Bahia
state; Brazil. M.A. thesis, University of Oregon,
Eugene, 1965. microfilmed. -- Good bibliography.

1204. Plett, Donnie W. Evangelical literature in Brazil. M.A.
thesis, Graduate School of Missions, Columbia Bible
College, Columbia, S.C., 1959.

1205. Read, William R. New patterns of church growth in Brazil.
Grand Rapids Erdmann, 1965. 239 p. -- Trans. into
Portuguese as Fermento religioso nas massas do Brasil.
Campinas, Livraria Crista Unida, 1967. 250 p. Good
bibliography. Basic information on Brazilian Pentecostal churches and a comparison of their growth with
that of the older denominations. Reveals some judgments of Brazilian Protestantism which are controversial.

1206. Ribeiro, Domingos. Origens do evangelismo brasileiro.
       Rio de Janeiro, Centro Brasileiro de Publicidade,
       1946. 135 p. -- A good historical study with some
       polemical overtones.

1207. Rio, João do. As religiões no Rio. Rio de Janeiro,
       Carniero Libeiro, 1906. 245 p. -- An interesting
       report on worship services and organizations in Rio
       in 1906.

1208. Silva, Ismael da. Notas históricas sobre a missão
       evangelizadora do Brasil. Rio de Janeiro, 1960.
       2 v. -- Chronological but poorly documented. Treat-
       ment of work begun by Dr. R. R. Kalley.

1209. Testa, Michael P. The apostle of Madeira. *Presbyterian
       historical review* 2:244-71, 1961. Part of M. Th.
       thesis on Robert R. Kalley at Hartford Seminary
       Foundation.

1210. _____. O apóstolo da Madeira. -- Cf. no. 509. p. 92-
       105 deals with Brazil.

1211. Tucker, Hugh C. The Bible in Brazil. New York, Revell,
       1902. 292 p. -- A thrilling narrative of 14 years
       of colportage. Good illustrations. Reveals Brazil-
       ian character.

1212. Van Rossum, R. G., S. S. Cc. Braziliaans protestantismus.
       Het missierwerk 4:231-44, 1966.

1213. Weaver, Blanche C. Confederate immigrants and evangelical
       churches in Brazil. *Journal of southern history*
       108:466-68 November 1952.

1214. Wheeler, W. Reginald, et al. Modern missions in Chile
       and Brazil. Philadelphia, Westminster Press, 1926.

1215. Willems, Emilio. Protestantism and culture change in
       Brazil and Chile. *In* Religion, revolution and
       reform (Cf. no. 164).

Reports of Evangelical Conferences of Brazilian Churches

1216. A accão christã na América Latina. Rio de Janeiro,
       Centro Brasileiro de Publicidade, 1923. 144 p. --
       Includes report of 2° Congresso regional commerativo

do centenário da independência do Brasil and summary
of other cooperative efforts.

1217. A igreja e as rápidas transformaçoes sociais do Brasil.
Rio de Janeiro, Confederacão Evangélica do Brasil,
1958. 46 p. -- A study of the role of the church
as it faces rapid social change.

1218. Christian cooperation in Brazil. Rio de Janeiro, Evangelical Confederation of Brazil, 1937. 23 p. --
Review of situation in 1937 for the national Evangelical Congress of that year.

1219. Congresso regional da obra christã na América Latina.
Rev. Francisco de Souza, ed. Rio de Janeiro, Casa
Publicadora Batistia, 1917. 148 p.

1220. Cristo e o processo revolucionário brasileiro; a confer-
ência do Nordeste. Recife, julho 1962. Rio de
Janeiro, Editora Loqui, 1962. 2 v. -- v. 1, 128 p.,
record of conference proceedings; v. 2, 190 p.,
addresses.

1221. Echos da segunda convencão nacional da Assoc. Crista da
Moços no Brasil. São Paulo, 1906. 159 p. -- Report
of YMCA convention. Messages by John R. Mott and
Brazilians. Reveals deep insights and vision.

1222. Perspectivas e realizaçoes: 2ª conferencia de currículo
e congresso de cultura evangélica: fevereiro 1947.
Rio de Janeiro (ca. 1947). 180 p.

1223. Presenca de igreja na evolucão de nacionalidade. Rio de
Janeiro, Confederacão Evangélica do Brasil, 1960.
68 p. -- Report of third study meeting of the
social responsibility of the Church. Includes study
of rapid social changes in Brazil and the role of
the Church in these changes.

1224. Teses apresentadas ao seu I congresso de cultura
religiosa. São Paulo, 1941. 340 p. -- Essays prepared to consider possible evangelical solutions to
problems on the Brazilian scene. Reflects the
ecclesiastical atmosphere at that time in the
country.

Denominational History
See also p. 325.

Adventist

1225. Holliwell, Leo B. Light bearers to the Amazon. Nash-
       ville, Southern Publishing Assoc., 1945. 160 p.

Assemblies of God

1226. Conde, Emílio. História das assembléias de Deus no
       Brasil. Rio de Janeiro, Casa Publicadora Assembléias
       de Deus, 1960. 355 p.

1227. Jasson, Erik. Pa indianstigar i Brasilian. Orebro,
       Obrebro Missions-forenings Förlag, 1945. 103 p.

1228. Törnberg, Allen, Fram Amazonas till la Plata. Stockholm,
       Förlag, 1955. 136 p. (Med. svenska pingstmission-
       arër i Sydamerica).

Baptist

1229. Album do Brasil batista. Rio de Janeiro. Publicâdora
       Batista, 1955. 259 p. illus. -- General review of
       work.

1230. Almanaque batista: Depto. de estatística da Convencao
       Batista Brasileira. Rio de Janeiro, Casa Publicâ-
       dora Batista (n.d.).

1231. Bell, Lester Carl. Factors influencing doctrinal
       developments among Brazilian Baptists. Th. D.
       thesis, Southwestern Baptist Theological Seminary,
       Fort Worth, Texas, 1957.

1232. _____. Which way in Brazil? Nashville, Convention
       Press, 1965.

1233. Bratcher, Lewis M. Francisco Fulgêncio Soren, Christ's
       interpreter to many lands. Nashville, Broadman
       Press, 1938. 124 p. -- For many years the outstand-
       ing Southern Baptist leader in Brazil.

1234. _____. Mule tales from inland trails. 2. ed. Nashville, Broadman Press, 1948. 124 p.

1235. _____. The apostle of the Amazon. Nashville, Broadman Press, 1951. 138 p.

1236. Crabtree, A. R. Baptist in Brazil. Rio de Janeiro, Baptist Publishing House, 1950.

1237. _____. Antônio N. de Mesquita. Historia dos Batistas do Brasil. Rio de Janeiro, Casa Publicâdora Batista, 1940. 2 v. -- v. 1, to 1906; v. 2, 1906-42.

1238. Deter, Arthur B. Forty years on the land of tomorrow. Nashville, Broadman Press, 1946. 207 p.

1239. Gill, Everett. Pilgrimage to Brazil. Nashville, Broadman Press, 1954. 144 p.

1240. Hawkins, Dorine Cobb. The development and influence of the women's missionary training schools in Brazil. D.R.E. thesis, Southwestern Baptist Theological Seminary, Fort Worth, 1957.

1241. Key, Jerry S. The rise and development of Baptist theological education in Brazil, 1881-1963: a historical and interpretive survey. Th. D. thesis, Southern Baptist Seminary, Dallas, 1965.

1242. Mein, David. The contribution of the Baptists to the life of Brazil. Th. D. thesis, Southern Baptist Theological Seminary, Louisville, 1945.

1243. Soares Ferreira, Ebenezer. Rev. A. B. Christie no Brasil. Rio de Janeiro, Casa Publicadora Batista, 1959. 210 p.

1244. Stover, S. S. The beginning and progress of religious educational agencies of the Baptist Convention of Minas Gerais, Brazil. mss, Southwestern Baptist Theological Seminary, Fort Worth, 1958.

Congregacão Cristã no Brasil

1245. Breve história, fé, doutrina e estatutos. São Paulo, Indústrias Reunidas Irmãos Spina, S.A. (n.d.).

Congregational

1246. Gomes da Rocha, João. Lembrancas do passado. Rio de
       Janeiro, 1945. 3 v. -- Detailed history of the
       Igreja Evangélica Fluminense but not very well
       organized.

1247. Luz, Fortunato. Esboço histórico de escola dominical da
       igreja evangélica fluminense, 1855-1932. Rio de
       Janeiro, Rua Camerino, 102, 1932. 542 p. illus. --
       This book covers a larger range than its title pre-
       supposes; it is in fact the best history of the
       Congregational church in Brazil.

Episcopal

1248. Kinsolving, Arthur B. Biografia de um dos primeros
       misionários da Igreja Episcopal no Brasil. Porto
       Alegre, Publicâdora Ecclesia (n.d.). 80 p. -- A
       portrait sketch of the Rt. Rev. Lucien Lee Kinsolv-
       ing. Available in English. New York, Protestant
       Episcopal Church (n.d.). 22 p.

1249. Krischke, George Upton. História da igreja episcopal
       brasileira. Rio de Janeiro, Gráfica Tupy (n.d.).

Lutheran

1250. Almanaque do Sínodo riograndense: jahriveiser für die
       evangelischen Gemeindens in Brasilien, 1955. São
       Leopoldo, Oficinas Gráficas Rotermand, 1955. 227 p.

1251. Begrich, Martin. Kirchengeschichte Brasilius un abrib.
       Göttingen, 1963. (Die kirche in inhrer Geschichte.
       Ein Handbuch, Vondeerhoeck e Ruprecht Volumen S., Pa.
       23-34). -- First comprehensive church history of
       Brazil with bibliographical notes: the Protestant
       churches are dealt with on p. 27-34, from the colonial
       time on, 1548-1649.

1252. Igreja evangélica no Rio Grande do Sul, Sínodo Riograndense.
       São Leopoldo, Editora Sinodal (ca. 1957). 54 p.
       illus.

1253. Schlatter, Wilhelm. Geschichte der Basler Mission, 1815-
       1915. Basel, Basler Missionsbuchkandlung, 1916. 3
       v. -- Based especially on primary sources.

1254. Schröder, Ferdinand. Brasilien und Wittenberg, urspring
       and gestaltung deutschen evangelische kirchentums in
       Brasilien. Berlin, Walter de Gruyter, 1936. 413 p.
       -- Story of the Barmen missions.

1255. Setenta e cinco anos de existência do Sínodo Riograndense,
       1886-1961. São Paulo, Editora Sinodal, 1961. 114 p.
       illus. -- Historical review.

Methodist

1256. Buyers, Paul Eugene. Autobiografia. São Paulo, Imprensa
       Metodista, 1952.

1257. _____. História de metodismo. São Paulo, Imprensa
       Metodista, 1945.

1258. Kennedy, James L. Cincoenta annos de metodismo no Brasil.
       São Paulo, Imprensa Metodista, 1928. 439 p. -- A
       review of fifty years of Methodism with some
       statistics.

1259. Moore, Jennie Marie. Women's work in Brazil of the
       Methodist Epistocal church, south. M.A. thesis,
       George Peabody College, Nashville, Tenn., 1939.

Missions Among Indigenous Groups

1260. Cunningham, Rosemary. Under a thatched roof in a Brazil-
       ian jungle: a missionary story. Toronto, Evangelical
       publishers, 1947. 127 p.

1261. Grubb, Kenneth G. The lowland Indians of Amazonia. (Cf.
       no. 376).

1262. Hay, Alexander R. Saints and savages, Brazil's Indian
       problems. London, Hodder and Stoughton (n.d.). viii,
       91 p.

1263. Moennich, Martha L. Pioneering for Christ in Xingu jungles.
       Grand Rapids, Zondervan, 1942. 196 p.

1264. Nelson, Emrico Alfredo. O apóstolo da Amazônia. Rio de
      Janeiro, 1945. 74 p. -- Story of a Swedish pioneer
      missionary who arrived in 1889 in Natal.

1265. Roome, W. J. W. The three Freds: martyred pioneers for
      Christ in Brazil. London, Marshall, Morgan and Scott,
      1936. 124 p.

Nazarene

1266. Reza, Honorato. Brazil's open door. Kansas City,
      Nazarene Publishing House, 1958.

Pentecostal

1267. O Espírito Santo e o movimento pentecostal. São Paulo,
      Asociacão de Seminários Teológicos Evangélicos, 1966.

1268. Yuasa, Key. A study of the Pentecostal movement in
      Brazil, its importance. *The Reformed and Presbyterian
      world* 39:2:63-72. -- Statement by a minister of the
      Evangelical Holiness Church of Brazil.

Presbyterian

1269. Bear, James Edwin. Mission to Brazil. Nashville, BWM,
      PCUS, 1961. -- Includes sketch of work in North
      Brazil.

1270. _____. The mission work of the Presbyterian church in
      the United States in south Brazil, 1869-1958. Nash-
      ville, BWM, PCUS, 1960. 2 v. -- A mss. based on
      English sources.

1271. Brown, Charles Malverns. A history of the Presbyterian
      Church, U.S.A., in Brazil. Ph. D. thesis, Ohio State
      University, Columbus, 1947. -- Also based on English
      sources.

1272. Fernandes Braga, Henriqueta Rosa. Música sacra evangélica
      no Brasil: contribucao à sua história. Rio de
      Janeiro, Livraria Kosmos Editôra, 1961. 448 p.

1273. Ferreira, Júlio Andrade. O apóstolo de Caldas. Franca,
      S.P., Editora Gráfica Renascenca, 1950. 228 p. --
      The life and work of the Rev. Miguel Conclaves Torres.

1274. _____. História da igreja presbiteriana do Brasil, 1859-
      1959. São Paulo, Casa Editora Presbiteriana, 1960.
      2 v. -- A collection of primary sources in Portu-
      guese.

1275. Gammon, Clara G. M. So shines the light: a biography of
      Samuel Rhea Gammon, 1865-1928. mss, BWM, PCUS,
      Richmond, Va. (n.d.).

1276. Graham, Ann Elizabeth. The contribution of Ashbel Green
      Simonton to mission work in Brazil. M.A. thesis,
      Biblical Seminary, New York, 1952.

1277. Landes, Philip S. Asbel Green Simonton; a model pioneer
      missionary of the Presbyterian church of Brazil.
      Fort Worth, Cowan, 1956. 67 p. -- A privately
      published monograph. A concise bibliography.

1278. Lane, Edward E. History of the West Brazil mission.
      mss, Presbyterian Museum, Campinas, 1944.

1279. Léonard, Emile G. L'eglise presbytérienne du Brésil et
      sus expériences ecclésiastiques. Etudes evangéliques
      9:1:1-108 Janiere-Mars 1949.

1280. McIntire, Robert L. José Manoel da Conceicão. Th. M.
      thesis, Princeton Theological Seminary, N.J., 1946.
      -- Life of a converted priest who evangelized large
      areas in Central Brazil.

1281. _____. Portrait of a half-century: 50 years of Presby-
      terianism in Brazil, 1859-1910. Th. D. thesis,
      Princeton Theological Seminary, 1959. mimeographed.
      -- The origin of the Presbyterian church in Brazil
      and its history to 1910.

1282. Midkiff, Harry P. The sketch of a life on two continents.
      Privately printed by author, 1965. -- Memories of a
      Presbyterian Church, U.S.A. missionary in Brazil,
      1911-1952.

1283. Presbiterianismo no Brasil, 1859-1959 (Presbyterianism in
      Brazil). s.l., 1959. 157 p. -- A centennial bi-
      lingual survey with pictures and summary review of
      Presbyterian history.

1284. Read, William R. A program for accelerating the develop-
ment of an indigenous Presbyterian church in Central
Brazil. Th. M. thesis, Louisville Presbyterian
Theological Seminary, 1957.

1285. Ribeiro, Americo J. *and* Julio Andrade Ferreira. The
Brazilian Presbyterian church in the picture of the
universal church. *Revista teológica presbiteriana*
(Campinas Seminary) 1963.

1286. Ribeiro, Boanerges. O padre protestante. São Paulo,
Casa Editora Presbiteriana, 1950.

1287. Simonton, Ashbel Green. Journal of the Rev. Ashbel Green
Simonton, first Presbyterian missionary to Brazil.
mss, UPML (n.d.). 195 p.

1288. Smith, James P. An open door in Brazil. Richmond, Fa.,
Presbyterian Committee on Publication, 1925. 235 p.
-- Brief survey of work of Presbyterian Church of the
U.S. in Brazil since 1869. Accepts all reports at
face value, yet interesting.

1289. Syndenstricher, Margarida. Carlota Kemper. Sao Paulo,
privately published, 1941. 95 p. -- Trans. by Jorge
Goulart. Miss Kemper taught many years in Lavras,
Minas Gerais.

1290. Themudo Lessa, Vincente. Annaes da igreja presbiteriana
de São Paulo, 1863-1903. São Paulo, 1938. 720 p.
-- Principally a chronicle of the first Presbyterian
church in São Paulo and some Presbyterian work in the
state.

1291. _____. Padre José Manoel de Conceicão. 2. ed. São Paulo,
Cruzeiro do Sul, 1935.

1292. Waddell, William A. History of the Brazil mission, 1859-
1936. mss, COEMAR library, New York (n.d.). --
Anecdotal in character.

Spiritism (or Spiritualism) and Related Cults

1293. de Camargo, Cándido Procópio. Aspectos sociológicos do
espiritismo en São Paulo. Madrid, FERES, 1961. 125
p. Title and text in Portuguese.

1294. Carneiro, Edison, Candomblés da Bahia. Bahia. Secretaria
       de Educaçao e Saude, 1948 (Publicacoes do museu de
       estado, no. 9).

1295. Dos Santos, Deoscoredes M. Axé opo Afonjá. Rio de Jan-
       eiro, Instituto Brasileiro de Estudos Afro-Asiáticos,
       1962.

1296. Ferreira, Júlio Andrade. O espiritismo, uma avaliaçao.
       Sao Paulo, Casa Editôra Presbiteriana, 1959. 182 p.
       -- Good bibliography.

1297. Freitas, Torres de, Byron e Tancredo da Silva Pinto.
       Camba de Umbanda. Rio de Janeiro, Grárica Editora
       Aurora (n.d.). (Colecão espiritualista, no. 19).

1298. Kloppenburg, Boaventura. O espiritismo no Brasil.
       Petrópolis, Editora Vozes, 1960. -- Study of the
       evolution of Spiritism in Brazil. Polemical approach.

1299. Major, Alfred Roy. The origin and development of spiri-
       tualism in Brazil. Th. M. thesis, New Orleans
       Theological Seminary, 1958.

1300. Meneses, Heraldo. Caboclos na Umbanda. Rio de Janeiro,
       Coleçao Afro-Brasileira (n.d.).

1301. Renshaw, Parke. A new religion for Brazilians. *Practical
       anthropology* 13:4:126-132. -- Deals with Spiritism
       and related mystical religious sects.

1302. Ribeiro de Souze, José. O jogo dos Búzios e as grandes
       cerimônias ocultas da Umbanda. Rio de Janeiro,
       Gráfica Editora Aurora, 1963.

1303. Souze Franco, Florisbela Maria de. Umbanda. 2. ed. Rio
       de Janeiro, Gráfica Editora, 1957.

                         Roman Catholic Publications

1304. Crivelli, Camilo. Directorio protestante de la América
       Latina. (Cf. no. 596).

1305. Franca, Leonel, S. J. O protestantismo no Brasil; Lutero
       e el Sr. Frederico Hansen. Rio de Janeiro, Agir,
       1952. 339 p. -- Reply to two Protestant pastors.
       See also *his* Catolicismo e Protestantismo.

1306. Rossi, Agnelo. Directório protestante no Brasil. Campinas, Tipografia Paulista, 1928. 221 p. -- By a student of Father Crivelli in Rome. Longtime director and professor at the Catholic University in Campinas, S.P.; Roman Catholic expert on Protestantism and ecumenical movements inside the Protestant church.

1307. Silva, Paulo Wailler da. An ethical analysis of the sermons of Antonio Vieira, S. J. Th. D. thesis, Southwestern Baptist Seminary, Dallas, 1962. -- A Protestant writes on the preaching of an outstanding Jesuit who defended the Indians, Jews and African slaves.

Periodicals

1308. Evangelical papers and magazines published in Brazil. Bulletin no. 2a, February 1965. Missionary Information Bureau, Rua da Constituacão, 14, Rio de Janeiro, AC-58, Brazil. -- A list of 127 publications.

WEST COAST REPUBLICS

Bolivia
See also p. 327.

Bibliography
See also p. 327.

1309. Boletín bibliográfico boliviano. La Paz, 1965-. Modest attempt to record recent titles and authors.

1310. Guttentag, T. Werner. Bibliografía boliviana. Cochabamba, Editorial Los Amigos del Libro, 1962-. Annual. The best in current Bolivian bibliography.

1311. Inter-mission language school: orientation course reading list. Cochabamba (n.d.). -- A list for new missionaries. Periodically revised.

1312. René-Moreno, Gabriel. Biblioteca boliviana. -- The most

important work which lists, with its supplements,
some 6818 titles.

General Background
See also p. 327.

1313. Alexander, Robert J. The Bolivian national revolution.
       New Brunswick, N.J., Rutgers University Press, 1958.

1314. Alonso, Isidoro, et al. La iglesia en Perú y Bolivia.
       Madrid, Sucesores de Rivadeneyra, 1962. 271 p. --
       A history of the Catholic church in this area. (Cf.
       no. 218).

1315. Antezana, Fernando. Los braceros bolivianos. La Paz,
       Icthus, 1965. 44 p. -- A study promoted by the
       Methodist church on one of Bolivia's worst social
       problems. Also appears in abbreviated form in
       Migration today (Geneva) 7:4-18 November 1966.

1316. Arnade, Charles W. The emergence of the republic of
       Bolivia. Gainesville, University of Florida Press,
       1957. 205 p. -- A well-researched account of
       Bolivian history up to Independence.

1317. Barrado Manzano, Archangel. Las misiones franciscanas
       en Bolivia. Sevilla, Imprenta San Antonio, 1946.
       82 p.

1318. Duguid, Julian. Green hell. London, Pan Books, 1931.
       220 p. -- An English adventurer relates his exper-
       iences in eastern Bolivia. Very exciting reading
       and a good introduction to this region.

1319. García Quintanillo, Julio. Historia de la iglesia de las
       Charcas o la Plata. Sucre, Don Bosco, 1963. 2 v.
       -- Very technical and detailed chronicle of the
       Catholic church in Sucre.

1320. López Menédez, Felipe. Compendio de história eclesiás-
       tica de Bolivia. La Paz, El Progreso, 1965. 274 p.
       -- A Catholic work.

1321. Osborne, Harold. Bolivia, a land divided. London, RIIA,
       1954. 135 p. -- The best on the geography of
       Bolivia. Chap. 1 is the most important.

1322. Patch, Richard W. Social implications of the Bolivian

agrarian reform. Ph. D. thesis, Cornell University,
Ithaca, N.Y., 1956. Microfilmed.

1323. Zook, David H. The conduct of the Chaco war. s.l.,
Bookman, 1960. 256 p. -- This is the only full his-
tory ever written in English of this important phase
of Bolivian history. See also Colección sondeos,
CIDOC. El universo religioso de los Aymaras de
Bolivia.

Protestantism in General
See also p. 329.

1324. Browning, Webster E., John Ritche *and* Kenneth G. Grubb.
The west coast republics of South America. (Cf. no.
1383).

1325. Cottingham, Catherine. Bolivia as a field of missionary
endeavor. M.A. thesis, San Francisco Theological
Seminary, San Anselmo, Calif., 1956.

1326. Hamilton, Keith D. Church growth in the high Andes.
Lucknow, Institute of Church Growth, 1962. 146 p.
-- Study of growth of Evangelical movement in Bolivia,
Peru and Ecuador.

1327. Hudspith, Thomas. El cincuentenario de la obra evangélica
en Bolivia. *La Biblia en la América Latina*, júlio-
agosto 1948.

1328. Manifesto a la nación. La Paz, Movimento Social Evangélico Boliviano, 1962. 12 p. -- A public declaration
of Protestant socio-political viewpoint.

1329. Wagner, C. Peter, ed. Consulta nacional de educación
teológica. Cochabamba, 1963. 58 p. -- Papers presented by a cross-section of Protestant leaders.

1330. _____. Theological education in Latin America. *Christianity today* p. 21-22, 15 March 1963. -- A general
survey from a conservative point of view.

1331. _____. Today's missions in the Latin American social
revolution. *Evangelical missions quarterly* 1:2:19-27,
1965.

1332. Zurita, Pablo, ed. Instituto de evangelismo a fondo.

Cochabamba, Iglesias Unidas, 1963. 42 p. -- Papers
presented by Latin American Mission personnel.

Denominational History
See also p. 330.

Adventist

1333. Hayden, Gwendolen. From football field to mission field
      with Richard Hayden. Washington, D.C., Review and
      Herold, 1951. 318 p. -- An Adventist missionary in
      the Amazon valley and then Lake Titicaca.

Andes Evangelical Mission (formerly Bolivian Indian Mission)

1334. Hawthorne, Salley Reese. Cloud country soujourn.
      London, Bolivian Indian Mission (n.d.). 128 p. --
      Colorful personal experiences.

1335. Hudspith, Margarita Allan. Ripening fruit. Harrington
      Park, N.J., Harrington Press, 1958. 158 p. -- The
      history of the A.E.M.

1336. Wagner, C. Peter *and* Jos. S. McCullough. The condor of
      the jungle, pioneer pilot of the Andes. Westwood,
      Revell, 1966. 158 p. -- A biography of Wally Herron.

Canadian Baptist Mission

1337. The church overseas. p. 62-88. Report of Baptist work
      in Bolivia by the Canadian Baptist Convention.

1338. Dabbs, Norman H. Dawn over the Bolivian hills. Toronto,
      Canadian Baptist Foreign Mission Board, 1952. 269 p.
      -- Story of the Canadian Baptist work in Bolivia.

1339. St. Uwell, H. Pioneering in Bolivia. Toronto, Canadian
      Baptist Publishing House, 1923. -- The early history
      of Canadian Baptist work.

Evangelical Union of South America

1340. Payne, Will *and* Charles T. W. Wilson. Pioneering in
      Bolivia. London, H. A. Raymond (n.d.). 148 p. --
      Missionary pioneering in Bolivia. Reflects spiritual

conditions reigning in the early period in Bolivia
and the north of Argentina.

Methodist

1341. Arias, Mortimer. Los metodistas somos así. Cochamba,
       Icthus, 1965. 44 p. -- A simple primer on Methodism.

1342. Beck, Bessie D. A study of changing social attitudes in
       the American institutes of Bolivia. Private edition,
       University of Chicago Library, 1938. -- Part of a
       Ph. D. dissertation in the Chicago Divinity School,
       1935.

1343. Bolivian annual conference of the Methodist church, 1906-
       61. s.l. (n.d.). 228 p. The Methodist church in Boli-
       via, a bi-lingual survey, profusely illustrated. UML.

1344. Monti, Pablo. En la terraza del mundo. Buenos Aires,
       Methopres (n.d.). -- Experiences of an Argentine
       medical missionary in the Altiplano, director of
       the Clínica Americana in La Paz.

New Tribes Mission

1345. Johnson, Jean Dye. God planted five seeds. New York,
       Harper, 1966. 213 p. -- The martyrdom of five mission-
       aries at the hands of the Ayaré Indians in 1943.

1346. Porterfield, Bruce E. Commandos for Christ. New York,
       Harpers and Row, 1963. 238 p. -- Modern missionary
       adventures among stoneage savages.

South America Indian Mission

1347. Wagner, C. Peter. Defeat of the bird god. Grand Rapids,
       Zondervan, 1967. 256 p. -- The story of missionary
       Bill Pencille who risked his life to reach the Ayorés
       of Bolivia.

Friends

1348a. Cammack, Phyllis. Missionary moments. Newberg, Oregon,
       Barclay, 1966. 134 p. -- Well written and illus-
       trated account of thirteen years among the Aymara
       Indians of Bolivia and Peru.

1348b. Haines, Marie H. Friends in Aymara land, 1930-55.
       Portland, Oregon. Oregon Yearly Meeting Press
       (n.d.). 31 p.

Periodicals
See also p. 330.

Past Publications

1349. The Bolivian Indian. Cajón 514, Cochabamba, 1911-65.
       Organ of the Bolivian Indian Mission.

Current Publications

1350. Vision evangélica.   1959-1969.   Interdenominational and
       independent.

1351. The Andean outlook. Cajón 514, Cochabamba, 1966-. Organ
       of Andes Evangelical Mission.

1352. Avance. Casilla 2093, La Paz, 1966-. Organ of the Iglesia
       Metodista. Mimeographed prior to 1966.

1353. Centinela boliviana. Unión Bautista Boliviana, Casilla
       2056, Cochabamba, 1941-.

1354   Highland echos. Casilla 356, La Paz. Methodist.

Chile
See also p. 332.

Bibliography

1355. The works of Chile's outstanding bibliographer, José
       Toribio Medina, cover in general the bibliography of
       colonial Hispanic America. Of special value for stu-
       dents of Chilean history and culture of the period is
       Biblioteca hispano-chilena, 1523-1817. 3 v. (BLCU).

1356. Anuario de la prensa chilena, 1886-1913. 28 v.

1357. Revista de bibliografía chilena y extranjera, 1913-1918, 1919-1926 and in 1930 was suspended.

1358. Vaisse, Emilio. Bibliografía de bibliografías chilenas by Ramón A Laval. Laval's listing was up dated in 1930 by Herminia de Ochsenius.

General Background
See also p. 332.

1959. Alonso, Isidoro, et al. La iglesia en Chile. (Cf. no. 210).

1360. Amunategui Solar, Domingo. El sistema de Lancaster en Chile y en otros países Sudamericanos. Santiago, Imprenta Cervantes, 1895. 371 p. -- UPL. Most valuable section concerns Chile and provides useful documentation. Inadequate research on other countries. Admires Thomson but is suspicious of his proselitizing activity in Scripture distribution.

1361. Clissold, Stephen. Chilean scrap book. New York, Praeger,1952. 316 p. -- An artful weaving together of geography and history.

1362. Cohen, Alvin. Economic change in Chile, 1939-59. Gainesville, University of Florida Press, 1960. 48 p. -- In Latin American Monographs, School of Interamerican Studies.

1363. Cruchaga, Miguel. De las relaciones entre la iglesia y el estado en Chile. Santiago, El Independiente, 1883. 186 p. -- Useful excerpts from documents.

1364. Domínguez, Oscar. El campesino chileno y la acción católica rural. (Cf. no. 221).

1365. Donoso, Ricardo. Las ideas políticas en Chile. Santiago, Editorial Pacífico, 1952.

1366. Edwards Vivas, Alberto. La fronda aristocrática. 4. ed. Santiago, Editorial Pacífico, 1952.

1367. Galdames, Luis. A history of Chile. Isaac Joslin Cox, ed. and trans. Chapel Hill, University of North Carolina Press, 1941. xii, 565 p. Title and text in Spanish. -- A standard text by a Chilean scholar.

1368. Gil, Federico G. The political system of Chile. Boston,
       Houghton, Mifflin, 1966.

1369. Hall, Basil. Extracts from a journal, 1820-22. 2. ed.
       Edinburgh, Constable, 1824. -- Impressions of an
       early visitor.

1370. Halperin, Ernst. Nationalism and communism in Chile.
       Cambridge, Mass., M.I.T. Press, 1965. 267 p. -- Good
       study on subject by a researcher at M.I.T.'s
       Communist Affairs Center.

1371. Hendricks, Frances K. Church and state in Chile before
       1891. Ph. D. thesis, University of Illinois, Urbana,
       1931. 241 p.

1372. Paul, Catherine M. Amanda Labarca; educator to the women
       of Chile. Ph. D. thesis, New York University, 1966.
       -- By the wife of a Protestant missionary to Chile
       and Argentina.

1373. Pendle, George. The land and people of Chile. New York,
       Macmillan, 1960. (The land and people series).
       -- Descriptive.

1374. Pike, Frederick B.. Chile and U.S. relations, 1880-1962.
       Notre Dame, University of Notre Dame Press, 1963.
       446 p. -- The emergence of Chile's social crisis and
       the challange to U.S. diplomacy. p. 305-446 provide
       extensive notes and reference to diplomatic corres-
       pondence in Chilean an U.S. archives.

1375. Silva Catopas, Carlos. Historia eclesiástica de Chile.
       Santiago, Imprenta de San José, 1925. viii, 387 p.
       -- Written by a bishop.

1376. Silvert, Kalman H. Chile. New York, Rinehart and Winsoton,
       1966. 212 p. (Contemporary civilizations series).

1378. Subercasuaux, Benjamín. Chile o una loca geografía.
       10. ed. Santiago, Ediciones Escilla, 1954. Title
       and text in English. -- Prologue by Gabriela Mistral.
       Five distinct Chiles are depicted in these fascinating
       pages by a forceful and charming Chilean author.

Protestantism in General
See also p. 334.

1379. Alexander, Addison M. The church in Chile facing an
immediate crisis. M.A. thesis, University of Wichita,
Kansas, 1935. 190 p.

1380. Araya, Samuel E. An approach to evangelism in Chile on
an ecumenical basis. S.T.M. thesis, Union Theological Seminary, New York, 1960. -- A good descriptive
statement on the churches but weak on conclusions.

1381. Arms, Goodsil F. History of William Taylor self-support-
ing mission in South America. New York, Methodist
Book Concern, 1921. 225 p. -- An important historical record of the William Taylor work in South
America, but also of Methodist work up to about 1904.

1382. Arnold-Foster, Frances. Heralds of the cross. London,
Hatchards, 1885. 499 p. -- Includes description of
work of Allen Gardiner.

1383. Browning, Webster E. The west coast republics of South
America. London, World Dominion, 1930. 183 p. --
Contains important surveys of missionary situation
in each country. Statistical tables, 1938 supplement.

1384. Eddy, Norman. A movement of the Holy Spirit-pentecostal-
ism in Chile. November 1963. Mimeographed. -- A
description mostly of the Assemblies of God work in
Chile.

1385. Kessler, John B. A., Jr. A study of the older protestant
missions and churches in Peru and Chile, with special
reference to the problems of division, nationalism and
native ministry. Goes, Netherlands, Oosterbaan, Le
Cointre, N.V., 1967. 369 p. -- A penetrating and
revealing study, based largely on primary sources and
extensive research. Available through Evangelical
Alliance, 30 Bedford Place, London, W.C.1.

1386. Lalive d'Epinay, Christian. La formación pastoral en
Chile y sus problemas. Santiago, Comunidad Evangélica
Teológica de Chile, 1966. 36 p. mimeographed. --
See also *his* La expansión protestante en Chile.
Cristianismo y sociedad, no. 9 y 10, 1965.

1387. Oyarzún, Arturo. Reminiscencias históricas de la obra
evangélica en Chile. Valdivia, Imprenta Alianza,
1921. -- A good review of early days.

1388. Paul, Irven. Acculturation in Chile: a study of the
       relation of evangelical Christianity to Christian
       culture with a view to the formation of effective
       missionary principles and practices. Ph. D. thesis,
       Hartford Seminary Foundation, Hartford, Conn., 1946.

1389. _____. A Yankee Reformer in Chile; the life and work of
       David Trumbull. South Pasadena, Ca., William Carey
       Library, 1974. 157 p. A biography of a towering per-
       sonage, a real maker and shaper of history. Draws upon
       diaries of Dr. Trumbull. Well-documented and insightful.

1390. Wheeler, W. R. Modern missions in Chile and Brazil.
       (Cf. no. 1214).

1391. Willems, Emilio. (Cf. no. 164). Section on Protestantism
       and cultural change in Brazil and Chile.

                         Denominational History
                            See also p. 335.
Anglican

1392. The birth of a native church in southern Chile. London,
       South American Missionary Society, 1944.

1393. Every, Bishop E. E. The Anglican church in South America.
       London, SPCK, 1915. -- Traces history of Anglican
       church in Peru and Chile, p. 86-94 and 103-107.

1394. Gardiner, Capt. Allen. Records of the South American
       Missionary Society. 4. ed. London, South American
       Missionary Society, 1894. -- A good description of
       the beginnings of the South American Missionary
       Society's work in Chile, Argentina and Paraguay, but
       with no attempt to analyze the problems.

1395. Hodgson, C. H. Sketch of the Anglican chaplaincy at
       Valparaiso, 1825-1909. Valparaiso, South Pacific
       Mail, 1917. -- Historical details without interpre-
       tation.

1396. Marsh, John W. *and* W. H. Stirling. Commander Allen
       Gardiner. 3. ed. London, Nisbet, 1874.

1397. Under the foothills of the Andes. London, South American
       Missionary Society, 1960. 231 p. reprint. -- A
       review of Anglican work among the Araucanians in
       southern Chile. See also no. 331 Ultimos documentos
       del Capitan Allen Gardiner.

Baptist

1398.   Cincuentenario de la Conferencia Bautista. Temuco, 1958.

1399.   Graham, Agnes. Pioneering with Christ in Chile. Nashville,
        Broadman, 1942. 140 p. -- Good review of Baptist
        work. Author does not enlarge upon internal problems,
        but neither does she ignore the issues.

1400.   Moore, Robert Cecil. Piety and poverty in Chile. Nash-
        ville, Broadman, 1946. -- General description of
        religious and social conditions in Chile and a review
        of Baptist development in Chile.

1401.   Pacheco, Elizabeth Condell. The apostle of the Chilean
        frontier: Wm. D. T. McDonald; a story of his life.
        Nashville, Broadman, 1941. 84 p. -- A fair presen-
        tation of the life of one of the Baptist pioneers.

Methodist

1402.   *Christian advocate* 3 November 1910. -- An interview with
        Bishop Briston reflecting apparent underestimation of
        the Pentecostal movement.

1403.   LaFetra, Ira H. The Chile mission of the Methodist
        Episcopal Church, 1878-1893. Santiago, Mission
        Publishing Dept., 1894. 92 p. -- Complements Goodsil
        Arm's book no. 1381. Includes details of William
        Taylor's self-supporting missions which may in part
        have laid the basis for the present Pentecostal move-
        ment in Chile.

1404.   Martin, Eldon H. Dorothy Mary Richard: her alabaster
        box. New York, Revell, 1931. 183 p. -- Copies of
        letters of 1910-11 shed interesting light on the
        Pentecostal revival.

1405.   Methodist letter book. New York, MML, 1908-11. v. 154-
        156. -- Copies of letters written by missionaries in
        Chile during cirtical period of Pentecostal revival.

1406.   Torregrosa, Moisés. Cuarenta años de lucha, vida y obra
        de José Torregrosa. Santiago, 1921. -- Torregrosa
        was one of the great Methodist preachers in Chile.

1407.   Wesley, Arthur J. The vintage of the years. Buenos

Aires, 1956. 132 p. -- An autobiography of the
founder of Sweet Memorial Institute.

Pentecostal

1408. Breckenridge, David C. Pentecostal progress in Chile.
       World dominion September-October 1951. -- A Bible
       agent who was permitted a very close association
       with Pentecostal churches writes his impressions.

1409. Hollenweger, Walter J. (Cf. no. 557). -- Collection of
       data includes considerable amount on Pentecostal
       movement in Chile.

1410. Hoover, Willis C. Histŕia del avivamiento pentecostal
       en Chile. Santiago, Imprenta El Esfuerzo, 1931.
       125 p. -- A review of his own life as a Methodist
       missionary, the events leading up to the Pentecostal
       revival in 1909 and the break with the Methodist
       church in 1910. Written in 1927 and has the marks
       of later reflection, yet fairly accurate. Reprinted
       Valparaiso, Imprenta Excelsior, 1948.

1411. _____. Pentecost in Chile. *World dominion* April 1932.
       -- An article on the early development of the
       Pentecostal movement in Chile.

1412. Lalive d'Epinay, Christian. Le pentecostalisme en Chile.
       s.1. (n.d.).

Presbyterian

1413. Erickson, Margaret Gilbert *and* Catherine Busler, comp.
       A cross of iron is his tribute; to the memory of
       Nathaniel P. Gilbert. New York, 1960. 48 p. --
       Letters and notes of an early Presbyterian missionary.

1414. Lester, W. H. Historia de la obra evangélica presbiter-
       iana de Chile. Unpublished mss.

1415. McLean, J. H. Historia de la iglesia prestiberiana en
       Chile. Santiago, Escuela Nacional de Artes Gráficas,
       1954. 100 p. -- A historical review of
       the Presbyterian Church in Chile, but considers in
       detail the work only until 1900.

1416. Presbyterian letters. New York, UPL. microfilmed. --

v. 31-43, 1872-1900; v. 28-40, 1900-1910. Of special
interest in the study of Presbyterian beginnings.

1417. Speer, Robert E. Modern missions in Chile and Brazil.
Philadelphia, Westminster Press, 1926. 164 p. --
Review of Presbyterian work but also refers to other
Protestant work.

Soldier and Gospel Mission of South America

1418. Nanz, Edith. Soldiering for Christ; the story of the
Soldier's and Gospel Mission of South America. Grand
Rapids, Zondervan, 1942. -- Description of work
begun in 1924 out of which has grown the "Centro
Bíblicos." Only book on this particular development.

1419. Strong, William, Sr. God's irregulars. Chicago, Good
News Publishers (n.d.). -- Stories of Strong's work
for the Soldier's and Gospel Mission in Chile.

Christian and Missionary Alliance

1420. Diener, W. Medio siglo de testimonio para Cristo. Temuco,
Imprenta Alianza, 1927. 151 p.

Roman Catholic Publications on Protestantism

1421. Anales de la facultad de teología, no. 11. Santiago,
Universidad Católica de Chile, 1960. -- CET. Three
articles on Protestantism in Latin America and Chile.
Distinguished by their fair-mindedness, factual
accuracy as promotion of inter-confessional understanding.

1422. Vergara, Ignacio. El protestantismo en Chile. 3. ed.
Santiago, Editorial del Pacifico, 1962. 259 p. --
A careful study of the whole Protestant church
in Chile. The history and doctrinal background of
each church is traced. Vergara is usually accurate.
He is interested in Protestantism for its own sake.
The work is largely devoid of polemics. Padre Vergara
was a worker priest.

Periodicals
See also p. 336.

Past Publications

1423. La alianza evangélica. 1877–?

1424. Chile cristiano. 1936 and a few years later.

1425. Chile evangélico. 1909–1910.

1426. Chile pentecostal. 1910–1915.

1427. El heraldo cristiano. A periodical of Methodist and
        Presbyterians.

1428. La piedra. 1872–1877. Became La alianza evangélica.

1429. The record. 1873–1886. For English-speaking Protestants
        in Chile.

1430. Verdad y justicia. Organ of the Iglesia del Señor in
        Chile.

Current Publications

1431. El anglicano. 1964–. Organ of the Anglican Church.
        Casilla 675, Santiago.

1432. Chile pentecostal. Organ of the Iglesia Metodista
        Pentecostal.

1433. El cristiano. Methodist periodical. Casilla 7035,
        Santiago.

1434. El despertar. Organ of Iglesia de Dios Pentecostal in
        Chile.

1435. Fuego de pentecostés. Organ of the Iglesia Evangélica
        Pentecostal in Chile.

1436. El heraldo evangélico. Organ of the Presbyterian Church
        in Chile.

1437. Reflexiones. Baptist University Student Association,
        1967–. Quarterly. US$3.00/annually.

1438. Salud y vida. Christian and Missionary Alliance, 1913-.
       Casilla 297, Temuco.

1439. Sembrando. Organ of Misión Iglesia Pentecostal in Chile.

1440. Teología y vida. Universidad Católica de Chile, Santiago.
       Quarterly. US$3.00/annually. Casilla 114-D, Facultad
       de teología Universidad.....

1441. La voz bautista. Santiago. Casilla 233, Chillan·

Peru
See also p. 331.

Bibliography
See also p. 331.

1442. The literature of Peru is of manifest importance. As a
       work of general scope, the Biblioteca peruana, 1896
       of Paz Soldan (BLCU) is perhaps the most important
       single work of bibliographical character.

1443. Alberto Tauro's Bibliografía peruana de historia, 1940-
       1953 (BLCU) is of help for that period. The Boletín
       bibliográfico de la Universidad de San Marcos reviews
       current publications. Rubén Vargas Garte's works are
       quite indispensable, i.e., Manual de estudios peruan-
       istas, 4. ed., 1959. (BLCU).

General Background
See also p. 331.

1444. Basadre, Jorge. La iniciación de la república. Lima,
       F. y E. Rosay, 1929. Tomo 1.

1445. Cabada Dancourt, Octavio. La inquisición en Lima,
       síntesis de una historia. Lima, Librería El Inca,
       1935.

1446. Dávalos y Lissón, Pedro. La primera centuria; causas
       geográficas, políticas y económicas que han detenido
       el progreso moral y material del Pruú en el primer
       siglo de su vida independiente. Lima, Libería e
       Imprenta Gil, 1919-1926. 4 v.

1447. Izaguirre, Bernardino. Historia de las misiones francis-
       canas y narración de los progresos de la geografía en

el oriente del Perú. Lima, Tipografías de la
Penitenciaría, 1925-1926. v. 10-12.

1448. Kantor, Harry. The ideology and progress of the Peruvian
aprista movement. Berkeley, University of California
Press, 1953. -- See also *his* bibliography on the
literature related to the Aprista movement, published
separately. (BLCU).

1449. Lecuna, Vicente, comp. and Harold A. Bierk, ed. Selected
writings of Bolivar. New York, Colonial Press, 1951.
2 v. -- Trans. by Lewis Bertrand.

1450. Medina, Francisco de Armas. Cristianización del Perú,
1532-1600. Sevilla, Escuela de Estudios Hispano-
Americanos, 1953. 635 p. -- The material and
spiritual conquest of its inhabitants. Profuse documentation. Appendix of documental and bibliographical
sources.

1451. Prescott, William H. The conquest of Peru. New York,
Dutton, 1908. xxxii, 648 p. -- This classic is now
available for $.50, abridged form, MD 314, Mentor
books. See also *his* History of the conquest of
Mexico and History of the conquest of Peru, New York,
Random House. 1288 p. (The modern library series).
Both books now in one paperback volume.

1452. Sáenz, Moisés. The Peruvian Indian. *In* The strategic
index of the Americas. Washington, Coordinator in
Inter-American Affairs, 1944.

1453. Stanger, Francis M. The relations between church and
state in the Peruvian republic. M.A. thesis, Univer-
ity of California, 1926. 85 p. -- Text also in
Spanish as Ph. D. thesis, La Iglesia y el Estado en
Peru Independiente, Universidad de San Marcos, Lima,
1925, Imprenta Luz.

1454. Tibesar, Antonine, O.F.M. Franciscan beginnings in
colonial Peru. Washington, D.C., Academy of American
Franciscan History, 1953. -- An interesting account
of the affairs of the Roman Catholic Church to build
up a native ministry.

1455. Urubamba! misiones dominicas en el Perú. s.l. (n.d.).
-- Condemnation of various Protestants in Peru, all
foreigners in second half of 16th century.

1456. Valcárcel, Luis E. Ruta cultural del Perú. México, Fondo de Cultura Económica, 1945.

1457. Villagomes, Pedro de. Exortaciones e instrucción acerca de las idolatrías de los índios, 1649. Lima, Imprenta y Librería San Martí, 1919. (Colección de libros y documentos referentes a la historia del Perú, tomo 12).

1458. Wiesse, Carlos. Historia del Perú, la república. 2. ed. Lima, Editorial E. y F. Rosay, 1926.

Protestantism in General
See also p. 332.

1459. Bahamonde, Wenceslao O. The establishment of Evangelical Christianity in Peru, 1822-1900. Ph. D. thesis, Hartford Seminary Foundation, Conn., 1952.

1460. Browning, W. E., The west coast republics of South America. (Cf. no. 1383).

1461. Christophersen, E. A. An examination of some indigenous factors in the evangelization of Peru. Th. M. thesis, Dallas Theological Seminary, Texas, 1952.

1462. Goslin, Thomas S. Protestantism in Peru. *Presbyterian historical society* v. 26, 3 September 1948.

1463. Grubb, Kenneth G. The lowland Indians of Amazonia. (Cf. no. 376).

1464. Hamilton, K. E. Church growth in the high Andes. (Cf. no. 1326).

1465. Kessler, J. B. A., Jr. (Cf. no. 1385).

1466. Mackay, John A. Protestant work in Peru. *The monthly record of the Free Church of Scotland* v. 17, 1918. -- Also see *his* Religious currents in the intellectual life of Peru. *The Biblical review* 6:2:192-211, 1921.

1467. Penzotti, F. G. Spiritual victories in Latin America. New York, American Bible Society, 1916. -- Trans. by Martha Bell. Duplication of no. 466.

Denominational History

Adventist

1468.   Maxwell, E. L.   Up and down the Andes on a burro.   Mountain
        View, Calif., Pacific Press, 1921.

1469.   Stahl, F. A.   In the land of the Incas.   Mountain View,
        Calif., Pacific Press, 1920.

1470.   Westphal, Barbara.   Ana Stahl of the Andes and Amazon.
        Mountain View, Calif., Pacific Press, 1906.   48 p.

1471.   Wilcox, E. H.   In perils oft.   Nashville, 1961.

Christian and Missionary Alliance

1472.   Clark, Raymond B.   Under the southern cross.   Harrisburg,
        Pa., Christian Publications, 230 p.   -- By the
        pioneer C.M.A. missionary in Peru.   Also served in
        Chile.

1473.   Stull, Ruth.   Sand and stars: missionary adventures on
        the jungle trails.   New York, Revell, 1951.   189 p.
        -- C.M.A. work among Indians across the Andes on an
        Amazon tributary.

Evangelical Union of South America

1474.   Barreto, Ladislao.   Apuntes históricos de la iglesia
        libre del Perú.   Morococha, 1942.   48 p.   -- Describes
        the division of the Morococha Church around 1940.

1475.   Case, Kenneth G.   History of the work in the Apurimac
        region of Peru.   London, mss.   -- A review of the
        advent of Protestantism in this remote province from
        1935 onward.

1476.   Grubb, Kenneth G.   The E.U.S.A. at home and in South
        America.   1961.

1477.   Guiness, Geraldine.   Perú.   London, Marshall, Morgan and
        Scott, 1909.

1478.   Jardine, Alex and Maisie.   First the blade.   London,
        E.U.S.A., 1946, 32 p.

1479. McNairn, S. A. McNairn's letter to all E.U.S.A. mission-
       aries. London, E.U.S.A., 1933.

1480. Milnes, David, M.D. Inca stronghold. London, E.U.S.A.
       (n.d.). 72 p. illus., maps.

1481. Muñoz, Alfonso. Mis memorias. London, E.U.S.A. (n.d.).

1482. Ritchie, John. Apuntes para la historia del movimiento
       evangélico en el Perú durante el primer siglo. London,
       E.U.S.A., 1942.

1483. _____. The gospel in the high Andes. London, E.U.S.A.,
       1942.

1484. _____. The indigenous church in Peru. London, World
       Dominion Press, 1932.

1485. _____. Indigenous church principles in theory and prac-
       tice. New York, Revell, 1946. 144 p.

1486. _____. Sheep having no shepherd. London, E.U.S.A., 1912.

1487. _____. With the E.U.S.A. in central Peru. London,
       E.U.S.A., 1922.

1488. Savage, John. On trek in the Andes. London, E.U.S.A.,
       1946. 64 p.

1489. _____. Peru today. London, E.U.S.A., 1953.

Free Church of Scotland

1490. Cameron, J. Kennedy. Peru and its free Church in Scotland
       mission. Edinburgh, 1921.

1491. Free church missionary enterprise. Edinburgh, 1947.

1492. Mackay, John A. Reports on founding of this mission.
       The monthly record of the Free Church of Scotland
       v. 17-18, 1918.

Lutheran

1493. De la iglesia alemana evangélica-luterana en Lima y Callao.
       34 p. -- Commerative review on occasion of IV Lutheran
       Congress of Latin America, 1965.

Nazarene

1496. Taylor, Lucille. Tribes and nations from the south.
       Kansas City, Nazarene Publishing House, 1960.

1497. Winans, Roger S. Gospel over the Andes. Kansas City,
       Nazarene Publishing House, 1955.

Pilgrim Holiness

1498. Rundell, Merton R., Jr. The mission of the Pilgrim Holi-
       ness Church in Peru. M.A. thesis, Butler University,
       Indianapolis, 1957.

Regions Beyond Missionary Society

1499. Holmes, Kenneth. The cloud moves. London, Regions Beyond
       Mission Union, 1962. -- A short account of the
       R.B.M.U.

1500. Jarrett, J. L. Fifteen years in Peru. London, R.B.M.U.,
       1908. 24 p. -- Reflects struggle on behalf of
       religious liberty.

1501. Millham, William T. T. Peru activities of the R.B.M.U.
       London, R.B.M.U., 1893-1911.

1502. Newell, Mrs. For Christ and Cuzco. London, E.U.S.A.,
       1904. -- A memorial of W. H. Newell written by his
       mother.

1503. Thompson, Phyllis. Dawn beyond the Andes: the life and
       labors of Miss Annie G. Soper. 2. ed. London,
       R.B.M.U., 1958. 125 p. -- Story of the founding of
       missions in inland Peru. Colorful narrative of hard-
       ships in the early days.

1504. Watson, James. Lima, the city of kings. London, Harley
       House, 1909. 24 p. -- Leaves from the diaty of
       James Watson.

Periodicals

Past Publications

1505.   El cristiano. 1916-1921. Independent publication by
John Ritchie.

1506.   Renacimiento. 1921-1955.

Current Publications

1507.   Adelante. 1930-. Organ of the Iglesia Evangélica
Peruana.

1508.   El heraldo. Evangelical Union of South America.

1509.   El peregrino evangélico. Pilgrim Holiness publication.

1510.   Peru calling. Methodist mission publication.

GRAN COLOMBIA
See also p. 336.

Colombia

Bibliography
See also p. 336.

1511.   Posada's Bibliografía bogotana, 1917 and 1925 is valuable
(BLCU).

1512a. Available also is Geraldo Jarmillo's Bibliografía de
bibliografías colombianas, 1960 (BLCU).

General Background
See also p. 336.

1512.   Bernal Segundo E. Religious life of the Paez Indians of
Colombia. M.A. thesis, Columbia University, New York,
1956.

1513.   Castillo Cárdenas, Gonzalo. The Colombia concordat in the
light of recent trends in Catholic thought concerning

church-state relations and religious liberty. M.S.T.
thesis, Union Theological Seminary, New York, 1962.

1514.   Chapman, Phillip. Church and state in Colombia, 1810-
        1867. M.A. thesis, University of Chicago, 1940. 124
        p.

1515.   El caso del padre Camilo Torres. Comité de Redación.
        Bogotá, Inquietudes, Aptdo. Aéreo 11012, 1965. 81 p.
        (Inquietudes: laicos a la hora del concilio, no. 5).
        -- Nine documents on the ill-fated Padre Torres.
        Statements on reaction of clergy and laity to these
        documents. (Cf. Camilo Torres: biografía, plataforma,
        mensaje. Medellín, Ediciones Carpel-Antorcha (ca.
        1966). 104 p. See also *his* La revolución; imperativo
        cristiano. Bogotá, Ediciones del Caribe, 1965. 58 p.).

1516.   Escalante, Aquiles. El negro en Colombia. Bogotá,
        Universidad Nacional de Colombia, Facultad de Socio-
        logía, 1964. 196 p. (Monografías sociológicas, no.
        18).

1517.   Fals Borda, Orlando. La subversión en Colombia: visión
        del cambio social en la historia. Bogotá, Ediciones
        Tercer Mundo, 1967. 294 p. -- English translation
        published by Institute of Latin American Studies,
        Columbia University, 1967. An excellent consideration
        of national social history in its totality and in the
        light of its dynamic character. The author places
        the concept "subversion" in positive perspective.

1518.   _____. Campesinos de los Andes: estudio sociológico de
        Saucio. Bogotá, Editorial Iqueima, 1961. 340 p. --
        Available in English. Perhaps the best work available
        on the culture and personality of the *campesino* in
        sociological literature. See chapter on the role of
        religion in life of the peasant.

1519.   Fluharty, Vernon Lee. Dance of the millions: military
        rule and the social revolution in Colombia, 1930-1956.
        Pittsburgh, Pittsburgh Press, 1947. 336 p. -- Treats
        economic and political situation in a short historical
        span in Colombia with a final summary and conclusions.
        This book is marred by author's belief that Gustavo
        Rojas Pinilla, military dictator, 1953-57, was ushering
        in a genuine revolution to better the working class in
        Colombia.

1520. Graham, R. B. Cunninghame. The conquest of New Granada being the life of Gonzalo Jimenez de Quesada. Boston, Houghton, Mifflin, 1922. 272 p. -- Life of the founder of Bogotá. Reprinted Cooper Square Publishers, 1968.

1521. Guzmán, German, Orlando Fals Borda y Eduardo Umaña Luna. La violencia en Colombia; estudio de un proceso social. Bogotá, Universidad Nacional, Facultad de Sociologia, 1962. 2 v. -- The definitive study of the period of violence of 1948-1958.

1522. Henao, Jesús María y Gerardo Arrubla. Historia de Colombia para la enseñanza secundario. Bogotá, Librería Voluntad, 1952. 970 p. -- A standard work on Colombian history from the conservative Catholic point of view.

1523. _____. History of Colombia. J. Fred Rippy, ed. and trans. Chapel Hill, University of North Carolina Press, 1938. 578 p. -- A history of Colombia written by Colombians. Sound throughout with some conclusions. Written from a conservative Catholic point of view.

1524. Liévano, Aguirre. Los grandes conflictos socio-economicos de nuestra historia. Bogotá, Editorial Tercer Mundo (n.d.).

1525. Martz, John D. Colombia: a contemporary political survey. Chapel Hill, University of North Carolina Press, 1962. 384 p. -- A political survey of contemporary Colombia, 1948-1961 with special reference to the overthrow of Rojas Pinilla and the advent of the bipartisan government under Lleras Camargo. Vivid sketches of the various recent political leaders.

1526. Monografías sociológicas de la facultad de sociología de la universidad nacional de Colombia. From 1959-. -- Valuable studies of aspects of Colombian life by leading sociologists.

1527. Perez, Rafael, S.J. La compañia de Jesús en Colombia y Centro América después de la Restauracion. Valladolid, Imprenta de Luis N. de Gaviria, 1896. 453 p. -- Mostly on Colombia and Ecuador.

1528. Santa Teresa, Severino de. Historia documentada de la iglesia de Urabá y el Darién. Bogotá, 1957. 5 v.

1529. Shaw, Carey Jr.   Church and state in Colombia as observed
       by American diplomats, 1834-1906. *Hispanic American
       historical review* 21:4 November 1941.

1530. Valencia, Hector G. Theories and practices of secondary
       school organization and administration in the republic
       of Colombia. Ph. D. thesis, Ohio State University,
       Colombus, 1953. -- UPL. An examination of systems
       of education in Colombia from the colonial times to
       recent times by a leading Presbyterian educator.

1531. Whiteford, Andrew.   Two cities of Latin America.   Garden
       City, N.Y., Doubleday, 1964.   266 p.   -- A comparative
       description of social classes, referring to studies of
       Popoayan, Colombia and Querétaro, Mexico. One of the
       few studies of this kind.

1532. Wilgus, A. Curtis, ed.   The Caribbean: contemporary
       Colombia. Gainesville, University of Florida Press,
       1962. -- Extensive bibliography.

1533. Williamson, Robert C.   El estudiante colombiano y sus
       actitudes. Bogotá, Universidad Nacional, Facultad de
       Sociologia, 1962. -- See also Colección sondeos,
       CIDOC. Actitudes de los estudiantes panemeños frente
       al sacerdote.

1534. Parra Sandoval, Rodrigo. Las actitudes de los seminar-
       istas. Bogotá, Universidad Nacional, Facultad de
       Sociologia, 1964. 60 p. (Monografia no. 17). --
       Brief bibliography. See also Colección Sondeos,
       CIDOC. Un municipio católico. A socio-religious
       study of an Andean parish.

Protestantism in General
See also p. 339.

1535. Allan, Alexander M.   Recuerdos: el Protestantismo en
       Colombia, 1910-1945. Medellín, Tipografia Unión
       (n.d.).   61 p.   -- Reminiscences by a well-known
       pioneer Presbyterian missionary.

1536. Clark, Allen D.   Tentative history of the Colombia mission
       of the Presbyterian church in the U.S.A. with some
       accounts of other missions working in Colombia.
       Unpublished mss., UPL, 1946.   117 p.   -- A carefully
       written history by a Presbyterian missionary.

1537. Cronkhite, Stanley C. Developing an indigenous church in
       Colombia. M.A. thesis, Seattle Pacific College,
       Washington, 1955.

1538. Directorio evangélico y calendario de oración. Medellín,
       Tipografia Unión (n.d.). -- Annual directory of
       Protestant workers, churches, schools and institutions
       of 28 denominations and agencies.

1539. Goff, James E. Censo de la obra evangélica en Colombia;
       parte 1, introducción y membresía. Bogotá, Confedera-
       ción Evangélica de Colombia, February, 1969. --
       Statistics and church membership of 46 denominations
       in Colombia and comparison with previous studies.
       Parte 2, schools and other institutions, October 1966.
       Copies available from author. Also published
       Protestant census for 1967 and 1968.

1540. _____, ed. News service of the Evangelical confederation
       of Colombia, CEDEC. Ibagué, Barranquilla, Bogotá,
       1951-1963. Mimeographed. -- A series of 81 news
       bulletins dealing with the religious persecution of
       1948-1958 and the progress of the Protestant churches.
       Bul. 10, 17 August 1953 gives the report of the census
       of Protestant Christianity taken that year; Bul. 66,
       31 January 1961 of the census of 1960.

1541. _____. The persecution of Protestant Christians in Colom-
       bia, 1948-1958 with an investigation of its background
       and causes. Th. D. thesis, San Francisco Theological
       Seminary, San Anselmo, Calif., 1965. -- The defini-
       tive history of the persecution written by a United
       Presbyterian missionary, then Secretary of the Office
       of Information of the Evangelical Confederation of
       Colombia.

1542. _____. U.S. aid to Colombia's schools -- has it promoted
       democracy? *Latin America evangelist* p. 4-7 September
       1964. -- The story of our dubious investment in
       Colombia's clerically controlled 'public' schools.

1543. _____. What's behind the persecution in Colombia? *Latin
       America evangelist* p. 2-5 May 1961. -- A review of
       the religious persecution of 1948-1958 and the discrim-
       ination and harrassment which continued for years.

1544. Grubb, Kenneth. The northern republics of South America:
       Ecuador, Colombia and Venezuela. London, World Dominion

Press, 1931. -- The first careful survey of Protestant
Christianity in northern South America. (Cf. no. 377).

1545. Ordóñez, Francisco. Historia del cristianismo evangélico
en Colombia. Cali, La Alianza Cristiana y Misionera,
1956. 379 p. -- The only published history of
Protestantism in Colombia up to recent times. Although
not extensively documented, the history was carefully
compiled. Published to commemorate the centenial of
Protestant Christianity in Colombia.

1546. Quiring, Wilmer A. The establishment of evangelical Christianity in Colombia, South America, 1825-1900. M.A.
thesis, Hartford Seminary Foundation, Hartford, Conn.,
1957. 134 p. -- A scholarly written history based on
extensive research in early Presbyterian historical
archives.

1547. Schutmaat, Alvin L. Evangelical education in Colombia.
International review of missions p. 429-435 October
1954. -- A leading missionary educator analyses
Protestant education during the religious persecution
of 1948-1958.

1548. Wheeler, W. Reginald *and* Webster E. Browning. Modern
missions on the Spanish Main. Philadelphia, Westmin-
ister Press, 1925. 234 p.

Denominational History
See also p. 340.

Evangelical Mission Alliance

1549. Anderson, Isabel. Counted worthy. Chicago, Moody Press,
1964. 190 p. -- A novel. The names of people and
places are fictitious but the events are factual.
Experiences of Colombia Christians in the 20th century.
Reflects some of the work of the Evangelical Alliance
missionaries over twenty-five years in Colombia.

Gospel Missionary Union

1550. Chapman, Charles P. With the Bible among the Andes. Kansas
City, Gospel Missionary Union (ca. 1948). -- An account
of early Gospel Missionary Union work in Colombia and
Ecuador by a pioneer missionary.

New Tribes Missions

1551. Muller, Sophie. Beyond civilization. Chico, Calif. Brown
       Gold Publication, 1952. 62 p. illus. -- Protestant
       missionary work among the Kuripako Indians of Colombia
       by the pioneer New Tribes missionary. A collection of
       letters written in the jungles of South America. Ori-
       ginal drawings by the author.

1552. _____. Jungle methods. Curwensville, Pa., News, 1960.
       48 p. illus. -- Missionary methods of New Tribes
       missionary Sophie Muller, in her work with Colombian
       Indians who were totally ignorant of reading and writ-
       ing and without any knowledge of the Bible.

Presbyterian

1553. Evaul, Philip O. Alexander M. Allen: Presbyterian mission-
       ary to Colombia, 1910-1946. Th. M. thesis, Presbyterian
       Theological Seminary, Louisville, Ky. (ca. 1964). 133
       p.

World Wide Evangelization Crusade

1554. Easton, William C. Colombian conflict. London, Christian
       Literature Crusade, 1954. -- A report on the work of
       the World Wide Evangelization Crusade in Colombia dur-
       ing the 1948-1958 religious persecution by one of their
       missionaries.

1555. Symes, A. Patrick. Action stations Colombia. London,
       Christian Literature Crusade, 1955. -- An account of
       World Wide Evangelization crusade work in Colombia by
       the founder.

Roman Catholic Works on Protestantism

1556. Ministerio de gobierno. La cuestión de la religiones
       acatólicas en Colombia. Bogotá, Imprenta Nacional,
       1956. 83 p. -- Government decrees limiting the rights
       of Protestants: declarations restricting Protestantism
       by government officials.

1557. Ospina, Eduardo, S. J. The Protestant denominations in
       Colombia. Bogotá, National Press, 1954. 212 p. --

Father Ospina examines the charge of persecution,
denies it and makes numerous accusations against
Protestant Colombians and missionaries. His arguments
form the backbone of most of the discussion of the persecution by Roman Catholic writers. Copies were dis-
tributed abroad by Colombian embassies and consulates.
This book constituted the official government answer
to the Protestant accusation of persecution.

1558. Restrepo Uribe, Eugenio. El protestantismo en Colombia.
Bogotá, Ed. Lumen Christi, 1944. -- An evaluation of
Colombia Protestantism by a Roman Catholic priest and
a program to extirpate it. A published doctoral
dissertation at the Jesuit Xaverian Pontifical University of Bogota which laid the foundation for the
religious persecution of 1948-1958.

1559. Struve-Haker, P. Ricardo. El problema del protestantismo
en Colombia. Bogotá, Centro Mariano, 1958. 53 p. --
Critique of Protestantism in Colombia made by a
Catholic converted from Protestantism.

Periodicals
See also p. 341.

1560. Avivamiento. Interamerican Missionary Society, Aptdo.
Aéreo 1141, Medellín. Monthly.

1561. Colombian clippings. UPL, New York. Last issue published
December 1961 by fraternal workers of Presbyterian
Church in Colombia.

1562. Colombia news. Information service of the Mennonite
Mission in Colombia, Sptdo. 1966, Cachipay, Cund.,
Colombia. News of denominational activities; General
Conference Mennonite Church, Box 347, Newton, Ka.,
67114.

1563. Evangelische nachrichten für kilumbien. German Lutheran
publication.

1564. El evangelista colombio. Javier Zarate, ed. Barranquilla,
Sinodo de la Iglesia Presbiteriana. 16 page periodical
with news of the Presbyterian church of Colombia.
Founded by Alexander M. Allan in 1912. Last issue in
December 1965.

1565. El heraldo de la unión colombo-venezolana (Adventista).
Félix Fernández F., ed. Medellín, La Unión Colombo-
Venezolana, Aptdo. Aéreo 609. A report on activities
of the denomination by geographical sections.

1566. The messenger of the Episcopal church. Balboa, Canal Zone.
Includes also news on Panama and Colombia.

1567. The news. Jeanne W. Heinbuch, ed. Bogotá, Union Church of
Bogota, Carrera 4, No. 69-06. US$3.00/annually. News
sheet of activities of Union Church and St. Alban's
Episcopal Church.

1568. Wesleygrama. Carlos Gonzalez G., ed. Medellín, Tipografía
Union, Aptdo. Aéreo 964. Organ of the Iglesias Evangélicas Metodistas Wesleyanas.

Ecuador
See also p. 341.

Bibliography

1569. Espinosa Cordero's *Bibliografia ecuatoriana* may be consulted with profit. Rivera has also provided students
of literature with a useful list in *his* Tentative
bibliography of the belles-artes of Ecuador, 1934.

General Background
See also p. 341.

1570. Collier, John *and* Anita Buitrón. The awakening valley.
Chicago, University of Chicago Press, 1949. 199 p.
-- A narrative and photographic record of the life of
the commerce-wise Otavalo Indians.

1571. Franklin, A. B. Ecuador and portrait of a people. Garden
City, N.Y., Doubleday, Doran, 1943.

1572. Huerta Rendón, Francisco. Historia del Ecuador. Guayaquil,
Publicaciones Educativas Ariel, 1966. -- Concise and
readable. Written by a liberal Ecuadorian citizen
with considerable national pride. Endeavors to present real issues in Ecuadorian history.

1573. Icaza, Jorge. Huasipungo. Buenos Aires, Editorial
Losada, 1953. A classic novel.

1574. Larrea, Juan I. La iglesia y el estado en el Ecuador.
      Sevilla, Escuela de Estudios Hispanoamericanos, 1954.
      168 p. -- La personalidad de la Iglesia en el *modos
      vivendi* celebrado entre la Santa Sede y el Ecuador.
      A general survey which is friendly to the Roman
      Catholic Church.

1575. Linke, J. Ecuador; country of contrasts. 2. ed. London,
      Royal Institute of International Affairs, 1960. 173
      p. -- A factual account of the country and the way
      of life of the people.

1576. Pattee, Richard. Gabriel García Moreno y el Ecuador de
      su tiempo. Quito, 1941. -- Favorable work on García
      Moreno, a controversial figure, who bestowed on the
      Church a more exalted position than it enjoyed even
      in colonial times.

1577. Pérez Concha, Jorge. Ensayo histórico-crítico de las
      relaciones diplomáticas del Ecuador con los estados
      limítrofes. Casa de Cultura Ecuatoriana, 1961. 870
      p. (2 v.). -- The official government position
      reflected.

1578. Ruiz N., José Mario, ed. Proyecto de plan de aplicación
      del Concilio en el Ecuador. Ambato, Editorial Pio
      XII, 1966. 100 p. -- This is the report of an
      Episcopal committee charged with planning the applica-
      tion of the conciliar reform to the Catholic Church
      in Ecuador. It contains an unusually frank evalua-
      tion of the situation of the Catholic Church in
      Ecuador and of the effect of Protestant growth.

Protestantism in General
See also p. 342.

1579. Browning, Webster E. The republic of Ecuador. New York,
      CCLA, 1920. 30 p. -- Social, intellectual and
      religious conditions of early 20th century.

1580. Cabezas Almeida, Salomón. La renovación de la iglesia
      para su encarnación en el Ecuador. B. D. thesis,
      Seminario Evangélico de Puerto Rico, Río Piedras,
      1966. -- Contains list of missionaries, founding
      dates, principal founders, together with a brief
      statement of each national church and mission.

1581. Duey, Carlos. Ensayos evangélicos. Guayaquil, Editorial
       Cervantes (n.d.). 101 p. -- A personal reaction and
       contribution to the charges which are presently
       underway in the Evangelical church.

1582. Elliott, Elizabeth. No graven image. New York, Harper
       and Row, 1966. -- An excellent missionary novel
       dealing with struggles of adjustment and searching
       for personal vocation.

1583. _____. The savage my kinsman. New York, Harper and Row,
       1961. 159 p. -- A widow of one of the "Auca martyrs"
       returns with her little daughter to live among them.
       Profusely illustrated by the author and Cornell Capa.

1584. _____. The shadow of the Almightly. New York, Harper,
       1958. 256 p. -- The life and testament of Jim
       Elliott, one of the five "Auca martyrs."

1585. _____. Through gates of splendor. New York, Harper,
       1957. 256 p. -- The story of the five martyrs among
       the Aucas. See also Rolf Blomberg, The naked Aucas;
       an account of the Indians of Ecuador. s.l., Essential
       Books, 1957. 191 p. See also R. Savage and J.
       Andrade, El drama del eraray, 1956.

1586. Hitt, Russell T. Jungle pilot; the life and witness of
       Nate Saint. New York, Harper, 1959. 303 p.

1587. Padilla, Washington. Pastoral letter from the president
       of the confraternidad evangélica ecuatoriana in
       reaction to "Despertar." Quito, CEE, 1964. --
       Important statement on self-determination of national
       churches.

1588. Streich, Paul H. The unique place of Ecuador in the
       Latin American scene. Unpublished report, 1959.

1589. Wallis, Ethel Emily. The Dayuma story; life under the
       Auca spears. New York, Harper, 1960. 288 p. --
       Gives motivation for massacre of the five missionar-
       ies and evidences of the changes of fear-ridden Aucas
       into Christian believers.

Denominational History
See also p. 342.

Christian Missionary Alliance

1590. Jordan, W. F.   Ecuador, a story of missionary achievement.
       New York, The Christian and Missionary Alliance
       Publishing Co., 1926.   130 p.

Church of the Brethren Mission

1591. Crouse, Merle *and* Arlen Streitzel.   Which way in Ecuador?
       Elgin, Ill., Brethren Press, 1962.   32 p.   -- An
       evaluation of past work and present task of the
       Church of the Brethren in Ecuador.

1592. Long, Inez.   Faces among the faithful.   Elgin, Ill.,
       Brethren Press, 1962.   194 p.   -- p. 174-178 contain
       a biographical sketch of Matlide Benalcazer, an
       evangelical teacher in Calderón, Ecuador.

1593. Rhoades, J. Benton.   Brethren mission in Ecuador.   Elgin,
       Ill., Brethren Press, 1955.   -- A summary of Brethren
       work since its founding in 1945 by the author.

Evangelical Covenent Mission

1594. Duey, Charles J.   Covenent missions in Ecuador.   Chicago,
       Board of Missions of the Evangelical Covenent Church,
       1965.

Gospel Missionary Union

1595. Chapman, C. P.   With the Bible among the Andes.   Kansas
       City, Gospel Missionary Union, 1945.   111 p.   -- An
       historical sketch of the work of the Gospel Mission-
       ary Union in Colombia and Ecuador by one of its
       pioneer missionaries in both fields.

1596. Drown, Frank *and* Marie.   Mission to the head-hunters.   New
       York, Harper, 1961.   248 p.   illus., tables.   -- The
       book contains the autobiographical account of Frank
       and Marie Drown's ministry among the Jívaro Indians of
       the Ecuadorian jungle.

1597. Nickel, Ben J. Along the Quichua trail. Smithville, Mo.,
      Gospel Missionary Union (n.d.). 134 p.

United Andean Indian Mission

1598. Darnell, J. Millen. An evaluation of the UAIM in the light
      of Paul's missionary practices. Th. M. thesis,
      Columbia Theological Seminary, Decatur, Ga., 1963.

1599. Reyburn, William *and* Marie. Picalquí. Unpublished report
      submitted to the UAIM, Quito, 1955.

1600. Stewart, Richard. The significance of future Christian
      medicine in Latin America. Unpublished paper presented
      to First Latin American Congress on Medical Missions,
      1964. 11 p. By a UAIM doctor.

World Radio Missionary Fellowship, H.C.J.B.

1601. Jones, Clarence W. Radio, the new missionary. Chicago,
      Moody, 1946. 147 p. -- By the founder of the famous
      radio station HCJB in Quito.

1602. Roberts, Paul W. Medicine the magnate. Talcottsville,
      Conn., The Voice of the Andes, 1955. 64 p.

1603. Savage, Robert. At your orders, Lord. Grand Rapids,
      Zondervan, 1957. 64 p. -- An interpretative auto-
      biography.

Periodicals
See also p. 343.

1604. Despertar. A single issue opinion paper in Quito, April
      1965. Contains highly controversial opinions of
      Ecuadorian churchmen.

1605. Ecuador. Official monthly bulletin of the Christian and
      Missionary Alliance, Quito.

1606. El mensajero evangélico. Periodic publication of the
      Iglesia Evangélica Unida since 1965.

1607. Renovación. Organ of the Confraternidad Evangélica
      Eduatoriana, Quito.

Venezuela
See also p. 343.

Bibliography
See also p. 343.

1608. Sánchez, M. S. Bibliografía venezolanista. Caracas, 1914.
-- This scholarly bibliography is devoted primarily to
works on Miranda, Bolívar and Sucre.

1609. The bibliographies of Venezuela are covered in detail by
the authoritative bibliographer Manuel Segundo Sánchez,
whose Bibliografía venezolanista, 2 v., was reprinted
in 1964 (BLCU).

General Background
See also p. 343.

1610. Alexander, Robert J. The Venezuela democratic revolution;
a profile of the regime of Rómulo Betancourt. New
Brunswick, N.J., Rutgers University Press, 1964. 345
p. -- A competent study of political development in
Venezuela since 1958.

1611. Arcaya, Pedro. The Gómez regine in Venezuela and its
background. Caracas, 1947.

1612. Briceño, Olga. Cocks and bulls in Caracas; how we live
in Venezuela. New York, Houghton, Mifflin, 1945.
161 p. -- Life and customs among the upper class of
Venezuela. Rapidly becoming outdated.

1613. Espejo, Carlos Sánchez. El patronato en Venezuela.
Caracas, 1953. lxi, 198 p.

1614. Fergusson, Erna. Venezuela. New York, Knopf, 1939. --
General description of Venezuela from the viewpoint
of a writer who spent little time in the country.
Her observations are interesting but faulty at times
from lack of the understanding of the real life of
the people. A rather long travelogue.

1615. Graham, R. B. Cunninghome. José Antonio Páez. Philadelphia,
Macrue, Smith (n.d.). 328 p.

1616. Holstein, H. L. V. Ducoudray. Memories of Bolivar...
with an introduction... Boston, Goodrich, 1829. 383
p. -- See also Angell. Bolivar; Also de Madariaga.

1617. Jankus, Alfred P. *and* Neil M. Malloy. Venezuela, land of
       opportunity. New York, Pageant, 1956. 259 p. --
       Study of Venezuela of the 1950's from the standpoint
       of a businessman. Generally reliable but some factual
       errors.

1618. Lavin, John. A halo for Gomez. New York, Pageant, 1954.
       466 p. -- An attempt to dispel legends without creat-
       ing new ones.

1619. Oviedo y Baños, José de. Historia de la conquista y
       poblicaión de la provincia de Venezuela. New York,
       Scribner (n.d.). 667 p. -- A facsimile reproduction
       of an edition in 1824.

1620. Petre, F. Loraine. Simón Bolívar, "El Libertador." London,
       John Lane, 1910. xv, 459 p. -- The story of the chief
       leader in the revolt against Spain in Venezuela, New
       Granada, Peru.

1621. Rippy, J. Fred *and* Jean Thomas Nelson. Crusaders in the
       jungle. Chapel Hill, University of North Carolina
       Press, 1936. x, 401 p. -- Origin, growth and decline
       of the principal missions on the frontiers of South
       America during the colonial period.

1622. Rourke, Thomas, *pseud.* Gomez, the tyrant of the Andes.
       New York, Wm. Morrow, 1942. -- Story of Juan Gomez,
       the President and dictator of Venezuela, 1908-1935;
       his early life, military life, rise to power as
       President and dictators for 27 years.

1623. Thorning, Jos. F. Miranda; world citizen. Gainesville,
       University of Florida Press, 1952. 324 p.

1624. Watters, Mary. A history of the church in Venezuela,
       1810-1930. Chapel Hill, University of North Carolina
       Press, 1933. ix, 260 p. -- Based on careful research.
       A doctoral thesis on the history and situation of the
       Roman Catholic Church from early times to 1930. Based
       on extensive reading of publications in the Central
       Library in Caracas. She also consulted the extensive
       library of Rudolph Dolge, classified as the best private
       library on Venezuela in existence.

1625. Wise, George S. Caudillo, a portrait of Antonio Guzmán
       Blanco. New York, Columbia University Press, 1951.
       190 p. -- A study of Guzmán Blanco as the most
       typical of the dictator-statesmen of Venezuela.

Extensive background given for rise of Guzmán and
other "caudillos" to power. Good bibliography.

Protestantism in General
See also p. 344.

1626.   Goff, James E. *and* J. MacDonald.   Censo de la obra
        evangélica en Venezuela.   In preparation since 1966
        but still uncompleted.   Partial report available from
        author.

1627.   Manifesto al pueblo y al gobierno de los Estados Unidos
        de Venezuela.   s.l., 1945.   8 p.   -- Declaration of
        the first *Convención Evangélica Unida.*

Denominational History

Presbyterian

1628.   Phillips, C. Arthur.   A history of the Presbyterian Church
        in Venezuela.   Caracas, Presbyterian Mission Press,
        1958.   72 p.   illus., maps.   -- Spanish trans. by
        Robert E. Seel.   Brief history of the work of the
        Presbyterian mission, 1897-1958.

Others

1629.   Christiansen, John.   Under the southern cross.   Chicago,
        1932.   220 p.   -- Printed by the author.   History of
        the Scandinavian Alliance Mission (now the Evangelical
        Alliance Mission) from its founding 1900-1932.

1630.   Cott, Elizabeth Bahler.   Trailing the Davir Indians.
        Mountain View, Calif., Pacific Press, 1936.   95 p.
        -- A mission to the Indians on the edge of Venezuela,
        Guyana and Brazil.

1631.   Grubb, Kenneth C.   The Lowland Indians of Amazonia.   ---
        Cf. no. 376. for chapter on Indians in Venezuela's
        Amazonia.

Periodicals

1632.   Once-in-awhile from Venezuela.   Caracas, Mission Press.
        -- New Venezuela vistas.   News items and stories of
        individuals as met in the work of Presbyterian Church
        in Venezuela.   Apartado 5151-Este, Caracas.

1633.   La estrella de la mañana.   Evangelical Alliance Mission,
        1908-.   Apartado 402, Maracaibo.   Monthly.

CENTRAL AMERICA AND PANAMA
See also p. 345.

Costa Rica
See also p. 347.

Bibliography

1634.   Segreda, Dobles.   Indice bibliográfico de Costa Rica.   --
        See also Anuario bibliográfico costarricense, 1963
        and 1964.

General Background
See also p. 347.

1635.   Alers-Montalvo, M.   Cultural change in a Costa Rican
        village.   *Human organization* 15:6-8, 1957.

1636.   Biesanz, John B. *and* Mavis.   Costa Rican life.   New York,
        Columbia University Press, 1944.   x, 272 p.   -- The
        authors reflect Costa Rican life and activities in
        the early '40's.   One chapter on religion.   Good
        bibliography.

1637.   Fernández G., Ricardo, comp.   Costa Rica en el siglo XIX.
        San José, Imprenta Gutemberg, 1928.   508 p.   --
        Description and observations written by men who
        visited, lived in or were acquainted with Costa Rica
        during the century.   Contains references to European
        and North American Protestants living in Costa Rica
        and efforts in church organizations.

1638.   González, Luis F.   Historia de la influencia extranjera
        en Costa Rica.   San José, Imprenta Nacional, 1921.
        317 p.

1639. Monge Alfaro, Carlos. Historia de Costa Rica. 7. ed.
       San José, Imprenta Las Américas, 1957. 389 p. -- A
       general history of Costa Rica by the present rector
       of the Universidad de Costa Rica.

1640. Moritz *y* Scherzer. La república de Costa Rica en
       Centroamérica. San José, Lehman, 1944. Title and
       text in German. Trans. by Jorge Lines. -- A report
       on trip to Costa Rica made by three Germans in 1853-
       1854. Occasional and extremely interesting references
       to Protestants in Costa Rica.

Protestantism in General
See also p. 347.

1641. British and foreign Bible society reports. v. 42, 1846;
       v. 44, 1849. -- Reports of colportage activity of
       the British sea captain Wm. LeLacheur, in Costa Rica,
       the first evangelical activity known in the country.

1642. Celada, Claudio. Un apostol contemporáneo. -- Cf. no.
       356. Contains account of Penzotti's visit to Costa
       Rica.

1643. Nelson, Wilton M. A history of Protestantism in Costa
       Rica. Lucknow, India, Institute of Church Growth,
       1963. 258 p. -- Condensation of Ph. D. thesis,
       Princeton Theological Seminary, 1957. Entrance of
       individual Protestants, formation of foreign Protes-
       tant church, origin, development of the Evangelical
       movement. Available through Editorial Caribe, Aptdo.
       901, San José.

Denominational History
See also p. 348.

Central American Mission

1644. Spain, Mildred. And in Samaria. 2. ed. Dallas, Central
       American Mission, 1954. 328 p. -- Story of the
       origin and development of the Central American Mission
       whose work began in Costa Rica.

Episcopal Church

1645. Church of the Good Shepherd, 1865-1965. San José, 1965.
       20 p. -- Brief centenary pamphlet on the first
       Protestant chapel in Costa Rica.

Latin American Mission

1646. Saborio, Rodolfo. La contribución social de la Misión
       Latinoamericana a Costa Rica. B.D. thesis, Seminario
       Biblico, San José.

Methodist

1647. Bideaux, René O. Los metodistas en Costa Rica. Alajuela,
       C.R., 1964. 8 p. -- Brief historical and statictical
       review.

1648. Miller, George. Twenty years after. s.l., 1936. --
       Memoirs by a missionary bishop, one of the founders
       of the Methodist church in Costa Rica and Panama.
       See also *his* Growing up, based on letters to his
       daughter.

1649. Woods, Marion F. A training program for Methodist
       preachers in the Pacific zone of Costa Rica. M.A.
       thesis, Scarritt College for Christian Workers,
       Nashville, Tenn., 1965.

Periodicals
See also p. 348.

1650. Alianza. Dorothy Cabezas, ed. Alianza Evangélica
       Costarricense, Aptdo. 5134, San José, 1961-.

1651. The Central American bulletin. Central American Mission,
       Box 28005, Dallas, Texas, 75228, 1891-. Bi-monthly.

1652. The Latin America Evangelist. Latin American Mission,
       285 Orchard Terrace, Bogota, N.J., 07603.

1653. Lumbrera. Southern Baptist Convention in Costa Rica,
       Aptdo. 1713, San José.

1654. Prospecto. Seminario Bíblico Latinoamericano, Aptdo. 901,
       San José.

1655. Vocero, El. Asociación de Iglesias Bíblicas Costarricen-
       ses, Aptdo. 901, San José. Monthly.

Guatemala
See also p. 349.

Bibliography

1656. The current output of literature is covered by the
       valuable Boltein de la biblioteca nacional.

General Background
See also p. 349.

1657. Brigham, Wm. T. Guatemala; the land of the Quetzal.
       Wilson Popenoe, ed. Gainesville, University of
       Florida Press, 1887. reprint.

1658. Burgess, Paul. Justo Rufino Barrios. New York, Dorrance,
       1926. -- Cf. Robert Claxton's biography of Montufar,
       foreign minister under Barrios. Tulane University,
       (Cf. no. 2858).

1659. Chinchilla, Ernesto. La Inquisición en Guatemala.
       Guatemala, Ministerio de Educación Pública, 1953.
       335 p. -- A history of a branch of the Mexican
       tribunal. Relates cases of Protestants who came
       before the tribunal in Central America during the
       Colonial era.

1660. Griffith, Wm. J. Empires in the wilderness; foreign
       colonization and development in Guatemala, 1834-1844.
       Chapel Hill, University of North Carolina Press,
       1965. 332 p. -- Important to understanding work of
       Frederick C. Crowe, first Protestant missionary to
       Guatemala.

1661. Holleran, Mary P. Church and state in Guatemala. New
       York, Columbia University Press, 1949. -- Analysis
       of the Catholic situation and a fairly accurate
       resumé of Protestant beginnings. Discusses the
       reasons *ladinos* are not satisfactory converts - yet
       Indian converts are small in number. A good critical
       discussion of certain weaknesses in Catholic belief
       and practice.

1662. Oakes, Maud. The two crosses of Todos Santos; survivals
       of Mayan religious ritual. New York, Bollinger
       Foundation (n.d.). xiii, 274 p. — Important.

Protestantism
See also p. 352.

Indian Congregations and the Process of Ladinization

Books, Monographs and Theses

1663. Adams, Richard N. Encuestra sobre la cultura de los
       ladinos en Guatemala. Guatemala, Editorial del
       Ministerio de Educación Pública, 1956. 228 p.
       tables. — Available in Guatemala through the Semi-
       nario de Integración Social Guatemalteca. p. 169-
       174 discusses briefly Protestantism among *ladinos* -
       gives reasons for lack of success among *ladinos* due
       to lack of religious enthusiasm among *ladino* men.
       Discussion of differentiating customs; cigarettes,
       dancing, liquor, padrinos. Estimate of percentage
       of Protestants is inaccurate.

1664. _____, comp. Political changes in Guatemala Indian
       communities; a symposium. New Orleans, Tulane
       University, Middle American Research Institute, no.
       24, 1957. 54 p. — An excellent and thought-pro-
       voking analysis of political change in nine Indian
       communities. Reina, p. 34-35, discusses conversion
       of *ex-alcalde* whom he calls *hombre de verdad*. Inter-
       esting discussion of deviant behavior. Amir and
       Adams also discuss Protestantism in their articles.

1665. _____. Social change in Latin America today; its impli-
       cations for United States policy. New York, Vintage
       Books, 1960. 347 p. — Short discussion from p.
       262 on Protestant influence and innovations as a
       factor in breaking down Indian culture and causing
       uncertainity in religion.

1666. Emery, Gennet M. The influence of Protestantism on the
       bicultural situation in Guatemala, with reference to
       the Roman Catholic background. M.A. thesis, Hartford
       Seminary Foundation, Hartford, Conn., 1964. — A
       study of the innovation of Protestantism, its char-
       acteristics and structure, how it has been communicated
       (by whom and how) and how it has been re-interpreted by

the receivers; personally, in church life and in
social matters. This is discussed in each field with
regard to ladino/Indian differences. Factual and
technical. Copies in Hartford Seminary and UPL.
Sondeos series. No. 65, 1970.

1667. Hirshberg, Richard Irwin. The process of ladinization
in the Guatemala highlands. Ph. D. thesis, Syracuse,
N.Y., Syracuse University, 1958. microfilmed. --
Includes Protestantism as a factor in ladinization.
Some inaccurate statistics and information (e.g.,
hospital *only* service mission in Guatemala).
Attributes considerable culture change (disruptive)
to Protestantism without considering other factors.
However, his analysis of a Protestant Indian and
his role in the community is important.

1668. LaFarge, Oliver. Santa Eulalia; the religion of a
Cuchumatán Indian town. Chicago, University of
Chicago Press, 1947. -- Analysis of Roman Catholic
and pagan religion in Indian town. Very anti-
Protestant but his biases report of fanatical
Protestant missionaries has just enough truth to
hurt. Mentions attacks on Indian customs and over-
emphasizes "hell-fire-and-damnation." However, he
wrongly identifies the group of missionaries. Good
picture of Indian beliefs about Protestants.
Analyzes Catholic work also.

1669. Saler, Benson. Religious conversion and self-aggrandizement; a Guatemalan case study. In *Practical
Anthropology*, Vol. 12, May-June, 1965. 107-114 p.
Hypothesizes that Protestantism is an alternative to
sorcery in terms of maximizing self-aggrandizement;
that religious conversion gives a way for individuals
(those who would ordinarily be *shamans*) a way to show
their uniqueness while idealizing humility and self-
effacement.

1670. _____. The road from El Palmar. Ph. D. thesis, University of Pennsylvania, Philadelphia, 1960. microfilmed.
-- An anthropologist has good but not always accurate
judgments of Protestantism in the picture of culture
change. Mentions early missionaries and way Protestants have adapted their Indian customs to fit into
Protestant mold and the carry over of Catholic
practices. Excellent study.

1671. Tax, Sol. Panajachel field notes. Chicago, University
of Chicago Library, 1950. (Microfilm collection of
manuscripts on Middle American cultural anthropology,
no. 29). -- p. 2154-2895 have many references to
Protestants, which emphasize confused ideas and moral
restrictions. Biased against Protestantism but very
informative.

Articles

1672. Arias, Jorge B., ed. Aspectos demográficos de la
población indígena de Guatemala. *Guatemala indígena*
(Guatemala) 1:2:5-29. -- Available from the publisher in Guatemala. This article gives statistics
for Roman Catholic and Protestants among ladinos and
Indians. He estimates 4.3% of ladinos are Protestant,
1.5% of the Indians.

1673. McArthur, Harry S. La estructura político-religiosa de
Aguacatán. *Guatemala indígena* (Guatemala) 1:2:41-56,
1961. -- An article dealing with what happened
politically in the town structure when inhabitants
became Protestant.

1674. Paul, Benjamin D. *and* Louis. Changing marriage patterns
in a highland Guatemala community. *Southwestern
journal of anthropology* 19:2:131-148, 1963. -- In
college libraries. An article showing culture change
in marriage in San Pedro La Laguna. Discusses
Protestantism as a force which polarized the
Catholics into conservatives and progressives.
Marriage now has a "counter" in Protestant-Roman
Catholic competition.

1675. Reina, Rubén E. Chinautla, A Guatemalan Indian community;
a study in the relationship of community culture and
national change. New Orleans, Tulane University, 1960.
illus. (Middle American research institute, no. 24:
55-130). -- An excellent analysis of Protestant
Indians in this village outside Guatemala City.
Analyzes a church split, Protestant education, Sunday
School lessons, attempts to improve living conditions,
Indian beliefs which linger on, political affiliation
of Protestant Indians, ladinos, etc. A good-fair study
by an anthropologist.

1676. Sibley, Donald N. *and* George M. Beal. Adoption of
agricultural technology by Indians in Guatemala.
Iowa State University, 1966. -- Dr. Sibley is a

United Presbyterian missionary-agronomist. Object of
this research is to determine the variable related to
rate and intensity of the adoption of agricultural
technology among Quiche Indians.

1677. Smalley, William, ed. *and* Arden King. Changing cultural
goals and patterns in Guatemala. *American anthropologist* (Wisconsin) 54:1:139-143. -- p. 141 has a
few statements on the effect of Protestantism on
Indians' views of religious goals.

Protestantism in General

1678. Crowe, Frederick. The gospel in Central America contain-
ing a sketch of the country, physical and geographical
--historical and political--moral and religious: a
history of the Baptist mission in British Honduras
and of the introduction of the Bible into the Spanish
American republic of Guatemala. London, Chas. Gelpin,
1850. -- Story of the first Protestant to enter
Guatemala, a British sailor. Includes comments on
the country, experiences in evangelization and the
establishment of a school in the capital. A definitive source.

1679. Grubb, Kenneth G. Religion in Central America. London,
World Dominion, 1937. 147 p. -- Discussion of
history, work and early missionaries of each original
major denomination in Guatemala and other Central
American countries. An accurate analysis of emphasis
but not always accurate in historical facts and
statictics.

1680. Haymaker, Edward M. Footnotes on the beginnings of the
evangelical movement in Guatemala. New York, UML,
1946. 137 p. mimeographed. -- Invaluable notes on
the beginnings of Protestant work in Guatemala by one
of the early missionaries who went to Guatemala in
1887. Freely expressed opinions of Presbyterian work
and that of others. Examples of early mission approach,
attitudes toward the Roman Catholic church, methods of
evangelizing, and the cultural influences the missionaries brought.

1681. Informe official del Congreso evangélico Centro-Americano.

1682. Scanlon, Clark. Church growth and theological education. Eugene, Ore., Institute of Church Growth (n.d.). -- A Southern Baptist missionary reviews subject summarily.

1683. Stahlke, Leonardo E., ed. Estadística de la obra religiosa-cristiana de Guatemala. Guatemala, Iglesia Luterana, 1966. 235 p.

1684. Varetto, Juan C. Federico Crowe en Guatemala. Buenos Aires, Justa Bautista de Publicaciones, 1940. 122 p. -- Story of the first Bible society colporter in Central America.

1685. Wilgus, A. Curtis, ed. *and* Harvey K. Meyer. Church and state in Central America. Gainesville, University of Florida Press, 1961. (The Caribbean: the Central American area, series i, v. 9). -- An article concerning the role of the church and education. discusses Protestantism in general -- considers the regions only nominally Catholic. Protestant evangelism is chiefly only successful in education and health services. Has a good bibliography.

Denominational History

Central American Mission

1686. Inter-republic missionary conference of the Central American missions. January 1962. 152 p. -- mimeographed. -- A report of the January meeting.

1687. Spain, Mildred. (Cf. no. 1644).

Presbyterian

1688. Bodas de diamante comité. Historia de la obra evangélica presbiteriana en Guatemala, 1892-1957. Quezaltenango, Guatemala, Noticiero Evangélico, 1957. 171 p. -- Written to celebrate the 75th anniversary of Presbyterian work. Reveals, especially in the preface, the attitude or condition of the church today. Hastily written and printed. Valuable to understand how "a national church talks about itself."

Lutheran Church - Missouri Synod

1689. Kuehn, Clarence T. The history of the Lutheran church --
       Missouri Synod in Guatemala until June 1949. B.D.
       thesis, Concordia Seminary, St. Louis, Mo., 1950.
       90 p. See also "Problems of Lutherans in Central
       America" by R. T. Hoeferkamp in *Concordia Theological
       Monthly*, April, 1965. 272-274 p.

                         El Salvador
                      See also p. 354.

No publications listed.

                          Honduras
                      See also p. 355.

                       Bibliography

1690. Revista de archivo y biblioteca nacional de Honduras,
       1904.

                    General Background
                      See also p. 355.

1691. Dúron, Rómulo E. Bosquejo historio de Honduras, 1502-
       1921. s.l., San Pedro Sula, 1927.

                  Protestantism in General
                      See also p. 355.

1692. Cáceres Perdomo, Oscar. Ensayo histórico parcial del
       movimiento evangélico en Honduras. Th. B. thesis,
       Seminario Bíblico, San José.

1693. The Mosquito coast and the story of the first Schwenkfelder
       missionary enterprise among the Indians of Honduras
       from 1768-1775. Andrew S. Berky, ed. Norristown,
       Pa., 1953. 31 p. Title and text in German, trans.
       by Selina G. Schultz. -- Largely correspondence
       between the Moravian missionary Christian Frederick
       Post and Schwenkfelder leader Christopher Schultz.

Denominational History

Moravian

1694. Erdman, Mabel H., ed. Creative personalities. --
       Pioneer of Moravian work in Honduras in 1930 and
       translator of new version of Mosquito New Testament;
       is among the missionaries presented.

United Church of Christ, former Evangelical and Reformed

1695. Brown, Betty. Week-day program for junior and intermed-
       iate girls in Honduras. M.A. thesis, Wheaton College,
       Ill., 1955.

1696. Melick, Edith M. Seed sowing in Honduras. St. Louis,
       Mo., Eden Publishing, 1927.

1697. Twente, Theophil H. Honduran rainbow. St. Louis, Mo.,
       Eden Publishing (n.d.).

Nicaragua
See also p. 356.

Bibliography

1698. Kalb, Courtenay de. A bibliography of the Mosquito
       coast of Nicaragua. *Journal of the American geo-
       graphical society*, 1894.

1699. Perhaps Nicaragua is best known by the bibliographical
       studies regarding its great poet, Ruben Dario.

General Background
See also p. 356.

1700. Conzemius, Eduard. Ethnological survey of the Moskito
       and Sumu Indians of Honduras and Nicaragua. Washing-
       ton, D.C., Government Printing Office, 1932. 191 p.
       glossary. -- Excellent bibliography of over one
       hundred works, mainly in Spanish, English, German and
       French.

1701.   Hamilton, Kenneth. Meet Nicaragua. Bethlehem, Pa.,
        Comenius, 1939. 66 p.

1702.   Hooker, Robert Montgomery. La reincorporación de la
        Mosquitia desde el punto de vista del derecho inter-
        nacional y patrio. Tesis para grado de doctor en
        Ley, Universidad Real de León de Nicaragua, 1945.
        -- The case of the last four Mosquito kings, 1866-
        1894.

1703.   Parsons, James J. The Mosquito pine savanna of Nicaragua
        and Honduras. March 1955. (Annals of association of
        American geographies, v. 45, no. 1). -- Description
        of economy and topography.

1704.   Pijoan, Michael. The Moskito Indians. *América indígena*
        4:255 October 1944.

1705.   Roberts, Orlando W. Narratives of voyages and excursions
        on the east coast and in the interior of Central
        America: describing a journey up the river San Juan
        and passage across the lake of Nicaragua to the city
        of León; a facsimile of the 1827 edition. Gainesville,
        University of Florida Press, 1965. 302 p.

Protestantism in General

1706.   Iobst, Robert A. Teaching the Bible to primitive people
        particularly the Moskito and Sumu Indians of
        Nicaragua and Honduras. Th. M. thesis, Princeton
        Theological Seminary, 1947. 120 p.

Denominational History
See also p. 357.

Moravian

1707.   Borhek, Mary Virginia. Watchman on the walls. Bethlehem,
        Pa., The Society for Propagating the Gospel, 1949.
        72 p. -- A centenary review publication.

1708.   Brincleau, A. Histoire de la mision morave a la cote
        des Mosquitos (Nicaragua) de 1849 a 1921. Strasbourg,
        Hitler, 1922. 41 p.

1709. Mueller, Karl A., Bishop. Among Creoles, Moskitos and
      Sumos: a survey of the Moravian mission from 1847-
      1930. Bethlehem, Pa., Comenius, 1932. 156 p. illus.

1710. Shimer, Conrad. A century of Moravian missions.
      Bluefield, Nicaragua, Scouts of Nicaragua, 1949. --
      Brief review by a veteran missionary on the occasion
      of Centenary celebration.

Note: In the Moravian Archives, Bethlehem, Pa., are to be
found several publications in German covering the period from
1847 to 1930 during which the Mosquito mission was administered
largely from Germany.

Panamá
See also p. 357.

Bibliography

1711. Pippin, Larry L. An annotated bibliography on Panama
      and the Canal Zone. Reno, University of Nevada,
      1966.

1712. Susto, Juan A., comp. Bibliografía de Panamá, 1928-.
      -- Complemented by Fco. A. Herrera's Bibliografía de
      Panamá de 1960 a 1963.

General Background
See also p. 357.

1713. Biesanz, John *and* Mavis. The people of Panama. New York,
      Columbia University Press, 1955.

1714. Howarth, David. Panama -- 400 years of history and
      cruelty. New York, McGraw-Hill, 1966.

1715. Miller, George A. Prowling about Panama. New York,
      Abingdon, 1919. 354 p. -- Travelogue by a North
      American Methodist missionary. Reflects the Panama
      of that day with some references to Protestant work.

1716. Rojas y Arrieta, Guillermo. History of the bishops of
      Panama. T. J. McDonald, ed. and trans. Panama, La
      Academia, 1939. xvi, 355 p. -- Original text in

Spanish. See Colección sondeos: actitudes de los
estudiantes panameños frente al sacerdote.

Protestantism in General

1717. Butler, Charles O. Protestant growth and a changing
       Panama. Thesis, Perkins School of Theology, Dallas,
       1964. -- A study of Foursquare Gospel and Methodist
       patterns.

1718. Rolofson, Robert H. Christian cooperation at the world's
       crossroads. Union Church of the Canal Zone, privately
       printed, 1950. 425 p.

Denominational History
See also p. 358.

Baptist

1719. Coope, Anna. Anna Coope, sky pilot of the San Blas
       Indians: an autobiography. New York, American
       Tract Society, 1917. viii, 180 p.

1720. Morgan, Christine Hudgins. I married a San Blas Indian:
       the story of Marvel Elya Iglesias. New York,
       Vantage, 1958. 81 p. -- A mission to the Indians
       of the San Blas islands, off the coast of Panama,
       ultimately supported by the Southern Baptists of the
       U.S.A.

MÉXICO
See also p. 359.

Bibliography

1721. Bibliographies related to the literature of Mexico inspire
       respect among students in the field of Latin American
       studies. There are special bibliographies to facili-
       tate research in various disciplines, i.e., Valle's
       Bibliografía Maya and Ramos' *Bibliografía de la*
       revolución mexicana.

1722.   Foster, Merlin H., comp. An index to Mexican literary
        periodicals. New York, Scarecrow, 1966. 276 p.

1723.   Ker, Anita Melville. Mexican government publications.
        Washington, D.C., U.S. Government Printing Office,
        1940. 333 p. -- A guide to more important publica-
        tions of the national government of Mexico, 1821-
        1936. US$.75. (LC4.7:M2).

1724.   Ross, Stanley R., et al. A central guide to newspaper
        and periodical literature, 1910-1940. Mexico,
        Mexico City College (n.d.).

General Background
See also p. 359.

Religious Issues

1725.   Báez Camargo, Gonzalo. Pre-hispanic religion in modern
        Mexico. *International review of missions*, April
        1942.

1726.   Balderrama, Luis C. El clero y el gobierno de México;
        apuntes para la história de la crisis en 1926.
        México, Editorial Cuauhtémoc, 1927.

1727.   Bell, James D. Attitudes of selected groups in the
        United States toward Mexico, 1930-1940. Ph. D.
        thesis, University of Chicago, 1941.

1728.   Beltrán, Enrique. La lucha revolucionaria del protetar-
        iado contra la iglesia. México, Editorial L.A.R.,
        1931. 47 p.

1729.   Braden, Charles S. Religious aspects of the conquest of
        Mexico. Durham, North Carolina, Duke University
        Press, 1930.

1730.   Butler, William. Mexico in transition. 4. rev. ed.
        New York, Hunt and Eaton, 1892. 321 p. -- The
        transition from Roman Catholic political control to
        religious and civil liberty. Last chapter on
        Protestant missions.

1731.   Capistrán Garza, René. La iglesia católica y la
        Revolución mexicana; prontuario de ideas políticas.
        México, Atisbos, 1964. 202 p.

1732. Cronon, Edmund D. American Catholics and Mexican anti-
        clericalism, 1933-36. *Mississippi valley historical
        review*, September 1958.

1733. Cuevas, Mariano, S.J. Historia de la iglesia en México.
        El Paso, 1921-28. 5 v. -- The story from colonial
        times to 1910.

1734. Ellis, L. Ethan. Dwight Morrow and the church-state
        controversy in Mexico. *Hispanic American historical
        review*, November 1958.

1735. Greenleaf, Richard E. Zumárraga and the Mexican inquisi-
        tion. Washington, D.C., 1961. -- Enlightening work
        on the early operations of the Inquisition in Mexico
        before 1569.

1736. Hecketsweiler, Roy T. Church and state in Mexico since
        1910. Evanston, Ill., Northwestern, 1939. 102 p.

1737. Jiménez Rueda, Julio. Herejías y supersticiones en la
        Nueva España: los heterodoxos a México. México,
        Imprenta Universitaria, 1954. 307 p. -- Story of
        different types of aberrations of the Roman Catholic
        faith in Mexico during the colonial era. Some of
        these phenomena were "protestant" or quasi protestant
        in character.

1738. Madsen, William. Christo-paganism: a study of Mexican
        religious syncretism. Ph. D. thesis, Berkeley,
        Calif., 1955.

1739. Moctezuma, Aquiles P. El conflicto religioso de 1926.
        México, D.F., 1929.

1740. Pattee, Richard. The Catholic revival in Mexico.
        Washington, D.C., Catholic Association for Inter-
        national Peace, 1944. 60 p. -- Report to Inter-
        American Committee.

1741. Pérez. Lugo J. La cuestión religiosa en México. México,
        Publicaciones de Centro Cultural Cuauhetmoc, 1926.

1742. Porch, Robert S. The influence of the Aztecs upon con-
        temporary religious thought in Mexico. Columbia,
        S.C., Graduate School of Missions, Columbia Bible
        College, 1957.

1743.   Quirk, Robert E.   The Mexican Revolution and the Catholic
        church, 1910-29; an ideological study.   Bloomington,
        Ind., 1963.

1744.   Richard, Robert.   La conquista espiritual de México.
        México, 1947.   Title and text in French, trans. by
        Angel G. M. Garibay.   -- Describes early missionary
        endeavor (1523-72) in favorable terms.   English
        translation as The spiritual conquest of Mexico.
        Berkeley, University of California Press, 1966.
        423 p.

1745.   Rice, Elizabeth A.   The diplomatic relations between the
        United States and Mexico as affected by the struggle
        for religious liberty in Mexico, 1925-29.   Washington,
        D.C., Catholic University of America, 1959.

1746.   Ross, Stanley R.   Is the Mexican Revolution dead?   New
        York, Knopf, 1966.   -- A stimulating book for eval-
        uating the Mexican Revolution.   Properly belongs
        under following section.

1747.   Schmitt, Karl M.   Evolution of Mexican thought on church-
        state relations, 1876-1911.   Ann Arbor, University
        of Michigan, 1954.

1748.   Toro, Alfonso.   La iglesia y el estado en México.   México,
        Talleres Gráficos, 1927.   502 p.   -- A study of the
        conflicts between the clergy and the Mexican govern-
        ment from Independence to 1927.   A passionate denun-
        ciation of the Church and the clergy.

Political

1749.   Brandenburg, Frank R.   The making of modern Mexico.
        Englewood Cliffs, N.J., Prentice Hall, 1964.   379 p.
        -- Introduction by Frank Tannenbaum who writes "the
        author is kinder to the political machinery than he
        needs to be..."

1750.   Brenner, Anita *and* George R. Leighton.   The wind that
        swept Mexico.   New York, Harper, 1943.   302 p.   --
        A history of the Mexican Revolution, 1910-42.

1751.   Callahan, James M.   American foreign policy in Mexican
        relations.   New York, Macmillan, 1932.   Reprint by
        Cooper Square Publishers, 1968.   644 p.

1752. Cline, Howard F. The United States and Mexico. Washing-
      ton, Howard University Press, 1953. 453 p. -- A
      definitive study of U.S.-Mexico relations.

1753. Cosío Villegas, Daniel. La historiografía política del
      México moderno. México, 1953.

1754. Cumberland, Charles C. Mexican Revolution: genesis
      under Madero. Austin, University of Texas Press,
      1952.

1755. Dulles, John W. F. Yesterday in Mexico: a chronicle of
      the Revolution, 1910-36. Austin, University of Texas
      Press, 1961.

1756. Gonzalez Navarro, Moisés. La ideología de la Revolución
      mexicana. *Historia mexicana*, abril-junio 1961.

1757. Hackett, Charles W. The Mexican Revolution and the
      United States, 1910-26. Boston, World Peace Founda-
      tion, 1926.

1758. Johnson, John H. Political change in Latin America.
      Palo Also, Calif., Stanford University Press, 1965.
      -- Describes the post-revolution period in Mexico
      and the new orientation.

1759. Padgett, L. Vincent. The Mexican political system.
      Boston, Houghton, Mifflin, 1966.

1760. Prescott, William H. The conquest of Mexico. New York,
      Dutton, 1909. 2 v. -- Available in paperback
      edition Cf. no. 1451 together with The conquest of
      Peru. Both are classics.

1761. Quirk, Robert E. The Mexican Revolution, 1914-15. New
      York, Citadel Press, 1963. -- A good book for back-
      ground reading on the eventful years.

1762. Scott, R. E. Mexican government in transition. Urbana,
      University of Illinois Press, 1964.

1763. Tannenbaum, Frank. Mexico: the struggle for peace and
      bread. New York, Knopf, 1950. -- A survey of the
      events which have shaped present-day Mexico.

1764. _____. Peace by revolution: an interpretation of
      Mexico. New York, Columbia University Press, 1937.
      317 p. -- Published as Columbia paperback no. 68,

1966. In a brief bibliography on p. 310, references
are made to good bibliographies on Mexico and other
valuable listings.

1765. Townsend, William C. Lázaro Cárdenas, Mexican democrat.
Ann Arbor, Mich., George Wahr, 1952. -- A sympathetic
view by one who spent most of his life among the
Indians of Mexico and Guatemala.

Cultural, Educational and Social

1766. Bailey, Helen Miller. Santa Cruz of the Etla hills.
Gainesville, University of Florida Press, 1958. 292
p. -- Based on author's visits from 1934-54.

1767. Booth, George C. Mexico's school-made society. Palo
Alto, Stanford University Press, 1941.

1768. Brenner, Anita. Idols behind altars. New York, Harcourt,
Brace, 1929. 359 p. -- An interpretation of religion
and art in Mexico by one born and reared in Mexico.
The travail of a nation finds expression in mural and
other art forms.

1769. Bright, Roderick. The land and people of Mexico. New
York, Macmillan, 1958. 90 p.

1770. The broken spears, the Aztec account of the conquest of
Mexico. Miguel León Portillo, ed. Boston, Beacon
Press, 1962. 168 p. -- Trans. from Náhuatl to
Spanish and then to English.

1771. Cline, Howard I. Mexico, revolution to evolution, 1940-
60. New York, Oxford University Press, 1963.
tables. -- Good chapter on "The elusive Indian."

1772. Davis, Harold E. Latin American social thought. Washington, D.C., University Press, 1961. -- Excellent
material on José Vasconcelos and Antonio Caso.

1773. Díaz, May N. Tonalá: conservatism, responsibility and
authority in a Mexican town. Berkeley, University
of California Press, 1966. -- A study in culture
change through effects of industrialization of an
urban center upon a nearby small community.

1774.   Gruening, Ernest H. Mexico and its heritage. New York,
        Appleton-Century, 1940. -- Excellent general inter-
        pretative history of Mexico. Still useful for period
        before 1926. A social and economic history containing
        some analysis of the religious situation.

1775.   Hanke, Lewis. Mexico, land of sunshine and shadow.
        Princeton, N.J., Van Nostrand, 1967. -- A Search-
        light paperback, no. 31.

1776.   Herring, Hubert C. *and* Robert Weinstock. Renascent
        Mexico. New York, Freide, 1936. -- Chapter by Moisés
        Sáenz on "Indian Mexico."

1777.   Kneller, George F. The education of the Mexican nation.
        New York, Columbia University Press, 1951. --
        Comprehensive work with historical background from
        the colonial period.

1778.   Lewis, Oscar. See *his* A Mexican village; The children of
        Sánchez; Pedro Martínez; Life in a Mexican village;
        Five families. -- Five classics in the study of the
        culture of poverty in Mexico. Five families has
        appeared in paperback (MQ688).

1779.   McBride, George. The land systems of Mexico. New York,
        American Geographical Society, 1923. 204 p.

1780.   Parkes, Henry B. A history of Mexico. rev., enl. ed.
        Boston, Houghton Mifflin, 1958. 435 p. -- Good
        bibliography. Original edition, 1938.

1781.   Paz, Octavio. El laberinto de la soledad. s.l. (n.d.).
        -- English translation as The labyrinth of solitude.
        Grove Press, New York, 1961. 212 p.

1782.   Redfield, Robert. A village that chose progress, Chan
        Kom revisited. Chicago, University of Chicago Press,
        1964. -- A sociological study of a Mayan community.
        Contains section on the influence of Protestantism
        on this village. See also his Tepoztlán: a Mexican
        village.

1783.   Romanell, Patrick. Making of the Mexican mind. Lincoln,
        University of Nebraska, 1952. -- New philosophies in
        the making by Mexican thinkers.

1784.   Rosser, H. Edwin. "Beyond Revolution: The Social Concern
        of Moisés Sáenz, Mexican Educator, 1888-1941." Ann

Arbor, Mich.: University Microfilms, 1970. A
dissertation on the life and work of Prof. Moisés
Sáenz, his educational philosophy and planning (including the founding of the secondary schools in Mexico),
university reforms, sociological investigations,
diplomatic service, and efforts leading to the establishment of the Inter-American Indian Institute.
Extensive bibliography.

1785. Sáenz, Moisés. Carapán: bosquejo de una experiencia.
Lima, Librería e Imprenta, Gil, S.A., 1936. 352 p.
-- Deals with Indians of Mexico: culture, education
and government relations.

1786. _____. The Mexican situation discussed. Washington, D.C.,
Library of Congress, F1234.S124. -- A prominent
Mexican Presbyterian and former Under-Secretary of
Education discussed the Mexican Revolution.

1787. _____. Mexico, an appraisal and a forecast. New York,
The Committee on Cultural Relations with Latin
America, 1929. 16 p. -- A statement of the spiritual
ideals of the leaders of the new Mexico.

1788. _____. México íntegro. Lima, Imprenta Torres Aguirre,
1939. 264 p. -- Deals with Mexican civilization and
social conditions.

1789. _____ and H. I. Priestley. Some Mexican problems. Chicago,
University of Chicago Press, 1926. 175 p. -- Lectures
of the Harris Foundation.

1790. Sánchez, George I. The development of higher education in
Mexico. Austin, University of Texas Press, 1946.

1791. Simpson, Leslie Byrd. Many Mexicos. Berkeley, University
of California Press (n.d.). 353 p. -- A good
introduction for the general reader. Paperback
edition. 389 p.

1792. Vasconcelos, José and Manuel Gamio. Aspects of Mexican
civilization. Chicago, University of Chicago Press,
1926.

1793. Whiteford, Andrew H. Two cities in Latin America.
(Cf. no. 1531).

1794. Wilson, Irma. Mexico; a century of educational thought. New
Mexico, Albuquerque, Hispanic Institute, 1941.

1795. Zea, Leopoldo. El postivismo en México. México, El
       Colégio de México, 1943. 254 p. -- A definitive
       treatise.

Protestantism in General
See also p. 363.

1796. Báez Camargo, Gonzalo. The evangelical situation in
       Mexico. London, World Dominion, 1949.

1797. _____ and Kenneth G. Grubb. Religion in the republic of
       Mexico. New York, World Dominion, 1935. 166 p. --
       An excellent study. Still the best on the development
       of Protestant work in Mexico until 1935.

1798. Butler, J. W. Protestant Christianity in Mexico.
       Missionary review of the world, March 1911.

1799. Case, Alden B. Thirty years with the Mexicans; in peace
       and revolution. New York, Revell, 1917. -- Account
       of experiences of a rancher in Mexico during latter
       part of 1884-1915 who had served as a missionary of
       the American Board.

1800. Clawson, William M. The influence of the Catholic Church
       on the development of the Mexican government and its
       relationship to Protestant missions. Ph. D. thesis,
       Baptist Seminary, New Orleans, 1961.

1801. Conferéncia nacional de obreros evangélicos de México,
       1940. México, CUPSA (n.d.). 63 p. -- Report and
       addresses of meetings related to the visit of Dr.
       John R. Mott.

1802. Gandee, Lee R. The introduction and nineteenth century
       development of Protestantism in the republic of
       Mexico. M.A. thesis, Mexico City College, 1948.

1803. Garza, E., Gonzalo Báez Camargo *y otros*. La misión de la
       iglesia evangélica en México en la hora presente.
       s.l. (n.d.). 238 p. -- Report and recommendations
       of the first national evangelical conference, 1938.

1804. Gringoire, Pedro, *pseud*. El doctor Mora impulsor nacional
       de la causa Bíblica en México. México, Sociedad
       Biblica, 1965. 55 p. illus. -- Documented study of
       work carried on by Mora after Thomson's departure in
       1827.

1805. Leslie, Ruth R. The Protestant movement in Mexico. M.A. thesis, College of Mission, Eugene, Ore., 1923.

1806. McCarty, Jos. H. Two thousand miles through the heart of Mexico. New York, Phillips and Hunt, 1886. 288 p.

1807. McGavran, Donald, John Huegel *and* James Taylor. Church growth in Mexico. Grand Rapids, Erdmans, 1963. 136 p. maps, tables. Title and text in Spanish. -- An introductory study on Protestant church growth in Mexico, a virtually untouched area of research.

1808. McClelland, Alice J. Missions to Mexico. New York, BWM, Presbyterian Church, 1960.

1809. Marroquín, H. T. La agencia bíblica en México y su obra. México, Sociedad Bíblica Americana, 1953. 84 p. -- Review of work of 75 years.

1810. La misión de la iglesia evangélica de México en la hora presente; ponencias y resoluciones del primer congreso nacional evangélico, 1939. México, CUPSA, 1940. -- A conference strongly influenced by Madras.

1811. Moses, Jasper T. Today is the land of tomorrow; a study in the development of Mexico. Indianapolis, Christian Women's Board of Missions, 1907.

1812. Onderdonk, Frank S. A glimpse at Mexico. Nashville, Tenn., Board of Missions, Methodist Episcopal Church, 1930.

1813. Penton, Marvin J. Mexico's reformation; a history of Mexican Protestantism from its inception to the present. Ph. D. thesis, State University of Iowa, Ames, 1965.

1814. Rankin, Melinda. Texas in 1850. Waco, Texas, Texian Press, 1966. reprint. -- A vivid description of Miss Rankin who began work in Monterrey in 1866.

1815. _____. Twenty years among the Mexicans; a narrative of missionary labor. Cincinnati, Chase and Hall, 1875. 199 p. Title and text in Spanish, trans. by Joel Martínez Tamez, México, Casa Unida de Publicaciones, 1958. 164 p.

1816. Rembao, Alberto. Outlook in Mexico, New York, Friendship Press, 1942.

1817. Ross, William G. Sunrise in Aztec land. Richmond, Va.,
        Presbyterian Committee on Publications, 1922. 244 p.
        -- Highly sympathetic, personal history of develop-
        ment of evangelical work from its beginnings.

1818. Taylor, Jack E. God's messengers to Mexico's masses.
        Eugene, Ore., Institute of Church Growth, 1962. 82
        p. -- A study of the religious significance of the
        braceros.

1819. Westrup, E. T. Principios, relato de la introducción del
        evangélico en México. México, CUPSA, 1953. 140 p.
        -- Westrup dedicates one chapter to the work of James
        Thomson in Mexico and relates faithfully his activi-
        ties. Some find the style exaggerated. Biographies
        of five other pioneers.

1820. Wheeler, W. Reginald. Modern Christianity in Mexico.
        Missionary review of the world, March 1925.

1821. _____, Dwight H. Day *and* James B. Rodgers. Modern missions
        in Mexico. Philadelphia, Westminster Press, 1925.
        -- Covers many aspects of Presbyterian work in Mexico
        between 1910 and 1925, although it is not a comprehen-
        sive history.

1822. Winton, George B. Mexico today: social, political and
        religious conditions. New York, Missionary Education
        Movement of the U.S. and Canada, 1913. Pamphlet.

1823. Wonderly, William L. *y* Jorge Lara Braud. Los evangélicos
        somos así. México, La Comision Evangélica de Estudios
        y Comité de Literature Evangélica de México, 1964.
        62 p. -- A socio-religious survey of some attitudes
        which characterize the Protestant community of Mexico
        City. English re-write *in* Practical anthropology 14:1
        January-February 1967.

Denominational History
See also p. 365.

Associate Reformed

1824. Dale, James G. Mexico and our missions. Lebanon, Pa.,
        Sowers, 1910. 272 p. -- A review of early begin-
        nings from 1879 to 1910.

1825. Floyd, Olive Beatrice. Doctora en México; the life of Dr.
       Katherine Dale. New York, Putnam, 1944. x ,240 p.

1826. _____. Katherine Neel Dale, medical missionary. Grand
       Rapids, Erdmann, 1943. 216 p.

Baptist

1827. Chastain, James Garvin. Thirty years in Mexico. El Paso,
       Texas, Baptist Publishing, 1927.

1828. Patterson, Frank W. Baptist missionary administration in
       Mexico. Th. D. thesis, Central Baptist Theological
       Seminary, Kansas City, 1957.

1829. Penton, Marvin J. Mexico's Reformation; a history of
       Mexican Protestantism from its inception to the
       present. Ph. D. thesis, University of Iowa, 1965.
       This entry belongs under section on Protestantism in
       General.

1830. Quigley, Robert E. American Catholic opinions of Mexican
       anticlericalism, 1910-36. Ph. D. thesis, University
       of Pennsylvania, Philadelphia, 1965. This entry
       properly belongs under section on Bibliography

1831. Treviño, Alejandro. Historia de los trabajos bautistas
       en México. El Paso, Texas, Casa Bautista de
       Publicaciones, 1939. 390 p. -- Dr. Montemayor is
       preparing a second volume to complete the history
       from 1930 to date.

Congregational

1832. Case, Alden B. (Cf. no. 1799).

Cumberland Presbyterian

1833. Sharp, J. M. A brief history of the work of the Cumber-
       land Presbyterian Church in Mexico, 1898. s.l.
       (n.d.).

Disciples

1834. McGavran, Donald. Church growth in Mexico. -- (Cf. no.
        1807).

Episcopal

1835. Barnett, Das Kelley, ed. The mission of the Anglican
        Mission to Mexico and Central America. Austin,
        Research Center in Christian Theology and Culture,
        1961.

1836. Creighton, Frank W. Mexico: a handbook of the missions
        of the Episcopal church. New York, National Council
        of Protestant-Episcopal Church, 1936. 111 p.

1837. Greenland, Fay Sharon. Religious reform in Mexico.
        Gainesville, University of Florida Press, 1958.
        124 p.

Mennonites

1838. Iretz, Jos. Winfield. Mennonite colonization in Mexico:
        an introduction. Akron, Pa., 1945. 40 p.

Methodist

1839. Báez Camargo, Gonzalo. Biografía de un templo. México,
        Ediciones Luminar, 1953. 109 p. -- History of a
        Methodist church in Mexico, once a Franciscan con-
        vent. An interesting study of the nationalization
        of church properties during the Revolution.

1840. Butler, John W. History of the Methodist Episcopal in
        Mexico. New York, Methodist Book Concern, 1918.
        153 p. -- Review of beginnings against the back-
        ground of the Mexican Revolution, mainly in anecdotal
        form.

1841. Drees, Ada M. C. Thirteen years in Mexico. New York,
        Abingdon, 1915. 276 p. -- Letters of Dr. Drees,
        Methodist missionary in Mexico and Argentina.

1842. Fox, Lillie F. History of women's work of the board of missions, Methodist Episcopal Church, South, 1879-1944. mss. 137 p. -- MML.

1843. Holding, Nannie E. A decade of mission life in Mexican mission homes. Nashville, Publishing House of Methodist Church South, 1895. 273 p. -- Human interest sketches of Methodist work in the 1880's.

1844. Libro conmemorativo de las bodas de diamante de la iglesia metodista de México, 1873-1948. México, Imprenta Nueva Educación, 1948. 302 p.

1845. Porter, Eugene O. A history of Methodism in Mexico. Ph. D. thesis, Ohio, 1939.

1846. Souvenir book of the golden anniversary of the Methodist Episcopal church in Mexico, 1879-1944. Mexico, CUPSA, 1924. 205 p. -- MML.

1847. Thomas, Ethel. The industrial school - escuela para Alarcón. Abiline, Ka., Shodinger and Wilson (n.d.). 148 p. -- MML.

1848. Verduzco,_____. Bosquejo histórico del metodismo mexicano. Nashville, Abingdon (n.d.).

1849. Wood, Thomas B. Report on a tour of consultation in Mexico. s.l., 1882. -- mss and an appendix of documents referred to in the Report, 1882. Of special interest is his case against recognition of "Romish orders" and admission of "converted papists."

Presbyterian

1850. Bennett, Charles. Tinder in Tabasco; a study of church growth in tropical Mexico. Grand Rapids, Michigan, Eerdman, 1968. 213 p. -- A good study of an area of significant Protestant growth. Complete bibliography.

1854. Minutes of the national Presbyterian church of Mexico, 1901-. *Missionary review of the world*, November 1930.

Roman Catholic Publications on Protestantism

1856.   Carillo y Ancona, Crescencio.   Orden circular contra la
        propaganda protestante... Mérida, Imprenta de la
        Revista de Mérica (n.d.).   -- He was Bishop of
        Yucatán, 1837-79.

1857.   Cassaretto, Mary A.   El movimiento protestante en México,
        1940-55.   M.A. thesis, Universidad Nacional de
        México, 1956.   mimeographed.   -- Rather detailed
        study on nature and growth of Protestant movement
        during this period.   Limited by lack of access to
        denominational records.   Study is of limited value,
        but is only one of its type available.

1858.   Esquivel Obregón, Toribio.   La propaganda protestante en
        México a la luz del derecho international.   México,
        Publicaciones de la Academia Mexicana de Jurispru-
        dencia y Legislación (ca. 1940).   67 p.

1859.   González, José B. *y otros*.   El protestantismo en México.
        México, Buena Prensa, 1946.   173 p.

1860.   Planchet, Regis.   La intervención protestante en México
        y Sud América.   El Paso, Revista Católica, 1928.
        199 p.

1861.   Rivera, Pedro, S.J.   Instituciones protestantes en México.
        México, Editorial Jus, 1962.   -- Lists Protestant
        denominations in Mexico, location and size of their
        work, and type of Protestant educational institutions;
        examines basis of Protestant financial support and
        significance of Protestant growth in Mexico.

1862.   _____.   Protestantismo mejicano; su desarrolo y estado
        actual.   México, Editorial Jus, 1961.   -- A signifi-
        cant study although polemical at some points.

1863.   Solé, Manual.   Las armas del protestantismo.   México,
        Imprenta de "El Tiempo", 1894.   146 p.

Periodicals
See also p. 369.

Past Publications

1864. El abogado (or El abogado cristiano). Organ od the
      Methodist Episcopal Church of Mexico. Published
      with *El Faro* from 1919-1928 as *Mundo Cristiano*.

1865. Mexican moments. Presbyterian Church, U.S.A.

1866. Antorcha evangelica. A Presbyterian publication from
      1875-1877 in Zacatecas by Thompson and Phillips.

Present Publications

1867. El amanecer. Aptdo. Postal 13-257, México, D.F. Monthly.

1868. La Bíblia en México. Aptdo. 1373, México 1, D.F. --
      Official organ of the Bible Agency in Mexico.
      Semi-annually.

1869. Charm and challenge of Chiapas. 475 Riverside Drive, New
      York. -- Organ of the Reformed Church in America.

1870. Down Mexico way. United Presbyterian Church, U.S.A.

1871. El evangelista mexicano. Organ of the Methodist Church
      of Mexico.

1872. El faro. Organ of the National Presbyterian Church of
      Mexico. Apartado 21-965, Mexico, D.F. 1885-1914;
      1916-1919; 1928-. Complete collection available at
      Presbyterian Theological Seminary, Mexico, D.F.
      Microfilm collection at LAC-UT of v. 1-9 (1885-1893);
      v. 13-17 (1897-98); v. 26 (1910). El Faro was
      published from 1919-1928 together with El Abogado as
      Mundo Cristiano. Also *Nuevo Faro* was published 1921-
      1928.

1873. El heraldo. Organ of Iglesia Episcopal Mexicana. 1939-45
      copies in CHS.

1874. El noticiero de la fé. Aptdo. 111, Guatemala City.
      Monthly. Includes Lutheran work in Mexico.

Problems Related to U.S.-Mexico International Border

1875. D'Antonio, William V. Influentials in two border cities.
      South Bend, Ind., Notre Dame Press (n.d.).

1876. Madsen, William. Society and health in the lower Rio
       Grande valley. Austin, Hogg Foundation of the
       University of Texas (n.d.).

1877. Rubel, Arthur J. Across the tracks. Austin, University
       of Texas Press, 1966. -- A study of the structures
       of Mexican American society by an outstanding
       Mexican Americanist, Professor at Notre Dame Univer-
       sity.

1878. Samora, Julian, ed. La raza - forgotten Americans. South
       Bend, Ind., Notre Dame Press (n.d.). -- Extensive
       lists of bibliographies.

                      THE INSULAR LATIN CARIBBEAN

                           Caribbean Region
                           See also p. 370.

1879. Blanshard, Paul. Democracy and the empire in the
       Caribbean. s.l. (n.d.).

1880. Fagg, John E. Cuba, Haiti and Domican Republic. Engle-
       wood Cliffs, N.J., Prentice Hall, 1965. -- A
       Spectrum pocketbook.

1881. Guerin, Daniel. The West Indies and their future. London,
       Dodson, 1961.

1882. Munro, Dana G. Intervention and dollar diplomacy in the
       Caribbean, 1900-21. Princeton, N.J., Princeton,
       University Press, 1964. 553 p.

1883. _____. The United States and the Caribbean area. Boston,
       World Peace Founcation, 1934. 316 p. -- Includes
       treaties between the United States and the Caribbean
       states.

1884. Wilgus, A. Curtis, ed. Caribbean series. Gainesville,
       University of Florida Press, 1950-66.
       v. 1. The Caribbean at mid-century.
       v. 2. The Caribbean: people, problems and prospects.
       v. 3. The Caribbean: contemporary trends.
       v. 4. The Caribbean: its economy.
     **v. 5. The Caribbean: its culture.
      *v. 6. The Caribbean: its political problems.

```
*v.  7. The Caribbean:  contemporary international
                        relations.
 v.  8. The Caribbean:  British, Dutch, French and
                        the United States.
 v.  9. The Caribbean:  natural resources.
 v. 10. The Caribbean:  contemporary education.
 v. 11. The Caribbean:  the Central American area.
 v. 12. The Caribbean:  contemporary Colombia.
 v. 13. The Caribbean:  Venezuela development, a case
                        study.
 v. 14. The Caribbean:  Mexico today.
 v. 15. The Caribbean:  health today.
 v. 16. The Caribbean:  current United States relations.
 v. 17. The Caribbean:  its hemispheric role.
```

*   v. 6 and 7 have good sections on "Caribbean bibliography."

**   Chapter by W. S. Rycroft, "The contribution of Protestantism in the Caribbean" in Part V together with two other chapters on religion and culture.

Cuba
See also p. 370.

Bibliography
See also p. 370.

1885. Two outstanding works are by the distinguished biblio-
      grapher Dr. Carlos Manuel Treller, *Bibliografía
      cubana del siglo XIX* and *his* Bibliografía cubana del
      siglo XX. Current bibliography listed recently has
      been reprinted by the Revista bibliografía cubana.
      Guia de bibliotecas de la república de Cuba (La
      Habana) 1965 is an informative internal document in
      national and provincial libraries.

General Background
See also p. 371.

1886. Cuban economic research project. José R. Alvarez Díaz,
      chrm. Gainesville, University of Florida Press,
      1963.

      Labor conditions in communist Cuba. 1963. 158 p.
      Social security in Cuba. 1963.

A study of Cuba;   the colonial and republican periods,
the Socialist experiment. 1965. 774 p.

1887. Cuadernos (Cuba) marzo-abril 1961. -- Special issue;
supplement to no. 47. Articles by Cuban intellectuals.

1888. A decade of revolution and communism: IV institute on
the dynamics of leadership in Cuba. San Germán,
CISLA, 1967. -- Papers and addresses.

1889. Dewart, Leslie. Christianity and revolution; the lesson
of Cuba. New York, Praeger, 1963. -- Critique of
the role of the Roman Catholic Church by a Roman
Catholic.

1890. Goldenberg, Boris. The Cuban revolution and Latin
America. New York, Praeger, 1965. 376 p. --
Considers the Cuban revolution as perhaps the most
important event of this century in Latin America.
Quotes Haya de la Torre: "For Europe imperialism
is the last stage of capitalism; for Latin America
it is the first."

1891. Jenks, L. H. Our Cuban colony. New York, Vanguard,
1928. -- Revealing study of American economic
dominance in Cuba.

1892. Leuschenring, Emilio R. de. Martí y las religiones. La
Habana, Acción, 1941. 64 p.

1893. Mackay, John A. Cuba revisited. *The Christian century*
12 February 1964. -- See also *his* A fresh look at
Cuba, *ibid*. 5 August 1964.

1894. Matthews, Herbert L. The Cuban story. New York,
Braziller, 1961. 318 p.

1895. _____. Return to Cuba. *Hispanic American report* 1964.

1896. Mills, C. Wright. Listen yankee. New York, Ballantine,
1960. 192 p. -- Paperback and original publication
by McGraw-Hill.

1897. Pflaum, Irving Peter. Tragic island; how communism came
to Cuba. Englewood Cliffs, N.J., Prentice Hall,
1961. 196 p.

1898.   Política internacional. Instituto de Política Interna-
        cional, Ministerio de Relaciones Exteriores, La
        Habana, 1963-. Monthly.

1899.   Rankin, Victor L. Aspects of the Cuban mind. S.T.M.
        thesis, Union Theological Seminary, New York, 1957.
        -- Deals with main Catholic tradition through Spain
        and Cuban modifications especially in Valon.

1900.   Rivero, Nicolas. Castro's Cuba; an American dilemma.
        Washington, D.C., LUCE, 1962.

1901.   Robertson, C. Alton. The political role of the Protes-
        tants in Cuba, 1958-1962. *Occasional bulletin*
        18:1, 2 January-February 1967. -- MRL. Two parts.
        An impartial analysis of a complex subject.

1902.   Seers, Dudley, ed. Cuba: the economic and social
        revolution. Chapel Hill, N.C., University of North
        Carolina Press, 1962. 432 p. -- A serious work
        done in Cuba by British and Chilean researchers.

1903.   Smith, Robert F., ed. Background to revolution; the
        development of modern Cuba. New York, Knopf, 1966.
        224 p. -- Twenty-five essays on ideological,
        sociological and economic topics including a brief
        chronology of Cuba history.

1904.   _____. The United States and Cuba, business and diplomacy,
        1917-60. s.l. (n.d.).

1905.   Tellon, Edwin. An eye on Cuba. New York, Harcourt, Brace
        and World, 1966. 291 p.

Protestantism in General
See also p. 376.

1906.   Davis, J. Merle. The Cuban church in a sugar economy.
        London, IMC, 1942.

1907.   Rodríguez, Alfonso Alejandro. Implications of the
        doctrine of justification by faith; a comparative
        study on justification in the Roman Catholic and
        Reformed theology with reference to the Protestant
        movement in Cuba... Th. D. thesis, Princeton Theo-
        logical Seminary, 1955. viii, 243 p. -- States
        some teaching of the Roman Catholic and Reformed
        theology on the doctrine of justification by faith,

offers some reflections on the theological and
ethical implications of this doctrine in both of
these traditions. Examination also of the doctrine
in the teachings of the Council of Trent and in
several of the early Protestant catechisms and
confessions.

Denominational History
See also p. 377.

Baptist

1908. Delgado, Primitivo. The history of the Southern Baptist
        mission in Cuba to 1945. Th. D. thesis, Southern
        Baptist Theological Seminary, Louisville, Ky., 1948.

1909. Greer, Harold E., Jr. History of the Southern Baptist
        mission work in Cuba, 1886-1916. Ph. D. thesis,
        University of Alabama, 1965.

1910. Rodríguez Garcia, Alfredo S. La obra bautista en Cuba
        occidental. La Habana, Imprenta Bautista (n.d.).
        172 p.

Episcopal

1911. Alard, Leopoldo J. Proceso histórico de la iglesia
        episcopal en Cuba. mss, Seminário Episcopal del
        Caríbe, Carolina, Puerto Rico, 1966.

1912. Blankingship, Rt. Rev. A. Hugo. Cuba celebrates fiftieth
        anniversary. *Forth*, April 1954. -- Historical
        review.

Methodist

1913. Mitchell, Paul D. Cuba calling; a golden anniversary
        volume. Buenos Aires, Imprenta Metodista, 1950.
        135 p. -- A narrative survey, with biographical
        sketches.

1914. Neblett, S. A. Methodism in Cuba; the first thirteen
        years. Wesleyan College, Ga., 1966. 78 p.
        (Wesleyan studies, no. 1). -- Written by a missionary
        pioneer since 1902. Chairman of the "Protestant
        Conference," the first inter-denominational

organization formed in Cuba. This small volume is
part of a 347 p. typescript "Fifty years of Methodist
in Cuba." Copies of this script are available at
Emory University and Scarritt College.

Presbyterian

1915. Cepeda, Rafael. El forjador de hombres; vista y hechos de
 Roberto L. Wharton. La Habana, La Progresiva, 1953.
 133 p.

Periodicals
See also p. 377.

1916. El evangelista cubano. Official organ of the Iglesia
 Metodista. Salud 218, La Habana.

Dominican Republic
See also p. 378.

Bibliography

1917. Henríquez Ureña, Pedro. Bibliografía literaria de Santo
 Domingo. 1929. (Reportorio americano, no. 7, 12,
 14).

1918. A good bibliography is in Sumner Welles's *Naboth's vine-*
 yard... as listed below.

General Background
See also p. 378.

1919. Clark, James A. Church and crisis in the Dominican
 Republic. New York, Newman, 1966. Deals mainly
 with the role of the Church in the political and
 social crisis, especially from 1960-1966.

1920. Crassweller, Robert D. Trujillo: the life and times of
 a Caribbean dictator. New York, Macmillan, 1966.
 -- A carefully researched and detailed study of the
 Trujillo period but fails to probe the agony of the
 country's problems. Includes an excellent bibliography p. 451-59.

1921. Galíndez, Jesús de. La era de Trujillo. Santiago de
      Chile, Editorial del Pacifico, 1956. -- A signifi-
      cant study of Trujillo's rise to, use of, and
      perpetuation of power. Contains summary of earlier
      Dominican history but is incomplete since it was
      terminated before Trujillo's assassination in 1961.

1922. Incháustegui, J. M. Historia deomincana. Ciudad
      Trujillo, Impresora Dominicana, 1955. 2 v. --
      First volume and a brief part of second carry the
      history of the Republic from the discovery to time
      of Trujillo. Second volume is largely Trujillo
      propaganda.

1923. Lugo, Américo. Historia de Santo Domingo, 1556-1608.
      Ciudad Trujillo, Editorial Librería Dominicana,
      1952. -- Written in 1938. Excellent historical
      interpretation of an important period in Dominican
      colonial history. Significant comments on church-
      state relationships.

1924. Marrero Aristy, Ramón. La república dominicana. Ciudad
      Trujillo, Editora El Caribe, 1957. 2 v. -- Good
      survey history of the Dominican Republic from
      discovery until 1930. Excellent picture of church-
      state relations in colonial and early Independence
      periods.

1925. Martin, John B. Overtaken by events. Garden City, N.Y.,
      Doubleday, 1966. -- A good survey of events from
      the death of Trujillo until April 1966.

1926. Rodríguez Demorizi, Emilio. Relaciones históricas de
      Santo Domingo. Ciudad Trujillo, Archivo General de
      la Nación, Editora Montalvo, 1957. -- Important
      documents from the colonial period. Useful for
      research on early Roman Catholicism and church-state
      relations. Includes correspondence of significance.

1927. Schoenrich, Otto. Santo Domingo; a country with a future.
      New York, Macmillan, 1918. xiv, 418 p.

1928. Welles, Sumner. Naboth's vineyard; the Dominican Republic,
      1844-1924. New York, Payson and Clark, 1928. 2 v.
      Title and text in Spanish. -- Excellent survey by a
      political scientist of the internal confusion and
      foreign intervention in the political affairs of the
      Republic.

Protestantism in General
See also p. 380.

1929. Drury, Marion. Mission triumphs in Puerto Rico and Santo
Domingo. Ponce, P. R., 1924.

1930. Inman, Samuel G. Through Santo Domingo and Haiti. New
York, 1919. -- A brief study prepared by the author
prior to the establishment of the unified work of
Methodist, Presbyterian and E. U. Brethren denomina-
tions in 1922. Contains remarks of Roman Catholic,
Episcopal and African Methodist work.

1931. Johnson, Pearl V. Our neighbors the Dominicans. Winona
Lake, Ind., Women's Missionary Society, Free Methodist
Church, 1924.

1932. Lajara Romero, Juan José. Situación religiosa en la
República Dominicana. B. C. thesis, Seminario
Evangélico de Puerto Rico, Río Piedras, 1945. 72 p.
-- Rather sketchy.

1933. Wipfler, William L. The churches of the Dominican Republic
in light of history; a study of the root causes of
current problems. S.T.M. thesis, Union Theological
Seminary, New York, 1964. Cuernavaca, CIDOC, 1967.
214 p. Sondeos series no. 10. -- A detailed study
study of Christian bodies at work in the Dominican
Republic with special emphasis on the Roman Catholic,
Dominican Evangelical and Episcopal churches. A
history of each of these bodies is given with an
analysis of contemporary problems as they are related
to past history and the present socio-political
situation.

Denominational History
See also p. 381.

Iglesia Evangélica Dominicana

1934. Montalvo Francisco, Sadrach. Responsibilidad social de
la iglesia Evangélica dominicana. B.D. thesis,
Seminario Evangélico de Puerto Rico, 1965. -- A
study of several denominational streams which influences the Iglesia Evangelical Dominicana and the
image the public holds of the denomination.

1935. Morgan, Barney. Serving the least of these. New York,
         Board of Christian Work in Santo Domingo, 1949.

1936. Morgan, Carol M. The tale of two islands. New York,
         BNM-PCUSA, 1952.

1937. Odell, Edward. It came to pass. New York, BNM-UPCUSA,
         1952. -- Includes excellent summary, p. 147 ff.,
         on early missionary work begun by churches of Puerto
         Rico.

1938. Thomas, Felix Manuel. Actas de la asemblea evangélica
         dominicana en la misión renovadora. B.D. thesis,
         Seminario Evangélico de Puerto Rico, 1965.

Episcopal

1940. Moore, Jos. G. A study of the Episcopal church in the
         missionary district of the Dominican Republic. New
         York, 1959. -- Detailed survey of the work of the
         Episcopal church by congregations. Contains histor-
         ical sketches, statistics, maps to cover Episcopal
         work, as well as projections for future development.

Periodicals
See also p. 382.

1941. Journals of convocation, 1959-. Episcopal.

1942. The spirit of mission, 1839-1939. Episcopal. Contains
         reports of missionaries. Important sources for
         early history.

1943. Nuestro amigo. Iglesia Evangélica Dominicana.

Haiti
See also p. 382.

Bibliography

1944. A good bibliography in J. L. Williams' *Voodoos and
         obeahs...*, below.

General Background
See also p. 382.

1945. Breathett, George A. The religious missions in colonial
      French Saint Domingue. Ph. D. thesis, Iowa Univer-
      sity, 1954.

1946. Williams, Jos. L. Voodoos and obeahs; phases of West
      Indian witchcraft. New York, Dial, 1933. xvii,
      257 p. -- See also El voudou y cristianismo en
      Haiti. Colección Sondeos. Is a study of
      voudouistic influence and tactics used in
      evangelism. A case in modern syncretism in Latin
      America.

Protestantism in General

1947. Oyala, Paul Richard. Some implications of Haitian culture
      from leadership education in the evangelical church
      in Haiti. M.A. thesis, Kennedy School of Missions,
      Hartford Seminary Foundation, Conn., 1956.

1948. Pressoir, Catts. Le protestantisme haitien. Port-au-
      Prince, Imprimerie de la Société Biblique et des
      livres religieu d'Haiti, 1946. 3 v. -- v. 1. and
      v. 2. by a Methodist and one of the most erudite of
      Haitians. v. 3. which dealt with the Baptists and
      others was unpublished when the author died and the
      manuscript is apparently lost.

1949. Vilaire, Maurice, comp. Prosateurs protestants haitiens.
      Port-au-Prince, Impretimerie des Antilles, 1964.
      (Premiér). -- A biographical sketch of poets and
      writers, excerpts from their works and a listing of
      their published and unpublished works. Also a book
      of poetry compiled by the same author.

Denominational History

Baptist

1950. Detweiler, Charles S. The waiting isles. Valley Forge,
      Pa., Judson, 1930. -- Chapter on the Baptists in
      Haiti and two Baptist pioneers, Elie Marc and
      Nossirél Lhérisson.

1951. Stevens, Dorothy. Neighbor voices. Philadelphia, Pa.,
      Judson, 1958. 21 p.

1952. Stupka, V. P. Go y. Chicago, Czechoslovak Baptist
      Convention of the U.S. and Canada, ca. 1950.

Episcopal

1953. Dalzon, W. Coup d'oeil sur l'histoire de l'Eglise
      épiscopale d'Haiti, 1911-38. mss, Seminario Episco-
      pal del Caribe, Cardino, Puerto Rico, 1964.

1954. Millien, J. E. Une idée du premier cinguantenaire de
      l'Eglise épiscopale d'Haiti, 1861-1911. mss,
      Seminario Episcopal de Caribe, Carolina, Puerto
      Rico, 1964.

1955. A short history of the Episcopal church of Haiti. New
      York, Overseas Dept. of the Executive Council of
      the Episcopal Church (n.d.). Mimeographed.

Methodist

1956. See volumes 1 and 2 of *Le protestantisme Haitien* by
      Catts Pressoir.

Other Denominations

1957. Pudney, Edwin J. Haiti, white already to harvest.
      Toronto, Unevangelized Fields Missions, 1964.

Periodicals

Past Publications

1958. La bonne nouvelle.

1959. La concorde.

1960. Le courrier baptiste.

1961. L'écho de l'orthodoxie.

1962. Haiti-évangile.

1963.　La jeunesse.

1964.　Le lien.

1965.　Le messager évangélique.

1966.　La mission.

1967.　Le Phare.

1968.　Zétoile métodiste.

Puerto Rico
See also p. 383.

Bibliography
See also p. 383.

1969.　Anuario bibliográfico puertorriqueño.　G. Velásquez, ed.
　　　　　Río Piedras, Universidad de Puerto Rico, 1957-58.
　　　　　1964.

1970.　Bibliografía puertorriqueña: de fuentes para investiga-
　　　　　ciones sociales, 1930-45.　Augusto Bird, ed.　Río
　　　　　Piedras, Centro de Investigaciones Sociales, Universi-
　　　　　dad de Puerto Rico, 1946.　547 p.　mimeographed.

1971.　Munden, Kennecott *and* Milton Greenbaum, comp.　Records of
　　　　　the insular affairs, relating to Puerto Rico: a
　　　　　list of selected files.　Washington, D.C., National
　　　　　Archives, 1943.　47 p.

1972.　Pedreira, Antonio S.　Bibliografía puertorriqueña, 1493-
　　　　　1930.　Madrid, Imprenta de la Librería, Casa Editorial
　　　　　Hernando, S.A., 1932.　707 p.　-- The standard
　　　　　reference work for the Island.

1973.　Puerto Rico and the Puerto Ricans.　Clarence Senior *and*
　　　　　Josephine de Román, comp.　New York, Dept. of Labor
　　　　　of Puerto Rico, 1951.　Mimeographed.

1974.　The southeastern Latin Americanist.　September 1958.　--
　　　　　Listing of over 125 Ph. D. theses on Puerto Rico.

General Background
See also p. 383.

1975. Anderson, Robert W. Party politics in Puerto Rico. Palo
        Alto, Stanford University Press, 1965. 269 p. --
        A survey of party politics 1940-64.

1976. Fenton, Jerry F. Understanding the religious background
        of the Puerto Rican. B. D. thesis, Union Theological
        Seminary, New York, 1964. -- Excellent bibliography
        of available materials in English in relation to
        Catholicism, spiritism and Protestantism. Cuernavaca,
        Mexico, CIDOX, 1969. Sondeos no. 52.

1977. Lewis, Oscar. La vida: a Puerto Rican family in the
        culture of poverty. New York, Random House, 1965.
        669 p. -- A shattering account of three generations
        of the Ríos family in the slums of San Juan and the
        Puerto Rican enclaves of New York.

1978. Lockett, Edwin P. The Puerto Rico problem. New York,
        Exportation, 1964. 190 p. -- An independent study
        by the Richmond Professional Institute.

1979. Mills, Charles W. The Puerto Rican Journey. New York,
        Columbia University Press, 1950. -- New York City's
        newest migrants.

1980. Mintz, Sidney. Worker in the cane; a Puerto Rican life
        history. New Haven, Conn., Yale University Press,
        1960. -- Life story of a sugar cane worker who
        becomes a Pentecostal: includes considerable detail
        about his conversion.

1981. Monclava, L. Cruz. Historia de Puerto Rico, siglo XIX.
        San Juan, 1958. 3 v.

1982. Page, Homer. Puerto Rico: the quiet revolution. New
        York, Viking, 1963. 175 p. -- Largely black and
        white photographs but also a good introduction to
        problems and realities of the Island today.

1983. Steward, Julian H., et al. The people of Puerto Rico:
        a study in social snthropology. Urbana, Ill.,
        University of Illinois Press, 1956. -- Penetrating
        comments in relation to the people and their history
        in relation to spiritism, evangelicalism and Roman
        Catholicism.

1984. Tugwell, Rexford G. The stricken land. New York,
       Doubleday, 1947. 704 p. -- Story of Puerto Rico
       by a former governor of the Island.

               Protestantism in General
                  See also p. 385.

1985. Alvarez Pérez, Carmelo. ¿Como podrá el evangélico ayudar
       en la solución de los problemas fundamentales del
       campesino puertorriqueño? B.D. thesis, Seminario
       Evangélico, Río Piedras, Puerto Rico, 1934. --
       Discusses such problems as self-support, denomina-
       tionalism, and relationship of mission boards and
       Puerto Rican churches.

1986. Bidot Pamias, Juan. The origin and development of
       Christian education in Puerto Rico. M.A. thesis,
       McCormick Seminary, 1940. -- Thorough treatment of
       all phases of educational work.

1987. Cooperative planning conference, April 13-18, 1959. San
       Germán, Universidad Interamericana. mimeographed.
       -- Reports tracing past history with plans for pro-
       jecting the work in the future.

1988. Custer, Watson S. A decade of church-state relations in
       Puerto Rico, 1952-62. Ph. D. thesis, Dept. of
       Religion, Temple University, 1965. -- Clear, pene-
       trating analysis of decade, plus overview of previous
       eras.

1989. Grose, Howear B. Advance in the Antilles; the new era in
       Cuba and Puerto Rico. New York, Missionary Education
       Movement, 1911. -- Early statistics on missions in
       each country (p. 244-45), description of religious
       situation upon the entrance of Protestantism in 1898
       and terms of the comity agreement.

1990. Handy, Robert T. We witness together; a history of
       cooperative efforts in Puerto Rico.

1991. Hill, Chas. Edwin. Christian work in Puerto Rico, 1898-
       1918. M.A. thesis, Columbia University, New York,
       1919. -- Brief synthesis of work of historic
       denominations.

1992. Material de estudio para nueva estrategia de la iglesia
       en Puerto Rico. July 1965. Mimeographed. --

Prepared for the Comisión de Estudio y Planificación
Eclesiástica de Puerto Rico.

1993. McAfee, J. Ernest. Today in Puerto Rico. *The missionary
review of the world* 38:577-85 August 1915. --
Contains a map of the comity agreement prior to its
change in the 1920's.

1994. McLean, R. H. *and* Grace P. Williams. Old Spain in new
America. New York, Association, 1916. -- Details
of founding of early medical and educational institutions in Puerto Rico.

1995. Mead, Frank. On our own doorstep. New York, Friendship
Press, 1948. -- "The whole story of Protestant home
missions in Puerto Rico will never be read in
statistics, but in the working of Christian leaven."

1996. Mercado, Juan Emilio. Practical methods of evangelism
for Puerto Rico. S.T.M. thesis, Union Theological
Seminary, New York, 1956. -- Description of Puerto
Rican society and churches; review of evangelism in
continental United States among Puerto Ricans.

1997. Mier, Elpidio de. Rompiendo el molde; episódios de una
vida. Madrid, privately published, 1923. 3 v.
(Biblioteca cristiana). -- One of the first
expressions of "native" vs. American missionary
friction. The author was a controversial figure
across decades. "Only about a dozen American
missionaries have been really cultured ... ni ... a
estilo de San Pablo que pueden ir a una academia a
sostener al doctrina que propagan..." (p. 79-80).

1998. Morales Alamo, Robert. A consideration of some factors
involved in the development of church planning in
Puerto Rico. M.A. thesis, Butler University,
Indianapolis, 1964. -- A thorough study of the
distribution of Protestants in Puerto Rico; analysis
of some of the Council and non-Council church distribution; tables on average family income, etc.,
in different municipalities. Offers material for
additional research in correlation and interpretation.

1999. Morgan, Carol McAfee. Rim of the Caribbean. New York,
Friendship Press, 1942. -- A review of missionary
work of several denominations in the Caribbean.

2000.   Moore, Donald T.   Puerto Rico para Cristo; a history of
        the progress of the evangelical missions on the
        island of Puerto Rico.   Th. D. thesis, Southwestern
        Baptist Theological Seminary, 1967.   -- First com-
        prehensive study of Protestantism in Puerto Rico
        with complete bibliography.   Cuernavaca, Mexico,
        CIDOC, 1969.   304 p.   Sondeos no. 43.

2001.   Rosa Guzmán, Carlos.   El periodismo evangélico en Puerto
        Rico.   B.D. thesis, Seminario Evangélico, Río Piedras,
        Puerto Rico, 1952.   -- Author documents most of the
        Protestant periodicals since early 1900's with quite
        precise dates of the periods in which each was
        published.

2002.   Sáenz, Michael.   Economic aspects of church development;
        a study of the policies and procedures of the major
        Protestant groups in Puerto Rico from 1898-1957.
        Ph. D. thesis, University of Pennsylvania, Philadel-
        phia, 1961.   180 p.   Microfilmed and xerographed.
        -- Study of some major Protestant groups containing
        year by year statistics of the churches from
        beginning.

2003.   Santana, Jiménez, Benjamín.   La iglesia y el estado en
        Puerto Rico.   B.D. thesis, Seminario Evangélico,
        Río Piedras, Puerto Rico (n.d.).   218 p.   --
        Bibliografía especial lists articles in principal
        newspapers of the Island related to the organization
        of Partido Acción Cristiano.

2004.   Seda, Angel L.   Implications for Puerto Rico in a study
        of the hospital chaplaincy in the U.S.   Ph. D.
        thesis, Columbia University, New York, 1958.

2005.   Shope, John H.   Los puertorriqueños y la Biblia.
        Universidad Interamericana, San Germán, Puerto
        Rico, 1962.   -- A survey of the use and accessability
        of the Scriptures in Puerto Rico.

2006.   Vasquez Galloza, Tomás.   Características de los campesinos
        puertorriqueños y sus implicaciones para la educación
        cristiana.   B.D. thesis, Seminario Evangélico, Río
        Piedras, Puerto Rico, 1965.   116 p.   -- Written by a
        Puerto Rican minister "quien ha pulsado las más
        últimas emociones del campesino."   The results of
        his questionnaires on campesino attitudes are

interesting. (Refers to Fanfrías, Ernesto Juan.
Conversao en el Batay. San Juan, Editorial Club de
la Prensa, 1958.)

Denominational History
See also p. 385.

American Baptist Convention

2007. Beers, G. Pitt. Ministry to turbulant America: a history
of the American Baptist home mission society covering
its fifth quarter century. Philadelphia, Judson,
1957. -- Short summary of significant events between
1932-57.

2008. Dávila, Jaime E. A translation of selected chapters from
an unpublished history of Baptist mission work in
Puerto Rico, by José L. Delgado. mss, Central
Baptist Theological Seminary (n.d.).

2009. Detweiler, Charles S. The waiting isles; Baptist
missions in the Caribbean. Philadelphia, Judson,
1930. -- Discusses the early periods with frankness
that is unusual for missions publications.

2010. Riggs, G. A. Baptists in Puerto Rico, 1899-1939; brief
historical notes of forty years of Baptist work in
Puerto Rico. Ponce, Puerto Rico Evangélico, 1939.
-- Contains interesting pictures and historical data.

Christian and Missionary Alliance

2011. Varetto, Juan C. Héroes y mártires de la obra misionera.
Buenos Aires, Junta de Publicaciones de la Convención
Evangélica Bautista (n.d.). -- Contains concise
biography of Villamil, the founder of Puerto Rican
work.

Church of God (Cleveland, Tenn.)

2012. Conn, Charles W. Where the saints have trod; a history
of Church of God missions. Cleveland, Tenn., Pathway
Press, 1959. -- Most complete information available.

Church of the Nazarene

2013.   Prescott, Lyle. Light in Latin America. Kansas City,
        Nazarene Publishing House, 1961. -- Latest histori-
        cal treatment available of work.

Disciples of Christ

2014.   Carpenter, Vere C. Puerto Rican disciples; a personal
        narrative of fifty years with Christ in the island
        of enchantment. Tampa, Fla., Christian Press, 1960.
        -- Sub-title accurately describes evangelistic phase
        of Disciples' work.

2015.   Convención cuadragésima primera; cincuentenario de las
        iglesias de los discípulos de Cristo en Puerto Rico.
        Bayamón, P.R., Imprenta Moreno Hijos, 1949. -- Brief
        essays by Puerto Rican church leaders touching on
        different facets of work in the past 50 years.

2016.   McGavran, Donald A. Un estudio de la vida y crecimiento
        de la iglesia de los Discípulos de Cristo en Puerto
        Rico. Indianapolis, Board of Foreign Missions, UCMS,
        1955. Also English edition.

2017.   Morton, C. Manly. Kingdom building in Puerto Rico; a
        study of fifty years of Christian service. Indian-
        apolis, UCMS, 1949. -- The definitive history for
        fifty years.

Episcopal Church

2018.   Burset, V. The fifty years of the Protestant Episcopal
        church in Puerto Rico. B.D. thesis, General Theo-
        logical Seminary, New York, 1957. -- The careful
        history of first fifty years.

Iglesia de Diós Pentecostal

2019.   Hodges, Serena M., ed. Look on the fields; a missionary
        survey. Springfield, Gospel Publishing House, 1956.
        -- A brief view of a few phases of development of
        work.

2020.   Lugo, Juan L. Pentecostés en Puerto Rico o la vida de un
        misionero. San Juan, Puerto Rico Gospel Press, 1951.

-- An autobiographical eulogy and apology by one of
the early missionaries.

Mennonite Church

2021. Holsinger, Justus G. Serving rural Puerto Rico; a history
       of eight years of service by the Mennonite church.
       1952. Scottsdale, Pa., Herald Press, 1952. --
       Exhaustive study of initial years of Mennonite social
       service and evangelistic work.

Methodist Church

2022. Sprinkle, Henry, et al. Spanish doorways; American
       Methodists and the evangelical mission among Spanish-
       speaking neighbors. New York, World Outlook Press,
       1964. -- Not a history; one chapter with some past
       historical data but primarily showing present situa-
       tion of mission.

2023. Wellman, Coe R. A plan for the in-service training of
       teachers and leaders in the Methodist school in
       Puerto Rico. Ph. D. thesis, Columbia University,
       New York, 1936.

Seventh-Day Adventists

2024. Amundsen, Wesley. The advent message in Inter-America.
       -- Cf. no.   Provides concise information about
       first Puerto Rican colporteur and brief glimpse of
       missionary work in the early period.

2025. Neufeld., Don F., ed. Seventh-day adventist encyclopedia,
       v. 10. Washington, D.C., Review and Herald, 1955.
       -- A bird's eye view of development of work.

United Evangelical Church (formerly United Brethren in Christ
   and Congregational Christian churches)

2026. Arturet Meléndez, Antonio. Desarrollo histórico de la
       iglesia evangélica unida de Puerto Rico; análisis de
       un experimento. B.D. thesis, Seminario Evangélico,
       Río Piedras, P.R., 1965. -- Penetrating historical
       study of church union which has been unable to
       accomplish its ideal.

United Lutheran Church

2027. Swanson, S. Hjalmar. Foundation for tomorrow; a century
       of progress in Augustana world missions. Minneapolis,
       BWM, Augustana Lutheran Church, 1960. -- Brief
       historical account of beginnings.

United Presbyterian Church

2028. Colón Bonet, Victor M. Sostenimiento propio de la iglesia
       presbiteriana en Puerto Rico. B.D. thesis, Seminario
       Evangélico, Río Piedras, 1942. -- Frankly discusses
       church's failure to attain self-support.

2029. Lugo-Alvarez, José G. Bases para un programa de planifica-
       ción eclesiástica del presbiterio de Puerto Rico en
       la zona metropolitiana de San Juan. B.D. thesis,
       Seminario Evangélico, Río Piedras, 1965. -- Contains
       also maps and charts of growth patterns of other
       historic denominations.

2030. Odell, Edward A. It came to pass. New York, BNM-PCUSA,
       1952. -- One chapter, but most accessible single
       account of the origin of work in Puerto Rico.

2031. Rosado, Domingo I. La política del Presbiterio de Puerto
       Rico en el desarrollo de la obra en la zona rural.
       B.D. thesis, Seminario Evangélico, Río Piedras, 1958.
       -- Closely examines history and practices of rural
       work of Presbyterians.

2032. Zayas Mercado, Luis. Recursos de la iglesia presbiteriana
       para servir a la comunidad puertorriqueña. B.D.
       thesis, Seminario Evangélico, Río Piedras, 1956.
       31 p.

Defensores de la Fe

2033. Korrell, Geraldine W. Rodriguez of Puerto Rico. Wichita,
       Defendor Publishers, 1950. -- An idealizing biography
       of the founder of the Defensores in Puerto Rico.

Roman Catholic Publications on Protestantism in Puerto Rico

2034. Fitzgerald, William Ambrose. A survey of religious

conditions in Puerto Rico, 1899-1934. Ph. D. thesis,
Fordham University, 1934. -- Contains brief chapter
on Protestants with major focus on Episcopalians.

2035. See also Colección sondeos, CIDOC. Protestantismo y
catolicismo en Puerto Rico: su influencia en la
evolución de la personalidad portorriqueña.

Periodicals
See also p. 386.

Past Publications

2036. See Rosa-Guzmán for listing up to 1952. No. 2001.

Current Publications

2037. El boletín. Seminario Evangélico, Apartado C, Río Piedras,
P.R. 00928. v. 1-31.

2038. El defensor hispánico. Organ of the Defensores de la Fe.
A partado 20178, Río Piedras, P.R. 00928. 1931-.

2039. El evangelista pentecostal. Organ of Iglesia de Dios
Pentecostal.

2040. El nuevo evangelista. Organ of the Baptist Convention.
Apartado 1283, Hato Rey, P.R. 00919. 1967-. Monthly.

2041. Puerto Rico evangélico. Río Piedras, P.R. Organ of
denominations in the Evangelical Council.

2042. La voz apostólica. Juncos, P.R. Organ of the Iglesia de
Dios.

Miscellaneous

2043. Guía eclesiástica, Puerto Rico y Vírgenes. San Juan,
Archdioses de San Juan, 1961.

2044. Quién es quién en Puerto Rico. Conrado Asenjo, ed.
(Diccionario biográfico de record personal).
1ª ed. 1933-1934.   San Juan, Real Hermanos, 1933.
2ª ed. 1936-1937.   San Juan, Real Hermanos, 1936.
3ª ed. 1941-1948.   San Juan, Cantero Fernando, 1942.
4ª ed. 1948-1949.   San Juan, Imprenta Ven., 1949.

Part Two.
1976 Edition

Chapter 4.
Bibliographical Aids in the Field of Latin American Studies

BASIC RESOURCES AND STUDY TOOLS

Bibliographies and Indices
See also p. 3.

2045. Bibliography on Latin America, New York, NACLA, 1973. 49
      p. A selected list of writings on radical change in
      Latin America today. Includes both topical and
      country listings, largely concentrating on materials
      critical of imperialism in Latin America. No pre-
      tense is made of "bourgeois scholarly neutrality,"
      yet different viewpoints are included.

2046. Carlton, Robert J., ed. Oswald J. Gregory, trans. Soviet
      image of contemporary Latin America; a documentary
      history 1960-68. Washington, Library of Congress,
      1970. No. 3 in series Conference on Latin America on
      History publications. Compilation of translated
      Soviet Russing writings on the contemporary Latin
      American scene which presents a cross section of
      various official and academic viewpoints.

2047. Chilcote, Ronald H. Revolution and structural change in
      Latin America, Stanford, California. The Hoover

Institution, Stanford University, 1970. Two volumes.
668 p. and 603 p. Organized by country. A bibliography on ideology, development and the radical left
(1930-1965).

2048. Consuela, Sister Mary, I.H.M. Latin America: materials
for the knowledge gap in *Social Education*, journal
of the National Council for the Social Studies,
October 1970. 673-681 p. A special article for
teachers of Latin America in the school curriculum.
A good listing with ample descriptions of basic
materials available. Also lists names and addresses
of sixty agencies and publishers of these materials.

2049. Development and Underdevelopment. Toward a bibliography
on historical and consciousness and human meaning.
Center for the Study of Development and Social
Change. 1430 Massachusetts Ave., Cambridge, Mass.
02138. 1970. 7 p. -- Very abbreviated.

2050. Dorn, Georgette M. Latin America, Spain and Portugal:
an annotated bibliography of paperback books.
Washington, D.C. Library of Congress, 1971. 180 p.
Hispanic Foundation Bibliographical Series No. 13.
-- A good annotated list of books in paperback.

2051. Fleener, Charles J. *and* Ron L. Seckinger. The guide to
Latin American paperback literature. Gainesville,
University of Florida Press, 1966. 106 p.

2052. Griffin, Charles C. Latin America: A guide to the
historical literature. Washington, Library of
Congress, 1970. No. 4 in series of Conference on
Latin American History Publications. -- Provides a
scholarly bibliography, accompanied by critical
annotations, covering the whole field of Latin
American history. Basic organization of guide is
chronological, with main divisions devoted to the
colonial, independence and post-independence periods.
Graphical divisions are found within the major parts.

2053. Higher education in developing countries: a select bibliography (Occasional papers on international affairs,
24). Philip G. Altbach, Cambridge, Mass. Harvard
University, Center for International Affairs, 1970.
113 p.

2054. Inter-American Review of Bibliography. (Revista Interamericana de bibliografía). Pan American Union,
Washington, D.C.

2055. Paulston, Rolland G., ed. Non-formal education: an
annotated international bibliography. New York,
Praeger Publishers, 1972. 332 p.

2056. Sable, Martin H. Latin American studies in the non-western
world and Eastern Europe. Metuchen, N.J., The Scarecrow Press, 1970. 701 p.

2057. Select bibliography, Asia, Africa, Eastern Europe and
Latin America. New York, American Universities Field
Staff, Inc., 1960. 534 p.

2058. Social, economic and political dimensions of Latin America
today: a bibliography. Prepared by Centre Europe
Tiers Monde, Foyer John Knox, 27 Chemin des Crets,
1218 Grand-Saconex, Geneva. 1969. 19 p. Mimeographed.

2059. Zimmerman, Irene. Current national bibliographies in
Latin America: a state of the art study. Miami,
Center of Latin American Studies, 1971. 137 p. --
The first book devoted exclusively to a description of
the current national bibliographies on Latin America.
Includes a brief historical account of the annual
SALALM seminar and list of working papers which serve
as points of departure for future reference.

2060. Vivó, Paquita. *Latin America: A Selected List of Sources*.
Washington, D.C. The Latin American Service, 1972.
-- A compilation of current periodicals and organiza-
tions concerned with Latin American affairs.

Guides to Archival Material
See also p. 7.

2061. Bartley, Russell H. *and* Stuart L. Wagner. Latin America
in basic historical collections: a working guide.
Stanford, Ca. The Hoover Institution, 1972. 212 p.
-- A concise descriptive statement and bibliography
on major archives, libraries and special collections
germane to the study of Latin American history.

2062. Bartos, Anne, ed. Latin American archives and resources.
Los Angeles, Latin America Center of University of
California, 1967. 187 p.

2063. Gomez Cañedo, Lino, ed. Los archivos de la historia de
América. Mexico, Instítuto Panamericano de
Geografía e Historia, 1961. 2 v.

2064. Gropp, Arthur E. Guide to libraries and archives in
         Central America, the West Indies, Panama, Bermuda
         and British Guyana. New Orleans, Middle American
         Research Institute, 1941. 721 p.

2065. Hamer, Philip M. A guide to archives and manuscripts in
         the United States. New Haven, Conn. Yale University
         Press, 1961. 775 p. -- Organized by states of the
         Union, including one page on Puerto Rico.

2066. Hammond, George P. A guide to the manuscript collection
         of the Bancroft Library. Vol. II, Mexico and Central
         American manuscripts. 336 p. -- This is second in a
         three volume series of all the manuscript collections
         at the Bancroft Library, University of California and
         Berkeley. About 1500 are included in Vol. II.

2067. Keen, Rosemary. A survey of the archives of selected
         missionary societies. London, Historical Manuscripts
         Commission, 1968. Not paginated, n.p.s. -- A list-
         ing of the main resources of nineteen Protestant
         societies in Great Britain. Only a listing and does
         not indicate accessibility. Study sponsored by
         Conference of British Missionary Societies.

2068. Millares, Carlo Agustin, ed. Los archivos municipales de
         América Latina. (Libro de Actos y colecciones
         documentales). Maracaibo, Venezuela, Universidad de
         Zúlia, 1961. 220 p.

2069. New York (City) Public Library. Dictionary catalogue of
         the History of the Americas collection. 28 v.
         Boston, Hall, 1961. -- Covers all aspects of North
         and Latin American history for all periods. The
         Library's collection is outstanding for research in
         Latin American history.

2070. Suelflow, Augustus R., compiler. A preliminary guide to
         church records repositories. Church Archives
         Committee of the Society of American Archivists,
         Concordia Historical Institute, St. Louis, Mo. 1969.
         108 p. Mimeographed.

2071. The Acquisition of Latin American library materials. The
         final report and working papers of the 17th seminary
         of SALALM. Washington, D.C. Organization of
         American States, 1972. Available through Microcards
         Editions, Inc.

2072. The National Union of Catalogues of Manuscript collections.
       Ann Harbor, Michigan and other publishers, various
       dates. This catalogue is based on reports from the
       repositories of manuscripts themselves.

General Reference Materials
See also p. 10.

2073. Handbook of Middle American Indians.
       Vol. 1   Natural environment and early cultures.
       Vol. 2, 3 Archeology of southern Mesoamerica.
       Vol. 4   Archeological frontiers and external
                 connections.
       Vol. 5   Linguistics. Norman A. McQwown, ed.
                 Austin, University of Texas Press, 1968.
       Vol. 6   Social anthropology. Manning Nash, ed.
                 Austin, University of Texas Press, 1968.
       Vol. 7-11 Are now available. A total of fourteen
                 volumes is projected.

2074. Hilton, Ronald. The scientific institutions of Latin
       America, with special reference to their organiza-
       tion and information facilities. Stanford, 1970.
       748 p. maps.

2075. Latin America and Latin America periodicals. Cambridge,
       Mass. Harvard University Press, 1966. Vol. I -
       classification schedule: 675 p. Vol. II - alpha-
       betical and chronological. 187 p. (No. 5 in
       Widener Library Shelflist).

2076. Latin American Review of Books. London, Latin American
       Newsletters Ltd., 1973. First issue of an annual
       survey of books in all languages about Latin
       America. Includes a lengthy survey article on
       Latin America's "radical church".

2077. Latin American Research and Publications at the University
       of Texas at Austin, 1893-1969. Austin, University of
       Texas Press. 1971. 187 p. -- Lists over 1,000
       doctoral dissertations and Master's theses as well as
       over 300 titles of publications on Latin American
       subjects. Dissertations have brief summary.

2078. Latin American technical assistance program of U.S. non-
       profit organizations (TAICH) American Council of
       Voluntary Agencies, 200 Park Avenue S., New York.
       1965 and 1967 editions. 494 p. See also 1973

International Directory for Educational Liaison, OLC,
1 Dupont Circle, N.W., Washington, D.C. 20036;
International Directory of Cooperative Organizations
(ILO, 12th Ed., 1971); Statistical Directory of
Volunteer and Development Service Organizations.
ISVS, 10 chemin de Surville, 1213 Petit-Lancy, Geneva.

2079. Organization of the American States and human rights.
Washington, D.C. Organization of American States,
n.d. A bilingual record of the experience from
1960-67 of the Inter-American Commission on Human
Rights (IACHR) with basic documents, agreements and
a comprehensive bibliography. Available OAS.
Publication 341. ES-8133.

2080. Pan American Associations in the United States, with
supplementary lists of other inter-american associations. Washington, D.C. General Secretariat of
the Pan American Union, 1968. 99 p.

2081. Sable, Martin H. A guide to Latin American studies.
Vol. 1. Los Angeles, Latin American Center,
University of California, 1967. Reference series
No. 4. 783 p. 1st of two volumes.

Yearbooks and Handbooks
See also p. 11.

2082. Interamerican Statistical Yearbook. Compiled by Raul C.
Migone, etc. New York, 1940 and 1942. 2 v. 612 p.
and 1066 p. Only these two volumes were published.

2083. Ratliff, William E. Yearbook on Latin American Communist
Affairs. 1971. Stanford, Ca. The Hoover Institution,
1971. 194 p. -- A country by country description of
the Marxist-Leninist parties and movements in Latin
America during 1970 with an analysis of positions and
policies in and toward Latin America during the past
decade.

2084. Staar, Richard F. Yearbook on International Communist
Affairs. Stanford, Ca. The Hoover Institution,
1972. Sixth edition. 708 p. Comprehensive survey
of events in world communion, profiles of national
parties, positions, etc.

2085. Yearbook of American and Canadian Churches. 1973 edition
available through Office of Research, National

Council of Churches, 475 Riverside Drive, New York 10027.

GENERAL BACKGROUND

General History
See also p. 12.

2086. Alexander, Harley B. Latin American mythology. New York, Cooper Square Publishers. 1970. Volume XI of the series on Latin American History and Culture treats the various myths within their regional divisions. 42 full-page illustrations. 536 p.

2087. Davis, Harold E. *Latin American Thought: A Historical Introduction*. Baton Rouge: Louisiana State University Press, 1972. An examination of revolutionary trends in Latin American intellectual history, including the revival of Christian thought, both social and theological, in the twentieth century. Good bibliography.

2088. Fleener, Charles J. *and* Harry Cargas, eds. *Religious and Cultural Factors in Latin America*. St. Louis: St. Louis University, 1970. Papers presented at the Midwest Council of the Association of Latin American Studies, 1968.

2089. Guevara Bazan, Rafael. "Muslim Immigration to Spanish America" in the *Moslem World* (UML). -- A unique article by the president of the Instituto Peruano de Altos Estudios Islámicos, Lima, Peru. Documents the persecution of "Lutherans, Jews and Moors."

2090. Merrill, John C. The Elite Press. New York, Pitman, 1972. -- Portraits of newspapers such as Excelsior, La Prensa and O Estado de São Paulo. Models of concerned, knowledgeable, rational papers.

2091. Picon-Salas, Mariano. A cultural history of Spanish America. Berkeley, University of California Press, 1966. From Conquest to Independence. Trans. I.A. Leonard. 1972. Paperback.

Roman Catholicism in Latin America

Bibliographical Aids
See also p. 34.

2092. Delaney, John J. *and* James E. Tobin. Dictionary of
       Catholic Biography. New York, Doubleday and Co.,
       1961. 1245 p. -- Contains 16,000 entries, including
       13,000 biographies covering people in all walks of
       life, twenty centuries and every country where Roman
       Catholicism has been established.

2093. Directorio Católico Latinoamericano. Bogotá, Secretaría
       General de CELAM, 1968. 586 p. -- A complete list-
       ing of the organization of all Roman Catholic
       dioceses in every Latin American country, of church-
       related specialized organizations and other religious
       and secular organizations. Available through CELAM,
       Apartado Aéreo 5278, Bogotá.

2094. International. IDOC- North America, 235 E. 49th Street,
       New York, N.Y. 10017. IDOC Transconfessional docu-
       mentation on human and religious renewal begun in 1962
       to supply the Dutch bishops with background documen-
       tation for informed participation in the sessions of
       Vatican II, extending its services the following year
       to all bishops. In 1965 began interconfessional and
       available to all interested in trends and movements
       within the Christian churches.

2095. New Catholic Encyclopedia. Articles on Latin America of
       special interest to the church historian are:
       "The Church in Latin America" VIII, 448-69.
       "The Church and the Indian in Latin America" VIII,
         446-48.
       "The Church and the Enlightenment in Latin America"
         VIII, 440-41.
       "The Church and the Independence in Latin America"
         VIII, 441-69.
       "The Church and State in Latin America" III, 738-42.
       "Missions in Colonial America" I, Spanish, II
         Portuguese, IX, 944-64; 964-67.

2096. Ortega, Benjamin. Repertório para el estudio de las
       iglesias en la sociedad de América Latina: 1960-1969.
       Cuernavaca, CIDOC, 1970. 208 p. Sondeos No. 52. --
       Contains 1807 listings.

2097. Schmidlin, Joseph. Catholic Mission History. Trans. by
Matthias Braun, S.V.D., section on South and Central
America. 674-685 p.

2098. Turner, Frederick W. The Church in Latin America: A
Bibliography. Storrs, Conn., University of Connet-
icut, 1972. 40 p.

2099. U.S. Catholics Overseas 1968: a statistical directory.
Washington, D.C. Mission Secretariat of USCC, 1968.
79 p. -- Tables on each country, indicating states
and dioceses of origin, addresses of orders, etc.

2100. U.S. Personnel serving the Church in Latin America.
Fourth Report. January, 1970. Prepared by LAB-USCC.
142 p. The number was 4,211 in 1970, a decrease of
378 over 1968.

2101. Valenzuela Monges, Rodolfo. De la dependencia a la teología
de la liberación: notas bibliográficas. Cuernavaca,
Mex. CIDOC, 1973. 45 p. -- A draft of a more extensive work on the theology of liberation. Also
includes the bibliographies of the Boletín Bibliográfico Iberoamericano (Cf. no. 2261) and Osmundo
Alfonso Miranda (Cf. no. 2312).

2102. Boxer, C. R. "The Problem of the native clergy in the
Portuguese and Spanish empires from the sixteenth to
the eighteenth centuries," in G. J. Cuming, ed. The
Mission of the Church and the propagation of the
faith. Cambridge, Cambridge University Press, 1970.
85-105 p.

2103. Dussel, Enrique D. El Episcopado hispanoamericano:
institución misionera en defensa del indio. 1504-
1620. Cuernavaca, Mexico: CIDOC, 1969. Nine
volumes, with last two volumes being document
appendices. Sondeos No. 32-37 and other numbers of
this series.

2104. _____. Historia de la iglesia en America Latina. Barcelona.
Editorial Nova Terra, 1972. (Second edition) 348 p.

2105. Greenleaf, Richard E. The Roman Catholic Church in
Colonial Latin America. New York, Alfred A. Knopf,
1971. 272 p. -- Contains introduction and essays
from various viewpoints. Good bibliogrpahical essay
of selected works.

2106. Hanke, Lewis. Estudios sobre Fray Bartolomé de las Casas
       y sobre la lucha por la justicia en la conquista
       española de América. Caracas, Universidad Central
       de Venezuela, 1968. 428 p. No. 35 in series pub-
       lished by this institution and No. 12 of the series
       of the social sciences. Volume prepared over sev-
       eral years. Essays published first in several
       historical journals, yet book does have unity.
       Lewis Hanke evaluates critically the interpretations
       of Menendez Pidal, Juan Friede and others. Rich in
       footnotes and bibliography.

2107. History of the Church in Latin America. Part one of the
       CELAM project under the Commission on the History of
       the Latin American Church (CEHIL) coordinated by
       IPLA, Quito. CEHIL, Casilla 2026, Quito. -- An
       extensive ten volume project begun in 1972 to
       include country by country studies. Protestant
       church history will be covered in these latter
       studies and will be prepared by Protestant histor-
       ians who now form part of CEHIL. Goal is to provide
       a critical history with a theological and pastoral
       approach.

2108. Hoffner, Joseph. Kolonialismus and Evangelium. Spanische
       Kolonialethik im Goldenen Zeitalter. Trier, Paulinus
       Verlag, 2nd. ed., 1969. 455 p. -- A second edition
       of his Christianity and Dignity of Men. An indispen-
       sable instrument for all who want to study the
       Spanish conquest of Latin America. A history of
       ideas (ideengeschichte) of the Spanish Conquest
       which attempts to show the unique nature of Spanish
       colonialism.

2109. Lopetigui, Leon *and* Felix Zubillaga. Historia de la
       Iglesia en la América Española desde el descubrimiento
       hasta comienzos del Siglo XIX. Mexico, America
       Central y Antillas. Madrid, Biblioteca de Autores
       Cristianos, 1965. 945 p. -- Excellent bibliography.
       The second volume by Padre Antonio Egana will deal
       with the history of the territory between Panama
       and the Straits of Magellan.

2110. Losada, Angel. Fray Bartolomé de las Casas a la luz de
       la moderna crítica histórica. Madrid, Editorial
       Tenos, 1970. 405 p. -- Recognizes both virtues
       and defects of Las Casas but considers him to be
       "a glory of Spain."

2111. Mendez Arceo, Sergio. Política e Iglesia en México en el
      Siglo XVI. Cuernavaca, CIDOC. n.d. 200 p. Sondeos
      Series.

2112. Rogel, Issac. Documentos sobre la realidad de la Iglesia
      en América Latina 1968-69. 410 p. Cuernavaca,
      CIDOC, 1970. Sondeos No. 54. -- A selection pre-
      pared by NADOC, Lima. Documents reflect the move-
      ments within the institutional church.

2113. Valtierra, Angel, S. J., Peter Claver, Saint of
      the Saints. Burns and Oates, 1960. 322 p. Trans.
      of "El Salto que libertará una raza." Bogotá,
      Imprenta Nacional, 1954.

Contemporary Roman Catholicism
See also p. 41.

General Literature

2114. Alonso, Antonio. Comunidades eclésiales de base.
      Salamanca, Spain, Ediciones Sígueme, 1970. 266 p.
      -- Discusses the reappearance of local groups for
      evangelization in our times.

2115. Aleixo, Jose Carlos. The Catholic Church and elections.
      Cuernavaca, CIDOC, 1969. Sondeos No. 62. A study
      of the Catholic thought on the moral obligation of
      voting.

2116. Antoine, Charles. Church and Power in Brazil. Maryknoll,
      N.Y., Orbis Books, 1972. Translation of L'eglise et
      el pouvoir au Bresil. Paris, Descleé de Brouwer,
      1971. 271 p. -- A French priest served in São
      Paulo and interprets attempts to mediate between
      people and government.

2117. Broucker, Jose de. Dom Helder Câmara. The Violence of
      a Peacemaker. Trans. by Herma Briffault. Maryknoll,
      N.Y., Orbis Books, 1970. A study of a leading
      Brazilian archbishop.

2118. Câmara, Dom Helder. The Church and colonialism: the
      betrayal of the third world. Denville, N.J.
      Dimension Books, 1969. 179 p. Original "Terzo Mundo
      Defradado" by Editrice Misionaria Italiana, Turin,
      1968.

2119. _____. The Spiral of Violence. Denville, N.J., Dimension
      Books, 1971. 82 p. -- The Archbishop of Recife and
      Olinda reaffirms his commitment to the cause of the
      poor and to social change through non-violence.
      Spanish translation, "Espiral de Violencia," Salamaca,
      Editorial Sígueme, 1970.

2120. _____. Revolution through Peace. Trans. from the
      Portuguese by Amparo McLean. New York, Harpers, 1971.
      Spanish translation, "Para llegar a tiempo."
      Salamanca, Editorial Sígueme, 1971.

2121. _____. Four significant addresses given in West Germany
      in 1972. Cuernavaca, Mexico, CIDOC, 1972. (Doc.
      I/I 72/376-379).

2122. Cardenal, Ernesto. Poemas. La Habana, Casa de las
      Americas, 1967. 196 p. -- Includes his well-known
      modern versions of several Psalms. Fr. Cardenal is
      a Nicaraguan priest.

2123. Castro Villagrana, Bernardo, et al. *La iglesia, el
      subdesarrollo y la revolución*. Mexico: Editorial
      Nuestro Tiempo, S.A., 1968. -- Problems of develop-
      ment analyzed in Christian perspective.

2124. "Catholicism in Latin America" in *ISAL Abstracts* No. 40.
      Special issue.

2125. Cleary, O. P., Edward L., ed. Shaping a New World: an
      orientation on Latin America. Maryknoll, N.Y., 1972.
      -- Written for anyone preparing to enter the new
      culture of Latin America.

2126. Colección IPLA. Publications of the Department of Pastoral
      CELAM. Instituto Pastoral Latinoamericano. Apartado
      2026, Quito, Fifteen publications by Segundo Galilea,
      José Comblin, Gregorio Smutko and others.
      1.   Pastoral y liberación humana.
      2.   Evangelización en América Latina.
      3.   Catolicismo popular.
      4.   Espiritualidad y renovación pastoral.
      5.   Cristianismo y desarrollo.
      6/7. Evangelizadores laicos para América Latina.
      8.   América Latina y conciencia cristiana.
      9.   Reflexiones sobre la evangelización.
      10. Reflexiones sobre la evangelización.
      11. ¿A los pobres se les anuncia el Evangélio?
      12. Fé y secularización an America Latina.

      13.   Comunidad de base y prospective pastoral en
            América Latina.
      14.   Pastoral popular y liberación en América Latina.
  15/16.   La Iglesia Latinoamericana y la política despues
            de Medellín.

2127. Colonnese, Louis M. Conscientization for Liberation: New
        dimensions in hemispheric realities. Washington,
        D.C. Division for Latin America, USCC, 1971. The
        1970 CICOP papers.

2128. _____., ed. Human rights and the Liberation
        of Man in the Americas. Papers presented at the 1969
        CICOP meeting. Washington, D.C., Division for Latin
        America, USCC, 1970.

2129. Cross Currents. Special issue on Latin America. Vol.
        XXI, No. 3. Summer, 1971. "Latin American in search
        of liberation," an excellent series of articles edited
        by Gary MacEoin. Available through University Micro-
        films, Ann Harbor, Mich.

2130. Damboriena, Prudencio. Tongues as of fire: Pentecostalism
        in contemporary Christianity. Washington, Corpus
        Books, 1969.

2131. Falnnery, Austin, Ed. Mission and religions: A commentary
        on the Second Vatican Council's decrees on the church's
        missionary activity and declaration on the Church to
        non-Christian religions. Dublin, Scepter Books, 1968.
        163 p.

2132. Freixado, S., S.M. Mi iglesia duerme! Un libro no apto
        para Católicos satisfechos. San Juan, Puerto Rico,
        ISAL Editorial, n.d. 267 p.

2133. Gallet, Paul. Freedom to Starve. Introduction by Michel
        Quoist and Rosemary Sheed. Trans. from French by
        Rosemary Sheed. Dublin, Gill and Macmillan, 1967.
        -- Letters to family by a worker priest in Brazilian
        favellas.

2134. Gheddo, Piero. Why is the Third World poor? Maryknoll,
        N.Y., Orbis Books, 1972. Highly readable survey of
        what the affluent, largely Christian nations can and
        must do to assist the integral development of peoples.

2135. Gheerbrant, Alain. La iglesia rebelde de América Latina.
        Mexico Siglo XXI, 1970. 319 p. Original in French,

L'eglise rebelle d'Amerique Latin, 1969. -- Collection of documents of the "rebel priests" with a
running commentary by the author/editor and articles
by Sergio Arce Martinez and Richard Shaull.

2136.   Gutiérrez, Gustavo.   A theology of liberation: History,
politics and salvation.   Maryknoll, N.Y., Orbis
Books, 1973.   232 p.   -- A solidly reasoned theological argument for radical change in our social structures.   One of the most important books of the decade.
(Spanish original, Una Teología de Liberación.   CEL,
Lima, 1971).

2137.   Houtart, Francois *and* Andres Rousseau.   The Church and
revolution.   Maryknoll, New York, Orbis Books, 1971.
371 p.   -- From the French revolution of 1789 to the
Paris riot of 1968 and from Cuba through Angola to
Vietnam.

2138.   "Iglesia Latinoamericana: Crisis y Revolución," in
Cuadernos de Marcha.   No. 24.   April, 1969.   Special
issue.

2139.   Illich, Ivan D.   Deschooling society.   New York, Harper
and Row, 1970, 1971.   -- A stinging critique of
education institutions and methods.

2140.   _____.   Celebration of awareness.   New York, Doubleday,
1970.   189 p.   -- The futility of schooling, the
planned poverty of technical assistance and the
absurdity of the U.S. concentration on contraception
as a solution for Latin American problems.

2141.   Institute superieur de pastorale catechetique.   Mentalidad
Religiosa Popular.   Cuernavaca, CIDOC, 1969.   Sondeos
No. 58.

2142.   Knadt Vitalis, Hellmut.   The significance of changes in
Latin American Catholicism since Chimbote, 1953.
S.T.M. thesis, Union Theological Seminary, New York,
N.Y., 1964.   Published Cuernavaca, CIDOC, 1969.
Sondeos No. 51.

2143.   Landsberger, Henry A., ed.   The Church and social change
in Latin America.   Notre Dame, University of Notre
Dame Press, 1970.

2144.   Laurentin, René.   Liberation, development and salvation.
Maryknoll, N.Y., Orbis Books, 1972.   -- By an

eminent Marian theologian and later historian of
Vatican II. Introduction to these themes which
challenge many theological concepts.

2145. _____. L'Amerique Latine a l'heure de l'enfantenent.
Paris, Editions du Seuil, 1968. 278 p. -- Result
of a prolonged visit by writer to Latin America in
connection with the 1968 Medellín Assembly. Critical
of bureaucratic tendencies to impose solutions.
Quotes full letter of 350 Brazilian priests sent to
Assembly.

2146. MacEoin, Gary. Agent for change: the story of Harvey
(Pablo) Steele. Maryknoll, N.Y., Orbis Books, 1972.
175 p. -- A Canadian missionary who served in China,
Dominican Republic and presently in Panama. About
what a missionary can and can not do in Latin America.

2147. _____. Latin American, the eleventh hour. New York,
Kennedy, 1962. 224 p. -- A presentation of the
socio-economic problems facing Latin America and
ways in which the developed world should respond to
the crisis. References to the weaknesses in the
Roman Catholic Church which have both aided the
crisis and also awakened the Church.

2148. Medina, Carlos Alberto *and* Dimas Furtado. Participação e
Igreja. Cuernavaca, CIDOC, 1971. 212 p. --
Questionnaires, tables, comparisons in the Church
and related organizations.

2149. Michenfelder, Joseph. Gringo volunteers. Photos by Fred
Albert. Maryknoll, N.Y., Maryknoll Publications,
1969. 96 p. -- Central theme is the Roman Catholic
laity in mission in Peru.

2150. Mutchler, David E. The Church as a political factor in
Latin America with particular reference to Colombia
and Chile. New York, Praeger Publishers, 1971. 640
p. -- A critical study both in the field of church
history and sociology which probes the sources of
institutional religion and political sociology.
Controversial but amply documented. Introduction by
Irving Louis Horowitz. The thesis of this book is
outlined in his article in *Social Research* , Vol. 36,
No. 2, summer, 1969.

2151. O'Connor, Edward Dennis. The Pentecostal movement in the Catholic Church. South Bend, Indiana, Ave Maria Press, 1971.

2152. Proaño, Luis E. Iglesia, Política y Libertad Religiosa. Quito, Editorial Ecuatoriana, 1968.

2153. Quigley, Thomas E., ed., Freedom and unfreedom in the Americas: Towards a theology of liberation. Introduction by Harvey Cox. New York, IDOC-North America, 1971. 140 p. -- Addresses at the 1971 CICOP Conference.

2154. Richardson, William J., ed. The Church as sign. Maryknoll, N.Y. Maryknoll Publications, 1969. 171 p. -- An ecumenical venture of essays on mission in the post-Vatican II period, with two appendices of documents of reappraisal undertaken by Maryknoll of its own activities.

2155. Rossi, Juan José, ed. Iglesia Latinoamericana: ¡Protesta o Profecía? Mexico, 1969. 462 p. -- An annotated collection of articles, essays and statements by laymen, priests and hierarchy concerning the Church and Latin American society and the prospects for change.

2156. Sanders, Thomas G. Catholic innovation in a changing Latin America. Cuernavaca, Mexico. CIDOC, 1969. 288 p. Sondeos No. 41.

2157. Schmidt, Karl. The Catholic Church in modern Latin America. 1972. 216 p. -- Ten essays, previously published. Sections are: (1) The Church's response to the political order; (2) Problems of Church and states; (3) The Church's response to new social demands.

2158. SEDOS symposium. Foundations of Mission Theology. Maryknoll, N.Y., Orbis Books, 1972. -- Papers of the first symposium of SEDOS, the international committee for documentation and research created by the major Roman Catholic missionary institutes.

2159. Segundo, Juan Luis. Social reality and theology in Latin America: Theology for Artisans of a new humanity. Maryknoll, N.Y., Orbis Books, 1973. 5 volume set. Translation of *Teología abierta para el laico adulto* (Buenos Aires, Carlos Lohle). -- Theology of liberation at a popular level.

2160. Shapiro, Samuel, ed., Integration of Man and Society in Latin America. Addresses given at 1966 meeting of the Catholic Inter-American Cooperation Program. South Bend, Indiana; University of Notre Dame Press, 1967. 356 p.

2161. _____, ed. Cultural Factors in Interamerican Relations. Papers and addresses given at the 1968 CICOP meeting. Washington, D.C., Division for Latin America, USCC, 1969. General subject is how to bridge the gap between the Americas.

2162. Turner, Frederick C. Catholicism and political development in Latin America. Chapel Hill, N.C.; University of North Carolina Press, 1971. 259 p.

2163. Tyson, Brady. "Dom Helder as a symbolic man" in *Catholic World*, August, 1971. pp 235-239.

2164. Vallier, Ivan A. Catholicism, social change and modernization in Latin America. New York, Prentice Hall, 1970.

2165. Vekemans, Roger, S.J. *La Revolución Latinoamericana*. Buenos Aires: Ediciones Troquel (for DESAL), 1970. Three essays on Latin American marginality and integration by a leading Jesuit priest.

2166. White P. "Can Catholics learn anything from Evangelical Protestants"? in *Catholic Today*, 30 (December, 1970) 12-21.

2167. Wipfler, William L. "The current Roman Catholic challenge to government in Latin America," in *South East Latin Americanist*, XVI (September, 1972) 1-4.

2168. Zañartu, Mario. Desarrollo económico y moral católico. Cuernavaca, CIDOC, 1969. 274 p. Introducción de Roger Vekemans. Special reference to the Church in Chile.

Documents of Regional Conferences and Consultations
See also p. 46.
2169. Between Honesty and Hope. Documents from and about the Church in Latin America. Issued at Lima by the Peruvian Bishops' Commission for Social Action. Trans. by John Drury. Maryknoll, New York;

Maryknoll Publications, 1969. 247 p. Pronounce-
ments, addresses and official statements. Includes
the working draft of the Medellin Conference, a lay
critique of the Medellin draft, the Medellin documents on peace, poverty and key addresses from that
meeting. A valuable collection of key documents
from 1966-69.

2170. Conclusiones de la Asamblea Extraordinaria del CELAM.
Departamento de Acción Social, Salvador (Bahia),
Brazil. Consultation held October, 1966.

2171. La Pastoral en las misiones de América Latina. Documents
and conclusions of the meetings in Melgar. (Primer
Encuentro Continental de Misiones en América Latina),
Caracas (Encuentro Continental de los obispos
presidentes de las comisiones episcopales de misiones
de América Latina and Iquitos (Encuentro sobre
misiones del Alto Amazonas). Indo-American Press
Service. Apartado aereo 53274, Chapinero, Bogota
2. Also "Antropología y Evangelización", the study
papers from Melgar and "Antropología y teología en
la Acción misionera" from Iquitos.

2172. Medellin documents. Washington, D.C., Latin American
Bureau, U.S. Catholic Conference, 1970. Translation
of position papers and of the final documents issued
by the Second General Conference of Latin American
bishops, 1968.

2173. Misión Abierta al Servicio de la Fe. September-October,
1972. Report of Latin American Conference on
"Christian Faith and Social Change in Latin America"
held July 8-15, 1972. El Escorial, Spain. Addresses
by Míguez, Gutiérrez, Galilea, Comblin, Borrett,
et al.

2174. Priests and Religious for Latin America. Proceedings of
the First Inter-American Conference on Religious,
Mexico City, February, 1971. $1.50. Division for
Latin America, USCC, P. O. Box 6066, Washington,
D.C.

2175. Richardson, William J., M.M., ed., Reappraisal: Prelude
to Change. Maryknoll, N.Y. Maryknoll Publications,
1965. 125 p. Papers given at symposium of the
Mission Secretariat of the U.S. Catholic Conference,
1965. Rethinking of training programs, methods and
the very nature of the missionary apostolate.

2176. The Church in the present day transformation of Latin
America in the light of the Council. August 24-
September 6, 1968. Position papers and conclusions
of the Second General Conference of Latin American
Bishops (CELAM). Bogotá, General Secretariat of
CELAM, Apartado aereo 5278, 1970. 2 volumes. 280
p. and 290 p. Also Spanish edition of same date
and publisher. (Cf. Laurentin, René, No. 2145).

Periodicals and Journals
          See also p. 49.
2178. Boletín CELAM. Includes episcopal documentation, studies,
reflections, etc. Official organ of The Latin
American Episcopal Council. Apartado aereo 5278,
Bogotá, D.E. Monthly. 1968-.

2179. Catholic Mind. 106 W. 56th Street, New York, New York
10019.

2180. Cuadernos de Documentación. Br. Oroño 1345, Rosario,
Argentina.

2181. Diálogo Ecuménico. Editado por el Centro Ecuménico
Juan XXIII de la Universidad de Salamanca, España.

2182. Ecumenical Trends. Graymoor/Garrison, New York 10524.
Monthly.

2183. Enlace. (Sacerdotes Tercermundistas). Zelada 4771,
Buenos Aires, Argentina.

2184. LADOC - A documentation service. Division for Latin
America, USCC, P. O. Box 6066, Washington, D.C.
Monthly material of significant statements, reports,
articles and talks, all in English, from or about
Latin America. $6.00 annually. $16.00 air mail
to Europe, Latin America.

2185. Latin America Calls. Division for Latin America, USCC,
P.O. Box 6066, Washington, D.C. Monthly. One
dollar annually. News of religious life and social
development. Maryknoll magazine. Monthly.
Maryknoll, New York.

2186. Misión Abierta al Servicio de la Fe. 1907-   Buen
Suceso 22, Madrid 3. T-28-21-01. Bi-monthly.

2187. Renovación Ecuménica. Editado por el Centro Ecuménico
Juan XXIII de la Universidad de Salamanca, España.

2188. Revista Bíblica. San Martin 3773, R. Calzada, Buenos
Aires, Argentina.

2189. Revista Eclesiástica Brasileira. Petropolis, RJ, Brazil.
Quarterly.

2190. Teología, PUC. José Cubas 3543, Rosario, Argentina.

Publications on or related to Fr. Camilo Torres

2191. Torres, Camilo. Compendium of his writings (1956-1966)
Cuernavaca, CIDOC, 1966. 377 p. Sondeos series
No. 5. Covers period of his student days in
Colombia, advanced studies in Belgium, chaplaincy
at the National University in Bogota and his last
months in confrontation with the Church and nation.

2192. _____, Liberación o Muerte. La Habana, Instituto del
Libro, 1967. 206 p. Collection of platform
strategy of *Frente Unido*. Camilo's statements from
August, 1965 to February, 1966. Introduction by
Francisco González, Cuban guerrilla leader in
Colombia.

2193. Caycedo, Olga de. El Padre Camilo Torres o la crisis de
madurez de América. Barcelona, Ediciones Aura, 1972.
462 p. Written by a Colombian congresswoman of a
prominent family.

2194. Guzman, Germán C. Camilo, El Cura Guerrillero. Bogotá,
Servicios especiales de Prensa, 1967. 257 p.
Biography by a friend and associate. Chapter 16
provides only official documents related to his
death. This is also published in English as *Camilo
Torres* (trans. by John D. Ring). New York: Sheed
and Ward, 1969. 310 p.

2195. Habegger, Norberto. Camilo Torres, El Cura Guerrillero.
Buenos Aires, A. Peña Lillo, ed., n.d. 312 p.

2196. Iglesia Católica y Revolución. La Habana, Impresora
Universitaria "Andre Voisin" 1969. 241 p. Includes
message from eighteen Third World bishops, statements from CELAM, Dom Helder Camara, rebel priest
movements throughout Latin America and *Camilismo*
movements in the continent.

2197. López Oliva, Enrique. Los Católicos y la revolución
       latinoamericana. La Habana, Instituto del Libro,
       1970. 186 p. Review by a Cuban journalist of the
       response of the Church to revolution in Latin
       America. Attempts to interpret social doctrine of
       the Church as expressed in different countries.

2198. _____. El Camilismo en la América Latina. Habana, Casa
       de las Américas, 1970. 97 p. Includes essay from
       "El Primer Encuentro Latinoamericano 'Camilo Torres'",
       Montevideo, 1968. Statements from Chilean Movimiento
       "Camilo Torres" and articles from *Cristianismo y
       Revolución*. Prof. López Oliva is a Cuban journalist
       and researcher on religious life in Cuba.

2199. Pareja, Carlos H. El Padre Camilo, El Cura Guerrillero.
       Mexico, Editorial Nuestra América, 1968. 262 p.
       Covers much of the same material of Guzmán and
       Habegger, but begins with an extended treatment of
       the periods of Jose Antonio Galan (1781), Nariño
       (1814) and Jorge Eliecer Gaitan (1948), thus placing
       Camilo Torres in historical perspective.

2200. Salazar, Maria Cristina, et al. Inquietudes. Laicos a
       la hora del Concilio. El "Caso del Padre Camilo
       Torres. Bogotá, Tercer Mundo, 1965. 81 p. Letters,
       declarations and editorials related to the specific
       details of the problems between the Church and
       Father Torres in 1965.

2201. Torres, Camilo. La Revolución, imperativo cristiano.
       Bogotá, Ediciones del Caribe, 1965. 58 p. State-
       ments on the essence of the Christian apostolate as
       Camilo understands his task, with concrete proposals
       for radical social, economic and political change in
       Colombian life.

Ecumenical Dialogue

2202. Butler, B.C. "Limits on ecumenism" in *The Tablet of
       London*. Vol. 225, No. 6822. March 6, 1971. p.
       222-224. Bishop Butler's refutation of Karl Rahner's
       Church unity proposal.

2203. Congar, Ives. "Les problemes nouveaux du monde seculier,
       rendent-ils l'ocumenisme superflu?" in *Concilium*.
       No. 54, February, 1970. p. 11-19. Discusses the
       progress of ecumenism and its present malaise and
       proposes social ecumenism as a solution.

2204. "Ecumenism in Latin America" in *ISAL Abstracts* Nos. 38/39.
       Special issue.

2205. Hoffman, Ronan. "Ecumenism and mission theology" in
       World Mission, Vol. 15, No. 3, Fall, 1964. 48-64.
       Reveals the intimate relation between ecumenism and
       mission, the missionary's influence, developments
       after the Second Vatican Council and the possibility
       of the entry of the Roman Catholic Church into the
       World Council of Churches.

2206. Lengsfeld, Peter. Tradición, escritura e iglesia en el
       diálogo ecuménico. Madrid, Fax, 1967. 343 p. A
       good summary of the developments and recent dis-
       cussions on this subject.

2207. McDonagh, Enda. Roman Catholics and Unity. London,
       Mowbrary, 1962. 98 p. A study of the ecumenical
       movement with an emphasis on Spiritual Ecumenism.

2208. Rahner, Karl. Teología actual, diálogo entre Protestantes
       y Católicos. Madrid, Guadarrama, 1960. 374 p.
       Obra católica romana de alto nivel.

2209. Romeu, Luis V., editor. Diálogos de Cristiandad.
       Salamanca, Ediciones Sígueme, 1964. 401 p. A
       survey of a number of well-known theologians and
       men of the church of several confessions ask how
       their ecumenical vocation was awakened and what
       they expect from the ecumenical movement.

2210. Tavard, George. Two centuries of ecumenism. Notre Dame,
       Fides Publishers, 1960. An historical treatment of
       the ecumenical movement, the Catholic Church's
       reaction to it and its eventual involvement.

Contemporary Religious Phenomena and Secular Movements
See also p. 49.

Marxism and Religion
See also p. 50.

2211. Baez Camargo, Gonzalo. El comunismo, el cristianismo y
       los cristianos. Mexico, Casa Unida de Publicaciones,
       1960. 101 p.

2212. Clasper, Paul D. The yoga, the commissar, and the Third
       World church. Valley Forge, Pa., Judson Press, 1962.
       95 p.

2213. Conway, James F. Marx and Jesus: Liberation Theology in Latin America. New York, Carleton Press, 1973. 232 p. Discusses the method and approach of the theology and liberation and the Marxist critique.

2214. Escobar, Samuel. Diálogo entre Cristo, Marx y otros ensayos. Lima, Publicaciones AGEUP, Lampa 1137-303. 1967. 89 p.

2215. Fromm, Eric. The Marxist Concept of Man. Also in Spanish. Uses earlier writings of Marx.

2216. Hromadka, James L. Evangélio para los ateos. Montevideo, Tierra Nueva, 1970. 107 p. A classic by the late chairman of the Christian Peace Conference, and a clear demonstration of the need of dialogue between Christians and Marxists.

2217. Miranda, José Porfirio. Marx y la Biblia: crítica a la filosofía de la opresión, Mexico, 1971. 263 p.

2218. O Cristão e o Comunismo. Confronta. Rio de Janeiro, Centro Cristiano de Literatura, 1963. 87 p.

2219. Ogletree, Thomas, ed., Openings for Marxist Christian Dialogue. Nashville, Abingdon Press, 1968.

2220. Petulla, Joseph. Christian Political Theology: A Marxian Guide. Maryknoll, N.Y. 1972.

2221. Raines, John C., *and* Thomas Dean. Marxism and radical religion. Philadelphia, Temple University Press, 1970. Articles by Richard Shaull, John C. Bennett and others.

2222. Vekemans, Roger, S.J. *Lo antidialéctico en la dialéctica de Marx*. Buenos Aires: Ediciones Troquel, 1970. An analysis of contradictions in Marxist thinking and a proposal of a new social organization based on coexistence.

Change in Latin America:
Rapid Social Change, Revolution, Inter American Tensions
See also p. 50.

2223. Alexander, Robert J., Prophets of the Revolution: Profiles of Latin American leaders. New York, Macmillan, 1967.

2224. _____. Trotskyism in Latin America. Stanford, Ca. The
      Hoover Institution, 1973. 250 p. The only history
      of Trotskyism in Latin America.

2225. Barreiro, Julio. Violencia y política en América Latina.
      Mexico, Sigle XXI, 1971. 205 p.

2226. Beals, Carlton. Great guerrilla warriors. Englewood
      Cliffs, N.J. Prentice-Hall, 1970. 248 p. Popular
      revolutionary heroes in Latin America who lead
      people toward independence.

2227. Debray, Regis. Revolution in the Revolution? New York,
      Monthly Review Press, 1967. The French Marxist who
      later followed Che Guevara to Bolivia writes of
      plans for revolution throughout the continent.

2228. Diary of Che Guevara. The secret papers of a revolution-
      ary. New York, Bantam Books, Inc. 1968. 190 p.
      Diary from Nov. 7, 1966 to October 7, 1967.

2229. Duncan, W. Raymond *and* James Nelson Goodsell, eds.
      *Quest for Change in Latin America: Sources for a
      Twentieth Century Analysis.* New York: Oxford
      University Press, 1970. Latin American thinkers,
      from Martí to Che Guevara.

2230. Fals Borda, Orlando. Subversión y Cambio Social en
      Colombia, Bogotá. Tercer Mundo, 1967 (published
      also in English, New York, Columbia University
      Press, 1969). Introduces a new definition into
      sociology of the term "subversion" as a social
      process set in historical realities. 238 p.

2231. _____. Subversión y Desarrollo: el caso de América
      Latina. Eleventh annual lecture, Foyer John Knox,
      Geneva. June, 1970. 18 p. Available at CETIM,
      27, chemin des Crets-de-Pregny, 1218 Gran Saconnex,
      Geneva.

2232. _____, Las Revoluciones Inconclusas en América Latina.
      Mexico, Siglo XXI, 1969. Published also in English.
      New Brunswick, N.J. Rutgers University Press, 1970.
      French edition, Paris, Artheme Fayard, 1970.

2233. _____. Ciencia propia y colonialismo intelectual.
      Mexico, Editorial Nuestro Tiempo, Mexico, 1970.

2234. Fleener, Charles J. *and* Harry J. Cargas. Religious and Cultural Factors in Latin America. St. Louis, Mo. St. Louis University Press, 1970. Papers given at Tenth annual meeting of the Midwest Association of Latin American Studies. Articles by Roger Vekemans, George Maier, Richard Millett and others.

2235. Franco, Pablo. La Influencia de los Estados Unidos en América Latina. Montevideo, Ediciones Tauro/ISAL, 1967. 130 p. Document produced by a team of young Latin American sociologists. Appendices and tables.

2236. Frank, André Gunder, Dale Johnson *and* James Cockcroft. Dependence and Underdevelopment: Latin America's Political Economy. 1972.

2237. Furtado, Celso. Desarrollo y Subdesarrollo. Buenos Aires, Editorial Universitaria de Buenos Aires, 1964. 247 p.

2238. _____. Desenvolvimiento y subdesenvolvimiento. Rio de Janeiro, Editora Fundo de Cultura, 1961.

2239. Gil, Frederico G. Latin American - United States Relations. New York, Harcourt, Brace Jovanvieh. 339 p. Paperback. Feels that U.S. relations with Latin America are "cyclical".

2240. Goulet, Denis. Is Gradualism Dead? Reflections on order, change and force. New York, Council on Religion and International Affairs, 1970. 34 p. By a pioneer in the field of the ethics and development.

2241. _____ *and* Michael Hudson. The Myth of Aid. Maryknoll, New York, 1972.

2242. Gray, Richard B. Latin America and the United States in the 1970's. Itasca, Illinois; Peacock Publishers, 1971. 369 p. A basic reader on the Alliance for Progress, changing Inter-American relations, common markets and U.S. policy changes toward Latin America. A collection of articles previously published in *Foreign Affairs*.

2243. Horowitz, Irving Louis, ed. *and* Josué de Castro *and* John Gerassi. Latin American Radicalism: a documentary report on left and nationalist movements. New York, Random House, 1969. 653 p.

2244. Humphreys, Robert A. Tradition and revolt in Latin
         America. New York, Columbia University Press, 1969.

2245. Inter-American Dialogues. On causes of North and South
         American misunderstandings. Resumes of five actual
         dialogues. New York, LAWG-NCCC, 1970. 20 p.
         Latinos and Anglos resident in Washington, D.C.
         dialogue in 1964. Reveals some key areas of our
         misunderstandings.

2246. Kane, Wm. Everett. Strife in Latin America: a legal
         history of U.S. involvement. Baltimore, John
         Hopkins Press, 1972. Attempts to give reasons for
         a century of interventionary activities. Written
         under auspices of American Society of International
         law: Panel on International Law of Civil Wars.

2247. Landsberger, Henry A., ed. Latin American Peasant move-
         ments. Ithaca and London, Cornell University Press,
         1972. A comprehensive study.

2248. MacEoin, Gary. Revolution next door; Latin America in
         the 1970's. New York, Holt, Rinehart and Winston,
         1971. 243 p. Critical analysis of the Decade of
         Development, neocolonialism, the Church, the armed
         forces, the CIA, etc.

2249. Needler, Martin C. The U.S. and Latin America Revolution.
         New York, Allyn and Bacon, 1972. 167 p. Paperback.
         A slim volume with style which evaluates U.S.
         foreign policy within the perspective of the revol-
         utionary, political and social changes of recent
         years.

2250. New Chile. Berkeley, North American Congress on Latin
         America, 1972. 177 p. Revised edition, 1973.
         Aimed at acquainting the non-specialist with some
         of the important issues related to the Socialist
         regime in Chile.

2251. Petras, James *and* Maurice Zeitlin. Latin America:
         Reform or Revolution? Greenwich, Conn., Fawcett
         Publisher, 1968. 511 p. A reader on fundamental
         issues of social structure and politics.

2252. Radler, D. H. El Gringo: The Yankee image in Latin
         America. Philadelphia, Chilton, 1962. 141 p.

2253. Rockefeller, Nelson A. The Rockefeller Report on the
Americas. New York. Quadrangle, 1969. 144 p. A
controversial document which evoked serious criticism.

2254. Seminario Latinoamericano del CETIM, III. Modalidades
Internas de la Dependencia en América Latina. Enero,
1970. 130 p. Seven lectures by Latin American and
European scholars. Available CETIM. 27, chemin des
Crets-de-Pregny, 1218 Gran Saconnex, Geneva.

2255. Seminario Latinoamericano del CETIM, IV. Dependance et
Structure de Classes en Amérique Latine. October,
1972. 458 p. The seminar offered twenty researchers
of the Left to encounter each other and their ideas.
Text in English, Spanish, French and Portuguese.

2256. Smith, David S., Prospects for Latin America. New York,
Columbia University, 1970. 385 p. Sixteen essays
presented in a seminar sponsored by the International
Fellows Program. Discusses conflicts between U.S.
policy and nationalism among other subjects. Particularly of value is "The Role of the churches in
U.S.-Latin American relations" by John B. Housley.

2257. Smith, Donald Eugene, ed. Religion, Politics and Social
Change in the Third World. New York, The Free
Press, 1971.

2258. Stockwell, Eugene L. Latin American Self-Determination/
Illusion or Reality? The 1970 Miller Lecture on
Inter-American Affairs, Scarritt College for Chris-
tian Workers, Nashville in *Religion in Life*, Summer,
1971. 16 p. Reprinted in 1972 by Division of
Education and Cultivation, United Methodist Church.
Available free, Service Center, 7820 Reading Road,
Cincinnati, Ohio 45237.

2259. Wagner, R. Harrison. U.S. policy toward Latin America:
a study on domestic and international politics.
Stanford University Press. 246 p. An advanced
apology for continued U.S. deterioating L.A. policy;
avoid facing cost to U.S. of radical policy shifts.

2260. Zea, Leopoldo. Latin America and the world. Trans.
Frances K. Hendricks and Beatrice Berler. Norman,
Oklahoma; University of Oklahoma Press, 1969.

PERIODICALS AND JOURNALS
See also p. 51.

2261. Boletín Bibliográfico Iberoamericano. Centro de Informa-
      ción y Sociología de la OCSHA, Ciudad Universitaria,
      Madrid 3.

2262. Boletín del Servicio para la Acción Liberadora en América
      Latina (Orientación no violenta). Agraciada 1531,
      Apt. 1104, Montevideo, Uruguay.

2263. Brazilian Information Bulletin. American Friends of
      Brazil. P. O. Box 2279. Station A., Berkeley, Cal.
      94072. Supplements inadequate press coverage in
      English of news from Brazil.

2264. Bulletin of Hispanic Studies. Liverpool University
      Press. The University, Box 147, Liverpool, England.
      1963 BX. Quarterly.

2265. Business Latin America. Business International Corp.
      757 Third Ave., New York, N.Y. 10017. Weekly.
      Expensive informative review.

2266. Canadian Journal of Latin American Studies/Revue
      canadienne des etudes latinoamericaines. Publication
      to be known by siglas "N_S". 1972-. Department of
      Spanish, Queen's University, Kingston, Canada.

2267. CIDOC Informa. Centro Intercultural de Documentación.
      Apartado 479, Cuernavaca, Mexico. Bi-weekly coverage
      of Latin America.

2268. Comparative Studies of Society and History. Morton and
      Co. Publishers. The Hague. The Netherlands. 1958-.

2269. Cross Currents. 103 Van Housten Fields, West Nyack, N.Y.
      10994. Quarterly.

2270. Cuadernos de CIDOC and CIDOC Dossiers. Centro Inter-
      cultural de Documentación, Apartado 479, Cuernavaca,
      Mexico. Continuing series of research publications.

2271. EPICA Newsletter. Ecumenical Program for Inter-American
      Communication in Action. 1500 Farragut St., N.W.
      Washington, D.C. 20011. Monthly. Situational
      analysis of crucial areas in Latin America.

2272.   Estudios Andinos.   Casilla 5887, La Paz, Bolivia.
        Published in cooperation with the Center for Latin
        American Studies, and Center for International
        Studies of the University of Pittsburg.   Quarterly.
        1970-.

2273.   Estudios Centroamericanos.   Apartado 668, San Salvador,
        El Salvador.   Monthly.

2274.   Estudios Sociales Centroamericanos.   San José, Costa
        Rica, 1972-.

2275.   Guatemala Report.   American Friends of Guatemala, Box
        2283, Station A.   Berkeley, Ca. 94702.   Occasional.
        Deals largely with human and civil rights issues.

2276.   Historical Abstracts.   800 East Micheltorena St., Santa
        Barbara, Ca.   Bibliography of world's periodical
        literature.   English summaries of historical articles.

2277.   International Development Review.   Quarterly.   Society
        for International Development, 1346 Connecticut Ave.,
        N.W., Washington, D.C. 20036.

2278.   Inter-American Economic Affairs.   Box 181.   Washington,
        D.C. 20044.   Quarterly.

2279.   ISLA.   Information Services of Latin America, Box 4267,
        Berkeley, Ca. 94704.   Monthly.   Provides complete
        clipping services from the following newspapers:
        *Christian Science Monitor, Journal of Commerce, Los
        Angeles Times, Miami Herald, Manchester Guardian,
        Le Monde, New York Times, Wall Street Journal,* and
        Washington Post.   Subscription price upon request.

2280.   Journal of Latin American Studies.   Cambridge University
        Press, London, 1969.   Twice yearly.

2281.   Journal for the Scientific Study of Religion.

2282.   Journal of Religious Thought.

2283.   Journal of Church and State.   Baylor University, Waco,
        Texas.

2284.   Latin America.   432 Park Ave., South, New York, N.Y.
        10016.   Weekly.

2285. Latin America. A weekly political and economic report.
        Published by Latin American Newsletter, Ltd. 69
        Cannon Street, London, EC 4. Edited by John Rettie
        and Hugh O. Shaughnessey.

2286. Latin America and Empire Report. North American Congress
        on Latin America (NACLA). Formerly *NACLA Newsletter*.
        1967-. Box 57, Cathedral Station, N.Y., N.Y. 10025
        and Box 226 Berkeley, Ca. 94701. Monthly. $10.00
        per year for individuals; $16.00 per year for non-
        profit institutions.

2287. Latin American Studies Association Newsletter. Box 13362.
        University Station, Gainsville, Fla. 32601. Quart-
        erly. Professional and news of Latin American
        Studies Association.

2288. LTC Newsletter. Land Tenure Center, University of
        Wisconsin, 310 King Hall, Madison, Wis. 53706. Semi-
        annual coverage of Latin America, Africa and Asia.

2289. Marcha. Talleres gráficos "33", Piedras 522, Montevideo,
        Uruguay. Weekly. (Closed by government in 1974).

2290. Notícias. National Foreign Trade Council, Inc. 10
        Rockefeller Plaza, New York, N.Y. 10020. Coverage
        of U.S. business perspectives on Latin America.
        Weekly.

2291. Pasos. Un documento de reflexión por semana. A service
        of Iglesia y Sociedad en América Latina (ISAL)
        Casilla 6112, Santiago 22, Chile. Fr. Hugo Assman,
        editor. (Closed by government in 1973).

2292. Rand Corporation Communications Department. Rand, 1700
        Main St., Santa Monica, Ca. 90406. One of the U.S.
        government's most crucial "think tanks" publishes
        regularly monographs on Latin America as well as on
        other areas.

2293. Revista Iberoamericana. Organ of the International
        Institute of Iberoamerican Literature. Quarterly.
        1894-. Sponsored by the University of Pittsburg.

2294. Revista Latinoamerica de Sociología. Virrey del Pino
        3230. Buenos Aires, Argentina. Tri-annual.

2295. Revista: Review Interamericana. A multidisciplinary
        quarterly published by the Inter-American University,

dealing with problems of education in Puerto Rico
and the Caribbean. P.O. Box 1293, Hato Rey, Puerto
Rico 00919. 1973-.

2296. Studies in Comparative International Development. Trans-
action Periodicals Consortium. Box A, Rutgers
University, New Brunswick, N.J. 08903. Deals with
application of political sociology to Third World
problems and events. 1965-. Three times yearly.

2297. Testimonies Uruguayos. 1973. Organ of diffusion of
human and civil rights issues in Uruguay.

2298. The Times of the Americas. A national weekly about all
of Latin America. Woodward Building, Washington,
D.C. 20005.

2299. Tricontinental News Service. Box 3441, Merchandise Mart
Station, Chicago, Ill. 60654. $25 per year. Monthly.
1972.

2300. Union of Radical Latin Americanists Newsletter. URLA.
c/o Edelstein-CCS, University of Wisconsin, Green
Bay, Green Bay, Wis. 54302. Quarterly. News and
notes on activities of radical Latin Americanists.

2301. USLA Reporter. 150 Fifth Ave., Room 737, New York, N.Y.
10011. Monthly. Deals with Latin American political
prisoners.

2302. Vozes. Revista de cultura. Petropolis, R.F., Brazil.
Ten issues yearly. Edited by Frei Clarencio Neoti.
Contemporary articles on sociology, communication
arts, literature, theology, etc.

Borzoi Books on Latin America
(All published by Alfred A. Knopf, New York, N.Y.)
See also p. 55.

2303. Aguilar, Luis E. Marxism in Latin America. 1969. 288
p. X002.

2304. Barager, Jos. R. Why Peron came to Power. 1968. 288 p.
X026.

2305. Bushnell, David, ed. The Liberator. Simon Bolivar, 1970.
256 p. X092.

2306. Delpar, Helen, ed. The Borzoi reader in Latin American
       history. A two-volume anthology. Vol. I - From the
       Colonial period to Independence; p. 224. Vol. II. -
       The Nineteenth Century and Twentieth Century. p.
       304. 1972.

2307. Graham, Richard, ed. A century of Brazilian History
       since 1865. Issues and problems. 1969. 256 p.
       X216. Valuable appendix "Suggestions for further
       reading." 228-233.

2308. Manden, John. The Unrevolutionary society. The power of
       L.A. in a changing world. 1969.

2309. Schmitt, Karl M., ed. The Roman Catholic Church in Modern
       Latin America. 1972. 225 p. Includes introduction
       and essays from various points of view. Good biblio-
       graphical essay.

2310. Wilkie, Jas. W. *and* Albert L. Michaels. Revolution in
       Mexico. 1969. 320 p. X477.

Chapter 5.
Protestantism in Latin America, General

BIBLIOGRAPHIES AND INDICES
See also p. 57.

2311. Minnich, R. Herbert, Willard H. Smith, *and* Wilmar Stahl.
        Mennonites in Latin America: an annotated biblio-
        graphy, 1912-1971. Reprinted from the *Mennonite*
        Quarterly Review, XLVI (April, 1972, 177-235).
        Available from *Mennonite Review*, Goshen College,
        Goshen, In. 46526. Contains more than 620 items
        originally published in five languages (German,
        English, Spanish, Portuguese and Dutch). A general
        section (159 items, excluding cross references)
        covers materials dealing with Mennonites in more
        than one country. Twelve additional sections cover
        each country for which significant publications have
        appeared. Those with the largest number are
        Paraguay (192), Brazil (80), and Mexico (65). In
        addition to books and articles, important archival
        collections and other unpublished material are
        included.

2312. Miranda, Osmundo Afonso. Bibliography of Third World
        theology of liberation. A partial listing. 10 p.
        Available from author, Tuscaloosa College, Tuscaloosa,
        Alabama. (Cf. Bibliography on the same subject in

Boletín Bibliográfico Iberoamericano. Centro de
Información y Sociologia de la OCSHA, Ciudad
Universitaria, Madrid - 3. 22 p.

2313. Valenzuela Monges, Rodolfo. De la dependencia a la
        teología de la liberación; notas bibliográficas.
        Cuernavaca, Mexico, CIDOC, 1973. 45 p. A draft
        preparatory to a more extensive work on the theology
        of liberation. Contains also the two bibliographies
        listed above or a part of Dec. 73/386 of CIDOC's
        series I/I (Idealogies/Iglesias).

2314. Vanderhoff, Frank. Bibliography: Latin America and
        Theology of Liberation. Ottawa, University of St.
        Paul, 1972. 44 p.

2315. Wagner, C. Peter. The Charismatic Movement in Latin
        America. Limited bibliography of about one hundred
        items prepared for the School of World Missions,
        1972. Mimoegraphed. ICG.

2316. Wilson, Stanton R. *and* C. Kenneth Goodpasture. Biblio-
        graphy of writings of John A. Mackey (from 1958-1970).
        SML.

GENERAL LITERATURE
See also p. 59.

2317. Beyerhaus, Peter. Shaken Foundations: Grand Rapids,
        Michigan, Zondervan, 1972. 1972 Lectures on Church
        Growth.

2318. Bradshaw, Malcom R. Church Growth through Evangelism-in-
        Depth. South Pasadena, William Carey Library, 1969.
        127 p. Written by a missionary to Colombia related
        to this movement.

2319. Beaver, R. Pierce. Pioneers in Mission. Grand Rapids,
        Michigan, Eerdmans, 1966. 278 p. Ten ordination
        sermons, charges and instructions between 1733 and
        1810. Reveals missionary passion before the rise
        of present missionary societies and the modern
        Protestant missionary movement.

2320. Castleman, Wm. J. Samuel Guy Inman (1905-1916). Indian-
        apolis, 1969. 468 p. Vol. 2. A historical, liter-
        ary biography of Christian cooperation and an
        advocate of Inter-American friendship (1877-1965).
        Details of his missionary service in Mexico, the

Edinburgh Conference of 1910 and the preparation for
the Panama Conference of 1916. Vol. 1, *On this
Foundation*, is by the same author. 176 p. A summary
of Inman's life and missionary service. Available
from the author, 9 S. Lynhurst Dr., Indianapolis,
Ind. 46241.

2321. Crossroads in Mission. A reprint of five books in one
binding of the IFMA-DFMA Green Lake conferences by
Johannes Blauw, Jas. A. Scherer, Beyerhaus, Lefeber,
T. Watson Street and R. Pierce Beaver. South Pasadena,
Ca., William Carey Library, 1973. 900 p. Introduc-
tion by Arthur Glasser.

2322. Castro, Emilio. Pentecostalismo y Ecumenismo. Santiago,
Centro de Difusion Ecuménica, Casilla 16477, Santiago.
1972.

2323. Cook, Harold. Historic Patterns of Church Growth. Grand
Rapids, Mich. Eerdmans, 1969. The 1969 Church Growth
Lectures.

2324. Castro, Emilio. "Evangelism in Latin America," in *Mission*,
7 (December, 1968). pp. 22-34.

2325. Cogswell, Jas. A. Response: the Church in mission to a
world in crisis. Richmond, Virginia, The CLC Press,
1971. 160 p. Deals with the interaction of the
Christian message and the world situation.

2326. Damboriena, Prudencio. Tongues as of Fire; Pentecostalism
in contemporary Christianity. Washington, Corpus
Books, 1969.

2327. Edwards, Richard E. Toward a critical understanding of
Protestant missions in Latin America. B.D. thesis,
Union Theological Seminary, New York, N.Y. Attempts
to show a functional relation between missions and
imperalism.

2328. Goodpasture, H. McKennie. "The Latin American Soul of
John A. Mackay." In *Journal of Presbyterian History*.
Vol. 48, No. 4 (Winter, 1970). 265-292 pp. An
excellent summary of an outstanding missionary
statesman of Latin America based on his life and
writings.

2329. Green, Dana S. Chasms in the Americas. New York, Friend-
      ship Press, 1970. A search for new understanding
      between North and South Americans.

2330. Grubb, Kenneth G. Religion in Central America. London,
      World Dominion Press, 1937. 147 p. A basic survey
      of Protestantism in that region. Comparable to Sir
      Kenneth's surveys on all other major areas in Latin
      America.

2331. _____. Crypts of Power: An autobiography. London,
      Hodder and Stroughton. 1971. 253 p. Grubb spent
      his early years as missionary and researcher in
      Latin America and has been an influential figure in
      British relationships with Latin America for half a
      century. A reluctant autobiography written at a
      publisher's request.

2332. Gullin, Gillian Lindt. Moravians in Two worlds. New
      York, Columbia University Press, 1968. The Moravians
      were the first Protestant missionaries in the
      Caribbean.

2333. Hamilton, J. Taylor. History of the Moravian Church,
      1722-1957. Bethlehem, Penn., Moravian Archives.
      n.d. Revised in 1968 by Bishop K. G. Hamilton.

2334. Hodges, Melvin. Growing young churches. How to advance
      indigenous churches today. Chicago, Moody Press,
      1970.

2335. Hollenweger, Walter J. "Pentecostalism and the Third
      World" in *Dialog* 9:1129. 1970.

2336. _____. The Pentecostals: The charismatic movement in
      the Churches, London: SCM Press, 1972. Also
      Augsburg, 1972. 572 p. The most comprehensive and
      authoritative study of international Pentecostalism
      in print. The author was an evangelist of the Swiss
      Pentecostal Mission from 1948-58, secretary for
      evangelism of the World Council of Churches and since
      1971 professor of mission at the University of
      Birmingham.

2337. Latourette, Kenneth Scott. Beyond the Ranges. Grand
      Rapids, Eerdmans, 1967. An autobiography published
      posthumously. 161 p.

2338. Liggett, Thomas J., Where Tomorrow struggles to be born: The Americas in Transition. New York, Friendship Press, 1970. A call for recognition by the United States government and church of Latin America desires for self-determination.

2339. Lores, Ruben. La Unidad y los misioneros extranjeros. San José, Costa Rica, Instituto de Evangelismo a Fondo, Apartado 1307. 1970.

2340. Mackay, John A. Christian reality and appearance. Richmond, Virginia. John Knox Press, 1969. English edition of portions of 1953 Carnahan lectures, published by La Aurora, Buenos Aires, 1970, under title Realidad e Idolatría en el Cristianismo contemporáneo. Refers to modern idols of doctrine, Christian emotion, institutional religion and legalism. Recognizes the powerful influences of Pentecostal and renewed Roman Catholic witness in Latin America.

2341. McCollough, Larry D. Latin American and Evangelism-in-depth: Factors involved in transdenominational and inter-mission cooperation in Evangelism in Depth. M.A. thesis. Deerfield, Illinois, Trinity Evangelical Divinity School, 1971.

2342. Miguez Bonino, José. "Protestants' contributions to Latin America," in *Lutheran Quarterly*, 22 (February, 1970) 92-98 p.

2343. Neill, Stephen C. Call to Mission. Philadelphia, Fortress Press, 1970. 113 p. A popular apologetic directed to the American laymen in particular.

2344. Paton, David M., ed. Reform of the ministry: a study in the work of Roland Allen. London: Lutterworth Press, 1968. 235 p. On the centenary of the birth of a missionary "prophet," a collection of his writings and comments on his work was prepared but a definite critical biography is still needed.

2345. Petersen, G. Leonard. Sor-Amerika: fremtidens kontient. Oslo, Filadelfia-forlaget, 1965 (?). 136 p. Record of tour of Norwegian of Pentecostal work in South America. No attempt to analize either socio-political or religious background of continent.

2346. Pickett, J. W. Dynamics of Church Growth. Nashville,
       Abingdon Press, 1962. The 1962 Lectures on Church
       Growth.

2347. Quick, Bernard. Money and Mission in a Revolutionary
       World. Ph.D. dissertation. Princeton Theological
       Seminary. 1973. In process. A critical approach
       to the factor of the power of foreign subsidy by
       personnel and funds for foreign mission.

2348. Rembao, Alberto. "Protestant Latin America: sight and
       insight" in *The International Review of Missions*,
       46 (January, 1957) 30-36.

2349. Roberts, W. Dayton. "Latin American Protestants: which
       way will they go?" in *Christianity Today*, XIV, No.
       1, 1969.

2350. _____. Revolution in evangelism: The
       story of Evangelism-in-Depth in Latin America.
       Foreward by Leighton Ford. Chicago, Moody Press,
       1967. 127 p.

2351. Rosales, Ray S. The Evangelism in Depth Program of the
       Latin American Mission. Cuernavaca, Mexico; CIDOC,
       1968. Masters thesis at Lutheran Theological
       Seminary. Sondeos series No. 21. Discusses methodo-
       logy as practiced in this movement and in particular
       in relation to Lutheran evangelism in Latin America.

2352. Scherer, James A. Justinian Welz: essays by an early
       prophet of mission; translated, annotated and with a
       historical introduction. Grand Rapids, Eerdmans,
       1969. 111 p. A predecessor to William Carey who
       worked on the North coast of South America where he
       died in 1668(?).

2353. Schwarze, W. N. *and* S. H. Gapp. A history of the begin-
       nings of Moravian work in America. Bethlehem, Penn.,
       Moravian Archives, 1955. Archives Publication No. 1.

2354. Shacklock, Floyd. Man of Two Revolutions. The story of
       Justo González. New York, Friendship Press, 1969.
       The life of Justo and Luisa González, literacy
       experts and founders of ALFALIT after leaving Cuba
       in 1961. The story of the founding of this organi-
       zation based in Costa Rica, appears in the last
       chapter.

2355.   Stockwell, Eugene L.   Claimed by God for mission.   The
        congregation seeks new forms.   New York, World Out-
        look Press, 1961.   159 p.   On the missionary
        structure of the congregation.

2356.   Strachan, R. Kenneth, ed.   Evangelism in depth; experi-
        menting with a new type of evangelism.   Chicago,
        Moody Press, 1961.   126 p.   The story or the origen
        of this movement and the record of its first two
        campaigns in Nicaragua and Costa Rica.

2357.   _____.   The Inescapable Calling.   Grand Rapids, Eerdmans
        Publishing Company, 1968.   (Cf. Who Shall Ascend
        No. 2846).

2358.   Stowe, David M.   Ecumenicity and Evangelism.   Grand
        Rapids, Michigan, Eerdmans, 1970.   94 p.   The 1967
        Church Growth Lectures at Fuller Theological
        Semianry.   An important contribution to the post-
        Uppsala debate on the "meaning, substance, aim and
        imperative" of evangelism.

2359.   Taylor, John V.   The Pentecostal Movement in *Christian
        Missionary Society Newsletter*, No. 137, 157 Waterloo
        Road, London, 1972.

2360.   Tippett, Alan R., ed.   God, Man and Church Growth.   A
        festschrift in honor of Donald A. McGavran.   1973.
        447 p.   Grand Rapids, Mich., Eerdmans.

2361.   _____.   Church Growth and the Word of God: The Biblical
        basis on the church growth viewpoint.   Grand
        Rapids: Eerdmans, 1970.   82 p.   A solid work by a
        competent missionary anthropologist and seminary
        teacher.

2362.   Thompson, Betty, ed.   The Healing Fountain: Voices from
        Contemporary Christians.   New York, United Methodist
        Board of Global Ministries, 1973.   204 p.   A
        compendium of brief statements including several
        Latin American church leaders.

2363.   Tschuy, Theo.   "Latin American Protestants, the coming
        crisis," in *Christian Century*, 26 (December, 1962),
        39-46.

2364.   Uehling, Carl T., ed.   Special issue of *World Encounter*
        on Latin America.   February, 1972.   Vol. 9, No. 3.

Series of articles under theme "South America, marxists, Catholics, Lutherans and the future."

2365. Wagner, C. Peter. "The Latin American Crisis in Evangelistic Impact," in *Evangelical Missions Quarterly*, (Winter, 1972), 65-72.

2366. Winn, Wilkins B. "Reports of British Diplomats concerning the status of Protestantism in Latin America in 1851," in *A Journal of Church and State*, X (Autumn, 1968). pp. 437-444. A good overall view of Protestantism (Brazil excluded) in Latin America in the middle of 19th century as seen by British diplomats.

2367. Woods, James E. "The Rise and Growth of Religious Pluralism in Latin America," in *A Journal of Church and State*, 12 (Winter, 1970), 1-12.

2368. Yoder, Sanford Calvin. Down South America Way. Herald Press, Scottsdale, Pa. 1943. 148 p. Review of Mennonite work in Argentina, Uruguay and Paraguay.

BASIC RESOURCES AND STUDY TOOLS
See also p. 80.

Surveys, Histories of Missions
and Comprehensive Mission Studies
See also p. 81.

2369. Boberg, John T. S.V.D. and James Scherer, editors. Mission in the Seventies, Chicago Cluster of Theological Studies, 1972. 208 p. Addresses given at 1971 Mission Institute. Reflect common missionary concern of participating theological institutions.

2370. Burgess, Andrew S., ed. Lutheran churches in the Third World. Minneapolis, Minnesota, Augsburg Publishing House, 1970. 176 p. A symposium with an area by area account of Lutheran presence in Africa, Asia, and Latin America. A table of statistics for 1969.

2371. *Concepto Latino-Americano*, I, II, III. Special issue, No. 26, March 1970. I. Articles by Manoel de Melo. Alfredo Ramirez Ramirez, Walter J. Hollenweger in "El Consejo Mundial de Iglesias y el Pentecostalismo"; II. Estudios Bíblicos; III. Minutes on Bible Seminars.

2372. Fey, Harold E., ed. A history of the ecumenical movement.
London, SPCK, 1970. Vol. II. "The Ecumenical
advance." 524 p. A continuation of the work com-
pleted by Ruth Rouse and Stephen C. Neil, beginning
with the WCC founding to the General Assembly in
Uppsala in 1968. Of special interest are developments in Latin America.

2373. Gerber, Vergil, ed. Mission in creative tensions. South
Pasadena, William Carey Library, 1972. The papers
of the Green Lake conference in 1971 on this theme.

2374. Gonzalez, Justo L. Historia de la misiones. Buenos
Aires: La Aurora, 1970. An important survey volume.

2375. Hollenweger, Walter J., ed., The Church for others and
the Church for the world. A quest for structures
for missionary congregations. Geneva, World Council
of Churches, 1967. 135 p. Final report of the
Western European Working Group of the Department on
Studies in Evangelism.

2376. *International Review of Mission.* Special issue on Latin
America and the Caribbean. Vol. LX, No. 238, April
1971. 314 p. An excellent review with key interpretative articles.

2377. Jones, Aziel W. Organizational development of the Central
American Mission. M.A. thesis, Columbia Bible
College, Columbia, S.C. 1967.

2378. Kane, J. Herbert. A global view of Christian missions"
From Pentecost to the present. Baaker Book House,
1971. Comprehensive survey of the Christian mission
effort through history and with country-by-country
sections on current activity.

2379. Kirby, Gilbert. Evangelism alert" a strategy for the
Seventies. World Wide Press, 1972. Papers of the
1971 European Congress on Evangelism.

2380. "Lutheran Plunge in Latin America." In *Lutheran
Quarterly*, February, 1970. Vol. XXII, No. 1. pp.
4-100. Entire issue on Lutheranism in Latin America.

2381. Martin, Malcolm, S.A. The missionary influence in the
origens of the Ecumenical movement and its development in Latin America. M.A. thesis. Ottawa, St.
Paul's University, 1972. 127 p. A survey of the

role of the missionary in ecumenical awakenings in
the context of the modern missionary movement in
Latin America since the Second Vatican Council.

2382. McGavran, Donald, ed. Eye of the Storm: The great
       debate in mission. Waco, Texas; Word Publishers,
       1973. Focuses on the central conflict in mission
       today, giving various points of view. A collection
       of historic documents by leading mission spokesmen.

2383. _____, ed. Crucial Issues in Mission Today. Chicago,
       Moody Press, 1972. Twelve leaders in contemporary
       mission thought including Peter Byerhaus and John
       Mbiti find expression in this book.

2384. Read, William R., Victor Monterroso *and* Harman A. Johnson.
       Latin American Church Growth. Grand Rapids,
       Michigan, Eerdmans Publishing Co., 1969. 421 p.
       Covers countries of mainland Latin America and
       documents the growth of Protestant community in
       Latin America. Project funded by Lily Foundation
       and several mission boards. Data provided is
       superior to previous data available in World
       Christian Handbooks and Taylor-Coggins survey of
       1961. (Cf. No. 536, 535). Tends to evaluate impact
       of the Evangelical movement in Latin America on the
       basis of numerical growth. A deeper analysis is
       needed. (Spanish edition, "Avance Evangélico en
       La America Latina"). Portuguese edition, "O cres-
       cimento da igreja no America Latina." São Paulo,
       Editora Mundo Cristao, 1969. 473 p. Trans. by João
       Marques Bentos.

2385. Rouse, Ruth *and* Stephen R. Neil, eds. A history of the
       ecumenical movement. Vol. I. London, SPCK, 1967.
       600 p. An excellent history of the entire ecumeni-
       cal movement from the beginnings in the Protestant
       Reformation to the founding of the World Council of
       Churches in 1948.

2386. Sinclair, John H. Congregational life as a factor in
       church growth; illustrated from some First Century
       and Twentieth Century churches. 1971 Church Growth
       Lectures at the School of World Mission of Fuller
       Theological Seminary. 62 p. Unpublished. Available
       at the UML and ICG.

2387. Taylor, John F. Indigenous churches of the Christian and
       Missionary Alliance. Ph.D. dissertation. New York
       University. 1966.

2388. Wagner, C. Peter, ed. Church/mission tensions today.
      Chicago, Moody Press, 1972. 237 p. Symposium by
      thirteen mission leaders at Green Lake Conference,
      1971. Discusses the role of sending churches,
      mission agencies, the receiving churches and the
      missionaries.

2389. _____. "Missiological research in the Fuller Seminary
      School of Missions." Mimeographed. 9 p.
      Describes research program and lists completed and
      current theses topics.

2390. _____. Frontiers of mission strategy. Chicago, Moody
      Press. 1971. 222 p. Guidelines for a strategy
      which seeks to be evangelical and biblically
      oriented, yet pragmatic and effective. Outgrowth
      of lectures at School of World Mission, Fuller
      Theological Seminary, 1970-71.

2391. Warren, Max. To apply the Gospel. Grand Rapids,
      Michigan, Eerdmans, 1971. A publication in series
      of the Christian World Mission. R. Pierce Beaver,
      general editor. Collection of writings of Henry
      Venn and the concept of the voluntary missionary
      society working within church structures.

2392. Wieser, Thomas, ed., Planning for Mission. Working
      papers on the new quest for missionary communities.
      New York, the U.S. Conference for the World Council
      of Churches, 1966. 228 p.

2393. Winter, Ralph D. The twenty-five unbelievable years:
      1945-1969. South Pasadena, California; William
      Carey Library, 1970. 116 p. Review of extensive
      and radical changes in mission structures during
      this period and attempts to interpret the meaning
      of these changes. Graphs and charts.

2394. _____ *and* R. Pierce Beaver. The Warp and the Woof:
      Organizing for mission. South Pasadena, California;
      William Carey Library, 1970. 63 p. Proposes
      diversity in mission strategy in contrast to central-
      ization, emphasizing values of the voluntary
      missionary order.

2395. Wong, James. Missions from the Third World. Singapore,
      Church Growth Study Center, 1973. 135 p. Survey
      study of Third World missionaries in this decade.
      Statistical base appears sketchy.

2396. World Update: Latin America, 1973. Summary of "The
       mood and the mode" for mission in the 1970's with
       significant articles by Latin American church
       leaders, facts and figures. New York, Friendship
       Press, 1973. 12 p.

                          Directories
                        See also p. 87.

2397. Anderson, Gerald H. *and* Andrew F. Walls. Seven hundred
       basic books for studies in the Christian World
       Mission. A bibliographical guide. In preparation.

2398. Beguin, Oliver, ed., Directory of Bible Societies.
       London, United Bible Societies, 1970. 188 p.

2399. Neill, Stephen C., Gerald H. Anderson *and* John Goodwin
       (editors). Concise Directory of the Christian World
       Mission. Nashville, Abingdon Press, 1971. 682 p.
       Alphabetized descriptions of the status of the
       church in countries and areas of the world; bio-
       graphies of church leaders, past and present; major
       Christian organizations. (also London, Lutterworth
       Press, 1971).

2400. North American Protestant Ministries Overseas. 1970, 1973
       editions. 320 p. A comprehensive listing of over
       600 agencies, showing their fields of service,
       country by country breakdown, analysis of income,
       expenditures, numbers of personnel, association
       membership, etc. Color coded sections. $4.50
       (rustic); $7.50 on four microfiche (microfilm);
       $2.50. Missions Advance Research and Communication
       Center, 919 West Huntington Drive, Monrovia,
       California 91016. $4.50.

2401. World Directory of Mission-related educational institu-
       tions. Edited by Raymond B. Buker and Ted Word for
       CAMEO, 1972. 900 p. William Carey Library, South
       Pasadena, Ca. 1972.

         REPORTS OF CONTINENTAL AND REGIONAL CONFERENCES

                      Interdenominational
                        See also p. 88.

2402. Deudores del Mundo. Tercera Conferencia Evangélica
       Latinoamericana. U.N.E.L.A.M. Montevideo, 1969.
       Addresses and reports of this continental conference.

2403. Misioneros norteamericanos en America Latina ¿Para qué?
       Montevideo, UNELAM, 1971. 117 p. Addresses and
       resolutions of consultation in Oaxtepec, Mexico,
       November, 1970.

Denominational
See also p. 93.

Methodist
See also p. 94.

2404. Evangelización y revolución en America Latina. Iglesia
       Metodista en América Latina. Documentos previos,
       trabajos y conclusiones de la Consulta Continental
       de Evangelización. Cochabamba, Bolivia, 1966.

2405. Latin America and the World Division. Report on the
       Latin American Task Force of the Board of World
       Missions of the United Methodist Church, 1972. 55
       p. Policy and program recommendations for involve-
       ment in mission in Latin America today. Available
       free. Service Center, 7820 Reading Road, Cincinnati,
       Ohio 45237.

Presbyterian
See also p. 94.

2406. Illusion and Reality in Inter-American Relations. Social
       Progress, July-August, 1969. 20 p. Statement and
       recommendations approved by the United Presbyterian
       Church. Result of a three year study of inter-
       american relations by the Advisory Council on Inter-
       American Affairs of that denomination.

LITERATURE ON THE SPECIAL CONCERNS
OF PROTESTANTISM IN LATIN AMERICA
See also p. 96.

Work Among Indigenous Groups

Books, Essays and Pamphlets
See also p. 96.

2407. Consulta Indígena Latinoamerica.   Crítica a Barbados.
       Published by Asociación Indigenista del Paraguay.
       Asunción, Paraguay. Editorial Toledo, 1972. 671 p.
       Results of a consultation held in Asunción in March,
       1972 to follow through on the implications in Paraguay
       of the Barbados document.

2408. Dostal, W., ed. The Situation of the Indian in South
       America; Contributions to the study of inter-ethnic
       conflict in the non-Andean regions of South America.
       Geneva, World Council of Churches, 1972. 510 p.
       Also a publication of the Department of Ethnology,
       University of Bern, No. 3, 1971. Spanish edition.
       La Situación del Indígena en la América del Sur.
       Montevideo, Tierra Nueva, 453 p. The papers pre-
       sented at the Barbados Consultation in 1971 on
       Venezuela, Colombia, Ecuador, Perú, Bolivia,
       Paraguay, Argentina, Brazil and the Guianas.
       Valuable tables, charts and maps. Also critical
       bibliographies.

2409. El indígena de los Andes. Estudios sobre Nuevas Formas
       de Obra Cristiana entre los Indígenas Andínos.
       Montevideo, ISAL, 1966. Papers and reports on the
       II Consulta Andiana. 122 p.

2410. Hefley, James *and* Marti. Dawn over Amazonia. Waco,
       Texas, Word Books, 192 p. Describes the rapid
       expansion of the Wycliffe Bible Translators from a
       handful of people to 2,500 missionaries in 38
       years. The Hefleys spent a summer observing and
       investigating the inner machinery of the organiza-
       tion and its outreach in Peru.

2411. Kroeker, Peter J. "Lenguas and Mennonites: A study of
       cultural change in the Paraguayan Chaco, 1928-1970.
       M.A. thesis, Dept. of Anthropology, Wichita State
       University, Wichita, Kan., 1970. 172 p. Copy in
       files of Mennonite Board of Missions and Charities,
       Elkhart, Indiana. Student examines Lengua Indian
       sociocultural change resulting from contact with
       German-speaking Mennonite neighbors: long historical
       introduction to both Lenguas and Mennonites: ethno-
       graphic description of Lengua social organization
       and brief evaluation of Mennonite programs of
       religious and social services to Indians. Commend-
       able effort for master's thesis.

2412. Morner, Magnus, ed. *Race and Class in Latin America.* New York: Columbia University Press, 1970.

2413. Williams Garcia, Roberto. El mito en una comunidad indígena. Pisaflores, Vera Cruz. Cuernavaca, CIDOC, 1970. Sondeos No. 61.

Articles
See also p. 96.

2414. Loewen, Jacob A. "A Mennonite Encounter with the 'Innermost' of the Lengua Indians" in *Practical Anthropology*, XIII, N.D. 1966, 252-72. Study demonstrates how Paraguayan Mennonites failed to understand behavior of motivation of Indian neighbors because they did not comprehend the existence or meaning of Lengua "innermost."

2415. _____. "Mennonites, Chaco Indians and the Lengua Spirit World" in *Mennonite Quarterly Review*, XXXIX (0 1965), 280-306. Analysis of aboriginal Lengua Indian religious belief and practices. Suggests ways Mennonite missionaries can approach Lengua culture.

2416. _____. "The Way to First Class: Revolution or Conversion?" in *Practical Anthropology*, XII (S/O 1965) 193-209. Background to the Chulupi Indian "purising" which resulted from unresolved difficulties with the Paraguayan Mennonite colonists over land disputes, theft, etc.

2417. Metraux, Alfred. Myths of the Toba and Pilagá Indians of the Gran Chaco. Philadelphia. American Folklore Society, 1946. 167 p. (Vol. 40 of the Memoirs of the American Folklore Society, 1946). Good bibliography.

Youth and University Students
See also p. 99.

Youth (Non-University)
See also p. 99.

2418. Miguez Bonino, José, ed. Out of Hurt and Hope, Voices of Latin American youth. New York, Friendship Press, 1970. Selections made by Latin American high school

youth of portions of their literature which North
American youth should read.

University Student Work
See also p. 99.

2419. Dani, B. Thomas *and* R. B. Craig. "Student dissent in
Latin America: toward a comprehensive analysis" in
Latin American Research Review, Vol. VIII, No. 1,
Spring, 1973. 71-97 p.

2420. Sensening, Jay Vernon. The Gospel and the Latin American
Student. M.S. thesis. Columbia Bible College,
Columbia, S.C. 1967.

2421. Van den Heuvel, Albert H. Estos Poderes Rebeldes.
Translation from English by Roberto Mariano.
Montevideo, Paysandú 983, ULAJE, 1967. 185 p.
Presentation of the issues youth face in today's
world by the former WCC Youth secretary.

2422. Voekel, Janvier W. "The Eternal Revolutionary: Evangelical Ministry to the University Student in Latin
America". Unpublished M.A. thesis, 1971. School
of World Missions and Institute of Church Growth,
Fuller Theological Seminary, Pasadena, Ca.

Literature and Literacy
See also p. 100.

(See works of Paulo Freire under section on Church and Society)

Church and Society
See also p. 100.

2423. Alves, Rubem, et al. De la Iglesia y la Sociedad.
Montevideo, Tierra Nueva. 1971. Biblioteca Mayor.

2424. Amaya, Ismael E. "The Present status of the theology of
Revolution in Latin America" in *Latin American Pulse*,
Vol. VIII, No. 1, January, 1973. Disagrees with
Alves, Assman and others on "social sin" and affirms
"injustice, crime and sin in general are not found
either in things or systems."

2425. Assman, Hugo. Opresión-Liberación, Un desafio a los
       cristianos. Montevideo, Tierra Nueva, 1971.

2426. _____, ed., Habla Fidel Castro sobre los cristianos
       revolucionarios. Montevideo, Tierra Nueva, 1972.
       111 p. Prologue gives the setting for the conversa-
       tions Premier Castro held in Chile in late 1971 with
       Christians, Cardinal Silva Henriquez, priests and
       students.

2427. Barbieri, Flavio Ermio. The revolutionary situation in
       Latin America and its significance for the Church.
       S.T.M. thesis. Boston University School of Theology,
       Boston, Mass., 1964.

2428. Blanquart, Paul, et al. Pueblo Oprimido, Señor de la
       Historia. Montevideo, Tierra Nueva, 19 . 280 p.
       Discussion by seventeen social scientists and
       theologians of the great themes related to theology
       and liberation in the economic, social and political
       context of Latin American society.

2429. Carvajal, Rafael Tomas, Filemón Escobar, et al. American
       Latina: Movilización popular y fe cristiana.
       Montevideo, ISAL, 1971. 172 p. Contains the docu-
       ments and conclusions of the last General Assembly
       of the Church and Society held in Naña, Peru in 1971.

2430. Christianity and Crisis. Special issue on Latin America.
       Vol. 32, No. 5, April 3, 1972. Articles by William
       Wipfler, Sheperd Bliss, James and Margaret Goff and
       John Bennett. 84 p.

2431. Cesar, Waldo, et al. Protestantismo e imperialismo na
       America Latina, Petrópolis, 1968.

2432. Costas, Orlando. "Latin American Revolutions and the
       Church," in *Foundations*, XIV, April-June, 1967.
       116-127.

2433. de Hainaut, Raymond. Faith and ideology in Latin
       American perspectives. Ph.D. dissertation. Drew
       University, Madison, N.J., 1970. Sondeos Series
       No. 85.

2434. del Valle, Luis G. "Identidad del cristiano revolucion-
       ario" en *Contact* (Mexico City). Vol. 9, Nos. 3, 4.
       August, 1972. 43-50 p.

2435. Dumas, Andre. Ideologia y Fe. Montevideo, Tierra Nueva,
      1970. 85 p. Also in Portuguese Ideologia e Fe,
      Tempo e Presenca. Written by Professor of Social
      Ethics at the Protestant Facultad in Paril and a
      well known student of Marxism in France.

2436. Freire, Paulo. La educación como práctica de la libertad.
      Montevideo, Tierra Nueva, 1972. Cuarte edición.

2437. _____. "La misión educadora de la iglesia en América
      Latina" in *Pasos*, July 10, 1972. Doc. I/II, 72/38.

2438. _____. Pedagogía del Oprimido. Montevideo, Tierra
      Nueva, 1972. Tercera edición.

2439a. Furter, Pierre. Educación y Reflexión. Montevideo.
       Tierra Nueva, 1971.

2439b. _____. Educación y Vida. Montevideo. Tierra Nueva,
       1973.

2440. Gente Comprometida. Montevideo, ULAJE, 1970. 63 p.
      Reflections of older youth of Argentina, Bolivia,
      República Dominicana and Uruguay about the situa-
      tion to be faced as Christians who have committed
      themselves to the Lord of History.

2441. Gingrich, Melvin. The Christian and Revolution. Scotts-
      dale, Penn. Herald Press, 1968.

2442. Institute on the Church in Urban Industrial Society
      (ICUIS). Publication includes: "Notes on Urban
      Industrial Mission" published three times a year,
      free of charge; "Abstract Services," a monthly
      indexed publication ($15.00 per year) and "Quarterly
      Index Cumultions" ($5.00 per year or accompanying
      Abstract Services at no extra charge). ICUIS pro-
      vides a world-wide information service and reference
      center and serves as an international clearing house.
      ICUIS operates in cooperation with the Division of
      World Mission and Evangelism of the World Council
      of Churches. Address of ICUIS: 800 W. Belden
      Avenue, Chicago, Ill. 60614.

2443. Lalive, Christian D'epinay. "La Iglesia Evangélica y la
      Revolución Latinoamericana" in *Cristianismo y
      Sociedad*. Vol. VI, No. 16:17. 1968. 21-30 p.
      Also in English. Trans. by James E. Goff. October
      25, 1969. Mimeographed.

2444. Lara-Braud, Jorge, trans., Social Justice and the Latin
          Churches, Richmond, Va. John Knox Press, 1969.
          137 p. Original contributions to Protestant thinking
          in Latin America on issues of Church and Society.
          Discussions and reports from the Church and Society
          Conference in El Tabo, Chile, January, 1966. Reviews
          movement since 1961 and analyzes the historical
          juncture in 1966 (Spanish edition, America Hoy,
          Iglesia y Sociedad en America Latina, Montevideo,
          1966. 132 p.).

2445. Lara-Braud, Jorge, ed. Our Claim on the Future. New
          York, Friendship Press, 1970. A controversial
          collection from six Latin Americans on social and
          economic revolution and the role of the Protestant
          and Catholic churches.

2446. Leeuwen, A. Th. Van. Desarrollo y revolución. Buenos
          Aires, Aurora, 1967.

2447. Macin, Raul. Jaramillo, un profeta olvidado. Montevideo,
          Tierra Nueva, 1970. 182 p. Story of Mexican
          revolutionary figure, a Methodist lay preacher in
          the early 1900's.

2448. Miguez Bonino, José. "Church and the Latin American
          Social Revolution," in *Perspective*, IX, Fall, 1968.
          213-232 p.

2449. _____, "Christians and the Political Revolution" in
          Risk, Vol. III, Nos. 1 and 2, 1967. 100-110 p.

2450. Miranda Osmundo, Afonso. Third World Theology of
          Liberation. A partial bibliography. (Cf. No. 2312).

2451. Mosley, J. Brooke. Christians in the Technical and
          Social Revolutions of our Time. Suggestions for
          study and action. Cincinnati, Ohio; Forward Move-
          ment Publications, 1966. Summary of the World
          Council of Churches conference on Church and
          Society in 1966.

2452. Perez, Pablo. The Theology of the Mission of the Church
          in Latin America in the Light of the Current Debate
          on Revolution (written in Spanish). D. Miss.
          Research in progress. School of Missions and
          Institute of Church Growth, Fuller Theological
          Seminary, Pasadena, Ca.

2453. Rountree, Estelle *and* Hugh F., Halverstadrt, editors.,
       Sometimes they cry. A study-action book. New York,
       Friendship Press, 1968. Prepared to document world
       hunger, theological aspects of the problem and
       poverty in affluent societies. 144 p.

2454. Sabanes, Julio. El Cristo de las elites políticas.
       Santiago, UNELAM, Casilla 1773, 1972.

2455. de Santa Ana, Julio, "Latin American Masses: the Unsat-
       isfied Ones," T. W. Duee, in Student World, XVII:
       1(1964) 21-30 p.

2456. Seifert, H. El sí de la no violencia. Montevideo,
       Movimiento de Reconciliación, 1969. Translation
       of English original, Westminster Press.

2457. Se vive como se puede. Montevideo, Editorial Alfa, 1969,
       123 p. Unique experiment of concientizacion in a
       barrio of Montevideo among marginalized people.
       Conversations over several months were recorded and
       woven together into a fabric which reveals both the
       misery and yet the yearnings of the masses. This
       small book takes one inside "the culture of poverty"
       of Oscar Lewis.

2458. Sodepax. In Search of a Theology of Development. Geneva,
       WCC, Com. on Development and Peace, 1970.

2459. Wagner, C. Peter. Latin American Theology: radical or
       evangelical? Grand Rapids, Eerdmans, 1970. 118 p.
       Spanish translation. Teología Latinoamericana
       ¿Izquierdista o evangélica? Miami, Florida,
       Editorial Vida, 1969. 176 p. A critical analysis
       of the development of radical theology among Latin
       American Protestants, with contemporary evangelical
       alternative.

Mass Communications
See also p. 102.

2460. Bulletins of several Protestant communication groups:
       Intercom. Liverpool 65-206. Mexico 6, D.F. Mexico.
       Rev. Rolando Zapata, Director of CAVE-Mexico. See
       especially No. 13, September-October, 1972 with
       article "El Pato Donald ha muerto." Also El
       Cavernario. Published by CAVE-Mexico.

2461. Cavito. Apartado Aereo 51092, Bogota, Colombia. CAVECOL
       publication.

2462. Communícala. Report on international pilot project in
       mass communications in which training media special-
       ists was carried out through a six-months internship
       program with commercial media and university resources.
       Available from Intermedia, Room 670, 475 Riverside
       Drive, New York, N.Y. 10027. 65 p.

2463. El Cavernícola. Lautaro 245, Buenos Aires, CAVER-Rio
       Platense.

2464. Intermedia Newsletter. November, 1972. Special issue on
       Latin America. Available from Room 670, 475 River-
       side Drive, New York, N.Y. 10027.

2464a. Mattelart, Armando *and* Ariel Dorfman. Para leer al Pato
       Donald. Santiago, Universidad de Chile, 1972. A
       psyco-sociological study of influence of North
       American mass media on Latin America.

2465. Nida, Eugene. Understanding Latin Americans. South
       Pasadena, Ca., William Carey Library, 1973. A
       valuable anthropolical perspective. Written with
       sympathy and perspective of many years related to
       Latin America.

2466. _____. Communication of the Gospel in Latin America,
       Cuernavaca, Mexico: CIDOC, 1969. Sondeos No. 53.
       145 p. A series of articles which appeared in
       Practical Anthropology and also an anthropological
       analysis of the major themes of Latin American life.

2467. World Directory of religious radio and television broad-
       casting, South Pasadena, Ca., William Carey Library,
       1973. 900 p. Exhaustive listing for each country
       of the world, arranged by continents and overviews
       of regions.

2468. Resúmen de la Telecomunicación. Apartado 2470, San José,
       Costa Rica. Published by DIA - Difusiones Inter-
       Americanas.

2469. WACC Journal. 6 Frankfurt-Main, Friedrichstrasse 34,
       Germany. Special issue on Latin America, December,
       1972. 56 p. Spanish and English.

2470. Wells, Alan. Picture-tube imperialism? The impact of
       U.S. television on Latin America. Maryknoll, N.Y.,
       Orbis Books, 1972. 192 p. A professor at Tulane
       University challenges the assumption that increasing
       the mass communication in a country stimulates
       economic development. Wells has the interest of
       both the United States and the "poor nation" at
       heart.

                     Sociology of Protestantism
                        See also p. 103.

2471. Alcantara Matos, Domingo. Cien Años de Presencia del
       Protestantismo en Centro-America. (Cf. No. 2828).

2472. Alves, Rubem A. "Protestantism in Latin America: its
       ideological function and utopian possibilities" in
       The Ecumenical Review, January, 1970.

2473. Cesar, Waldo A. Para uma sociologia do Protestantismo
       Brasileiro. Petropolis, R.J., Editores Vozes Ltda,
       1973. 48 p. Excellent essay on three aspects of
       Protestantism: importation, relation to other
       religions and relation to Brazilian society.

2474. Denton, C. F. "Protestantism and the Latin American
       Middle Class," in *Practical Anthropology*, 18:24-28.
       January-February, 1971.

2475. Drekonja, Gerhard. "Religion and Social Change in Latin
       America," in *Latin American Research Review*, VI
       (Spring, 1971), 53-72 p.

2476. Fals Borda, Orlando. "Protestantes y el cambio social
       en American Latina," in *CIDOC Informa*, Cuernavaca,
       Mexico. 3(13), 220-225 p., July 1, 1966.

2477. Lalive d'Epinay, Christian. Changements sociaux et
       developpement d'une secte (Chile). In *Archives de
       Sociologie des Religions*. No. 23, 1967, 23 p.

2478. _____, Penetration culturelle et presse religieuse. Les
       cas d'une revue protestante argentine. Cuernavaca,
       CIDOC, 1971. 182 p. San Jeos No. 10.

2479. _____, "Les protestantismes latino-americains: un modele
       typologigue" in *Archives de Sociologie des Religion*,
       No. 30, 1970.

2480. _____, "Culture, religion et dependence en Amérique Latine," in *Archives de Sociologie des Religions*, No. 32, Paris, 1971 (trad. espagnole in: *Cuadernos de la Realidad Nacional*, No. 7, Santiago, Chile, 1971).

2481. _____, "Les Eglises du transplant: le protestantisme d'immigration en Argentine" in *Social Compass*, No. 18/2, 1971 (Louvain, Belgique).

2482. _____, "L'esprit et le champ ecuménique de pasteurs sud-américains," in *Social Compass*, 14:5-6, 1967 (Louvain, Belgique).

2483. _____. Sociéte globale, classes populaires et millénarisme: les possibilités de mutation d'un systeme religieux dans une sociéte revolutionnaire (Chile)" in *Dependencia y Estructura de Clases en America Latina*, C.E.T.I.M. (27 chemin des Crets, 1218 Grand Saconnex, Genéve, Suisse), 1972.

2484. Nida, Eugene A. "The Relationship of Social Structure to the Problems of Evangelicals in Latin America" in *Practical Anthropology*, Vol. 5, No. 3, 1958.

2485. Parsons, Anne. "The Pentecostal immigrants: a study of an ethnic central city church" in *Practical Anthropology*, 14 (6), 249-266 p. Nov.-Dec., 1967.

2486. de Santa Ana, Julio. *Protestantismo, Cultura y Sociedad*. Buenos Aires: Editorial y Librería Aurora, S.R.L., 1970. Analyzes influence of Protestantism in Latin American life.

2487. _____. *Cristianismo sin religión: ensayo*. Montevideo: Editorial Alfa, 1969. Examines events affecting religious attitudes and behavior in Latin America since the Conquest.

2488. Troutman, Charles H. "Evangelicals and the Middle Classes in Latin America," in *Evangelical Missions Quarterly*, (Summer, 1972) 202-208 p.

Christian Education
See also p. 105.

2489. Educación Hoy. Apartado 3994, Lima. 1972 - Trimestral. Boletín de la Oficina de Educación del CMI y CELADEC.

2490.   Encuentro. New Perspective for Christian Education.
          Geneva, World Council of Christian Education. 1972.
          186 p. Two editions. Addresses, reports on
          seventeen "Encuentros" in Latin America. Interviews
          with delegates. Illustrated well with photos and
          cartoons. Biographical listing of delegates.
          Article on impact of meetings on Latin America.

2491.   Primera Consulta sobre el Rol y Misión de los colégios
          evangélicos en el dia de hoy. Lima, CELADEC, 1970.
          70 p. Preparatory meeting for this consultation,
          the addresses given and conclusions approved by
          consultation.

                        Theological Education
                          See also p. 106.

2492.   Conferencias de la Consulta sobre Educación Teológica,
          2-6 de Agosto, 1971 held in Cali, Colombia. James
          E. Giles, editor. 128 p. Available through
          Seminario Internacional Bautista, Cali, Colombia.
          Addresses by Cecil McConnell, A. Jack Glaze, Marvin
          Pitts, Albert Lopez, Daniel Tinao, Pat Carter,
          Clark Seanlon, Oscar Pereira, Carlos Garcia and
          Jorge Diaz. Mimeographed.

2493.   Consulta Brasileira de Educacão Teologica - Teología
          Viva. ASTE, São Paulo, 1971. 35 p. Addresses
          presented at the Brazilian Consultation on theolo-
          gical Education. September 8-10, 1971. Deals with
          priorities for Brazilian seminaries in search of
          greater relatedness with emerging missiological
          demands. Mimeographed.

2494.   Lalive d'Epinay, Christian. "Training of Pastors and
          Theological Education: the case of Chile, in
          International Review of Missions, 56:185-192,
          April, 1967.

2495.   Hopewell, J. F. "Protestant Theological Education in
          Latin America," in *Lutheran World*, XV, 4 (1968),
          329-334 p.

2496.   Ministry in context. The third mandate program of the
          Theological Education Fund, 1970-77. London, The
          Theological Education Fund, 1972. 107 p. Appendices
          on various associations of theological schools which
          participate in the TEF are of particular value.

2497. Primera y segunda consulta sobre educación cristiana en
       seminarios de teología. Lima, CELADEC, 1968. 2
       volumes. 74 p. and 85 p.

2498. Qué significa educar teológicamente. Buenos Aires, ASIT-
       Southern Latin American Theological Association,
       1971. 36 p. Summary of presentations and debate
       at the Latin American Consultation on the Meaning
       of Theological Education held in São Paulo, August
       25-28, 1970.

2499. Simposio. ASTE publication, numbers 5, 6 and 7 (June,
       1970; June, 1971; and December, 1971 respectively)
       deal with various aspects of theological education
       in Latin America. Articles by J. C. Marashin, Rubem
       Alves, Ralph Winter, A. Sapsezian, Werner Kaschel,
       and Marialice Foracchi.

2500. Ward, Ted W. *and* Margaret. Programmed instruction for
       theological education by extension. East Lansing,
       Mich., Committee to assist missionary education
       overseas, 1970. 131 p.

2501. Winter, Ralph D., ed. Theological Education by Extension.
       Pasadena, California. William Carey Library, 1969.
       589 p. and 28 p. of bibliography. Series of articles,
       essays and reports edited by a former missionary to
       Guatemala and member of the faculty of the School of
       Missions at Fuller Theological Seminary. These docu-
       ments review the first years of experiments in this
       field, and describes grass roots experiments of
       training the natural leader where he lives through
       a plan geared to the resources of younger churches.

2502. Weld, Wayne, ed. The World Directory of Theological
       Education by Extension. South Pasadena, Ca., William
       Carey Library, 1973. Covers each of more than 200
       schools working in this new fashion. Documents all
       the workshops held, support agencies, associations,
       periodicals and publications. Also one hundred
       pages given to philosophy and method of this move-
       ment.

Church and State; Religious Liberty
See also p. 106.

2503. Del Monte, Carlos, Julio de Santa Ana, et al. Problema
       de la Libertad Religiosa. Essays. Montevideo,

Ediciones Tauro, 1967. 125 p. A publication of
the Center for Christian Studies of the Rio de la
Plata.

Women in Latin American Society

2504. Beaver, R. Pierce. All Loves Excelling. Grand Rapids,
Michigan; Eerdmans, 1968. Part of series on
Christian World Mission. Story of women in mission
and role to which little attention has been given.
Women's liberation concerns today will undoubtedly
revive such interest.

2505. Bettencourt Thome, Yolanda. A Mulher no mundo de hoje.
Ed. Vozes, Limitada. Petropolis, Brasil, 1968.

2506. Boletin Documental sobre la Mujer. A quarterly Bulletin
of articles and excerpts from books (many translations) published by CIDAL, Rio Fuerte 3, Cuernavaca,
Morelos, MEXICO. Now in its third year of publication. Back numbers available at $6.00 U.S. for a
volume of four issues.

2507. Borges Costa, Leticia, Carmen Hernández Penelas, Beatriz
Melano de Couch, Emilio Castro, *y* Esther Moore de
Sainz. El Rol de la Mujer en la Iglesia y en la
Sociedad. Montevideo, Uruguay, Editorial UNELAM,
1968. Papers presented at an ecumenical conference
held in Piriapolis, Uruguay in December, 1967.

2508. Carrel, José. Hilda, Protestan contra una Madre. Hilda
personifies the millions of women of Latin America,
curbed by injustice and oppression which limits them,
but which cannot kill their consciences nor the
creative capacity of being human. Montevideo,
Tierra Nueva, 1970.

2509. Colección "Materiales de Estudios." Biblioteca del CEDAL.
Responisabilidad Política de la Mujer - The report
and papers presented of a Seminar on this subject
held in La Catalina. Santa Barbara de Heredia,
August, 1970. Biblioteca de CEDAL, Apartado 874,
San José, Costa Rica.

2510. Derby, Marion. "Where have all the women gone?". Address
on the contribution of women in the nursing enterprise.

Mimeographed, New York. Board of Global Ministries of the United Methodist Church, 1971. 12 p.

2511. Elu de Leñero, María del Carmen. Hacia dónde va la mujer Mexicana. The conclusions of a research project based on family studies conducted on a national level. Instituto Mexicano de Estudios Sociales. 1969.

2512. Instituto Mexicano de Psicoanálisis. La Guerra de los Sexos. Nine papers on this subject. Ed. Instituto Mexicano de Psicoanálisis, A. C. Odontologia 9, Copilso Universidad, Mexico 20, D.F.

2513. Magalis, Elaine. Conduct Becoming to a Woman. New York, Women's Division, Board of Global Ministries, U.M.C., 1973. Stories of United Methodist missionaries - not a "mission story book" but interpretation of role of women in mission. 140 p.

2514. Mass, Bonnie. Political economy of population control in Latin America. Montreal, Quebec: Editions Latin America, 1972. An analysis of U. S. population control programs.

2515. Matterlart, Armand y Michele. La Mujer Chilena en una Nueva Scoiedad. An exploratory study on the situation and image of women in Chile. Ed. del Pacífico, S.A., Santiago, Chile, 1968.

2516. Navarrete, Ifigenia M. de. La Mujer y los Derechos Sociales. An exposition of the present situation in which women in Mexico find themselves and an appendix giving the legal status of women in Mexico. Ediciones Oasis, Mexico. 1969.

2517. Pescatello, Ann. "The female in Ibero-America: an essay on research bibliography and research direction" in *Latin American Research Review*, Vol. VII, No. 2. Summer, 1972. 125-141 p.

2518. Scott Kinzer, Nora, ed. Special issue on women in Latin America in *Journal of Marriage and the Family*. May, 1973. The selections include many different disciplines and political leanings but are of generally a high quality.

Latin American Theology

2519. Alves, Rubem. A theological interpretation of the meaning of revolution in Brazil. U.S.T.M. thesis.
Union Theological Seminary, New York. 1964.

2520. _____. A theology of Human Hope. Washington, Corpus
Books, 1969. Also Abbey Press, 1972. Paperback. A
prophetic view of Christian faith in the face of our
human struggle by a great Third World theologian from
Brazil. Spanish trans. Religión: ¿Opio o instrumento
de liberación? Montevideo, Tierra Nueva, 1970.

2521. _____. Tomorrow's Child. New York, Harpers, 1973. A
continuation of the main theme of his Theology of
Human Hope.

2522. _____, Jurgen Moltman, Julio de Santa Ana, Hubert
Lapargneur and Gilberto Gorgulho. Liberdade e Fe.
Rio de Janeiro. Tempo e Presenca. 1972. 134 p.
Reflects growing convergence of Catholic and Pro-
testant theologians around human issues to which
categories of faith must be applied.

2523. Amaya, Ismael E. Teología Bíblica del evangelismo.
Miami, Fla. Editorial Vida, 1971.

2524. Castro, Emilio. Un Pueblo Peregrino. Buenos Aires, Editorial La Aurora. 1966. Reflects on the mission of
the church in today's world. 67 p. The writer is
now Secretary of the Commission on World Mission
and Evangelism of the World Council of Churches.

2525. _____. Realidad y Fe. Montevideo, Tierra Nueva, 1973.

2526. Costas, Orlando F. La Iglesia y su Misión Evangelizadora.
Buenos Aires, Editorial La Aurora, 1971. 123 p.
Forwarding looking and insightful of present
realities of the church in Latin America.

2527. León, Jorge A. Teología de la Unidad. Buenos Aires, La
Aurora, 1971. 166 p. By a Cuban Methodist theologian. The book is the subtance of his doctoral
thesis at the University of Montpellier and based
on the Biblical images of unity in Ephesians.

2528. Miguez Bonino, José. Integración humana y unidad cristiana. Conferencias Ecuménicas sobre la Iglesia y

su misión universal (No. 1). Rio Piedras, P.R.
Seminario Evangélico de Puerto Rico, 1969. 102 p.

2529. _____. Ama y haz lo que quieras. Buenos Aires, America
2000, 1972; 133 p. A noted Protestant theologian
deals with ethical problems within the Biblical
perspective. Bibliography.

2530. Moncada, Camilo, et al. Liberación en América Latina.
An *encuentro teológico*. Bogotá, Julio, 1971.
208 p.

INTERPRETATION OF PROTESTANTISM IN HISPANIC CULTURE

By Protestants
See also p. 107.

Protestants and the Second Vatican Council
See also p. 109.

2531. Miguez Bonino, José. Concilio Abierto. Buenos Aires,
Editorial La Aurora, 1967. 110 p. Una interpreta-
ción protestante del Concilio Vaticano II.

*Spanish Mystics, the Reformation
in Spain and Related Subjects*
See also p. 110.

2532. Motta, Jorge Cesar. O influxo da Biblia na vida e no
pensamento de Dom Miguel de Unamuno. Doctoral
thesis. Universidade de São Paulo. 1973. 550 p.

PERIODICALS AND JOURNALS
See also p. 113.

Bibliography of Periodicals and Journals

2533. Lee, Robert Joe. Guia de revistas y boletines religiosos.
Over 1500 listings. 1973. Does not include publications in Portuguese. SML.

Current Publications
See also p. 114.

2534. ASM Newsletter. Of the American Society of Missiology.
       Occasional. 1973-. 135 N. Oakland Avenue,
       Pasadena, California 91101.

2535. Bulletin of the Scottish Institute of Missionary Studies.
       1967-. Andrew F. Walls, editor, Dept. of Religious
       Studies, University of Aberdeen, Kings College,
       Aberdeen AB9 2UB Scotland.

2536. Carta Circular. Del Departamento de Ecumenismo del CELAM,
       Buenos Aires.

2537. C.E.I. Centro Ecuménico de Información. Tempo y Presenca,
       Editora Ltda. Caixa Postal 16-082 ZC-01, Rio de
       Janeiro.

2538. Estudios Ecuménicos. Guty Cardenas No. 131, Mexico 20.
       D.F. Occasional. Trimestral. 1969-. Variety of
       documentation on religious issues in relation to
       society and church structure.

2539. El Rincón Teológico. Publication of Mennonite Seminary,
       Avenida Millan 4392, Montevideo. 1972.

2540. Encuentro. Publicacion conjunta de publicaciones El
       Escudo y el Consejo Unido de Educación Cristiana,
       sucesor de *Orientacion* y *Educacion Cristiana.*
       Simbron 4667, Buenos Aires. Suscripción annual
       $1.50.

2541. Fichas de Isal. Monthly service of information of the
       Church and Society in Latin America. Casilla 179,
       Montevideo. $10.00 annually.

2542. Información Ecuménica. Simbron 4667, Buenos Aires,
       Argentina. Published monthly by UNELAM. $2.00
       annually. Estados Unidos, Europe, Asia y Africa.
       U.S. $4.00.

2543. Jornadas Ecuménicas Latinoamericanas. Montevideo,
       Paysandu 893. A publication of U.L.A.J.E.

2544. LADOC. A documentation service of the Division for
       Latin America--USCC. P. 0. Box 6066, Washington,
       D.C. 20005. $6.00 per year. Monthly translations
       and reprints of significant articles on the life

and problems of the Church in Latin America. Covers all Christian churches and all Latin American countries. 1969-(?).

2545. Latin American Pulse. Box 794. Wheaton, Ill. 60187. 1966. A monthly publication designed to inform IFMA-EFMA missions in Latin America. Other area editions on Africa, Asia and Europe.

2546. Missiology, an International Review. Quarterly. 1973. 135 N. Oakland Ave., Pasadena, California 91101. $8.00 per year (Note: Practical Anthropology, 1953-1972, Cf. No. 967, has merged with this new journal).

2547. New World Outlook. 475 Riverside Drive, New York, N.Y. 10027. Monthly. Joint mission magazine of United Presbyterian and United Methodist churches.

2548. Occasional Publications. Documentation service of the United Presbyterian Church for Latin America. Dr. and Mrs. James E. Goff, editors, Apartado 1024, Cuernavaca, Mor. MEXICO. Addresses, articles, book reviews and essays taken from a wide variety of Latin American publications and church leadership. Emphasis is on reform elements in religious life and Christian movements seeking radical social change.

2549. Testimonio Cristiano. Editorial La Aurora, Buenos Aires.

2550. World Encounter. 2900 Queen Lane, Philadelphia, Penn 19129. Published five times yearly by the Board of World Mission of the Lutheran Church in America.

Chapter 6.
Protestantism in Latin America,
Country by Country

RIO DE LA PLATA

Argentina
See also p. 121.

Bibliography
See also p. 121.

2551. Bibliografía Argentina de Artes y Letras. Vol. 1-48.
Buenos Aires, Fondo Nacional de las Artes, 1959-.
BLCU.

2552. Boletín Bibliográfico Argentina. Vol. 1-33. 1937-1956.
Buenos Aires, Publicación oficial de la Comisión
Nacional.

General Background
See also p. 121.

2553. Auza, Néstor Tomás. Historia de los Congresos Católicos
Argentinos: 1884-1921. Cuernavaca, CIDOC, 1968.
276 p. Sondeos Series No. 14.

2554.   _____. Católicos y liberales en la generación del 80.
Cuernavaca, CIDOC, 1966. 558 p. Sondeos Séries
No. 6-7.

2555. Castro, Nestor W. Expresiones religiosas en el folklore.
Cuernavaca, Mexico: CIDOC, 1969. 129 p. Sondeos
No. 42. Thesis at the Facultad Evangélica de
Teología in Buenos Aires on folklore in Northern
Argentina by a Protestant minister who refers to a
society and folklore which developed largely out of
popular catholicism.

2556. Reina, Ruben E. Paraná; social boundaries in an Argentine
city. Austin, University of Texas Press, 1972. 466
p. Latin American monograph No. 31. A study of the
former capital of the Argentine confederation and
its social structure, focusing primarily on the
middle class.

2557. Sweeney, Ernest S. Foreign missionaries in Argentina,
1938-1962; a study of dependence. Cuernavaca,
CIDOC, 1970. 363 p. A study of both Roman
Catholic and Protestant missionaries. Sondeos
No. 68.

Protestantism in General
See also p. 122.

2558. Enns, Arno W., Man, Milieu and Mission in Argentina. A
close look at church growth. Grand Rapids, Eerdmans,
1971. 258 p. Reviews beginnings and growth of ten
main denominations. A historical study and analysis
of the religious situation in Argentina.

2559. Larson, Peter. Receptivity among the migrants in Northern
Argentina. D. Miss. Research in progress. School
of Missions and Institute of Church Growth, Fuller
Theological Seminary, Pasadena, Calif.

2560. Miller, Elmer S. "Pentecostalism Among the Argentine
Toba." Ph.D. dissertation. Dept. of Anthropology,
University of Pittsburgh, 1967. 277 p. Copy
available Mennonite Board of Missions and Charities,
Elkhart, Indiana. Objective of study is "to des-
cribe and analyze the intense religious movement
which is the dominant dynamic feature of contemporary Toba society and to contribute to a clearer
comprehension of those social movements associated

with the revitalization process by demonstrating
the essential and active role played by religious
belief systems."

2561. Monti, Daniel P. Presencia del Protestantismo en el
        Río de la Plata durante el Siglo XIX. Buenos Aires,
        Editorial La Aurora, 1969. 261 p. A carefully
        documented and detailed history of Protestantism in
        the River Plate area. Expands greatly on the
        chapters in the survey volume by Dr. Goslin (Cf. no.
        370).

2562. Protestantismo de immigración en Argentina. Lista
        bibliográfica. Centro de Estudios Cristianos,
        Cangallo 1644, Buenos Aires. 1966. 19 p.

2563. Romero, Joel E. Church Planting Evangelism: An Argentine
        Case Study. Unpublished. M.A. thesis. 1970.
        School of Missions and Institute of Church Growth,
        Fuller Theological Seminary, Pasadena, Calif.

2564. Valle, Carlos A. Culto: Crítica y Búsqueda. Buenos
        Aires, Centro de Estudios Cristianos, 1972. 146 p.
        The result of five years of research, selection and
        discussion by a study group involved in liturgical
        renewal in the evangelical churches of the Río de
        la Plata area. The essays are not exhaustive, but
        each provides an introduction to a variety of sub-
        jects related to worship in 20th Century Latin
        America.

2565. Villalpando, W., ed., Christian Lalive d'Epinay and Dwain
        Epps. La Iglesia del Transplante. Protestantismo
        de Immigración en la Argentina. Buenos Aires,
        Centro de Estudios Cristianos, 1970. 237 p. Tables
        and bibliography. Historical, sociological and
        theological study of the immigrant churches in the
        Argentine. Excellent socio-religious research.

Denominational History
See also p. 124.

Mennonite

2566. Suarez Vilela, Ernesto. 50° aniversario de la Iglesia
        Evangélica Menonita Argentina, 1969. 124 p. Well
        written, concise summary of Old Mennonites in

Argentina, yet brief and understandably uncritical. Maps and illustrations.

Indigenous Churches

2567. Henneberger, James. Quo Vadis Ielux? A case study of the Iglesia Evangélica Unida en Argentina. Unpublished M.A. thesis, 1968. School of World Missions and Institute of Church Growth, Fuller Theological Seminary, Pasadena, Calif.

2568. Mast, Michael M. Theological training among the Tobas of Argentina. M.A. thesis, 1972. School of World Missions, Fuller Theological Seminary, Pasadena, Calif.

Periodicals
See also p. 129.

2569. Certeza. Bernardo de Irigoyen 840, Buenos Aires, 1959. Trimestral publication de la Comunidad Internacional de Estudiantes Evangélicos.

2570. El Expositor Bautista. Tucmán 358, 60. K, Buenos Aires, 1908-. Mensual. Publicación de la Convención de Iglesias Bautistas Argentinas.

2571. El Luterano. Casilla de Correo No. 5, José L. Suárez, Buenos Aires. 1944-. Mensual. Publicación de la Junta de la Misión de la Iglesia Evangélica Luterana Argentina.

2572. El Pregonero Cristiano. Maipú 466, Loc. 30, Buenos Aires. 1945-. Mensual.

2573. Encuentro con Dios. Unión Bíblica, Tucuman 358, 60. L. Buenos Aires. Trimestral. 1972-. Interdenominacional (meditaciones, devocionario).

2574. Información Ecuménica. Simbrón 4667, Buenos Aires. 1970-. Mensual. Publicación de UNELAM: Publicaciones El Escudo.

2575. Testimonio Cristiano. Doblas 1753, Buenos Aires. 1972-. Trimestral. Publicación de UNELAM.

2576. Unción. Hidalgo 353, Buenos Aires (5). 1969-. Bimestral.
       Publicación de la Unión de las Asambleas de Dios.

Paraguay
See also p. 129.

2577. Monterroso, Victor. Evangelism-in-depth and Church
       Growth in Paraguay. D. Miss. Research in progress.
       School of Missions and Institute of Church Growth,
       Fuller Theological Seminary, Pasadena, Calif.

2578. Shumaker, John T. Church Growth in Paraguay. Unpublished
       M.A. thesis, 1972. School of Missions and Institute
       of Church Growth, Fuller Theological Semianry,
       Pasadena, Calif.

Denominational History
See also p. 130.

Mennonite

2579. Hack, Hendrick. Die Kolonisation der Mennoniten im
       paraguayischen Chaco. Amsterdam: Königliches
       Tropeninstitut, 1961. 232 p. Perspective study
       utilizing statistical indices, tables, and graphs
       and providing analysis of social, economic, educa-
       tional and religious life of the three Chaco
       colonies. English summary included. Good scholarly
       synthesis.

Uruguay
See also p. 132.

Bibliography
See also p. 132.

2580. Bibliografía Uruguaya. Compilado por la Biblioteca del
       Poder Legislativo. 1962-1968. Montevideo,
       Biblioteca del Poder Legislativo, 1971. 395 p.
       BLCU.

Denominational History
See also p. 133.

Southern Baptists

2581. Bullis, Wm. Orrick. A history of the Southern Baptists
in Uruguay, M.A. thesis. Baylor University, Waco,
Texas. 1965.

Periodicals
See also p. 134.

Current Publications

2582. El Universitario Adventista. Casilla 286, Montevideo.
1967-.

BRAZIL
See also p. 134.

Bibliography
See also p. 134.

2583. Sacramento Blake, Aug. V.A. Diccionario bibliográfico
brasilero. Rio de Janeiro. 1883-1902. Reprinted
by Nedeln/Liechtenstein, 1969. BLCU. Vol. 1-7.

2584. Sodre, Nelson Warneck. O que se deve ler para conheccer
a Brasil. Rio de Janeiro, Publication of Instituto
Nacional de Estudios Pedagógicos (INEP). New
edition prepare by Editora Civilização Brasileira
(Rio). 388 p. Contains bibliographic information
on 700 works and more than 1,000 related publications in areas of historical development, special
studies and Brazilian culture.

General Background
See also p. 135.

2585. Alarcón, Rodrigo. Brasil: represión y tortura. Santiago,
Chile, ORBE, 1971. A study on repression and torture
in Brazil.

2586. Alves, Marcio Moreira. A Grain of Mustard Seed. New York,
Archon, 1973. An autobiographical account of events

in Brazil since 1964 written by an opposition ex-congressman now in exile.

2587. Andrade, Manoel Correia de. Nordeste, Espaço e Tempo. Petropolis, R.F. Editora Vozes, 1971. 184 p. An analysis of the problems of the Northeast, with information about the socio-economic structures and the physical realities of the region.

2588. Antoine, Charles. Church and Power in Brazil. A study by a French priest whose activity both as a student chaplain and editor led to his exile.

2589. Backlanoff, E. N. New perspectives of Brazil. Nashville, Vanderbilt University Press, 1966.

2590. Bastide, Roger. As religioes africanas no Brasil. Universidade Sao Paulo, S.P., 1971. Two volumes, 1966.

2591. Bastos, Abguar. Prestes e a revolucion social. Rio de Janeiro, Calfino, 1946. A sympathetic biography of Brazil's most famous communist leader.

2592. Bruneau, Thomas C. The political transformation of the Brazilian Catholic Church. Cambridge University Press, 1973.

2593. Burns, E. Bradford. A History of Brazil. New York, Columbia University Press, 1970.

2594. _____. Nationalism in Brazil: a historical survey. New York, Praeger Publishers, 1969.

2595. de Camargo, Candido Propcopi F. Igreja e Desenvolvimento. Rio de Janeiro, CEBRAP, Editora Brasileira de Cincias Ltda, 1971. A review of recent trends in the Church.

2596. de Britto, Jomar Muñiz. Do Modernismo a Bossa Nova. Rio de Janeiro, Editora Civilização Brasilera, 1966.

2597. de Castro, Josue. Death in the Northeast: Poverty and revolution in the Northeast of Brazil. New York, Vintage, 1969. 207 p. A study of current conditions in Brazil's most poverty-stricken area. (Also Random House, N.Y., 1966).

2598. de Holanda, Sergio Buarque. Raises do Brasil. Rio de
       Janeiro, Livraria Jose Olympio, Editora, 1956 (third
       edition).

2599. de Kadt, Emmanuel. Catholic Radicals in Brazil. New
       York, Oxford University Press, 1970. A sympathetic
       study of Catholic action for social reform in the
       mid-1960's focusing on grass-roots consciousness
       raising.

2600. della Cava, Ralph. Miracle at Joaseiro. New York,
       Columbia University Press, 1970. Account of a
       saint nearly destroyed in politics but triumphed
       to rise to regional and political prominence. Study
       of life of Padre Cicero of Crato, Ceará.

2601. _____. "Torture in Brazil" in *Commonweel*, Vol. XCII,
       No. 6, April 24, 1970. 135-141 p. One of the
       first exposés on the torture of political prisoners
       by the present military regime.

2602. de Queiroz, Maricio V. inhas. Messianismo e Conflicto
       Social: A Guerra Sertanejo do Contestado (1911-
       1914). Rio de Janeiro, 1966. A study of welfare
       and messianism in Brazil's southlands.

2603. de Souza, Luis Alberto G. Brasil Duas Geraçoes de
       Cristaos 1960. Cuernavaca, Mexico. CIDOC, 1966.
       139 p. Sondeos No. 2. Documents of controversy
       in the newspaper Metropolitana with the Union
       Metropolitana de Estudantes de Rio (1959-1964).

2604. Fernandez, Florestan. The Negro in Brazilian Society.
       New York, Columbia University Press, 1969. An
       excellent sociological study of racism in a
       society where it supposedly does not exist.

2605. Furtado Celso, et al. Inflaçao e desenvolvimiento.
       Petropolis, RJ. Editora Vozes, 1972. 320 p. The
       debate about the origins of inflation between the
       two principal currents of thought: the monetary
       orthodox and the "heretical" structuralists.

2606. _____, Analise do "Modelo" Brasileiro. Rio de Janeiro.
       Editora Civilização Brasileira, 1972. 122 p. An
       analysis of the virtues and defects of the
       "Brazilian model." Divided into two essays which
       poses the issues to be faced in this debate.

2607. Graham, Richard, ed. A century of Brazilian history
       since 1965. New York, Alfred Knopf, 1969. 256 p.
       X 216. Borzoi Books. Issues and problems. Valuable
       appendix on further readings.

2608. _____. Britain and the Onset of Modernization in Brazil,
       1850-1914. Cambridge University Press, Cambridge,
       England, 1968.

2609. Ianni, Octavio. Crisis in Brazil. Trans. Phyllis Eveleth.
       New York, Columbia University Press, 1970. A good
       analysis of the present crisis by a leading Brazilian
       sociologist.

2610. Johnson, Allen W. Sharecroppers of the Sertao; economics
       and dependence on a Brazilian plantation (Ceará),
       Palo Alto, California, Stanford University Press,
       1971.

2611. Juliao, Francisco. Cambao: The yoke, the hidden face
       of Brazil. Harmondsworth, England, Pelican, 1972.
       A progressive leader of peasant leagues now in exile
       writes about rural conditions and peasant movements.

2612. Keith, Henry H. *and* S. F. Edwards, eds. Conflict and
       Continuity in Brazilian Society. Colombia, S.C.,
       University of South Carolina Press, 1970. 312 p.
       Informative essays on key areas of Brazilian history
       and cultures: its economy, polity and its religious
       developments.

2613. Kosinski, Jose de Cavalcanti, e Godofredo Deelen. Brasil:
       Igreja em Trasiçao. Cuernavaca, Mexico: CIDOC,
       1970. Sondeos No. 45. 286 p. Written by a Brazilian
       journalist and a Dutch sociologist. Studies the
       leadership of the Church in Brazil today--the age,
       style and orientation of Brazilian bishops.

2614. Lima, Alceu Amoroso. Violencia ou não. Petropolis, R.J.,
       Editora Vozes, 1971. 252 p. The struggle against
       the spirit of violence. Peace must be a continuing
       creation and love the resistence against hate and
       indifference.

2615. Martelli, Amalia. Amazonia, nova dimensao do Brasil.
       Petropolis, R.J., Editora Vozes, 1972. 152 p. The
       Amazonas, the greatest extension of virgen lands and
       the greatest potential of natural resources in the

world. The question of how this immense territory
is to be incorporated into national life is faced.

2616. Melo, Antonio. The Coming Revolution in Brazil. New
York, Exposition Press, 1970. 54 p. Interview
with a Brazilian priest who is prevented from publishing his views in Brazil. Foresees civil strife.

2617. Monteiro, Cecilia *and* Valentina Borremans. Bibliografía
de Dom Helder Camara. Cuernavaca, CIDOC, 19__.
450 p. Sondeos Series No. 42.

2618. Oliveira Filho, José Jeremias. Organizaçao burocratica
e ideologia. Rio de Janeiro, 1972. Unpublished
doctoral thesis at the Dept. of Social Sciences of
the Faculty of Letters, Philosophy and Sciences of
the University of São Paulo.

2619. Pereira de Queroz, Maria Isaura. Images messianiques du
Bresil. Cuernavaca, CIDOC, 1972. 164 p. Summary
volume of her previous writings with new data. (See
also Historia y etnología de los movimientos
mesiánicos, Mexico Siglo XXI, 1969).

2620. _____. O Messianism no Brasil e no Mundo. São Paulo,
Dominus Editora, 1965. Basis of her doctoral dissertation showing that messianism is not confined to
Brazil's *sertão*. Shows ways in which movement has
functioned to transform profane society and to renew
the local political frameworks by substituting traditional chiefs.

2621. Poppino, Rollie E. Brazil, the Land and People. Oxford,
Oxford University Press, 1968.

2622. Prado, Caio, Jr. The Colonial Background of Modern
Brazil. Berkeley, Calif., University of California
Press, 530 p. (Paperback edition $3.45).

2623. _____, et al. Agricultura subdesenvolvida. Petropolis,
R.J. Editora Vozes, 1969. 276 p. Research on food
requirements of the Brazilian economy, comparative
studies on the agricultural situation in Latin American countries, a study of the internal structure of
latifundismo in Brazil and other subjects.

2624. Quartim, João. Dictatorship and Armed Struggle in Brazil.
New York, Monthly Review, 1972. Examines legacy of
Getulio Vargas and the presidencies of his successors

as well as the events which lead to the military coup
in 1964. Describes revolutionary struggle from 1968-
1970 as a part of a world-wide struggle against
imperialism.

2625. Roett, Riordan. The politica of foreign aid in the
Brazilian Northeast. Nashville, Vanderbilt Press,
202 p. Shows the short-sightedness of U.S. programs to understand Furtado's priorities for radical
change and the nature of political power in northeast
Brazil.

2626. Schaden, Egon. Homem, cultura e socidade no Brasil.
Petropolis, R.J., Editora Vozes, 1972. 450 p. A
study of a broad area of Brazilian reality including
studies on Indian populations, Afro-Brazilians,
rural and immigrant groups.

2627. Skidmore, Thomas. Politics in Brazil, 1930-1964: An
experiment in democracy. New York, Oxford University
Press, 1969. Contains useful information but has a
conservative orientation, especially regarding U.S.
involvement in relation to the 1964 military takeover.
Well organized bibliography.

2628. Stepan, Alfred. The military in politics: Changing
patterns in Brazil. Princeton, N.J., Princeton
University Press, 1971. The best establishment
study of the military by an ex-Rand Corporation
member.

2629. Tinhorão, José Ramos. Musica Popular, teatro e cinema.
Petropolis, R.J. Editora Vozes, 1972. The first
study of the relations between popular music and
two of the most important propaganda instruments,
radio and television, to the musical record.

2630. Torres, Joao Camilo de Oliveira. Historia das ideias
religiosas no Brazil. Igreja e a sociedade
brasileira. Sao Paulo, Editorial Grajalbo Ltda.,
1968. 324 p. The author, a Catholic, describes
very thoroughly and consistently the religious
evolution of Brazil. A brief and superficial
chapter given to Protestnatism and ecumenism.

Protestantism in General
See also p. 143.

2631.   Balhana, Altiva Pilatti, et al. Campos Gerais: Estructuras Agrarias. Curitiba, Faculdade de Filosofia,
Universidade Federal do Paraná, 1968. 268 p. First
book length publication dealing with a Mennonite
community in Brazil; extensive description of the
rural colony of Witmarsum; multi-disciplinary effort
with chapters by a geologist, a geographer, several
historians, a sociologist (North American, R.H.
Minnich) and several graduate students of economics
and education. Examination of historical backgrounds
of social and economic development of the Campos
Gerais, much statistical data on the colony's
internal life and demographic composition.

2632.   Bombart, Jean Pierre. "Les cultes dans une favela de
Rio de Janeiro" in America Latina. July-September,
1969. 137-158 p. The evolution of Protestantism in
a Rio *favela* which considers the differences in the
variety of cults, the changes and growth of the
different groups. Classifies these into five groups:
traditional, developing, foreign-oriented, antagon-
istic and isolated. Also considers Protestantism
and the social development of the *favelados*.

2633.   Brazil Protestant Handbook. Monrovia, Ca., Missions
Advanced Research and Communications Center, 1973.
500 p. Results of a five-year research of Protestant Church growth in Brazil.

2634.   Braga, Erasmo. Religião e Cultura. São Paulo, União
Cultural Editora, 1944. 180 p. The first part
considers the spiritual direction of Luso-Brasilian
evangelism. The second part considers social and
international questions.

2635.   Cesar, Waldo A., ed. Protestantismo e imperialismo na
America Latina: questões abertas. Petropolis,
R.J. Editora Vozes, 1968. 119 p. Articles by
Waldo A. Cesar, Richars Shaull, Orlando Fals Bo
and Beatriz Muñiz de Souza on the social situation
of Latin America and the growth of Protestantism in
relation to the historic conditions in which it
developed.

2636.   _____. Urbanizaçao e religiosidade popular. 1970.
Unpublished manuscript. 22 p. The principal

doctrines of the Pentecostals as a collective and
individual response to urban phenomena approached
from three different angles: santification and
secularization, spiritual gifts and social class,
and the Second Coming of Christ and urbanization.

2637.   _____, Para uma sociologia do Protestantism Brasileiro.
Petropolis, Editora Vozes Ltda., 1973. 48 p. An
excellent essay on the writings from 1930 to the
present on this subject. Extremely valuable as to
bibliographical comprehensiveness and interpretive
insights.

2638. Continuing Evangelism in Brazil. A MARC MIB Study
Project. A working paper. 1971. 107 p.

2639. Curry, Donald Edward. Lusiada; an anthropoligical
study of the growth of Protestantism in Brazil.
Doctoral dissertation, Columbia University, New
York, 1968. 260 p. Study of the rise of sectarian
religion against the backdrop of the breaking down
of the traditional order. Setting is an agricultural
area in the litigated area between Espiritu Santo
and Minas Gerais. Thesis is that Protestantism is
growing in Brazil "as a form of voluntary association
especially congenial to the Brazilian political
economy..." University microfilms.

2640.   _____. "Messianism and Protestantism in Brazil's Sertão."
In *Journal of Interamerican Studies and World Affairs*.
Vol. XII. No. 3 (July, 1970). Article woven around
the story of Antonio Jose dos Santos and the evangelical movement centered in Fazenda Nova Vida. 416-
438 p.

2641. da Costa, Octavio Eduardo. "O Protestantism en Sertâo
Novo, Comunidade Rustica de Interior Pernambucano."
Unpublished manuscript. Referred to in William's
"Followers of the New Faith", (No. 2671).

2642. Directory of Missionaries in Brazil. São Paulo, Missionary
Information Bureau, 1973. 76 p. List of nearly 3,000
missionaries from North America serving in Brazil.
Addresses are quickly out of date. Also list of 162
missions.

2643. Edwards, Fred E. The Role of the Faith Mission: A
Brazilian Case Study. M.A. thesis. South Pasadena,
Calif., William Carey Library. 1969.

2644. Face, Rui. Cangaceiros e fanaticos. Rio de Janeiro, Editoria Civilizaçao Brasileira, 1972. 223 p. Studies the phenomena of worker and religious fanaticism as a form of reaction against the existing social structures.

2645. Fanstone, A. Baird. Missionary adventure in Brazil: the story of James Fanstone, OBE. Worthing, Sussex, England, Henry E. Walton Ltd., 1972. 144 p. The life of the founder of the Anapolis Evangelical Hospital. A sketchy biography which lacks perspective and perception of Brazilian life both yesterday and today.

2646. Frase, Ronald. A sociological analysis of Brazilian Protestantism: a study in social change. Doctoral dissertation in progress. Princeton Theological Seminary.

2647. Gates, C. W. Industrialization: Brazil's catalyst for church growth. South Pasadena, Ca., William Carey Library, 1972. 90 p.

2648. Gueiros Viera, David. Foreign Intervention in the Religious Problem of Brazil, 1855-1870. Ph.D. dissertation, American University, Washington, D.C. In process. Draws heavily on primary sources of missionary correspondence and publications of period.

2649. Hollenweger, Walter J. O movimento Pentecostal no Brasil. Simposio ASTE, São Paulo, June 1969. 5-35 p. Also "O Espiritu Santo e o Movimento Pentecostal" in Simposio ASTE, No. 3, Sao Paulo, 1966. A story of a worker-pastor, Daniel Berg, founder of the Assemblies of God in Brazil.

2650. _____. The Pentecostals. London, SCM Press Ltd. 1972. Trans. from German by R. A. Wilson. 572 p. Chapter eight is entitled "Brazilian illuminism; an attempt at an assessment of the Brazilian Pentecostal movement.

2651. Instituto Evangelico de Pesquisa. Pesquisa sobre literature crista no Brasil. (Relatorio final). Sao Paulo, I.E.P., 1968. 30 p. mimeographed. Analyses Christian literature in Brazil from the point of view of content, audience, language and

forms of Catholic-Protestant cooperation. Includes
survey of 5,767 publications from 1940-1968 of
sixty publishers in Brazil and four in Portugal.

2652. Leonard, Emile, "O Protestantismo Brasilero" in *Revista*
       de Historia, São Paulo, Apo II, No. 7, 8 (1951) and
       III, No. 11 (1962).

2653. Listing of U.S. Protestant Agencies working in Brazil.
       São Paulo, Missionary Information Bureau, 1968.

2654. MacLean, Grant. Toward an Operational Definition of
       Cultural Imperialism. A study project report
       carried out by a seminarian in several Latin
       American countries including Brazil over an 18
       month period. Attempts to focus on inpact of
       foreign missionaries on direction of church
       development in particular in relation to social
       and political commitment. A good beginning, but
       incomplete. UML.

2655. Mooy, Pe. Suitberto. O proselitismo dos Protestantes
       no Brasil. Rio de Janeiro. Secretariado de
       Teologia, Setor Ecumenismo, 1965. 16 p.
       mimeographed. Effect of proselitism on ecumenical
       dimensions of stagnated historical denomination.

2656. Moura, Abdalaziz de. "O Pentecostalismo como fenomeno
       religioso popular no Brasil" in *Revista Eclesiastica*
       Brasileira, No. 121, 1971. 78-94 p. Some hypoth-
       eses on significance of Pentecostal developments in
       Brasil.

2657. Murphy, Edward. "Brasil para Cristo". A research study
       project for the School of Mission, Pasadena, Ca.,
       1972. Unpublished.

2658. Novaes Garcez, Benedicto. Mackenzie. São Paulo, Casa
       Editora Presbiteriana, 1970. 215 p. A history of
       Mackenzie University upon its centenary. Traces
       the institution in its development as a Presbyterian-
       related school. Book written also to document the
       Presbyterian-relatedness of the institutions at a
       time in which the control of this institution is
       in court litigation.

2659. Petry, Leopoldo. O episodio de Ferrabraz: os mucker.
       São Leopoldo, Editora Rotermund, 1966. 200 p.
       Second edition. Maps and photography. Documents

on a movement of religious fanatics in Sao Leopoldo
(R.S.) in 1874.

2660. Pierson, Paul Everett. A Younger Church in Search of
       Maturity: The History of the Presbyterian Church
       of Brazil from 1910 to 1959. Doctoral dissertation.
       Princeton Theological Seminary, 1971. 538 p. Com-
       pletes the century of Presbyterian history on which
       Robert L. McIntire wrote on the 1859-1910 (Cf. 1281).
       Work of an hones and competent historian who care-
       fully portrays the church in its human as well as
       its spiritual dimensions. The roots of certain
       current problems of the Presbyterian Church of
       Brazil can be traced to conflicts in her past his-
       tory. University Microfilms, Ann Arbor, Michigan.
       Published by the Trinity University Press, San
       Antonio, Texas, 1973.

2661. Read, William. Church Growth as Modernization in Brazil.
       D. Miss. Research in progress. School of Missions
       and Institute of Church Growth. Fuller Theological
       Seminary, Pasadena, Calif.

2662. Richard, Kenneth G. An Introduction of Christian mission
       in Southern Brazil. Columbia Bible College, Columbia,
       S.C. 1967.

2663. Robinson, John L. "Historical factors in Protestant
       Growth in Brazil" in *Restoration Quarterly*. Vol.
       14, No. 2, 1971. 80-100 p.

2664. Rogers, Wm. W. *and* Richard Graham. Cornell-Brazil
       experiment in learning. Cuernavaca: CIDOC, 1969.
       151 p. The experiences and detailed reports of a
       three year study-action project of university stu-
       dents with the guidance of faculty and church
       related university ministries. One of the few
       valid *encuentros* of U.S. and Brazilians at the
       grass-roots level.

2665. Sanders, John van Dyke. The social organization of a
       Protestant congregation in the Federal District,
       Brazil, in Sociologia (rev.) XXII, XXIII. Master's
       thesis at Vanderbilt University, 1960-61. Three
       extended articles on the life of a congregation
       which demonstrates the isolated life of the
       believers resulting from both the positive and
       negative values which were required of them.

2666. Smith, Charlotte Hale. I remember, I remember. 1969.
       The life story of Layona Glenn, centenarian
       Methodist educational missionary to Brazil as told
       to author. Enjoyable, but with few insights into
       mission in Brazil.

2667. Steffen, Pauline. Social and Psychological Functions of
       the Pentecostal Protestantism in the city of São
       Paulo, Brazil. Master's thesis. University of São
       Paulo.

2668. Souza, Beatriz Muniz de, Candido P. Ferreira de Camargo.
       Mudancas de funcoes, do Cristianismo em Sao Paulo.
       São Paulo, CEBRAP, Feb. 72-June 74. Research in
       process. The objective is to analyze the functions
       of Catholicism and Protestantism in the process of
       social change, considering specifically the last
       two decades.

2669. Thomas, Ralph, S.A. "Ecumenism in Brazil" in *Ecumenical
       Trends*, Vol. 1, No. 12. March, 1973. A realistic
       assessment of the church under limitations.

2670. Wiarda, Ieda Siquira *and* Howard J. Wiarda. "The Churches
       and Rapid Social Change: Observations on the
       Differences and Similarities between Protestants
       and Catholics in Brazil," in *Journal of Church and
       State*, Vol. XII, Winter, 1970. 13-30 p.

2671. Willems, Emilio. Followers of the New Faith. Culture
       change and the rise of Protestantism in Brazil and
       Chile. Nashville, Vanderbilt University Press,
       1967. 290 p. A thoughtful and revealing study.
       Asserts the influence of Protestantism from intro-
       duction into Brazil and Chile in the early 1800's
       and analizes its function as agent of social change
       and subtle psychological change.

2672. _____. Uma vila Brasileira: tradiçao e trasicão. São
       Paulo, Difusao Europeia do Livro, 1961. 22 p. A
       study of the development of Itaipava in the Valley
       of Paraiba. Includes a chapter on the social
       structure which describes religious associations,
       including the Methodist Church, of some three
       hundred families.

2673. _____. "Validation of Authority in Pentecostal Sects of
       Chile and Brazil" in *Journal of Scientific Study of
       Religion*. 6:235-38, Fall, 1967.

2674. _____. "A formação da Santidade" in *Sociologia*, Vol. II, No. 3, 1946.

2675. _____. "Religious mass movements and social change in Brazil" in Erick N. Baklanoff, ed., *New Perspectives in Brazil*, Nashville, Vanderbilt University Press.

2676. Yuasa, Key. "A Study of the Pentecostal Movement in Brazil, its importance," in the *Reformed and Presbyterium World*, 39:2:63-72.

Denominational History
See also p. 149.

Assemblies of God

2677. Vingren, Ivar. Pionjarens dogbok. Brasilienmissionaren Gunnar Vingrens dagboksantechningar. Stockholm, Lewi Pethrus Forlag, 1968. 250 p. Written by son of a pioneer Pentecostal missionary in Brazil (1910-1933). Based largely on personal diaries.

Baptist

2678. Oliveria, Zaquez. Factors contributing to Baptist growth in Pernambuco, 1886-1965. Th.M. thesis. Southwestern Baptist Seminary, Ft. Worth, Texas, 1967.

Lutheran

2679. Fragmentos Historicos. Compiled for the occasion of the meetings of the second Latin American Congress of LWF in Petropolis, 1954. 123 p. A synthesis of the Lutheran history in Brazil.

2680. Bachmann, E. Theodore. Lutherans in Brazil: a story of emerging ecumenism. Minneapolis, Minn. Augsburg Publishing House, 1970. 79 p. Compressed and helpful as a general background book.

Methodist

2681. Rocha, Isnard. Historias da Historia do Metodismo no Brasil. São Paulo, Impresa Metodista, 1967. 167 p.

Prepared for first centenary of Methodism in Brazil.
Author analyzes the historic bibliography on
Brazilian Methodism.

Presbyterian

2682. Read, William. A program of an indigenous Presbyterian
church in Brazil. Cuernavaca, CIDOC, 1969. 198 p.
Sondeos No. 56. A survey of Presbyterian work in
Brazil and application of missionary strategy in
Central Brazil.

Pentecostal Churches (General)

2683. Souza, Beatriz Muñiz de. A experiencia da Salvação.
Pentecostais en São Paulo. São Paulo, Duas Cidades,
1969. 181 p. Bibliography. Systemic scientific
study of Pentecostal denominations. Describes
social and psychological condition of Pentecostalism
in São Paulo.

Spiritism and Related Cults

2684. Johnson, Harmon A. Authority over the Spirits: Brazilian
Spiritism and Evangelical Church Growth. Unpublished
M.A. thesis. Fuller Theological Seminary, School of
Missions, Pasadena, California, 1969.

2685. Kloppenburg, Boaventura. Umbanda no Brasil. Petropolis,
R.J. Editora Vozes Ltda. n.d. 264 p. Study of
Umbanda as a variant of Spiritism and tied to
superstitions.

2686. Mauro Batista, P. A religiosidade do povo no Brasil.
Also *his* A religiao do povo no brasil. Mimeographed
studies. (71 p. and 34 p.) Good bibliography.

2687. Renshaw, Parke. Updating Spiritism in Brazil. See also
his doctoral thesis at the University of Florida,
1969. "A Sociological Analysis of Spiritism in
Brazil." Also article in LASA Newsletter, 36-38 p.
Vol. III, No. 3, September, 1972.

2688. Rocha, Wagner Neves. Religioẽs de convers
sociedade em mudanca: Umbanda e Igreja Adventista
do Setimo Dia. 1972. Unpublished mss. Depto. of

Social Sciences of the Institute of Human Sciences
and Philosophy of the Federal University Fluminense,
Niteroi.

WEST COAST REPUBLICS

Bolivia
See also p. 157.

Bibliography
See also p. 157.

2689. Historical Dictionary of Bolivia. Metuchen, N.J.
Scarecrow Press, n.d. An exceptionally comprehensive bibliography.

General Background
See also p. 158.

2690. Almaraz, Sergio. El Poder y la Caida, Cochabamba, Los
Amigos del Libro, 1969.

2691. Arguedas, Alcides. Raza de Bronce, Puerta del Sol, La
Paz, Bolivia, 1970.

2692. Barton, Robert. A Short History of Bolivia. La Paz,
Los Amigos del Libro, 1968. 343 p. The best
general history of Bolivia in English.

2693. Bath, C. Richard, Ph.D. "The Bolivian MNR and the
Mexican PRI: A structural Functional Comparative
Analysis within the Context of their Respective
Political Systems." Tulane Univ., 1970. 515 p.
Order No. 71-8035.

2694. Buechler, Hans *and* Judith. The Bolivian Aymara. New
York Holt Rinchart, and Winston, 1971. An
anthropological study.

2695. Eder, George. Inflation and Development in Latin America:
A case study of Inflation and Development in Bolivia.
Ann Arbor, University of Michigan Press, 1971. An
economic stabilization program the author devised.

2696. Fifer, J. Valerie. Bolivia: Land, location and politics since 1835. Cambridge, Cambridge University Press, 1972. A convenient research tool.

2697. Grubb, Kenneth G. Amazon and Andes (Bolivia, Peru, Ecuador, Colombia, Venezuela). London: 1930. 296 p. Also about ninety plates. A valuable record by a careful researcher.

2698. Heath, Dwight, et al. Land reform and social revolution in Bolivia. New York, Praeger, 1969. Anthropologists discuss achievements and problems.

2699. Illich, Ivan. Bolivia y la Revolución Cultural. 1970. 65 p.

2700. Iriarte, Gregorio. Galerias de Muerte; Vida de los mineros bolivianos. Montevideo, Tierra Nueva, 1972. 212 p. Relates the plight of the Bolivian miner and the atmosphere in which he toils, his work and the injustices he suffers and his faint hopes for a better future. Discussion of the tin economy.

2701. James, Daniel, ed. The Complete Bolivian Diaries of Che Guevara and other captured documents. New York, Stein and Day, 1968. 330 p. This is an excellent diary and the editor provides ample background material to increase the reader's understanding.

2702. Klein, Herbert. Parties and Political Change in Bolivia, 1880-1952. New York Cambridge Press, 1969. A liberal history with information on the working class movement, the development of leftist ideology and U.S. oil companies.

2703. Lara, Jesus. La Cultura de los Incas. Cochabamba, Los Amigos del Libro. 1967.

2704. Lofstrom, Wm. L. Attitudes of an industrial pressure group in Latin America, The *Associación de industriales mineros de Bolivia*, 1925-1935. Ph.D. dissertation, Cornell University, 1970. No. 9 in Dissertation Series.

2705. Malloy, James M. *and* Richard S. Thorn, eds. Beyond the Revolution. Bolivia since 1952. Pittsburgh, University of Pittsburgh Press, 1971. 402 p. A

scholarly symposium analysing the after effects of
the Bolivian Revolution of 1952.

2706. McEwen, William. Changing Rural Bolivia. New York
Research Institute for the Study of Man. 1969.
A report on several communities.

2707. Monast, Jacques *y* Jordan Bishop. L'univers religieux
des Aymaras de Bolivie. Cuernavaca, CIDOC, 1967.
300 p. Jordan Bishop, superior of Dominicans in
Bolivia presents with author his observations
gathered over ten years about the religious ideas
of the Aymaras.

2708. Pardo Valle, Nazario. Poligrafía de Bolivia. La Paz,
Los Amigos del Libro, 1966. 245 p. One of the
best collections of statistical data on Bolivia,
with much background information on the country.

2709. Ponce Garcia, Jaime *and* Oscar Uzin Fernandez. El clero
en Boliviz, 1968. Cuernavaca, CIDOC, 1970. 224 p.
Based on a questionnaire by clergy and laity.
Sondeos No. 59.

2710. Wilke, James. The Bolivian Revolution and U.S. aid
since 1952. Los Angeles, University of California
Press, 1971. A chronicle.

Protestantism in General
See also p. 159.

2711. Mensaje de ISAL al pueblo boliviano en su tercer
encuentro. Published in *Cristianismo y Sociedad*,
IX, Nos. 26-27. 1971. A significant church and
society document, reflecting the conditions of
Bolivia in 1971 from a leftist point of view.

2712. Nordyke, Quentin. Animistic Aymaras and Church Growth.
Newberg, Oregon. Barcley Press, 1972. 200 p.
Anthropological study of the Aymara Indians with
emphasis on their animistic religion and a study
of the growth of the Protestant church among them.

2713. Pet, Gerardo, ed. El Indígena de los Andes de la comuni-
dad a la ciudad. Montevideo, ISAL, 1966. 122 p.
A sociological survey of the Indians of the Andes.
Report of Second Andean Consultation organized by
ISAL, Huampani, April, 1966.

2714. Phillips, David. Protestantism in Bolivia. 1952.
Unpublished M.A. thesis, University of Calgary,
Canada, 1968. An historical survey of Bolivian
Protestantism up to 1952 by a Canadian Baptist
missionary.

2715. Wagner, C. Peter. The Protestant Movement in Bolivia.
South Pasadena, Calif., Wm. Carey Library, 1970.
240 p. The first published history of the Protestant churches in Bolivia.

Denominational History
See also p. 160.

Methodist

2716. Arias, Mortimer. La Iglesia y la Revolución. In
Cristianismo y Sociedad, X, No. 31-32, 1972. A
significant article by the Bishop of the Methodist
Church in Bolivia.

2717. _____. Mutual Responsibility. An address to an American
church. In *International Review of Mission*. Vol.
LX, No. 238. April 1971. A significant statement
by Bishop Arias.

2718. Barber, Natalie, Dr. *and* Mrs. Fix-it, the story of Frank
and Bessie Beck. New York, Friendship Press, 1970.

2719. Palmer, Jim. Red Poncho and Big Boots; the life of
Murray Dickson. Nashville, Abingdon Press, 1969.
224 p. Dickson was one of the outstanding Methodist
missionaries in Bolivia who met an untimely death
in 1961. His influence had a marked effect on the
Methodist Church in Bolivia.

2720. Robinson, H. McAen. A training program for Methodist
lay preachers among the Aymara Indians of Bolivia.
M.A. thesis. Scarritt College for Christian workers,
Nashville, 1964.

Periodicals
See also p. 162.

Current Publications

2721. El Chasqui - 1967. Monthly. Editor: Carlos Lozada,

3942 Minerva Ave., Los Angeles, Calif. 90066.
Published by Bolivian Prayer Circle.

Peru
See also p. 171.

Bibliography
See also p. 171.

2722. Anuario Bibliográfico Peruano (1964-66). Lima, Ediciones
de la Biblioteca Nacional, 1969. 839 p.

2723. Campbell, Leon G. "The historiography of the Peruvian
guerrilla movement, 1960-65," in *Latin American
Research Review*, Vol. VIII, No. 1, Spring 1973,
45-70 p.

General Background
See also p. 171.

2724. Astriz, Carlos Alberto. Social Structure and Political
Power in Peru. Doctoral dissertation. Pennsylvania
State University, College Park, Penn. 1968. 439 p.

2725. Bourricaud, Francois. Power and society in contemporary
Peru. New York, Praeger Publishers, 1970. 356 p.
Trans. from French of a substantial social and
political analysis of Peru's development since the
1930's.

2726. Bourque, Susan C. Cholification and the campesino: a
study of three Peruvian peasant organizations in
the process of social change. Ph.D. dissertation.
Cornell University, 1970. No. 21 in Dissertation
Series.

2727. Delgado de Thays, Carmen. Religión y Magia en Tupe
(Yauyos). Cuernavaca, Mexico. CIDOC, 1968. 183 p.
Sondeos No. 28. Results of work of team 1948-52 in
the village of Tupe, Peru.

2728. Dew, Edward. Politics in the altiplano: the dynamics
of change in rural Peru. (Latin American monographs,
No. 15). Austin, University of Texas Press, 1969.
216 p. Analysis of more recent political, social
and economic developments.

2729. Sharp, Daniel A., ed. U.S. foreign policy and Peru.
       Austin, University of Texas Press, 485 p. A series
       of papers prepared for meetings organized by the
       Adlai Stevenson Institute for policy-conscious
       corporations working in Peru. Dan McCurry's paper
       "U.S. Church-Financed Missions in Peru" is a well
       thought-out critique. In general the papers post
       road signs in relation to the directions U.S.
       corporations will try to go in Latin America.

2730. Wallis, Ethel Emily. Tariri: My Story. As told to the
       author. New York, Harper and Row, 1965. 126 p.
       The story of the transformation of the Shapras of
       Peru from head-hunters to Christian tribe.

2731. Walsh, William B., M.D. Yanqui, come back! The Story
       of Hope in Peru. New York, E. P. Cutton and Co.,
       1966. 192 p. A warmly human account of a ten-
       month visit of the hospital ship "Hope" to Peru.

                      Protestantism in General
                         See also p. 173.

2732. Kessler, John B.A. A comparison of three churches in
       Peru. (Adventist, Iglesia Evangelica Peruana and
       Pentecostal). Mimeographed. A brief study by an
       eminent mission historian. Buurtweg 3, Doorn. In
       Dutch.

                              Chile
                         See also p. 162.

                      General Background
                         See also p. 163.

2733. Debray, Regis. The Chilean Revolution: Conversations
       with Allende. New York, Random House, 1971.

2734. Faron, Luis C. The Mapuche Indians of Chile. New York.
       Holt, Rinehart and Winston, 1968.

2735. Fidel in Chile. International Publishers, 1972. A
       collection of speeches delivered by Fidel Castro
       during visit to Chile November-December, 1972.
       Contains references to Christianity in Cuba today.

2736. Frank, Andre Gunder. Capitalism and Underdevelopment in Latin America. Historical Studies of Chile and Brazil. New York, Modern Reader, 1967.

2737. Hanisch Espindola, Walter. Las vocaciones en Chile, 1536-1850. Cuernavaca, CIDOC, 1970. 137 p. Sondeos No. 67.

2738. Johnson, Dale L., ed. Chilean Socialism. Garden City, N.Y., Doubleday/Anchor Press, 1973. 546 p.

2739. Meyer, Richard L. Debt repayment capacity of the Chilean agrarian reform beneficiaries. Ph.D. dissertation, Cornell University, 1970. No. 14 in Dissertation Series.

2740. New Chile. New York. North American Congress on L.A. (NACLA) 1972. 208 p. An excellent compendium of articles and statistics on the first two years of the Allende government in Chile. Available NACLA, Box 57, Cathedral Station, New York, N.Y. 10025. $2.50 - 1973 edition. See also "Chile under the Military," 1974.

2741. Paul, Catherine Manny. Amanda H. La Barca, Educator to the women of Chile. The work and writings of Amanda H. La Barca in the field of education in Chile: their importance; their value in the progress of education in Chile. Doctoral dissertation, New York University, 1967, Microfilm and xerography. 210 p. Published by Cuernavaca, CIDOC, 1968. 224 p. CIDOC Cuadernos No. 1.

2742. Petras, James. Politics and Social Forces in Chilean Development. Berkeley, University of California Press. 1970. 54 p.

2743. _____ and Hugo Z. Merino. Trans. by Thomas Flory. Peasants in Revolt. A Chilean case study, 1965-1971. Austin Texas, University of Texas Press, 1972. 154 p. Latin American Monography No. 28.

2744. _____. "Chile: Can we do business with Radical Nationalists?" In *Foreign Policy*, Summer, 1972.

2746. Rycroft, W. Stanley. "Fidel Castro visits Chile" in *The Churchman*, March, 1972. 9-10 p.

2747. Shiller, Herbert. "Chile: An end to Cultural Colonilism" in *Transaction*, March, 1972.

2748. Smith, Giles Wayland. The Christian Democratic Party in
      Chile: a study of politican organization and
      activity with primary emphasis on the local level.
      Cuernavaca, Mexico, CIDOC, 1969. 314 p. Sondeos
      No. 39. A selected fourteen page bibliography.

2749. Volkomener, Mary Theophane. Providence Community in
      Latin America: A Canadian Group of Sisters refounds
      itself in Chile. Cuernavaca, CIDOC, 1967. 156 p.
      Sondeos Series No. 17. The Order was founded in
      1853 in Valparaíso. Study reveals problems of
      restructuring to respond to new problems and
      realities.

2750. Weaver, Frederick S., Jr. Regional patterns of economical
      change in Chile, 1950-1964. Ph.D. dissertation,
      Cornell University, 1970. No. 11 in Dissertation
      Series.

2751. Unmasking Development. A collection of articles, per-
      spectives, program goals of Unidad Popular,
      chronology, etc. Prepared by Common Front for
      Latin America (COFFLA), 1500 Farragut St., N.W.,
      Washington, D.C. 20011. $2.00. Responsible
      material.

2752. Zammit, J. Ann, ed. The Chilean Road to Socialism.
      Austin, University of Texas Press, 1972. 465 p.
      Proceedings of an ODEPLAN-IDE round table Press,
      March, 1972. Papers and speeches of principal
      participants of the conference published in coopera-
      tion with the Institute of Development Studies at
      the University of Sussex, England.

Protestantism in General
See also p. 165.

2753. Housley, J. B. "Protestant Failure in Chile," in
      Christianity and Crisis, 26:244-46, October 31,
      1966.

2754. Lalive d'Epinay, Christian. El refugio de las masas.
      Estudio sociológico del protestantismo chileno.
      Santiago, Chile, Editorial El Pacífico, 1968. 295
      p. Tables and maps. English translation. Haven
      of the Masses. A study of the Pentecostal movement
      in Chile. London, Lutterworth, 1969. Portuguese
      translation. O refugio das massas. Estudo

sociologico do protestantism chileno. Rio de
Janeiro, Paz e Terra, 1970. The Spanish edition is
hard to find.

Denominational History
See also p. 166.

Anglican

2755. George, Kathleen. Among the Araucanians of South Chile.
London, South American Missionary Society, 1931.

2756. Pytches, David. "Anglicanism in Chile Today" in *The
Churchman*. LXXXI, Summer, 1967. 114-28 p.

Pentecostal

2757. Chacón, Arturo. "Pentecostal Movement in Chile" in
Student World, XVII, 1, (1964), 85-88 p.

2758. Johnson, Norbert E. The history, dynamic and problems
of the Pentecostal Church in Chile. Unpublished
Th.M. thesis. Richmond, Va. Union Theological
Seminary, 1970.

2759. Milmine, Douglas. "Pentecostalism in Chile". Lecture
by present Anglican bishop of Paraguay to the
Dutch Missionary Council, 1971. Mimeographed.
Pr. Hendricklaan 37, Amsterdam, 7. A thoughtful
synthesis.

2760. Tennekes, J. "De Pinksterbeweging in Chile, een uiting
van social protest" in *Sociologische Gids*, Vol. 17,
1970. 480-487 p.

2761. _____. "De Pinksterbeweging in Chile: een uitdaging"
in *Wereld en Zending*, Vol. 1, 1972. 148-163 p.

2762. _____. "De Pinksterbeweging in Chile." A provisional
report. Department of Cultural Anthropology, Free
University of Amsterdam.

2763. Willems, E. "Validation of Authority in Pentecostal
Sects in Chile and Brazil," in *Journal for the
Scientific Study of Religion*, 6:253-8. Fall, 1967.

Presbyterian

2764. Paul, Irven. A Yankee reformer in Chile: The life and
      works of David Trumbull, 1819-1889. South Pasadena,
      Wm. Carey Library, 1973. 155 p. Reflects the great
      influence of the United States and its predominantly
      19th century Protestant culture on Chilean political
      and social development.

                        Periodicals
                      See also p. 170.

Current Publications

2765. Betania. Casilla 720, Temuco, 1960. Bimensual. Women's
      magazine.

                        GRAN COLOMBIA

                        Colombia
                      See also p. 177.

                        Bibliography
                      See also p. 177.

2766. Anuario bibliográfico Colombiano. 1951-. Bogotá,
      Instituto Caro y Cuerva. Compiled by Fco. José
      Romero Rojas.

2767. Ramsey, R. W. "Critical bibliography on la violencia
      in Colombia," in *Latin American Research Review*,
      Vol. VIII, No. 1, Spring, 1973. 7-44 p.

2768. Peraza, Fermin. Bibliografia Colombiana. Vol. 1-13.
      1961-69. Last volume was finished shortly after
      his death in 1969 by his widow.

                    General Background
                      See also p. 177.

2769. Alzate R., Manuel. Libertad Religiosa en Colombia.
      Cali, Editorial Pacífico, 1969. 122 p. Judgment
      on the authoritarianism within the Catholic Church
      which denies religious liberty. Written by a priest
      deeply involved in the slums of Cali.

2770. Amaro, Peter W. An analysis of the changing patterns of
       elite residential areas in Bogotá, Colombia. Ph.D.
       dissertation, Cornell University, 1970. No. 7 in
       Dissertation series.

2771. Bonilla, Victor D., Gonzalo Castillo Cardenas, C. Duplat,
       Orlando Fals Borda, Augusto Libreros. Por Ahi es la
       Cosa. 127 p. Bogotá, Rosca de Investigación y
       Acción Social, 1972. Essays on the sociology and
       history of Colombia designed to raise the conscious-
       ness of leaders of the popular sectors to the forces
       which have molded and continue to form Colombian
       life and destiny. Chapters two and three touch on
       the religious problem, especially in its ideological
       function.

2772. Bonilla, Victor D., Gonzalo Castillo, Orlando Fals Borda
       and Augusto Libreros. Causa Popular, Ciencia Popular.
       Bogotá, Rosca de Investigación y Acción Social, 1972.
       78 p. Description of methods and techniques of
       "involvement research" through which social scien-
       tists cooperate effectively with popular sectors,
       not only to understand the situation but to trans-
       form it. Summary of nearly two years of research-
       action by members of ROSCA team.

2772a. Bonilla, Victor D., Servants of God or Masters of Men?
       The story of a Capuchin Mission in Amazonia. Trina
       Rosemary Sheed, London, Penguin Books, 1972.
       Fascinating and authorative research.

2773. Dunn, Marvin G. Radical Change in Latin America: A
       case study of the Golconda movement. M.A. thesis,
       Garrett Bible Seminary and Northwestern University,
       Evanston, Illinois. 1970.

2774. Garcia Marquez, Gabriel. Cien Años de Soledad. B.A.
       Editorial Sudamericana. 1967. 351 p. (Trans. by
       Gregory Rabussa. Several English editions). A
       New World epic called by some a *Don Quixote* of the
       Western hemisphere. A classic about a continent in
       which the Spanish conquest left tragic instability
       and inhumanity. A miniature "history" of the cen-
       turies of colonialism, civil war and political
       chaos dramatized in the life of the mythical
       Colombian village, Macondo. (See also his second
       major novel, Leaf Storm and other stories) N.Y.,
       Harper and Row, 1972.

2775. Haldox, Benjamin E. Sociedad y Religión en Colombia.
       Bogotá. Tercer Mundo, 1965. 180 p. No. 20 in
       monograph series of Facultad de Sociología de la
       Universidad Nacional.

2776. Holt, Pat M. Colombia Today--and tomorrow. New York,
       Frederick A. Praeger Publishers, 1964. Author is
       presently career congressional aide to Senate For-
       eign Relations Committee.

2777. Lamé, Manuel Quintin. Las luchas del indio que bajo de
       la montaña al valle de la civilización. Seleccion,
       arreglo y notas por Gonzalo Castillo Cardenas.
       Bogota, Comité de Defense del Indio, 1973. Una
       publicación de la Rosca de Investigación de Accion
       Social, Apartado 51012, Bogota, 2, Colombia. 86 p.

2778. _____. En Defensa de mi raza. Intro-
       ducción y notas por Gonzalo Castillo Cárdenas.
       Bogota, Comité de Defensa del Indio, 1971. 133 p.
       Published by Rosca de Investigación y Acción Social,
       Apartado 51012, Bogotá 2. Writings of Colombian
       Indian leader (1883-1967) who spent years in prison
       in protest to abuses toward dialect-speaking
       Colombian citizens.

2779. Parks, E. Taylor. Colombia and the United States 1765-
       1934. Durham, North Carolina; University of N.C.
       Press, 1935. 554 p.

2780. Payne, James L. Patterns of conflict in Colombia. New
       Haven, Yale University Press, 1968.

2781. Perez Ramirez, Gustavo. Planas: Las contradicciones del
       capitalismo, Bogotá, Tercer Mundo, 1971. 253 p.
       Persecution, torture and death of Guahibo Indians
       and a sociological interpretation of the Planas
       problems. Appendices and bibliography.

2782. Richardson, Miles. San Pedro, Colombia: small town in
       a developing society. New York, Holt, Rinehart and
       Winston, 1970.

2783. Rodriguez Forero, Jaime. Education catholique et
       secularization en Colombie. Cuernavaca, CIDOC,
       1970. Sondeos No. 63.

2784. Simmons, Alan B. The emergence of planning orientations
       in a modernizing community: migration, adaptation

and family planning in Highland Colombia. Ph.D.
dissertation, Carmel University. 1970. No. 15 in
Dissertation Series.

2785. Torres, Camilo. Cristianismo y Revolución. Mexico,
Ediciones ERA, 1970. 612 p. Prologue, selected
writings and notes by O. Maldonado, Guitmie
Olivieri and G. Zavala.

2786. Torres Giraldo, Ignacio. Maria Cano, Mujer Rebelde.
Bogota, Editorial Editextos, Ltda. 1972. A publication of Rosca de Investigación y Acción Social.
A political biography of militant revolutionary in
the 1920's who led Colombian workers in their early
stages of organization. One of the few women
socialist leaders of the early part of the century
in Latin America.

2787. Urrutia, Miguel. The development of the Colombian labor
movement. New Haven: Yale University Press, 1969.

Protestantism in General
See also p. 180.

2788. Allan, Alexander M. Before the Mast and behind the
Pulpit. Unpublished manuscript of the life of a
pioneer Presbyterian missionary in New Zealand and
Colombia (1876-1973) UML. DMC.

2789. Fajardo, Luis H. The Protestant Ethic of the Antioqueños:
Social Structure and Personality. Cali, Colombia;
n.d. 1968. 140 p. Bibliographical. Bilingual.

2790. Flora, Cornelia Butler. Mobilizing the Masses: the
sacred and secular in Colombia. Ph.D. thesis,
Cornell University, 1970. 285 p. No. 25 in
Cornell Dissertation Series. Excellent bibliography.
A sociological study related to the development of
the United Pentecostal Church in Colombia in past
two decades. Discusses lower class solidarity movements in Colombia, their internal structure, prece-
dent conditions and consequence of these movements.
Important.

2791. _____. "Response to the 'Protestant Persecution' in
Colombia by the U. S. religious press -- the search
for allies." Unpublished paper, Cornell University,
Ithaca, New York, 1967.

2792. Habegger, Howard. Toward a mission strategy to the
         emerging urban middle stratum in Colombia. 1970.
         Unpublished dissertation. General Conference
         Mennonite Church. 722 Main Street, Newton, Kansas
         67114. Also Spanish translation.

2793. Howard, David M., Hammered as Gold, New York, Harper and
         Row, 1969. The moving story of Ernest Fowler who
         was killed by bandits in 1968, a missionary, since
         1926 of the Latin America Mission in Colombia.

2794. Palmer, Donald C. The growth of the Pentecostal churches
         in Colombia. Deerfield, Illinois, Trinity Evangel-
         ical Divinity School. Unpublished M.A. thesis, 1972.

2795. Sinclair, John H. The History of Christian Mission
         in Gran-Colombia. In preparation. A survey
         volume of both Catholic and Protestant missions
         in Ecuador, Colombia, and Venezuela. Chapter on
         Indian and African influences in religion in this
         area.

2796. Wall, Martha. As a roaring lion. Foreward by Donald
         McGavran. Chicago, Moody Press, 1967. 254 p. A
         missionary novel on sufferings of small Protestant
         congregations. Uncritical presentation of the role
         of foreign missionaries in development of these
         rural churches.

2797. Winn, Wilkins E. "The issue of religious liberty in the
         United States commercial treaty with Colombia, 1824"
         in The Americas: *Quarterly Review of Inter-American
         Cultural History*, XXVI (January, 1970), 291-301 p.
         Indicates the importance of religion in negotiating
         this treaty, as the United States desired religious
         privileges for her citizens in Colombia engaged in
         economic affairs.

                        Denominational History
                          See also p. 182.

Cumberland Presbyterian

2798. Action, Lawrence. Growth of the Cumberland Presbyterian
         Church in Colombia. Research in progress. School of
         Missions and Institute of Church Growth, Fuller
         Theological Seminary, Pasadena, Calif.

Presbyterian

2799. Report of the Special Study Committee on Colombia.
Office of the General Assembly, United Presbyterian
Church, U.S.A., 1972. 15 p. Significant paper on
controversial grant to ROSCA, a social research-action
group in Colombia.

Periodicals
See also p. 184.

Current Publications

2800. Diálogo Teológico, Apartado Aéreo 6613, Cali. Abril de
1973. Cada seis meses. Publicación de ABITHA
(Asociación Bautista de Instituciones Teológicas
Hispanoamericanos).

2801. Daveto. Apartado Aéreo 29720, Bogotá. 1970-. Bimestral.
Noticiero de los evangélicos protestantes de
Colombia.

2802. La Voz de la Alianza. Apartado Aéreo 4725, Cali. 1964-.
Bimestral. Publicación de la Iglesia Alianza
Cristiana y Misionera en Colombia.

Ecuador
See also p. 185.

General Background
See also p. 185.

2803. Eichler, Arturo. Ecuador, snow peaks and jungles.
Gesemtherstellung, Gebr. Zummerman. Buchdruckerei
and Verlag Gmbh. Revised edition, 1970. 182 p.
One of the best books on Ecuador. English and
Spanish editions.

2804. Garza Zavala, Jaime. El festin del petroleo. Quito,
Ediciones Solitierra, 1972. 376 p. Controversial
analysis of the beneficiaries of the newly-developed
"black gold" of Ecuador.

Protestantism in General
See also p. 186.

2805. Dilworth, Donald. Evangelization of the Quichuas of
        Ecuador. Unpublished M.A. thesis, 1967. School of
        Missions and Institute of Church Growth, Fuller
        Theological Seminary, Pasadena, Calif.

2806. Elliot, Elisabeth. The liberty of obedience. Waco,
        Texas, Word Books, 1968. 71 p. Life among the
        Auca Indians and honest confrontation of the ethical
        categories of primitive people.

2807. Gold, Robert. "Problems of Protestantism in Ecuador,
        1966-1973." A *Journal of Church and State*, 12
        (Winter, 1970). 59-78 p.

2808. Jativa, Carlo, ed. Ecuadorian Protestant Census - 1966
        and 1968. Quito, Sociedad Biblica en el Ecuador.
        Mimeographed. 22 p. Available from Dr. James Goff,
        Apartado 5594, Lima, 1, Peru, as an appendix
        to the CEDEC Colombian Census of 1969. (Cf. No.
        1539).

2809. Weld, Wayne C. An Ecuadorian Impasse. Pasadena,
        California, Institute of Church Growth, 1968.
        135 p. Addresses the problem of an Evangelical
        Church whose membership includes only three-tenths
        of one per cent of the total population after
        seventy years of missionary activity. Maps and
        charts. Good in spite of paucity of material on
        church in Ecuador.

Denominational Work
See also p. 188.

World Radio Missionary Fellowship (H.C.J.B.)

2810. Cook, Frank S. Seeds in the Wind. Miami, World Radio
        Missionary Fellowship. n.d. 187 p. The story of
        HCJB.

2811. Landers, Jay. Antenna Country. Chicago, Moody Press.
        n.d. 95 p. The story of HCJB through the eyes
        of a missionary child.

2812. Turner, Faith H. Out of weakness strength. Miami, Fla.
        World Radio Missionary Fellowship. n.d.   286 p.
        A missionary autobiography.

Periodicals
See also p. 189.

2813. Mensajero. Monthly. Apartado 4100, Quito. Independent
        publication with distinct Christian orientation.

2814. C.E.T. Organo informativo del Centro de Estudios
        Teológicos. Casilla 32-31, Quito. Occasional.

Venezuela
See also p. 190.

Bibliography
See also p. 190.

2816. Anuario bibliográfico Venezolano. 1942-. Caracas,
        Biblioteca Nacional.

2817. Ensayo de un repertorio bibliográfico venezolano. (1808-
        1950). Compiled by Angel Raul Vilasana. Vol. I,
        II. Caracas, A. Bjorkman, 1969. Vol. III, IV,
        1970.

General Background
See also p. 190.

2818. Acedo de Sucre, María de Lourdes and Carmen Margarita
        Nones Mendez. La generación venezolana de 1928.
        Estudio de una elite popular. Caracas, Editorial
        Ariel, 1967. 182 p. The university class of 1928
        produced many of the political leaders of Venezuela
        in the 1940-70 period.

2819. Alexander, Robert J. The Communist Party of Venezuela.
        Stanford, Calif., The Hoover Institution, 1969.
        246 p. A history of the Communist Party of
        Venezuela, with emphasis on its failure to achieve
        its goals through violence.

2820. Bernstein, Harry. *Venezuela y Colombia.* Englewood
        Cliffs, N.J., Prentice Hall, 1965. 2nd ed. 157 p.
        A popular survey.

2821. Chacón, Alfredo *y* Miguel Cardona. Curanderismo en
      Venezuela. Cuernavaca, Mexico: CIDOC, 1970.
      Sondeos No. 18. 124 p. A study of the Afro-
      American magic superstitions by use of plants,
      prayers in the treatment of diseases. Originally
      appeared in CAL magazine in Venezuela in 1972 in
      eleven issues.

2822. Chen, Chi-Yi. Movimientos migratorios en Venezuela.
      Caracas: Instituto de Investigaciones Económicas
      de la Universidad Católica Andres Bello, 1968.
      Caracas. 276 p.

2823. Córdoba, Diego. Los desterrados y Juan Vicente Gómez.
      Memorias de Pedro Elías Aristeguieta. Caracas.
      n.p. 1968. 244 p.

2823a. del Corro, Alejandro. Venezuela: Violencia: 1960-68.
      Cuernavaca, CIDOC, 1968. 5 volumes and bibliography.
      Some 8,000 items.

2824. Peattie, Lisa Redfield. The view from the barrio. Ann
      Arbor, University of Michigan Press, 1968. 147 p.
      An American anthropologist gives a warm personal
      account of life in a barrio of a planned city in
      Venezuela.

2825. Pollack-Eltz, Angelina. Vestigios africanos en la
      cultura del pueblo venezolano. Cuernavaca, Mexico:
      CIDOC, 1971. 135 p. Sondeos No. 76. Results of
      a ten year study in Barlovento region.

2826. Sierra, Jaime. Iglesia y Estado 1810-1821. Caracas.
      Ediciones del Cuatro-centenario de Caracas, 1967.
      363 p. Documents relations between ecclesiastical
      and civil authorities in period of Archbishop
      Narciso Coll y Prat.

Protestantism in General
See also p. 192.

2827. Johnson, Alfred E. Venezuela Survey Report, Potential
      for Revolutionary Church Growth. Worldwide evangel-
      ization Crusade. A master's thesis at the School of
      Missions and Institute of Church Growth, Fuller
      Theological Seminary, Pasadena, Calif.

CENTRAL AMERICA AND PANAMA
See also p. 193.
(Works referring to more than one Central American country.)

2828. Alcantara Matos, Domingo. Cien Años de presencia
        protestante en Centroamerica. Santiago, Chile.
        Iglesia y Sociedad, 1973. 105 p. A provocative,
        sociological study of Protestantism in its ecclesial
        reality, as institution as a community.

2829. Alonso, Isidoro *and* Gines Garrido. La Iglesia en América
        Central y el Caribe. Friburg, Germany, FERES, 1961.
        282 p. Regional volume for Central American in
        FERES Series on the Catholic Church in Latin America.
        Now somewhat dated. (Cf. no. 216).

2830. Enyart, Paul C. Friends in Central America. South
        Pasadena, William Carey Library, 1970. 224 p.
        Story of the growth of the work of the California
        Friends Yearly Meeting with a comparison to other
        evangelical churches in Guatemala, Honduras, and
        El Salvador.

2831. Gibson, Jeffry R. A demographic analysis of urbanization:
        Evaluation of a system of cities in Honduras, El
        Salvador and Costa Rica. Ph.D. dissertation.
        Cornell University, 1970. No. 20 in Dissertation
        Series.

2832. Huck, Eugene R. *and* Edward H. Mosely, eds. Militants,
        Merchants and Missionaries: United States
        Expansion in Middle America. University, Ala.
        University of Alabama Press, 1970, 172 p. A
        collection of essays which include three on Protes-
        tantism in Middle America: (1) "Southern Baptists
        in Cuba, 1886-1916," (2) "The Religious Impact of
        the American Occupation in Mexico City, 1847-1848,"
        and (3) "Albert Edward Bishop and the Establishment
        of the Central American Mission in Guatemala, 1899-
        1922."

2833. Parker, Franklin D. The Central American Republics.
        New York, Oxford University Press, 1964. 348 p.
        The series of the Royal Institute of International
        Affairs which is an excellent historical account
        of Central America as a whole and of the individual
        countries. Protestantism included in the section on
        religion. Useful but quickly out of date.

2834. _____. Travels in Central America, 1821-1840. Gaines-
       ville, University of Florida Press, 1970. 340 p.
       Largely a critical synthesis of ten travelers to
       Central America, 1821-1840, and therefore, presents
       their description of the area. Contains a chapter
       of religion, often through Protestant eyes, which
       includes statements on religious liberty. Last
       section is a topical index to thirty-five travel
       accounts for the period but also with considerable
       historical data.

2835. Pike, Frederick B. The Catholic Church in Central
       America. In *Review of Politics*, Vol. 21, January
       1959. 83-113 p. Presents good survey of R.C.
       Church in Central America up until the late 1950's.

2836. Rodriguez, Mario. Central America. Englewood Cliff,
       N.J., Prentice-Hall, 1965. 179 p. A brief survey
       of Central American history with emphasis on post-
       World War II period. Paperback.

2837. Taylor, William D. A diagnostic and remedial study of
       Christian education in Central America. M.A.
       thesis, Dallas Theological Seminary, Dallas, Texas.
       1967.

2838. Vega, Ramón y Greer Taylor. El Concubinato en América
       Central. Cuernavaca, Mexico: CIDOC, 1966. Sondeos
       No. 8. 289 p. Dissertation at Louvain by Ramón
       Vega, Causes du Concubinage in Amerique Centrale.
       1962. Father Vega concerns himself with solutions
       as well as analysis, affirming that the problem of
       concubinage is not simply one of family structure.
       Appendix by an Episcopal priest on "Concubinage and
       Communion in the Protestant Episcopal Church."

2839. Winn, Wilkins B. "A History of the Central American
       Mission as seen in the work of Albert Edward Bishop,
       1860-1922." Unpublished Ph.D. dissertation,
       University of Alabama, 1964. 285 p. Describes the
       efforts of a pioneer Protestant missionary in
       Honduras, 1896-1899, and in Guatemala 1899-1922,
       to establish the Central American Mission (inter-
       denominational), including problems and progress in
       evangelizing, institutionalizing the work, and
       some comments on social and political conditions.

Costa Rica
See also p. 193.

General Background
See also p. 193.

2840. Blanco Segura, Ricardo. Historia Eclesiástica de Costa
       Rica. San José, Editorial Costa Rica, 1967. 401 p.
       Extensive history of the Catholic Church in Costa
       Rica. Limited material on Protestants and the post-
       World War II period. Unfortunately it deals almost
       entirely with the Colonial Period with little con-
       cerning the 19th Century and nothing on the 20th.

2841. _____. Monseñor Sanabria. San José, Editorial Costa
       Rica, 1962. Biographical study of Costa Rica's
       first archbishop. Rather uncritical.

2842. Blutstein, Howard, et al. Area Handbook for Costa Rica.
       Washington, U.S. Government Printing Office, 1970.
       323 p. One of a series of summaries of social,
       political and economic data on Latin American
       nations prepared for the Department of Defense by
       the American University in Washington, D.C. Con-
       tains section on religion.

2843. Denton, Charles F. La política de desarrollo en Costa
       Rica. San José, Editorial Novedades, 1969. 164 p.
       A study of the economic and political structures of
       Costa Rica - some novel, semi-socialist.

2844. Lascaris, Constantino. Desarrollo de las ideas filosó-
       ficas en Costa Rica. n.p. 1965. 631 p. A resumé
       of the ideas of the principal thinkers of Costa
       Rica and of the currents of thought which have
       occupied their attention. Author is professor of
       philosophy in the University of Costa Rica.

2845. Lundberg, Donald E. Adventure in Costa Rica. San José,
       Juan Mora and author, 1968. 224 p. A popular pre-
       sentation of the geography, history, culture,
       economic and religion of Costa Rica. Heavily
       illustrated.

Protestantism in General
See also p. 194.

2846. Elliot, Elizabeth. Who shall ascend: the life of R.
       Kenneth Strachan of Costa Rica. New York, Harper

and Row, 1968. 171 p. A very readable study of
Strachan based on thorough research in the Strachan
papers. Reveals his weaknesses as well as the
struggles of a great soul.

2847. Millett, Richard L. Protestant-Catholic Relations in
Costa Rica. *Journal of Church and State*. Vol. XII
(Winter, 1970). 41-57 p. A review of the histor-
ical development of relations between Catholics and
Protestants with emphasis on changes produced by
Vatican II.

2848. Murillo Gutierrez, Jesús. La libertad de cultos y las
constituciones de Costa Rica. Unpublished thesis.
Facultad de Leyes, Universidad de Costa Rica, 1966.
Deals with legal aspects of religious freedom in
Costa Rica.

2849. Roberts, W. Dayton. Strachan of Costa Rica: missionary
insights and strategies. Grand Rapids, Eerdmans,
1971. 187 p. A very favorable treatment of
Strachan's life which traces his accomplishments in
relation to the entire Latin American scene and
world mission. Contains some worthwhile information
on Protestants in Costa Rica. Traces development of
Kenneth Strachan, a beloved missionary leader, from
an insecure young man to his great influence as a
mission strategist.

Denominational History
See also p. 194.

Central American Mission

2850. Sánchez, Manuel R. Historia de la Iglesia Centroamericana
en Costa Rica. Th.B. thesis. Seminario Bíblico
Latinoamericano, San José, C.R. A history of the
work of the Central American Mission in Costa Rica,
the pioneer mission of Costa Rica.

Periodicals
See also p. 195.

2851. ALET. Boletín de la Secretaria Ejecutiva, Apartado 2053,
San José, 1969-. Bimensual. ALET (Asociación
Latinoamericana de Escuelas Teológicas).

2852. Boletín de ALFALIT (ALFALIT news is title of English
        edition available from same address), Apartado 292,
        Alejuela, C.R.

2853. En Marcha Internacional. Apartado 1307, San José.
        Occasional, Publicación del INDEF (Instituto de
        Evangelización a Fondo).

2854. Pueblo. A Costa Rican weekly under ecumenical auspices.
        Javier Solis, editor. Calle 9, Av. 14-14 bis, San
        José, C.R.

2855. Resúmen de Telecomunicación Evangélica (English edition:
        Bulletin of Telecommunication Ministries), Apartado
        2470, San José. 1963-. (English edition, 1960-.).
        Trimestral. Publicación de "Difusiones Inter-
        americanas."

Guatemala
See also p. 196.

General Background
See also p. 196.

2856. Adams, Richard N. Crucifixion by Power: Essays on
        Guatemalan National Social Structure, 1944-1966.
        Austin, University of Texas Press, 1970. 553 p.
        Based on work of research teams (1963-66) under
        Professor Adams. One of the best books on Guatemala
        which shows the marked growth in that 22 year period
        of the power of the upper sectors in Guatemala and
        the limited extent to which the lower sectors bene-
        fited in national development. Excellent chapter
        on the Church. Emphasizes the dominant influence
        of the United States to the extent that Guatemala
        was not free to resolve its own problems but in
        reality was "crucified by unyielding and uncontrol-
        able power plays beyond its national borders."

2857. Aguilera Peralta, Gabriel Edgardo. La violencia en
        Guatemala como fenómeno político. Cuernavaca,
        CIDOC, 1971. 176 p. Study of guerilla and counter-
        guerilla activity in Guatemala. CIDOC Cuadernos No.
        61.

2858. Calder, Bruce J. Growth and Change in the Guatemala
        Catholic Church, 1944-1966. Unpublished M.A.
        thesis. Austin, Texas, University of Texas, 1966.

2859. Claxton, Robert Howard. "Lorenzo Montúfar: Central
       American Liberal." Ph.D. dissertation, Tulane
       University, 1970. 352 p. Indicates the influence
       of Protestantism on Montúfar (1823-1898) and his
       importance on the development of liberalism in
       Guatemala. (Order No. 70-24, 512).

2860. Del Corro, Alejandro, Compilador. Guatemala: La
       Violencia: Posiciones ante el uso de la violencia
       en el cambio social, 1960-68. 3 volúmenes. I
       Prensa nacional (1960-65) 115 p., II Prensa nacional
       (1966-67) 135 p., III Impresos clandestinos de
       tirajes reducidos: Prensa suprimida y marginal,
       1965-68. 434 p. The three volumes contain 2,232
       items.

2861. Dombrowski, John, et al. Area Handbook for Guatemala.
       Washington, U.S. Government Printing Office, 1970.
       361 p. One of a series of social, political and
       economic data on Latin American countries prepared
       for the Department of Defense by American University.

2862. Falla, Ricardo. "Evolución político-religiosa del
       Indígena Rural en Guatemala (1945-1965) in *Estudios
       Sociales Centroamericanos*. Enero-abril, 1972.

2863. Frankel, Anita. Political Development in Guatemala:
       1044-54: The impact of foreign military and
       religious elites. Ph.D. dissertation. University
       of Connecticut, 1969. Available at the University
       of Connecticut and copies through University micro-
       films. (Cf. Dissertation abstracts, February, 1970.
       3515 a. p.).

2864. Galeano, Eduardo. Guatemala: País Ocupado. Mexico,
       Editorial Nuestro Tiempo. 129 p. A study of
       violence by which the dominant class defends its
       privileges and the response of the people is
       through struggle and guerrilla action. (Also in
       English. Guatemala: Occupied Country, New York,
       Monthly Review, 1969).

2865. López Godínez, Rolando Ruperto. La ignorancia y la
       incomprensión de la ley penal en el medio indígena
       Guatemalteco. Estudio de casos de personas concep-
       tuadas como delincuentes por el derecho ladino.
       Graduate thesis of great value. Universidad de
       San Carlo, Guatemala City, 1972. 77 p.

2866. Melville, Thomas *and* Marjorie. The politics of land ownership. New York, Free Press, 1971. Provocative and controversial study of Guatemala by former priest and nun who became involved with Guatemalan guerrillas in 1960. Material covered is of a broader scope than indicated by the title.

2867. _____. Whose heaven, Whose earth? Knopf, New York, 1972. A contemporary drama of holy dissent with the missionary community and institutions of the United States. The story of the Melvilles' transformation from missionaries to revolutionaries--through their commitment to the disposessed of Guatemala. Both served sentences in federal prisons (1970-72) with the "Catonsville Nine" because of their protest to the draft system. An important missionary autobiography by a capable and committed couple.

2868. Miller, Hubert John. "The Church and State Question in Guatemala, 1871-1885." Ph.D. dissertation, Loyola University, Chicago, 1965.

2869. _____. Positivism and Educational Reform in Guatemala, 1871-1885. In *Journal of Church and State*, Vol. VII (June, 1967). 251-260 p. A study of some of the factors which led, among other developments to the introduction of Protestantism into Guatemala.

2870. Parrilli, Rita. The Church and Social Change in Guatemala. Thesis, 1969.

2871. Roberts, Bryan R. "Protestantism and Coping with Urban Life in Guatemala City," in *American Journal of Sociology*, Vol. 73 (May, 1968).

2872. _____. Organizing strategies. Austin, University of Texas Press, 1972. 418 p. A study of two poor neighborhoods in Guatemala City. A first major study of any Central American urban population.

2873. Schneider, Ronald S. Communism in Guatemala, 1944-1954. New York, Frederick A. Praeger, 1959.

2874. Snee, Carole A. Current types peasant-agricultural worker coalitions and their historical development in Guatemala. Cuernavaca, CIDOC, 1969. 129 p. Presentation by Charles Wagley. Includes case study of union in sugar cane finca. CIDOC Cuadernos No. 31.

2875. Weaver, Jerry L. Political Style of the Guatemalan
      Military Elite. Long Beach, California. California
      State College, 1968.

2876. Whetten, Nathan L. Guatemala: The land and the people.
      New Haven, Conn. 1961. Caribbean Series No. 4.
      Good description of Guatemalan society by a
      sociologist. Includes references to Protestantism.

2877. Williford, Miriam. "The Reform Program of Dr. Mariano
      Gálvez, Chief-of-State of Guatemala, 1831-1838."
      Ph.D. dissertation, Tulane University, 1964.

Protestantism in General
See also p. 197.

Indian Congregations and the Process of Ladinization

Books, Monographs and Theses

2878. Peck, H. Dudley. Practice and Training of Guatemala
      Mam Shamans. Ph.D. thesis. Hartford Theological
      Seminary, 1970. The researcher documents the thesis
      that Mam Shamans are community leaders who serve as
      witch doctors or healers as well as priests to
      their people. Dr. Peck spent from 1923-63 among
      the Mam Indians.

Articles

2879. Emery, James. "The preparation of leaders in a Ladino-
      Indian Church," in *Practical Anthropology* (May, 1963),
      8-15 p.

2880. Mayers, Marvin K., The two man feud in the Guatemalan
      Church. In *Practical Anthropology*, Vol. 13 (July-
      August, 1965). 115-125 p. Study of interpersonal
      conflicts on basis of church conflicts and divisions
      among Guatemalan Protestants.

2881. Thompson, Donald. Maya Paganism and Christianity. In
      Nativism and Syncretism. Published by Middle Ameri-
      can Research Institute, Publication No. 19. New
      Orleans, Tulane Press, 1960. 1-35 p. Valuable
      anthropological study, dealing primarily with
      Guatemala.

Note: Useful articles on religious aspects of the
Indian culture in Guatemala are found in *Guatemala
Indigena* and *Cuadernos del Seminario de Integracion
Social Guatemalteca.*

Protestantism in General

2882. Alcott, Georgiana Ruth. An historical survey of Evangelical North American missions in Guatemala. M.A.
thesis. Columbia Bible College, Columbia, S.C.
1970. 95 p. A brief description of historical
development of twenty-two Protestant organizations
in Guatemala.

2883. Barton, Edwin. Physician to the Mayas. Philadelphia,
Fortress Press, 1970. 207 p. The story of Dr.
Carroll Behrhorst, a former Lutheran medical
missionary in Guatemala who began an independent
community health program in which the training of
low-level practicioners became the focus of medical
services. Dr. Behrhorst's work has attracted world
wide interest because of his innovative techniques
and understanding of the Guatemala culture. The
book is hastily written, but important.

2884. Blakeney, Adolph L. The origin and growth of Protestantism in Guatemala. Unpublished M.A. thesis,
University of Alabama, 1956. Excellent, brief
account of the development of Protestant movement
in Guatemala. Good bibliography.

2885. Nash, June. "Protestantism in an Indian Village in
Western Highlands of Guatemala." In *Alpha Kappa
Delta* (Winter, 1960). 41-58 p. Article cites
various reasons, in addition to religious, why some
Indians are converted to Protestantism, i.e. social
betterment.

2886. Roberts, Bryan R. Protestant groups and coping with
urban change in Guatemala City. In *American Journal
of Sociology.* Vol. 53 (May, 1968). 753-67 p.
Study of Protestant influences in adaptation from
rural to urban living.

2887. _____. El Protestantismo en dos barrios marginales de
Guatemala. Guatemala, Seminario de Integración
Social Guatemalteca, 1967. 22 p. No. 2 Estudios
Centroamericanos.

2888. Smith, Robert J. Medical missionaries as agents of
       change in Guatemala. In *Michigan Academician*, 1970.
       67-72 p. Anthropological study of Presbyterian
       medical work in San Juan Ostucalco area.

2889. Thomas, Harold. Factors of church growth among the
       Chorti Indians of Guatemala. Research in progress.
       School of Missions and Institute of Church Growth,
       Fuller Theological Seminary, Pasadena, Calif.

2890. Weerstra, Hans M. Maya Peasant Evangelism: Communication,
       receptivity and acceptance factor among Maya campes-
       inos. Unpublished D. Miss. thesis. 1972. School
       of Missions and Institute of Church Growth, Fuller
       Theological Seminary, Pasadena, Calif.

                              Periodicals

2891. Boletín Divulgativo de JESSYC (Junta Evangélica de
       Servicio Social y Cultural), Apartado 904,
       Guatemala. 1971-. Quarterly.

2892. Corazón y Vida, Apartado Postal No. 8, Chiquimula. 1916-.
       Bi-monthly. Publicación de la Junta Anual de
       Iglesias Evangélicas "Amigos" de Centroamérica.

                           El Salvador
                        See also p. 202.

                        General Background

2893. Blutstein, Howard, et al. Area Handbook for El Salvador.
       Washington, D.C., U.S. Government Printing Office,
       1971. 257 p. One of series of studies of social,
       political and economic data on Latin American
       nations prepared for the Dept. of Defense by the
       American University. Contains section of religion,
       including brief summary of Protestant work. Useful
       reference source.

2894. Iglesias, Luis. Los misioneros redentoristas y la
       República de El Salvador. Mexico, 1956. 147 p.
       Lists and describes work of this order in El
       Salvador from 1928-55. Includes account of actions
       designed to counter Protestant influence.

2895. López Jiménez, Ramón. Mitras Salvadoreñas. San Salvador,
Ministerio de Cultura, 1960. Study of the history
of the Catholic Church in El Salvador from independence until 1960, told generally through the history
of its bishops.

Denominational History

Baptist

2896. Hutler, Grace. Land of the Lighthouse. Valley Forge,
Penn., Judson Press, 1966. 110 p. The personal
memoir of American Baptist work in El Salvador,
concentrating on educational aspects.

Periodicals

2897. Luz del Alba, Apartado Postal 347, San Salvador. Bimensual.
Publicación de la Asociación Bautista de El Salvador.

2898. Rápidas. Apartado (01) 142, San Salvador. 1971-. Mensual.
Boletín de la Novena Provincia de la Iglesia
Episcopal.

Honduras
See also p. 202.

General Background
See also p. 202.

2899. Blutstein, Howard, et al. Area Handbook for Honduras.
Washington, D.C., U.S. Government Printing Office,
1971. 224 p. One of the series of summaries of
social, political and economic data on Latin
American nations prepared for Dept. of Defense by
American University. Contains section on religion
including brief summary of Protestant development.
Useful reference work.

Protestantism in General
See also p. 202.

2900. Helms, Mary W. ASANG: adaptations of cultural contact
in a Miskito Community. Gainesville, Florida.

University of Florida Press, 1972. 268 p. Illustrations and tables. An ethnographic anthropological
and sociological interpretation of the Miskitos of
Honduras and Nicaragua with village life of typical
community, Asang, as a basis. Also good background
on the whole area of Mosquitia which provides an
excellent evaluation of the total effect of nearly
one hundred fifty years of Protestant missionary
effort mainly by Moravians. The presentation is
technical rather than popular. Wide and frequent
reference to other sources.

2901. Mathews, Edward F., Planting the Church in Honduras. M.A.
        thesis, Fuller Theological Seminary, Institute of
        Church Growth and School of Missions, 1970. Focuses
        on church growth problems and strategy with some
        treatment of general socio-political and religious
        situation in Honduras.

2902. Winn, Wilkins B. Pioneer Protestant missionaries in
        Honduras: A. E. Bishop and J. G. Cassel and the
        establishment of the Central American Mission in
        Western Honduras, 1896-1901. Cuernavaca, Mexico,
        CIDOC, 1973. 287 p. Sondeos Series. Edited diaries
        of two pioneer Protestant missionaries. The diaries
        reveal problems and progress in the work, attitudes
        and emotions of the missionaries, their daily routine
        and comments on social conditions. A historical
        introduction.

Nicaragua
See also p. 203.

General Background
See also p. 203.

2903. De cara al futuro de la Iglesia en Nicaragua. León,
        Nicaragua. Editorial Hospicio, 1969. 263 p.
        Documents presented at Primer Encuentro Pastoral in
        Nicaragua by both lay and clerical Catholic leaders
        in 1969. First indication of growing social and
        political within Nicaragua Catholic Church.

2904. Gallegos, Paco. Nicaragua, Tierra de Maravillas.
        Managua, Editorial San José, 1964. 300 p. Illus-
        trations. A publication of the Chamber of Commerce
        for students, professionals, business men and
        foreign visitors with coverage on population,

products, industries, physical features, and points
of attraction or interest.

2905. Ryan, John Morris, et al. Area Handbook for Nicaragua.
Washington, D.C., U.S. Government Printing Office,
1970. 393 p. One of series of summaries of social,
political and economic data on Latin American
nations prepared for the Dept. of Defense by the
American University. Contains sections on religion
in Nicaragua, including brief summary of Protestant
history. Useful for reference.

2906. Tweedy, Maureen. This is Nicaragua. Ipswich, England,
East Anglican Magazine, 1953. 116 p. A popular
tourist book with historical background and a
chapter on "legend, potions and philters."

Denominational History
See also p. 204.

Baptist

2907. Martinez, Melvyn de. Reseña Histórica de la Obra
Bautista de Masaya. n.p., 1968. 12 p. Brief
history of American Baptist work in Masaya.

Periodicals

2908. La Antorcha. Boletín de la Convención Bautista de
Nicaragua, Apartado 2593, Managua. 1918-. Mensual.

Panamá
See also p. 205.

General Background
See also p. 205.

2909. Alaides, Lozano R. Separación de la Iglesia y Estado;
O laicísmo en Panamá. Graduation thesis, Universidad
de Panamá, 1970. 66 p. A study of the church problems
in Panamá. Mimeographed copies available on Inter-
Library loan from Southern Illinois University,
Edwardsville, Illinois.

2910. Bravo, Francisco. The Parish of San Miguelito in Panama,
       history and Pastoral-Theological Evaluation.
       Cuernavaca, CIDOC, 1966. 340 p. In Spanish and
       in English. A significant experimental parish in
       techniques of evangelization which may prove epoch
       making.

2911. U. S. Army Area Handbook for Panama. Washington, D.C.,
       U.S. Government Printing Office, 1965. 488 p. One
       of the first of the series of studies of social,
       political and economic data on Latin American
       nations prepared by American University. Contains
       section on religion including some data on Protes-
       tants. Useful reference source but now rather out-
       dated.

Denominational History
See also p. 206.

Baptist

2912. Iglesias, Margaret G. Messenger to the Golden People.
       Nashville, Broadman, 1968. Study of Baptist work
       on the San Blas Islands near Panama. Spanish
       translation. Written for high schoolers.

2913. Knight, Walker L. Panama: The Land Between. Atlanta;
       Southern Baptist Home Mission Board, 1966. 106 p.
       Description of Southern Baptist work in Panama.

Methodist

2914. Alfonse, Efraim S. God at the Helm, London: Epworth
       Press, 1967. 139 p. Story of the Valiente Indian
       Mission (Methodist) of Northwest Panama on fiftieth
       anniversary. Founded by Jamaican Methodist in 1917.

2915. _____. Among the Valiente Indians. London, The Cargate
       Press, n.d. 104 p. Story of the founding of the
       Valiente Mission.

2916. Goodwin, E. Ray. Methodism in Panama. M.A. thesis,
       Wesley Theological Seminary, Washington, D.C., 1967.

MEXICO
See also p. 206.

General Background
See also p. 207.

Religious Issues

2917. Arenas, Reinaldo. *Hallucinations: Being an Account of the Life and Adventures of the Life and Adventures of Friar Servando Teresa de Mier.* Tr. by Gordon Brotherson. New York, Harper and Row, 1971. The story of a revolutionary priest, whose ideas contributed much to the independence Movement in Mexico.

2918. Avila, Manuel. Tradition and Growth. A study of four Mexican villages. New York, University of Chicago Press, 1969. 480 p. Compares results with anthpological studies done in the same villages in the 1930's. Concludes that these villages (Chan Kom, Soteapan, Mitla, and Tepoztlan) have not been stagnant but posses a unique dynamism and potential for economic and social growth.

2919. Bailey, David Charles, Ph.D. "The Cristero Rebellion and the Religious Conflict in Mexico, 1926-1929." Michigan State University, 1969. 459 p. Order No. 70-9493.

2920. Baird, Joseph Armstrong, Jr. *and* Hugo Rudinger. *The Churches of Mexico, 1530-1810.* Berkeley: University of California Press, 1962.

2921. Bazant, Juan. *Los bienes de la Iglesia en México.* Guanajuato: El Colegio de Mexico, 1971.

2922. _____. *Alienation of Church Wealth in Mexico.* Cambridge, England, Cambridge University Press, 1971. Church-State relations in the nineteenth century.

2923. Burland, C. A. *The Gods of Mexico.* New York: G. P. Putnam's Sons, 1967.

2924. Cadenhead, Ivie E., Jr. "Jesús González Ortega: Anti-clericalist" in *Journal of Church and State.* Vol. XII, Winter, 1970. 107-120 p.

2925. Callcott, Wilfred Hardy. Church and State in Mexico,
       1822-1887. Durham, N.C. Duke University Press,
       1926. Reprinted Octagon Books, New York, 1965.

2926. Gotshall, Jr., Ellwood Rufus, Ph.D. "Catholicism and
       Catholic Action in Mexico, 1929-1941: A Church's
       Response to a Revolutionary Society and the Politics
       of the Modern Age." Univ. of Pittsburgh, 1970.
       175 p. Order No. 21-15,948.

2927. Greenleaf, Richard E. The Mexican Inquisition of the
       sixteenth century. Albuquerque, New Mexico. Univ.
       of Mexico Press, 1969. 242 p. Study of records of
       Inquisition by an outstanding scholar in this field.
       Provides an overview of colonial life, best known
       through its heretics and dissenters.

2928. Krause, Corinne Azen, Ph.D. "The Jews in Mexico: A
       History with Special Emphasis on the Period from
       1857 to 1930." Univ. of Pittsburgh, 1970. 347 p.
       Order No. 71-8418.

2929. Macin, Raul. Jaramillo, un profeta olvidado. Montevideo,
       Tierra Nueva, 1970. 182 p. Story of a modern
       campesino revolutionary leader who was a Methodist
       lay leader.

2930. Murray, Paul V. *The Catholic Church in Mexico, 1519-1910.*
       Vol. I. Mexico: Editorial E.P.M., 1965.

2931. Nash, June. In the eyes of the ancestors: Belief and
       Behavior in a Mayan community. New Haven, 1970.
       368 p. 34 tables, glossary and bibliography. Study
       of Amatenango del Valle a Tzeltal-speaking community
       of highland Chiapas.

2932. Quirarte, Martín. *El Problema Religioso en México.*
       México: Instituto Nacional de Antropología e
       Historia. 1967.

2933. Ravicz, Marilyn Ekdahl. Early Colonial Religious Drama
       in Mexico; from Tzompantli to Golgatha. Washington,
       D.C. Catholic University of America Press, 1970.
       263 p. Study of drama as an active agent in an
       attempt to replace an indigenous religious culture
       with a Christian one. Seven extant plays, mostly
       written by Spaniards in the Indian Nahuatl language.

2934. Schmitt, Karl M. "The Mexican positivists and the Church-
       State Question" in *A Journal of Church and State*,
       Spring, 1966.

2935. Thompson, J. Eric. *Maya History and Religion*. Norman:
       Univ. of Oklahoma Press, 1970. A classic work on
       the Maya Indians.

2936. Timmons, Wilbert H. *Morelos of Mexico: Priest, Soldier,
       Stateman*. El Paso: Texas Western Press, 1970.
       (Revised ed., orign. pub. 1963).

2937. Wilkie, James W. "Statistical Indicators of the Impact
       of National Revolution on the Catholic Church in
       Mexico, 1910-1967, in *Journal of Church and State*,
       Vol. XII, Winter, 1970. 89-106 p.

Political

2938. Aub, Max. *Guía de Narradores de la Revolución Mexicana*.
       Mexico: Presencia de Mexico, No. 4, 1969.

2939. Cumberland, Charles C. *and* David C. Bailey. *Mexican
       Revolution: The Constitutionalist Years*. Austin,
       University of Texas Press, 1972.

2940. Goodman, Margaret Ann, Ph.D. "The Effectiveness of the
       Mexican Revolution as an Agent of Change in the
       State of Yucatan, Mexico," Columbia Univ., 1970.
       214 p. Order No. 71-23,594.

2941. Gutiérrez Lara, L. *and* Edgcumb Pinchon. *The Mexican
       People: Their Struggle for Freedom*. New York:
       Arno Press and the New Y ork Times, 1970. (orig.
       1914). Background book on Revolution of 1910,
       sympathetic to Mexicans.

2942. Hale, Charles A. *Mexican Liberalism in the Age of Mora*.
       New Haven, Yale University Press, 1968.

2943. Hansen, Roger D. *The Politics of Mexican Development*.
       Baltimore: The Johns Hopkins Press, 1971.

2944. King, Rosa E. *Tempest Over Mexico: A Personal Chronicle*.
       New York: Arno Press and The New York Times, 1970.
       (orig. 1935). Impressions of the Revolution of
       1910.

2945. Millon, Robert P. *Zapata: The Ideology of a Peasant
       Revolutionary*. New York: International Publishers,
       1969.

2946. Quirk, Robert E. An Affair of Honor. New York, W. W.
       Norton and Co., Inc. 1967. On U. S. involvement in
       Mexico.

2947. Smith, Jr. Arthur Kittredge, Ph.D. "Mexico and the
       Cuban Revolution: Foreign Policy-Making in Mexico
       under President Adolfo López Mateos (1958-1964)."
       Cornell University, 1970. 354 p. Order No. 21-14,
       598.

2948. Smith, Robert Freeman. *The United States and Revolution-
       ary Nationalism in Mexico. 1916, 1932*. Chicago:
       University of Chicago Press, 1972.

2949. Turner, Frederick C. *The Dynamic of Mexican Nationalism*.
       Chapel Hill, N. C.: University of North Carolina
       Press, 1968.

2950. Ulloa, Berta. *La revolución intervenida: Relaciones
       diplomáticas entre México y Estados Unidos* (1910-
       1914). México: El Colegio de México, 1971.

2951. Wright, Harry K. *Foreign Enterprise in Mexico: Laws
       and Policies*. Chapel Hill: University of North
       Carolina Press, 1971. Point of view of a Protes-
       tant businessman, born in Mexico.

Cultural, Educational and Social

2952. Balán, Jorge, Harley L. Browning *and* Elizabeth Jelin.
       Men in a developing society: geographic and social
       mobility in Monterrey, Mexico. Austin, University
       of Texas Press, 1972. Latin American monographs No.
       30. 432 p. A case study of 1,640 men, ages 21-60,
       in Monterrey.

2953. Cerwin, Herbert. Bernal Diaz, A Historial of the
       Conquest. Norman, Oklahoma, University of Oklahoma
       Press, 1963. 239 p. The first full biography on
       Diaz to be published in English.

2954. Childers, Howard Ray, Jr., Ph.D. "Response of an Estab-
       lished Latin American Revolution to the Cuban

Revolution: Mexican Symbols and Foreign Policy."
Washington University, 1970. 331 p. Order No.
71-11,028.

2955. Clifford, Roy A., Ph.D. "Sociological Study of the
Growth and Decline of Mexican Population Centers,
1940-1960." University of Florida, 1970. 182 p.
Order No. 71-24,417.

2956. Cook, Sherburne F. *and* Woodrow Borah. *Essays in Population History* (2 vols.). Berkeley, University of
California Press, 1971, 1973. Includes discussion
of concepts of family, househond, and census categories. Vols. I and II focus on Mexico and the
Caribbean.

2957. Fromm, Erich *and* Michael Maccoby. *Social Character in a
Mexican Village*. Englewood Cliffs, Prentice-Hall,
Inc., 1970. A study of the character and attitudes
of the Mexican *campesino* in relation to his socio-
economic conditions.

2958. González *y* González, Luis. San José de Garcia: A
microhistory of a Mexican village. Austin, University of Texas Press, 1972. Sees Mexican history
through the impact on the author's hometown in West
Michoacan. A solid piece of historical writing.

2959. Quirk, Robert E. *Mexico*. Englewood Cliffs: Prentice-
Hall, Inc., 1971. A succinct account of Mexico's
growth from a semi-feudal society to a modern
nation. Good bibliography.

2960. Sundel, Alfred. *A History of the Aztecs and the Mayas*.
New York, The Macmillan Co., 1967.

2961. Wauchope, Robert. *The Indian Background of Latin
American History*. New York, Alfred A. Knopf, 1970.

2962. Wilkie, James W. *and* Edna Monzón de Wilkie. *México visto
en el Siglo XX*. México: Instituto Mexicano de
Investigaciones Económicas, 1969.

Protestantism in General
See also p. 214.

2963. Aguirre Beltrán, Gonzalo. *Antología de Moisés Sáenz*.
Mexico: Ediciones Oasis, S.A. 1970. A compilation

of some of the writings of Prof. Moisés Sáenz and
an evaluation of his work by the Under-Secretary of
Public Education in Mexico.

2964. Bridges, Julian C. A Study of the Number, Distribution
and Growth of the Protestant Population in Mexico.
Master's thesis. University of Florida, Gainesville,
1969. Study covers period from 1857, using primary
and secondary sources. Distribution patterns are
significant and relation of growth rate to national
population increase. 109 p. Tables, graphs and
bibliography. UML.

2965. Chumacero, Rosalía de. *Perfil y Pensamiento de la Mujer
Mexicana.* Mexico, D.F.: Talleres Gráficos Olimpo,
1961. Includes a biography of Herlinda Treviño de
Sáenz.

2966. Goodman, Felicitas D. Speaking in tongues. A cross-
cultural study of glossalia. Chicago, The University of Chicago Press, 1972. 224 p. A study based
on research living with Apostolic congregations in
Mexico City, in Yucatan with Maya Indians and visits
with a congregation in Indiana.

2967. Greenleaf, Richard E. "North American Protestants and the
Mexican inquisition" in *A Journal of Church and
State*, Spring, 1966.

2968. Hefley, James C. Peril by Choice. Grand Rapids, Michigan,
Zonderman Publishing Company, 1968. 226 p. The
story of John and Elaine Beekman of the Wycliffe
Bible Translators in Mexico and Guatemala (1948-68).
Records the struggles of a pioneer missionary family
among the Chols, especially when challenged by
serious personal health problems. John Beekman is
now Chief Translation Consultant of Wycliffe in
Mexico.

2969. _____ *and* Hugh Steven. *Miracles in Mexico.* Chicago,
Moody Press, 1972.

2970. Macfarland, Charles S. Chaos in Mexico: *The Conflict
of Church and State.* New York, Harper and Bros.,
1935. Interpretations of Mexico's Church-State
Crisis of the thirties by a distinguished Protestant clergyman.

2971. Mejía Zúñiga, Raúl. *Moisés Saénz, Educador de México: su vida, su obra y su tiempo.* Monterrey, N.L.N. Talleres Linotipográficos Impresiones, S.A., 1962. A brief but enthusiastic biography of Moisés Sáenz.

2972. Nieto, Leo. Religion and Culture in Mexico. Th.M. thesis. Brite Divinity School, Texas Christian University, Ft. Worth, Texas, 1964.

2973. Pike, Eunice Victoria, ed. *Homenaje a William Cameron Townsend en el vigésimoquinto aniversario del Instituto Lingüístico de Verano.* México: I.L. de V., 1961. Essays on Indianism in Mexico, commemorating the founding of the Summer Institute of Linguistics by William Cameron Townsend.

2974. Ramos Pereira, Jovelino. The response of Protestants to the Mexican Revolution, 1910-1940. Doctoral dissertation in progress. Columbia University, 1973.

2975. Wilkie, James W. "The meaning of the Cristero religious war against the Mexican revolution," in *A Journal of Church and State*, Spring, 1966.

2976. Winn, Wilkins B. "The efforts of the United States to secure religious liberty in a commercial treaty in Mexico," in The Americas: *A Quarterly Review of Inter-American Cultural History*, XXVII (Jan. 1972). 311-332 p. Reveals difficulties of the United States to obtain religious privileges for her citizens in Mexico. The English and Spanish texts of the religious articles of the third and final treaty do not agree! Related to the policy of John Q. Adams and Henry Clary to bring about religious liberty in Latin America through commercial treaties.

Denominational History
See also p. 216.

Associate Reformed

2977. Mitchell, James E. The Emergence of a Mexican Church. The Associate Reformed Presbyterian Church of Mexico. South Pasadena, California, William Carey Library, 1970. 183 p. Tells the ninety-year story of the A.R.P. Mission in Mexico and the trials and hardships related to the emergence of a national

church body. Analyses the changing relationship
between mission board and national church.

Disciples

2978. Lee, Allan W. The Burro and the Bible. Jericho, N.Y.,
       Esposition Press Inc., 1968. 47 p. Largely the
       story of world and work of colporteurs.

Mennonites

2979. Redekop, Calvin Wall. "The Sectarian Black and White
       World." Ph.D. dissertation, Dept. of Sociology,
       University of Chicago, Chicago, Ill., 1959. 241 p.
       MUL. A close study of Old Colony Mennonites in
       Manitoba and Mexico.

2980. _____. The Old Colony Mennonites: Dilemmas of Ethnic
       Minority Life. Baltimore, The Johns Hopkins Press,
       1969. xiv, 302 p. Combines ethnographic approach
       with sociological analysis of dilemmas which
       threaten Old Colony culture with destruction; pre-
       sents the group's history with major focus on
       Mexico' studies implications of Old Colony sectar-
       ianism, as well as conflicts both within their
       systems and in their relations with outside world.

2981. Sawatsky, Harry Leonard. Mennonite Colonization in
       Mexico: A study in the survival of a traditionalist
       society. Ph.D. dissertation, Dept. of Geography,
       Univ. of California, Berkeley, 1967. vii, 506 p.
       Illustrated. Extensive and detailed examination of
       settlement patterns, size of holdings and agricul-
       tural and agro-business enterprises. Author pre-
       sents most complete picture currently available of
       Mennonite life and social organizations in Mexican
       geographical, biological and sociocultural milieu.

2982. _____. They Sought a Country: Mennonite Colonization
       in Mexico. Berkeley, University of California
       Press, 1971. xi, 387 p. Illustrated. Condensed
       version in popular style of doctoral dissertation.
       Contains a 37 page appendix on early years of
       Mennonite colonization in British Honduras.

Presbyterian

2983. Dame, Laurence. Maya Mission. Garden City, N.Y.
      Doubleday and Duran, 1968. 252 p. The story of
      the David Legters, independent Presbyterian
      missionaries in Yucatan.

2984. Erdman, Margaret Shelby. Un Jazmín floreció en Guerrero.
      Published privately by the author, 1966. 63 p.
      Story of Ms. Alice J. McClelland, a Presbyterian
      Church, U.S. educational missionary in Mexico.
      Work largely in Chilpancingo.

2985. Martinez López, Joel. Orígenes del Presbiterianismo en
      Mexico. Privately published. H. Matamoros,
      Tamaulipas, 1972. 238 p. The first book written
      by a recent seminary graduate upon the Centennial
      of the National Presbyterian Church of Mexico.
      Outlines the first years of Mexican Presbyterianism
      around the persons, contributions and colleages of
      Melinda Rankin, Grayson Mallet Prevost, Arcadio
      Morales and Leandro Garza Mora.

2986. McKaughan, James W. List and biographical sketches of
      the 213 missionaries of the Presbyterian Church,
      U.S.A. and the United Presbyterian Church, U.S.A.
      who served in Mexico from 1872-1973. Unpublished
      mss. UML.

2987. Morrow, Rufus C. El Almirante Misionero. México,
      Publicaciones El Faro, 1962. Translated to Spanish
      by L. P. Van Slyke. 90 p. The experiences of
      Captain Reginald C. Brenton of the Royal British
      Navy who established a naval school for Mexico
      under Porfirio Diaz (1891-97). He returned
      to serve as a lay colporteur until his death in
      Ometepec, Guer. in 1921.

Apostolic Faith in Jesus Christ Church

2988. Gaxiola, Manuel. La Serpiente y la Paloma. South
      Pasadena, Calif., Wm. Carey Library, 1970. 200 p.
      Impressive story of the rapid growth of the
      Apostolic Church of Mexico by a leader of this
      indigenous Mexican denomination.

Indigenous Churches

2989.   Pentecost, Edward C. A Church Growth Study of the
        Mexican Church founded by the Mexican Indian Mission.
        M.A. thesis, 1972. School of Missions and Institute
        of Church Growth, Fuller Theological Seminary,
        Pasadena, Calif.

Problems Related to U.S.-Mexico International Border

2990.   Arellano, Esteban, Tomás Atencio, Antonio Medina, et al.
        Entre Verde y Seco. Dixon, New Mexico. La Academia
        de la Nueva Raza, 1972. 119 p. The first of a
        series of publications on indigenous values in New
        Mexico folk culture, originating in sociological
        analysis and popular participation in self-deter-
        mination. La Academia is largely an effort of
        church-related groups.

2991.   Coker, William S., ed. "Research in the Spanish Border-
        lands: Bibliography," Austin: *Latin American
        Research Review*, Vol. VII, No. 2, Summer, 1972.
        Deals mainly with Spanish Borderlands east of Texas.
        Articles preceding the Bibliography make specific
        reference to works on religious history.

2992.   Helm, J. *Spanish-speaking People in the United States*.
        Seattle, Univ. of Washington Press, 1971. Survey
        of the Spanish-speaking people in the U.S. with
        bibliography.

2993.   Hester, Golda, ed. Select Bibliography on Mexican
        Americans. Mimeographed. 8 p. Hispanic American
        Institute, 100 East 27th St., Austin, Texas 78705.

2994.   Steiner, Sam. *La Raza: The Mexican Americans*. New
        York, Evanston, and London: Harper and Row, 1970.
        Background of the Chicano movement. Sources and
        suggested readings provided in appendix.

2995.   *The Spanish-Speaking in the U.S.* A bibliography.
        Washington, D.C. 20506. Committee on Opportunities
        for Spanish-Speaking People, 1800 G. St., 1971.
        175 p. Includes listing of bibliographies on the
        Spanish-speaking, books, articles, government
        publication, audio visual materials, Spanish lan-
        guage radio and T.V. station and dissertations on
        the subject.

2996. Winnie, William W., Jr., John F. Stegner, *and* Joseph P.
       Kopachevsky. *Persons of Mexican Descent in the
       United States: A Selected Bibliography.* Fort
       Collins, Colorado.

Mexican American Churches

2997. Holland, Clifton. The Religious Dimension in Spanish
       Los Angeles: A Protestant Case Study. Research
       in progress. School of Missions and Institute of
       Church Growth, Fuller Theological Seminary,
       Pasadena, Calif.

*Periodicals
See also p. 220.*

Current Publications

2998. Cruzada. Apartado 9292, México 1, D.F., 1972-. Tri-
       mestral. Publicación de la Cruzada Cultural de la
       Familia, A.C.

2999. Estudios Ecuménicos. Guty Cárdenas 131, México 20, D.F.
       1969-. Trimestral Publicación del Centro de
       Estudios Ecuménicos, A.C.

3000. El Mensajero, Apartado 1089, Cd. Juárez, Chich. 1966-.
       Mensual. Publicación de la Iglesia Evangélica
       Menonita.

3001. El Triángulo. Apartado Postal 8580, México 1, D.F.
       1968-. Bimestral. Publicación del Instituto
       Evangélico de Mexico.

3002. Gavillas Doradas. Apartado 334, México 1, D.F. 1933-.
       Bimestral. Boletín de las Asambleas de Dios.

3003. La Luz Bautista. Av. 16 de Septiembre No. 6. Despacho
       401, México 1, D.F. 1885-. Mensual. Publicación
       de la Convención Nacional Bautista de Mexico.

3004. Revista Teológica, Apartado 21-818, Coyoacán, México 21,
       D.F. 1969-. Trimestral. Publicación del Seminario
       "Juan Calvino."

THE INSULAR LATIN CARIBBEAN

Caribbean Region
See also p. 222.

3005. Audic, Fuat M. *and* Suphan Audic. "The role of the public
       sector in the development of the Greater Caribbean,"
       in *Latin American Research Review*. Vol. VIII, No.
       1, Spring, 1973. 97-134 p.

3006. Gonzalez, Justo L. The Development of Christianity in
       the Latin Caribbean. Grand Rapids, Michigan,
       Eerdmans, 1969. 136 p. Surveys Christianity under
       the colonial regimes before discussing the contem-
       porary periods in Cuba, Haiti, Dominican Republic
       and Puerto Rico.

3007. Crassweller, Robert D. The Caribbean Community; changing
       societies and the U.S. policy. New York, Praeger
       Publishers, 1970. 470 p. Published for the Council
       on Foreign Relations. Indicates the re-introduction
       of Caribbean area to priority policy concerns in the
       United States.

3008. de Kadt, Emanuel, ed. Patterns of Foreign Influence in
       the Caribbean, London, Oxford University Press,
       1971. 188 p. Published for the Royal Institute
       of International Affairs. High quality scholarship
       essays on impact of foreign interests on the
       quality of local life.

3009. Szulc, Tad, ed. The United States and the Caribbean.
       Englewood Cliffs, New Jersey, 1971. 212 p. Pre-
       pared for the Asmerican Assembly, Colombia Univer-
       sity. Papers of special value by Anthony Maingot
       and Frank McDonald on racist social structures and
       the rise of mass-based Black Power movements.

Cuba
See also p. 223.

Bibliographies
See also p. 223.

3010. Anuario Martiano. La Habana, Departamento Colección
       Cubana, 1970. Published by la Sala Marti de la
       Biblioteca Nacional de Cuba. 626 p. No. 2

(information lacking in No. 1). Extensive collection
of articles, essays, addresses and bibliography
martiano.

3011.   Bibliografía Cubana. Biblioteca Nacional "Jose Martí",
        Departamento Colección Cubana, Consejo Nacional de
        Cultura, Habana. 1959-62; 1963-64; 1965; 1967; 1968;
        1969.

3012.   Fort, Gilbert V., The Cuban Revolution of Fidel Castro:
        Annotated bibliography. Lawrence, Kansas, University
        of Kansas Press, 1969. Annotated list of all books
        about the Revolution published in Western Hemisphere,
        excluding Cuba and Canada, until 1965.

3013.   Pariseau, Earl J., ed. Cuban Acquisitions and Bibliography.
        Washington Library of Congress, 1970. 164 p. Pro-
        ceedings and working papers of an International
        Conference held at the Library of Congress, April,
        1970. Valuable review of resources in the Library
        of Congress, United Kingdom, Spain and Germany. List
        of book dealers offering Cuban research materials.

3014.   Peraza, Fermin, ed. Revolutionary Cuba: A Bibliographical
        Guide, Three English volumes of the former Anuario
        bibliográfico cubano. 1966, 1967, and 1968. Coral
        Gables, Florida; University of Miami Press, 1966-68.
        188 p., 244 p., and 262 p.

General Background
See also p. 223.

3015.   Blutstein, Howard I., Area Handbook for Cuba. Washington,
        D.C., U.S. Government Printing Office, 1971. 505 p.
        Another of a series on the social, political,
        economic and national security data on every Latin
        American country. Brief chapter on religion.
        Factually largely correct, but lacks any depth of
        interpretation of life in Cuba today.

3016.   Bonsal, Philip. Cuba, Castro and the United States.
        Pittsburgh, University of Pittsburgh Press, 1971.
        318 p. By a former U.S. diplomat in Cuba.

3017.   Boorstein, Edward. The Economic Transformation of Cuba.
        New York, Monthly Review Press, 1968. Socialist
        interpretation of economic change, especially during
        1960-63, by an American advisor to Cuban government.

3018. Clytus, John *and* Jane Rieker. Black Man in Red Cuba.
       158 p. Coral Gables, Florida; University of Miami
       Press, 1972. Story of a black American in Cuba.

3019. Crahan, Margaret E. The Roman Catholic Church in Castro's
       Cuba. Lehman College, City University of New York.
       Completion expected in 1973.

3020. Crassweller, Robert C. Cuba and the U.S. -- the tangled
       relationship. New York, Foreign Policy Association,
       1971. 61 p. In Headline series, No. 207.

3021. Cuba Economic Research Project. Labor Conditions in
       Communist Cuba. Coral Gables, Florida, University
       of Miami Press, 1972. 158 p. Analysis of the
       changes under the Castro regime as they relate to
       conditions of labor. Based largely on radio broad-
       casts, newspapers, texts of legislation and publica-
       tions on alleged "forced labor camps." Describes
       the "identity cards" workers carry.

3022. Cuba Review. Box 206, Cathedral Station, New York, N.Y.
       10025. Quarterly. Information on life in Cuba
       and in the churches in Cuba. U.S. $10.00 per year.
       Bibliographical section. Reprints of articles
       from Cuba in English translation. (Formerly "Cuba
       Resource Center Newsletter).

3023. Cuba Studies Newsletter. Center for Latin American
       Studies, University of Pittsburgh, Pittsburgh, Pa.
       15213. Quarterly. Published by University Center
       for International Studies. Editor, Carmelo Mesa-
       Lago. Vol. II, No. 2, June, 1972, has extensive
       bibliography on Cuba Creative Literature, 1958-71.
       Vol. III, No. 1, December 1972, lists books,
       pamphlets, articles and chapters in books mostly
       published in 1970 or later and announcements for
       1973 publications. Book reviews, commentaries and
       newspaper articles are excluded. 46 p.

3024. Cuba Center Survey. Vol. I, No. 19, Oct. 1972. Excellent
       six page summary on chronology, economic and political
       repression and resume of Revolutionary Cuba. Avail-
       able, Center for the Study of Power and Peace, 110
       Maryland Ave., N.E., Washington, D.C. 20002.

3025. del Quiaro, Robert. "Five Faces on Cuba" in *The
       Washington Post*, February 11, 1973.

3026. Dumont, Rene. Cuba: Socialism and Development. New York, Grove Press, 1970. (Translated from original in French, 1964). The early transition to collective agriculture described by a French agronomist-journalist.

3027. Fagen, Richard, R. et al, Cubans in Exile. Stanford, Stanford University Press, 1969. Study of refugees in Florida.

3028. _____. The transformation of Political culture in Cuba. Stanford, Stanford University Press, 1969. 271 p. Detailed material on the literacy campaign of 1961, on the Committees for Defense of Revolution, on Schools of Revolutionary Instruction, and all forms of "political socialization."

3029. Foner, Philip S. The Spanish-Cuban-American War and the Birth of Imperialism 1895-1902. New York, Monthly Review, 1973. 716 p. Two volumes. Also in paperback. The theme is "forget the Maine." Deals with broader perspective on the so-called "Spanish-American War."

3030. Gonzalez Ruiz, José Maria. "La Iglesia Católica en Cuba" in *Sabado Grafico*, Madrid, Setiembre, 1972. Careful analysis of the present situation of the Church in Cuba y a former professor of several members of the Cuban episcopacy.

3031. Hageman, Alice. "Santeria in the Black Experience" in the *Cuba Resource Center Newsletter*, Vol. II, No. 16, 15-20 p. A thoughtful assessment of this religious phenomena in Revolutionary Cuba.

3031a. _____. "Protestant Colonialism in the Spanish Caribbean" in *New World Outlook*, March, 1970.

3032. Horowitz, I.L., ed. Cuban Communism. Chicago, Adline, 1970. Articles of several authorities originally published in *Trans-Action*, April, 1969.

3033. IDOC Document. No. 49. December, 1972. "Papers toward trading with Cuba." Statement by nine church bodies together with statement of U.S. State Department and P.L. 87-733 of October, 1972. Compiled by Cuba Resources Center. Available IDOC, 235 E. 49th St., N.Y., N.Y. 10017.

3034. Le Riverend, Julio. Economic History of Cuba. La Habana, Instituto del Libro, 1967. 277 p. Traces the economic development of Cuba from the Conquest to the advent of the Socialist state.

3035. López Oliva, Enrique. La Semana Santa en Cuba. Abril, 1973. Noticias Prensa Lati a. A description of the life and practices of the Church in Cuba today.

3036. _____. La incorporacion de la mujer cristiana a la lucha revolucionaria, en *Revista OCLAE* (Organizacion Continental Latinoamericana de Estudiantes), La Habana, agosto de 1972. Specific reference to the late Casiana Ahumada, director of *Cristianismo y Revolucion*.

3037. _____. "Adios Mama Isabel." febrero, 1973. Noticias Prensa Latina. Report of the passing of the mother of the late Camilio Torres who went to live in Cuba after the death of her son.

3038. _____. ¿Revolucion en la teologia? Lima, Equipo Latino-americano del movimiento estudiantil Cristiano, 1972. Pamphlet on radical Christian theologians, with special emphasis on the work of the Peruvian theologian, Gustavo Gutierrez Merino.

3039. McCadden, Joseph *and* Helen. Father Varela, torch bearer from Cuba. New York, The U.S. Catholic Historical Society, 1969. XXVII in monograph series. 194 p. The life of one of Cuba's greatest patriots and educators. Documents part of life spent in New York City.

3040. Martínez, Estradam Ezequeil. Marti: El Héroe y su acción rvolucionaria. Mexico, Siglo XXI, 1966. Third and last part of a larger study of *Martí, revolucionario* under the Consejo Nacional de Cultura de Cuba. 266 p.

3041. Menton, Seymour. La novela y el cuento de la revolución cubana: 1959-1969. Cuernavaca, CIDOC, 1969. 10 p. Bibliography, mimeographed.

3042. O'Connor, James. Origens of Socialism in Cuba. Ithaca, N.Y., Cornell University Press, 1972.

3043. Ortega, Benjamín, ed. El Che Guevara; reacción de la prensa del Continente Americano con motivo de la

muerte; octubre-noviembre de 1967. Cuernavaca,
Mexico, CIDOC, 1968. 446 p. Listing of 2,934
items and 263 pages of documents.

3044. Plank, John N. "We should start talking with Castro" in
New York Times Magazine, March 30, 1969: 29-31, 76.

3045. _____, ed. Cuba and the United States: long-range perspectives. Washington, D.C. The Brookings Institution, 1967. 158-177 p. Written by a competent Cuba
scholar.

3046. Randall, Margaret. Mujeres en la revolución (originally
published as "La mujer en la revolucion." Havana,
Instituto Cubano del Libro, 1972). Mexico, Siglo
XXI, 1972. An excellent current study of the role
of women in the Cuba revolutionary progress based
on many interviews with woman at all levels of participation.

3047. Religion in Cuba Today, edited by Alice L. Hageman and
Philip E. Wheaton. New York, Associated Press,
1971. Writings on religion by Cubans living in
Cuba today. Reflects the search of a church for its
identity and place in a socialist society. An
introductory statement by Ms. Hageman challenges
some easy assumptions of North American mission
boards which worked in Cuba. One of the first
volumes in English of its kind and therefore a
valuable record of this decade.

3048. Rius. (pseud.) Cuba for Beginners. An illustrated
Guide for Americans and their government to
Socialist Cuba. New York, Pathfinder Press, Inc.,
1970. 153 p. This book is more than a hilarious
depiction of U.S.-Cuba relations by a famous
Mexican political cartoonist. It is the story of
Cuba as seen through the eyes of revolutionaries
in Cuba today.

3049. Rojas, Marta *and* Mirta Rodriguez Calderón. Tania, the
unforgettable guerilla. New York, Vintage Books,
1971. An informative and interesting account of
the life of the Argentine women who died in the
jungles of Bolivia with Che Guevara. Many personal
documents included.

3050. Smith, Robert Freeman. "Twentieth Century Cuba Historiography" in *The Hispanic American Historical Review,*

Vol. XLIV, No. 1, February, 1964. 44-73 p. An
excellent review by a noted Cubanologist who feels
that Cuba history has entered an exciting new age
and the exploration of its history offers a challenge
to scholars who seek to understand the complexities
of human activity.

3051. Suarez, Andres. Cuba: Castroism and Communism, 1959-
1966. Cambridge, Mass., The M.I.T. Press, 1967.
266 p. A survey of the events in Cuba from early
revolutionary days to the middle sixties.

3052. Suchlicki, Jaime, ed. Cuba, Castro and Revolution.
Articles by ten Cuba watchers who assess the international and international position of Cuba today.
Coral Gables, Florida, University of Miami Press,
1972. 350 p.

3053. _____. University Students and Revolution in Cuba, 1920-
1968. Coral Gables, Florida, University of Miami
Press, 1972. Supplemented by fifty interviews with
former leaders of student movements in Cuba. Does
not include positions held by student leaders who
remained in Cuba. 177 p.

3054. _____. The Cuban Revolution: A documentary guide.
Coral Gables, Florida, University of Miami Press,
1960. Includes resumes and quotes of some of most
significant documents and a guide to the library
collection at the University of Miami.

3055. Thomas, Hugh. Cuba: The Pursuit of Freedom, 1762-1929.
London, 1970. A monumental historical volume which
lacks some precision on interpretation despite the
extensive nature of the factual data.

Protestantism in General
See also p. 225.

3056. Clark, Ellen. "The Church in Cuba" in *New World Outlook*,
March, 1972.

3057. Directorio de Iglesias y Pastores pertenecientes al
Consejo de Iglesias Evangélicas de Cuba. La Habana,
Consejo Cubano de Iglesias Evangélicas, 1971. 33 p.
Complete list of names and addresses of church
leaders.

3058. Forrest, A. C. How Christians get along in Communist
       Cuba. United Church Observer. May, 1972. 28-32 p.

3059. Nottingham, Wm. J. "Two weeks in Cuba" in *World Call*,
       February, 1972.

3060. Tschuy, Theo., ed. Explosives Lateinamerika: Der
       Protestantismus inmitten der socialen Revolution.
       West Berlin, Germany: Lettner-Verlag, 1969. 207 p.

3061. _____. Von der Kolonie bis zur Sozialistischen Revolu-
       tion - Eine Gischichte des Kubanischen Protestantismus.
       Doctoral dissertation, University of Zurich:
       Institute of Reformation Theology. 600 p. 1973.
       By a former World Council of Churches representative
       for Latin America.

Denominational History
See also p. 226.

Baptist

3062. Greer, Harold Edward, Jr. "History of Southern Baptist
       Mission Work in Cuba, 1886-1916." Ph.D. disserta-
       tion, University of Alabama, 1965. Summary of thesis
       published as an essay in Eugene R. Huck and Edward
       H. Mosely, eds., Militarists, Merchants and Mission-
       aries: United States Expansion in Middle America.
       63-79 p. (Cf. No. 2832). Describes the Cuban-led
       Baptist mission work before the Spanish-American
       War and the problems and progress after the war as
       the Baptists built on their earlier foundations.
       By 1916 a strong Cuban Baptist denomination had
       developed in Western Cuba. (Order No. 66-2837).

Periodicals
See also p. 227.

3063. Impacto. Apartado Postal 85, Santa Clara, L.V., 1971-.
       Trimestral. Publicación del Movimiento de Iglesia
       y Sociedad en Cuba.

3064. Revista Encuentro. Salud 222 esq. Lealtad, La Habana.
       1953-. Publicación del MECC (Movimiento Estudian-
       tial Cristiano de Cuba).

Dominican Republic
See also p. 227.

General Background
See also p. 227.

3065.   Avelino, Francisco Antonio. Las Ideas Políticas en Santo
        Domingo. Santo Domingo, República Dominicana.
        Editorial Arte y Cine. 1966. 136 p. Ten pages of
        bibliography. The development of political ideas in
        the Dominican Republic from the colonial period,
        through the influence of the European bourgeois
        revolution ideologies and the period of the attain-
        ment of political independence from Spain, all the
        way to the contemporary ideological trends of
        nationalistic political-economic independence. The
        period of time covered reaches the publication of
        the 1963 National Constitution.

3066.   Bosch, Juan. Composición Social Dominicana, Historia e
        Interpretación. Santo Domingo, R.D. Publicaciones
        ¡Ahora! 1970. 309 p. This exile publication of
        Dr. Bosch is a classical example of the new Latin
        American sociology which has repudiated the canons
        of North American, technically objective, functional
        sociology. The interest of this book does not
        reside so much in the historical data on which it
        relies, as in the sweeping interpretations.

3067.   Corten, André. Cambio Social en Santo Domingo. Rio
        Piedras, Puerto Rico. Instituto de Estudios del
        Caribe. 1968. 180 p. The result of a series of
        sociological studies conducted with the aim of
        measuring the goal motivation of different
        segments of the Dominican population and its effect
        on socio-economic mobility. Of special interest to
        the student of church planning, is the quantitative
        description of the behavior of the newly-urbanized
        (after the death of Trujillo) population as it faces
        the multiplicity of choices offered by the urban
        setting.

3068.   Documentos de la Conferencia del Episcopado de la
        República Dominicana 1955-1969. Archdiocese of
        Santo Domingo, S.D. A complete collection of
        pastoral letters and statements of the Roman
        Catholic bishops of the Dominican Republic. The
        only collection available. It is of utmost impor-
        tance to church historians and analysts of the period.

3069. Dominican Republic Packet. Washington, D.C., EPICA,
1500 Farragut St., N.W. 1972. Articles on history,
economics, politics and suggestions for conscious-
raising activities. $2.50.

3070. Franco, Franklyn J. República Dominicana: Clases,
Crisis y Comandos. Habana, Cuba. Casa de las
Américas. 1967. 274 p. Socio-economic: classist
analysis of the Dominican history. The part dealing with the period of the Trujillismo is, in
itself, a major treatise. The penetration of foreign capital and its consequences upon the economic/
political process in the D.R. are described from a
marxistic analytical perspective, with a wealth of
data arranged in tables.

3071. Goff, Fred *and* Michael Locker. "The Violence of Domina-
tion: U.S. power and the Dominican Republic" in
Latin American Radicalism: a documentary on left
and nationalist movements, ed. by Irving Louis
Horowitz, et al. New York, Random House, 1969.
A Vintage Book, No. V429. 249-291 p.

3072. Jiménes Grullón, J. I. La República Dominicana - Una
Ficción. Mérida, Venezuela. Talleres Gráficos
Universitarios, 1965. 267 p. An example of socio-
political reconstruction of the Dominican historical past, by using the new points of view afforded
by the present. Describes the essence of "colonialism" (*coloniaje*) which still persists in the
Dominican Republic, is found in the history-long
denial of Negritude and its values by a Dominican
white-value seeking upper social echelon.

3073. Larrazábal Blanco, Carlos. Los Negros y la Esclavitud en
Santo Domingo. Santo Domingo, R.D. Julio D.
Postigo e Hijos Editores. 1967. 110 p. A documentary history of slavery in Hispaniola covering also
aspects in neighboring Haiti. The importance of
this book resides primarily in having brought together sources and data scattered in many out-of-
print older publications or still unpublished in
the national archives. Analyzes the far-reaching
consequences of the three centuries of "vinculación
negra" upon Dominican cultural and social institutions. This book is a necessary tool for understanding the dynamics of Dominican/Haitian inter-action.

3074. Lowenthal, Abraham F.   The Dominican Intervention.
Cambridge, Harvard University Press. 246 p.

3075. Moreno, José A.   Barrios in Arms, Revolution in Santo
Domingo. University of Pittsburgh Press, Pittsburgh. An excellent account of the Dominican
revolution of 1965 written by a priest who remained
within the Constitutionalist zone during hostilities.
It is one of the few studies that provides data on
the activity of the church in the zone and of the
Christian groups that identified with the armed
struggle.

3076. Slater, Jerome.   Intervention and Negotiation: The
United States and the Dominican Revolution. New
York, Harper and Row. 254 p. A forward by Hans
J. Morgenthau.

3077. Wiarda, Howard J.   Dictatorship and Development. Gainesville, University of Florida Press, 1968. A well
organized study of the political, economic, social
and religious developments that dominated the era
of Trujillo's rule.

3078. _____. Política y Gobierno en la Republica Dominicana
1930-1966. University Católica Madre y Maestra,
Santiago, R.D. 1968. A bibliography of major
books and publications dealing with the socio-
political factors of the period covered. Contains
numerous significant entries on the church.

3079. _____. "The Changing Political Orientation of the
Catholic Church in the Dominican Republic" in *A
Journal of Church and State*, Vol. VII, No. 2, Spring
1965. 238-254 p. An analysis of the factors that
have caused a more progressive outlook on social
and political issues on the part of the Roman
Catholic Church in the Dominican Republic, during
the years immediately following the assaddination
of Trujillo.

Protestantism in General
See also p. 229.

3080. Isais, Juan, ed.   The Other Revolution. Waco, Texas.
Word, Inc., 1970. 163 p. A well-edited, useful
collection of reports, articles and documents about
the Evangelism-in-Depth evangelistic campaign in

the Dominican Republic which coincided with the
year of revolt and turmoil. Covers all phases,
from early planning to evaluation in 1969.

3081. Woodward, Thomas E. Nonhistorical Protestantism in the
Dominican Republic, 1951-1971. A.B. history thesis,
Princeton University, 1972. Available in Firestone
Library on Inter-library loan. 105 p. A study of
the growth and development of the non-traditional
denominations in the decades before and after the
death of Trujillo. The impact of urban migration
and increasing political and socio-economic upheaval is closely studied on five groups: Adventists,
Assemblies of God, Free Methodists, Plymouth Brethren
and the West Indies Mission.

Denominational History
See also p. 229.

Free Methodist

3082. Lamson, Byron S. The Frontiers of Free Methodism.
Winona Lake, Indiana, Free Methodist Church, 1960.
255 p. Contains much valuable material about the
Dominican Republic work, spanning the early pioneering, growth and changes in the late 1950's.

3083. _____. Lights in the World. Winona Lake, Indiana, Light
and Life Press, 1951. The section on the mission in
the Dominican Republic (48-55 p.) is a good survey
of early history, including movement toward nation-
alization in the late 1940's.

Evangelical Mennonite

3084. Zimmerman, Marieta. Twenty-fifty Anniversary of the
Evangelical Mennonite Church in the Land Columbus
loved Best. Fort Wayne, Indiana, Commission on
Overseas Missions of the Evangelical Mennonite
Church by a veteran missionary. Contains biograph-
ies of national leaders and church statistics.

Southern Baptist

3085. Hefley, James. Intrigue in Santo Domingo. Waco, Texas,
Word Books, 1968. 183 p. The story of Rev. Howard

Shoemake, a Southern Baptist missionary, during and
after the 1965 civil war. It was written with a
very incomplete understanding of the basic issues
which face the Dominican people and a glaring insen-
sitivity to the historic role of the U.S. in
relation to that people. A sad commentary on the
role which some missionaries play in crucial moments
in the history of those whom they came to help.

Periodicals
See also p. 230.

Current Publications

3086. Ecos Evangélicos. 1927-. Dominican Free Methodist
       Church, published in Santiago, Dominican Republic.

Haiti
See also p. 230.

General Background
See also p. 231.

3087. Babin, Maria Teresa. Puerto Rican Spirit; their history,
       life and culture. New York, Collier, 1971. A short
       cultural history by an *independista*. A very tradi-
       tional approach which does not have a class analysis.

3088. Courlander, Harold *and* Remy Bastien. Religion and
       Politics in Haiti: Two essays. Institute for
       Cross-Cultural Research, 1966. 81 p.

3089. Lewis, Gordan. Puerto Rico: a socio-historic interpre-
       tation. New York, Random House, 1972. Probably the
       best single volume in terms of political analysis,
       but lacking in a clear description of different
       social groups and the roles they play.

3090. Motilus, Robert. Etudes sur le Vodou. Cuernavaca,
       CIDOC, 1967. 164 p. Sondeos Series No. 2.

3091. Orjala, Paul R. A dialect survey of the Haiten Creole.
       Ph.D. dissertation. Hartford Seminary, Hartford,
       Conn. 1970.

Puerto Rico
See also p. 233.

Bibliography
See also p. 233.

3093.　Bravo, Enrique R., ed.　Bibliografía Puertorriqueña:
　　　　selecta y anotada.　New York, Urban Center of
　　　　Columbia University, 1972.　200 p.　Listing of
　　　　works considered to be classics and those pertinent
　　　　to the contemporary Puerto Rican experience.
　　　　Excludes unpublished theses and magazine articles.
　　　　Comments in both English and Spanish.

3094.　Dessick, Jesse J.　Doctoral Research on Puerto Rico and
　　　　Puerto Ricans.　New York, New York University, 1967.
　　　　34 p.　Lists all doctoral dissertations about Puerto
　　　　Rico and by Puertoricans in U.S. and Canadian
　　　　university libraries until 1966.

General Background
See also p. 234.

3095.　Del Corro, Alejandro, ed.　Puerto Rico:　obispos nativos;
　　　　documentos y reacciones de prensa 1962-65.　Cuerna-
　　　　vaca, Mexico, CIDOC, 1969.　358 p.

3096.　Diaz Soler, Luis M.　Historia de la esclavitud negra en
　　　　Puerto Rico, n.p.　Rio Piedras, 1969.　3rd edition.
　　　　439 p.　Appendices and bibliography.

3097.　Dohen, Dorothy.　Two studies of Puerto Rico:　Religion
　　　　Data.　The background of consensual union.
　　　　Cuernavaca, CIDOC, 1966.　156 p.　Sondeos No. 3.

3098.　Ferre, William, Ivan Illich *and* Joseph Fitzpatrick, eds.
　　　　Spiritual care of Puerto Rican migrants; report on
　　　　the First Conference held in San Juan, Puerto Rico,
　　　　April, 1955.　Cuernavaca, CIDOC, 1970.　242 p.

3099.　López, Alfonso.　"Feliciano, Carlos:　History and
　　　　Repression."　New York, Committee to Defend Carlos
　　　　Feliciano, 1973.　An introduction by William

Kunstler, a chapter of historical material on
Puerto Rico and the story of a political prisoner
who spent 17 months in jail. Includes his letters
written in prison.

3100. López Oliva, Enrique. "El obispo de los independentistas:
Monseñor Antulio Parrilla-Bonilla," in *Revista CCLEA*,
La Habana, febrero-marzo de 1972. Interpretation
for the Cuba press of the controversial Puerto Rican
bishop.

3101. Parrilla-Bonilla, Antulio. Puerto Rico: iglesia y
sociedad, 1967-1969 and 1969-1971; conferencias,
discursos, entrevistas. Cuernavaca, CIDOC, 1970,
1971. Two volumes. Sondeos No. 66 and 84. By a
controversial bishop related to the Independence
movement.

3102. Puerto Rico: Showcase of Oppression. Division for Latin
America, USCC, Box 6066, Washington, D.C. $2.50.
An educational kit of six different pamphlets.
Designed to help understand better the struggle
going on in Puerto Rico for self-determination.

3103. Sales, Maria de. El sentimiento religioso en la lírica
puertorriqueña. Cuernavaca, CIDOC, 1966. 216 p.
Sondeos No. 15. Includes resume of Puerto Rican
religious poetry and bibliography.

3104. Senior, Clarence. Santiago Iglesias: Apóstol de los
trabajadores. Hato Rey, Puerto Rico, Editorial,
Universidad Interamericana, 1973. Prologue by
Herman Badillo. A biography prepared on the
centenary of his birth.

3105. Silen, Juan Angel. We, the Puerto Rican People: a
story of oppression and resistance. New York,
Modern Reader, 1971. Written by a young Puerto
Rican active in the Puerto Rican independence movement. A brief, empassionate, political document.
Challenges the concept of docility as Puerto Rican
cultural trait.

3106. Wagenheim, Kal, ed. (with Olga Jiménez de Wagenheim).
The Puerto Ricans: a documentary history. New
York, Praeger Publications, 1973. 322 p. A comprehensive study of the two Puerto Ricos, insular
and mainland U.S.

Protestantism in General
See also p. 235.

3107.   Carver, E. Earl.   Evangelical Church Growth in Puerto
        Rico.   Unpublished M.A. thesis.   1972.   School of
        Missions and Institute of Church Growth, Fuller
        Theological Seminary, Pasadena, Calif.   Objective
        value is lessened by lack of availability of
        original sources and *a priori* conclusions.

3108.   Orjala, Paul R.   Christ in the Caribbean.   Kansas City,
        Mo., Nazarene Publishing House, 1960.

3109.   Poblete, Renato.   Sectarismo portorriqueño: búsqueda de
        comunidad y expansión Pentecostal.   Cuernavaca,
        CIDOC, 1969.   134 p.   Sondeos No. 55.

3110.   Sáez, Florencio, Jr., M.D.   Entre Cristo y Che Guevara.
        Historia de la subversión política en las iglesias
        evangélica de Puerto Rico.   San Juan, Puerto Rico.
        Editorial Palma Real, 1972.   337 p.   Summarizes Sáez
        personal confrontation with pastors whom he consid-
        ers to be influenced by Marxism.   From a traditional
        insular perspective, he points to what he believes
        the source of influence and suggests ways to correct
        the tendency.

Denominational History
See also p. 238.
American Baptist

3111.   Rosario Ramos, Tomas, ed.   Abelardo M. Diaz Morales,
        profeta y escritor.   Santo Domingo, R.D.: Libreria
        Dominicana, 1971.   231 p.   Collection of tributes
        to and articles and speeches by an early Baptist
        pastor in Puerto Rico.   Diaz Morales was editor of
        Puerto Rico Evangélico, an articulate leader in
        Evangelical circles.

3112.   _____.   Los Bautistas en Puerto Rico.
        Apuntes históricos.   Santo Domingo, R.D.   Editorial
        Libreria Dominicana, 1969.   176 p.   A rough sketch.
        More than a systematic history.   The work is more
        nearly a "who's who" among Baptists.   Contains
        important data as witnesses by a participant in
        the Baptist movement.

Pentecostal

3113. Dominguez, Roberto. Pioneros de Pentecostés en el mundo
       de habla hispana. Madrid and Miami. Literatura
       Evangélica, 1971. 196 p. Primarily biographical
       and autobiographical data on early Puerto Rican
       leaders in Pentecostal movements. Provides basic
       information despite the author's uncritical judg-
       ments and division of space.

Periodicals
See also p. 242.

Current Publications

3114. Credo. Apartado 405, Manotí 00908. 1948-. Mensual.
       Publicación de la iglesia episcopal puertorriqueña.

3115. La Trompeta. Apartado 1112, Caguas 00625. 1929-.
       Mensual. Publicación de la Iglesia de Dios.

Appendixes

Appendix A.
References on Church Archives
and Records of Mission Boards

It is recommended that the researcher consult one or both of the following works for references on church archives and records of mission boards with work in Latin America and the Caribbean:

1. North American Protestant Ministries Overseas Directory. 9th edition, Monrovia, California, Missionary Advanced Research Center, 919 West Huntington Drive, 91016. 1973. pp. 320. This is the most up-to-date listing available for addresses and countries of missionary endeavors of United States and Canadian mission boards. (Cf. 2400).

2. Suelflow, Augustus R., compiler. A preliminary guide to Church Records Repositories. This is a 108 page mimeographed work published by the Church Archives Committee of the Society of American Archivists, 1969. Concordia Historical Institute, Concordia Theological Seminary, St. Louis, Missouri. (Cf. 2070). See also 2065 and 2072 for further key reference works on archives in the United States.

Appendix B.
Addresses of Publishers

(Reprinted with the permission of the North American
Congress on Latin America, Box 57, Cathedral Station,
New York, N.Y. 10025; Box 226, Berkeley, Calif. 10011)

American Univ. Press, The American Univ., Washington, D.C.
Anchor Enterprises, P.O. Box 1656, Manhattan Beach, Calif. 90266.
Archon Books, 60 Connolly Parkway, Hamden, Conn. 06514.
Arno Press, Inc. (A New York Times Co.), 330 Madison Ave., New
    York, N.Y. 10017.
Association Press, 291 Broadway, New York, N.Y. 10007.
Atheneum Publishers, 122 E. 42 st., New York, N.Y. 10017.
Augustus Kelley, 24 E. 22 St., New York, N.Y. 10010.

Basic Books, Inc., Publishers, 10 E. 53 St., New York, N.Y. 10022.
Beacon Press, 25 Beacon St., Boston, Mass. 02108.
Bobbs-Merrill Co., 4 W. 57 St., New York, N.Y. 10019.
Bookman Associates, 31 Union Square W., New York, N.Y. 10003.
Brookings Institution, 1775 Massachusetts Ave. N.W., Washington,
    D.C. 20036.

Cambridge Univ. Press, 32 E. 57 St., New York, N.Y. 10022.
Cineaste, 244 W. 27 St., New York, N.Y. 10001.
Collier, P.F., Inc. (Subs. of Crowell, Collier & Macmillan Inc.),
    866 Third Ave., New York, N.Y. 10022.
Columbia Univ. Press, 562 W. 113 St., New York, N.Y. 10025.
Commentary, American Jewish Committee, 165 E. 56 St., New York,
    N.Y. 10022.
Commonweal, 232 Madison Ave., New York, N.Y. 10016.
Cornell Univ. Press, 124 Roberts Pl., Ithaca, N.Y. 14850.
Council for Latin America, Inc., 680 Park Ave., New York, N.Y.
    10021.

Dial Press, Inc. (A wholly-owned subs. of Dell Pub. Co.), 750
    Third Ave., New York, N.Y. 10017.
Doubleday & Co., Inc., 277 Park Ave., New York, N.Y. 10017.

Emerson Hall, 62 W. 85 St., New York, N.Y. 10024.
EPICA, 1500 Farragut St. N.W., Washington, D.C. 20011.

Fawcett World Library, Crest, Gold Medal & Premier Books, 1
    Astor Plaza, New York, N.Y. 10036.
Free Press, Div. of Macmillan Co., 866 Third Ave., New York,
    N.Y. 10022.
Funk & Wagnalls, Inc., 53 E. 77 St., New York, N.Y. 10021.

Gordon Press, Box 459, Bowling Green Station, New York, N.Y.
    10004.
Greenwood Reprints, Greenwood Press, Inc., 51 Riverside Ave.,
    Westport, Conn. 06880.
Grossman Publishers, Inc. (Subs. of The Viking Press, Inc.),
    625 Madison Ave., New York, N.Y. 10022.
Grove Press, 53 E. 11 St., New York, N.Y. 10003.
Guardian, 32 W. 22 St., New York, N.Y. 10010.

Harper & Row Publishers, Inc., 10 E. 53 St., New York, N.Y.
    10022.
Harvard Univ. Press, Kittridge Hall, 79 Garden St., Cambridge,
    Mass. 02138.
Holt, Rinehart & Winston, Inc. (Subs. of Columbia Broadcasting
    System), 383 Madison Ave., New York, N.Y. 10017.
Hoover Institution Press, Stanford Univ., Stanford, Calif.
    94305.
Houghton Mifflin Co., 2 Park St., Boston, Mass. 02107.

Indiana Univ. Press, Tenth & Morton Sts., Bloomington, Ind. 47401.
Institute for the Comparative Study of Political Systems, A
    Division of Operations and Policy Research, Inc., Suite 505,
    4000 Albemarle St. N.W., Washington, D.C. 20016.
International Publishers Co. Inc., 381 Park Ave. So., New York,
    N.Y. 10016.

Johns Hopkins Univ. Press, Baltimore, Md. 21218.

            A. (Subs. of Random House, Inc.), 201 E. 50 St.,
    New York, N.Y. 10022

Latin American Center, University of California at Los Angeles,
    Los Angeles, Calif. 90024.
Latin American Research Review, Latin American Studies Assn.,
    Hispanic Foundation, Library of Congress, Washington, D.C.
    20540.
Liberated Guardian, 14 Cooper Square, New York, N.Y. 10003.
Lippincott, J.B. & Co., E. Washington Square, Philadelphia, Pa.
    19105.

Macmillan Co. (Subs. of Crowell, Collier & Macmillan, Inc.),
    866 Third Ave., New York, N.Y. 10022.
Maryknoll, See: Orbis Books.
McGraw-Hill Book Co., 1221 Ave. of the Americas, New York, N.Y.
    10020.
M.I.T. Press, 28 Carleton St., Cambridge, Mass. 02142.
Modern Reader, See: Monthly Review Press.
Monthly Review Press, 116 W. 14 St., New York, N.Y. 10011.
Morrow, William & Co. Inc. (Wholly-owned Subs. of Scott, Foresman
    & Co.), 105 Madison Ave., New York, N.Y. 10016.

Negro Universities Press, See: Greenwood Press, Inc.
Network Project, 104 Earle Hall, Columbia University, New York,
    N.Y. 10027.
North American Congress on Latin America (NACLA), Box 57, Cathe-
    dral Station, New York, N.Y. 10025; Box 226, Berkeley, Calif.
    94701.
Norton, W.W. & Co. Inc., 55 Fifth Ave., New York, N.Y. 10003.
Notre Dame Publishing Co., 129 Lafayette St., New York, N.Y.
    10013.

Octagon Books (Subs. of Farrar, Straus & Giroux, Inc.), 19 Union
   Square W., New York, N.Y. 10003.
Orbis Books (Pub. Div. of the Maryknoll Fathers), Maryknoll,
   N.Y. 10545.
Oxford Univ. Press, Inc., 200 Madison Ave., New York, N.Y. 10016.

Pacific Basin Reports, Custom House, Box 26581, San Francisco,
   Calif. 94126.
Pacific Studies Center, 1963 University Ave., E. Palo Alto,
   Calif. 94303.
Pageant, 205 E. 42 St., New York, N.Y. 10017.
Pan-American Union, Publications Division, 19 & Constitution Ave.,
   Washington, D.C. 20006.
Pathfinder Press, Inc., 410 West St., New York, N.Y. 10014.
Pelican, See: Penguin.
Penguin Books, Inc., 7110 Ambassador Rd., Baltimore, Md. 21207.
People's Press, 968 Valencia, San Francisco, Calif. 94110.
Phoenix Press, Box 342 Kennesaw, Ga. 30144.
Praeger Publishers, Inc., (Subs. of Encyclopedia Britannica Inc.),
   111 Fourth Ave., New York, N.Y. 10003.
Prentice Hall, Inc., Englewood Cliffs, N.J. 07632; 70 Fifth Ave.,
   New York, N.Y. 10011.
Princeton Univ. Press, Princeton, N.J. 08540.
Public Affairs Press, 419 New Jersey Ave. S.E., Washington, D.C.
   20003.
Public Documents Distribution Center, 5801 Tabor Ave., Philadel-
   phia, Pa. 19120.
Puerto Rican Socialist Party, Casa Puerto Rico, 106 E. 14 St.,
   New York, N.Y. 10003.
Putnam's, G.P., & Sons, 200 Madison Ave., New York, N.Y. 10016.

Quadrangle Press, Inc. (Subs. of New York Times Co.), 330 Madison
   Ave., New York, N.Y. 10017.

Rand Corporation, 1700 Main St., Santa Monica, Calif. 90406.
Random House, Inc. (Subs. of Radio Corporation of America), 201
   E. 50 St., New York, N.Y. 10022.
Russell & Russell Publishers (Div. of Atheneum Pubs.), 122 E.
   42 St., New York, N.Y. 10017.
Rutgers Univ. Press, 20 College Ave., New Brunswick, N.J. 08903.

Scarecrow Press, Inc. (Subs. of Grolier Inc.), 52 Liberty St.,
   Box 656, Metuchen, N.J. 08840.
Science & Society, 30 E. 20 St., New York, N.Y. 10003.

Simon & Schuster, Inc., 630 Fifth Ave., New York, N.Y. 10020.
Society, Rutgers University, New Brunswick, N.J. 08903.
Stanford Univ. Press, Stanford, Calif. 94305.
State Univ. of New York Press, 99 Washington Ave., Albany, N.Y. 12201.
Stuart, Lyle, Inc., 120 Enterprise Ave., Secaucus, N.J. 07094.
Studies in Comparative International Development (SCID), Sage Publications, Inc., 275 Wouth Beverly Drive, Beverly Hills, Calif. 90212.
Superintendent of Documents, U.S. Government Printing Office, Washington, D.C. 20402.

Transaction, See: Society.
Tulane Univ. Publications Dept., New Orleans, La. 70118
Twentieth Century Press, Inc., 320 So. Jefferson St., Chicago, Ill. 60606.

United Nations, Sales Section, Publishing Service, New York, N.Y. 10017.
UNESCO, Unipub, Inc., A Xerox Education Co., Box 433, New York, N.Y. 10016.
Univ. of California at Berkeley, 2223 Fulton St., Berkeley, Calif. 94720.
Univ. of California at Los Angeles, Willian Andrews Clark Memorial Library, Los Angeles, Calif. 90018.
Univ. of Florida Press, 15 N.W. 15 St., Gainesville, Fla. 32601.
Univ. of Michigan Press, 615 E. University, Ann Arbor, Michigan 48106.
Univ. of New Mexico Press, Albuquerque, N.M. 87106.
Univ. of North Carolina Press, Box 2288, Chapel Hill, N.C. 27514.
Univ. of Pittsburgh Press, 127 N. Bellefield Ave., Pittsburgh, Pa. 15213.
Univ. of Texas Press, Box 7819, University Station, Austin, Tex. 78712.
Univ. of Wisconsin Press, Box 1379, Madison, Wis. 53701.
URPE, Literature Clearing House, 2503 Student Activities Building, University of Michigan, Ann Arbor, Mich. 48104.
USLA, 150 Fifth Ave., Rm. 737, New York, N.Y. 10011.

Vanderbilt Univ. Press, Nashville, Tenn. 37235.
Vanguard Press, Inc., 424 Madison Ave., New York, N.Y. 10017.
Viking Press, Inc., 625 Madison Ave., New York, N.Y. 10022.
Vintage, See: Random House.

Yale Univ. Press, 92 Yale Station, New Haven, Conn. 06520.

Appendix C.
Evangelical Periodicals and Magazines
in Brazil

The following are the more important evangelical periodicals and magazines which are published in Brazil:

A CRUZ DO SUL
CAIXA POSTAL 6192
01000 - SÃO PAULO - SP

A.S.T.E. ASSOCIACÃO SEMINARISTAS
TEOLOGICOS EVANGELICOS
RUA REGO FREITAS, 530 APT. F-3
SÃO PAULO - SP

BÍBLIA NO BRASIL, A
CAIXA POSTAL 73
RIO DE JANEIRO, ZC-13 - GB

BRADO DE GUERRA
CAIXA POSTAL 8631
SÃO PAULO - SP

BRASIL CONGREGACIONAL
RUA JOÃO PINHEIRO, 100
PIEDADE, AC-13 - GB

BRASIL PRESBITERIANO
RUA HELVETIA, 732 APT. 2
SÃO PAULO, 2 - SP

CAMARA DE LITERATURE EVANGELICA
DO BRASIL
CAIXA POSTAL 8051
SÃO PAULO - SP

CEAS
RUA ARISTIDES NOVIS, 101
FEDERACÃO
40000 - SALVADOR - BA

CEDOC-JOVEM
RUA GRÃO MONGOL, 502
BELO HORIZONTE - MG

CEI - CENTRO ECUMÉNICO DE
INFORMAÇÃO
CAIXA POSTAL 16.082 (ZC-01)
RIO DE JANEIRO - GB

CENTRO INFORMATIVO CATÓLICO
CAIXA POSTAL 23
PETROPÓLIS - RJ

CONGREGACIONAL, O
RUA JOÃO PINHEIRO, 100
PIEDADE ZC-13 - GB

CRISTÃO, O
RUA ALEXANDRE MACKENZIE, 60
RIO DE JANEIRO, ZC-05 - GB

CRISTIANISMO
CAIXA POSTAL 6613
SÃO PAULO - SP

CRUZ DE MALTA
CAIXA POSTAL 8051
SÃO PAULO - SP

EDITORA LUTERANA
CAIXA POSTAL 11166
SÃO PAULO - SP

ESTANDARTE, O
CAIXA POSTAL 300
SÃO PAULO - SP

ESTANDARTE CRISTÃO
CAIXA POSTAL 33
PORTO ALEGRE - RGS

EXPOSITOR CRISTÃO
CAIXA POSTAL 8816
SÃO PAULO - SP

FOGO PENTECOSTAL
CAIXA POSTAL 2647
PORTO ALEGRE - RGS

FOLHA DOMINICAL
CAIXA POSTAL 14
SÃO LEOPOLDO - RGS

FUNDAMENTALISTA, O
CAIXA POSTAL 4500
SÃO PAULO - SP

HOMENS EM MARCHA
CAIXA POSTAL 2009
SÃO PAULO - SP

IMPRENSA METODISTA
CAIXA POSTAL 8051
SÃO PAULO - SP

INFORMAC
CAIXA POSTAL 1210
BELO HORIZONTE - MG

IGREJA EM NOSSOS DIAS
CAIXA POSTAL 14
SÃO LEOPOLDO - RGS

IGREJA LUTERANA
FACULDADE DO SEMINÁRIO CONCÓRDIA
PORTO ALEGRE - RGS

JORNAL BATISTA, O
BAIXA POSTAL 320
RIO DE JANEIRO, ZC-00 - GB

JORNAL EVANGÉLICO
CAIXA POSTAL 11
93.000, SÃO LEOPOLDO - RGS

PRESBITERIANO CONSERVADOR
LARGO 7 DE SETEMBRO, 52, 100
SÃO PAULO - SP

JORNAL DE HOJE
AV. SANTO AMARO, 4521 SOBRELOJA
BROOKLIN - SÃO PAULO - SP

PRESENCA
RUA SENHOR DOS PASSOS, 202-2
PORTO AKEGRE - RGS

LIVRARIA CRISTÃ UNIDA
RUA FRANCISCO GLICÉRIO, 1417
CAMPINAS - SP

REVISTA VIDA
CAIXA POSTAL 2600
SÃO PAULO - SP

LOUVOR PERENE
CAIXA POSTAL 1695
BELLO HORIZONTE - MG

REVISTA VOZES
RED. FREI CLARÊNCIO NEOTTI
CAIXA POSTAL 23 - PETRÓPOLIS - RJ

MENSAGEIRO DA PAZ
CAIXA POSTAL 3274
RIO, XC-00 - GB

SIMPÓSIO
(REVISTA TEOLÓGICA DA A.S.T.E.)
RUA REGO FREITAS 530, CONJ. F13
SÃO PAULO - SP

MENSAGEIRO LUTERANO, O
CAIXA POSTAL 916
PORTO ALEGRE - RGS

ULTIMATO
RUA GOMES BARBOSA, 618
VICOSA - MG

PALAVRA DE NOVA VIDA
CAIXA POSTAL 2734
RIO, XC-00 - GB

Index

index

EVANGELICALS IN LATIN AMERICA

COUNTRY	EVANGELICALS			POPULATION**	
	1967 COMMUNICANTS (Thousands)	ANNUAL GROWTH RATE 1960-1967	INDEX OF RELATIVE SIZE *	MID-1968 TOTAL (Millions)	CURRENT ANNUAL GROWTH RATE
ARGENTINA	249.5	5.0 %	107	23.4	1.5 %
BOLIVIA	45.4	11.5	116	3.9	2.4
BRAZIL	3,313.2	11.0	375	88.3	3.2
CHILE	441.7	8.5	485	9.1	2.2
COLOMBIA	73.9	12.0	38	19.7	3.2
COSTA RICA	14.2	7.0	89	1.6	3.5
ECUADOR	12.6	15.0	22	5.7	3.4
EL SALVADOR	35.8	5.5	109	3.3	3.7
GUATEMALA	77.2	9.0	158	4.9	3.1
HONDURAS	18.8	8.5	75	2.5	3.5
MEXICO	429.9	11.0	91	47.3	3.5
NICARAGUA	19.8	3.0	110	1.8	3.5
PANAMA	37.5	5.5	268	1.4	3.2
PARAGUAY	15.2	11.0	47	2.2	3.2
PERU	61.9	6.5	48	12.8	3.1
URUGUAY	21.8	7.0	78	2.8	1.2
VENEZUELA	46.9	14.0	48	9.7	3.6
TOTAL	4,915.4	10.0 %	204	240.4	3.0 %

* INDEX OF 100 EQUALS 1.00% OF POPULATION.
** POPULATION REFERENCE BUREAU 1968.

From *Latin American Church Growth* by William R. Read et al.,
William B. Eerdmans Publishing Company. Used by permission.

John H. Sinclair was born in 1924 in Belen, New Mexico, the son
of Scottish immigrant parents. As a son of the manse, challenged
by world mission at an early age, it was not strange that he
entered the Presbyterian ministry. He studied at Baker University and Princeton Theological Seminary and went to Latin America
at the age of twenty-four. His interest in church and mission
history started early since his father had written a history of
the Presbyterian Church in Kansas on its centenary in 1937.

As a missionary in Venezuela and Chile (1948-1960) he served
among *campesinos*, in villages and metropolitan areas as pastor,
teacher and church administrator. He collected and annotated
literature on Protestantism in Latin America across his years of
missionary service. Later as Secretary for Latin America of the
United Presbyterian Church (1960-1973), he garnered historical data
from both primary and secondary sources. He has been able to
put together the complex and scattered pieces of a century and
a half of Protestant literature on Latin America and edit this
data into one biographical volume. He also developed during
twenty-five years a wide circle of researchers and students on
Protestantism throughout the Americas. These friends and colla-
borators have shared greatly in the material found in this volume.
Protestantism in Latin America brings together the fruit of these
collective efforts.

The initial volume (1967 edition) was prepared primarily to
provide for missionaries on furlough a basic tool to encourage

and assist them in doing research on Protestant history. The
revised edition (1975) is directed to a wider group of researchers
and students and therefore includes a broader spectrum of literature.

From 1960-1963 Mr. Sinclair served as Secretary of the Advisory
Council on Inter-American Affairs of his denomination and thus
became immersed in the field of Interamerican relations. He
attended most of the major Latin American Protestant conferences
during the past decade. He served for several years as chairman
of the Latin American Department of the National Council of the
Churches of Christ and of the Hispanic American Institute. He
has traveled in every country in Latin America.

Mr. Sinclair is a member of the Latin American Studies Association and is listed in the National Directory of Latinamerican-
ists as a bibliographer. He is also a participant in the
Association for the Study of Religion in Latin America. As a
member of CEHILA (Comisión de Estudio de Historia de la Iglesia
en Latinoamérica), a Catholic-Protestant project, he is presently
sharing in the preparation of a nine-volume series by writing
the Protestant chapters on Colombia and Venezuela.

Mr. Sinclair has built relationships of academic respect and
ecumenical trust between Catholics, traditional Protestants and
the burgeoning family of Pentecostals in Latin America. His
broad sympathies for both the academican and the missionary have
been evidenced in his years of service. This bibliographical
guide is a small mirror which reflects his deep appreciation for
Latin American culture and his conviction that the Latin American
Church is a vital religious movement.

Presently Mr. Sinclair is serving as Associate Executive for
Program of The Synod of Lakes and Prairies and lives in Minnesota.
He is married to Maxine B. Sinclair and the father of three
grown sons.

OTHER BOOKS BY THE WILLIAM CAREY LIBRARY

General

The Birth of Missions in America by Charles L. Chaney, ISBN
0-87808-146-1, 1976: 352 pp. $7.95 paper
Christopaganism or Indigenous Christianity? edited by
Tetsunao Yamamori and Charles Taber. ISBN 0-87808-
423-1 1975: 262 pp. $5.95 paper
The Church and Cultures by Louis J. Luzbetak, ISBN 0-87808-
725-7, 1976: 448 pp. $5.95x paper
Church Growth and Christian Mission by Donald A. McGavran,
ISBN 0-87808-728-1, 1976: 252 pp. $5.95 paper
Church Growth and Group Conversion by Donald A. McGavran.
ISBN 0-87808-712-5 1973: 128 pp. $2.45 paper
*Culture and Human Values: Christian Intervention in
Anthropological Perspective* by Jacob A. Loewen.
ISBN 0-87808-722-2 1975: 443 pp. $5.95 paper
Customs and Cultures: Anthropology for Christian Missions
by Eugene A. Nida. ISBN 0-87808-723-0 1975: 306 pp.
$3.95x paper
Defeat of the Bird God by C. Peter Wagner. ISBN 0-87808-
721-4 1975: 256 pp. $4.95 paper
Growth and Life in the Local Church by H. Boone Porter.
ISBN 0-87808-141-0 1974: 124 pp. $2.95 paper
A Manual for Church Growth Surveys by Ebbie C. Smith, ISBN
0-87808-145-3, 1976: 144 pp. $3.95 paper
*Message and Mission: The Communication of the Christian
Faith* by Eugene A. Nida. ISBN 0-87808-711-7 1972:
253 pp. $3.95x paper
*Reaching the Unreached: A Preliminary Strategy for World
Evangelization* by Edward Pentecost. ISBN 0-87808-
418-5 1974: 256 pp. $5.95 paper
Spiritual Gifts and the Great Commission by Edward F.
Murphy (Mandate Press). ISBN 0-87808-144-5 1975:
352 pp. $5.95 paper
The 25 Unbelievable Years by Ralph D. Winter. ISBN 0-
87808-102-X 1970: 125 pp. $2.95 paper
Verdict Theology in Missionary Theory by Alan R. Tippett.
ISBN 0-87808-105-4 1973: 216 pp. $4.95 paper

Area and Case Studies

Aspects of Pacific Ethnohistory by Alan R. Tippett. ISBN
0-87808-132-1 1973: 216 pp. $3.95 paper
The Baha'i Faith: Its History and Teachings by William M.
Miller. ISBN 0-87808-137-2 1974: 450 pp. $8.95 paper
A Century of Growth: The Kachin Baptist Church of Burma
by Herman Tegenfeldt. ISBN 0-87808-416-9 1974:
540 pp. $9.95 cloth
Church Growth in Japan by Tetsunao Yamamori. ISBN 0-87808
412-6 1974: 184 pp. $4.95 paper
*Circle of Harmony: A Case Study of Popular Japanese
Buddhism with Implications for Christian Mission* by
Kenneth J. Dale. ISBN 0-87808-424-X 1975: 211 pp.
$4.95 paper
A New Day in Madras by Amirtharaj Nelson. ISBN 0-87808-
420-7 1975: 340 pp. $7.95 paper
People Movements in the Punjab by Margaret and Frederick
Stock. ISBN 0-87808-417-7 1975: 364 pp. $8.95 paper
The Protestant Movement in Italy by Roger E. Hedlund.
ISBN 0-87808-307-3 1970: 266 pp. $3.95 paper
*Protestants in Modern Spain: The Struggle for Religious
Pluralism* by Dale G. Vought. ISBN 0-87808-311-1
1973: 168 pp. $3.45 paper
*The Religious Dimension in Hispanic Los Angeles: A Prot-
estant Case Study* by Clifton L. Holland. ISBN 0-
87808-309-X 1974: 550 pp. $9.95 paper
*Solomon Islands Christianity: A Study in Growth and
Obstruction* by Alan R. Tippett. ISBN 0-87808-724-9
1975: 407 pp. $5.95x paper
Taiwan: Mainline Versus Independent Church Growth by
Allen J. Swanson. ISBN 0-87808-404-5 1973: 300 pp.
$3.95 paper
Understanding Latin Americans by Eugene A. Nida. ISBN
0-87808-117-8 1974: 164 pp. $3.95 paper

Theological Education by Extension

Designing a Theological Education by Extension Program
by Leslie D. Hill. ISBN 0-87808-312-X 1973: 224 pp.
$2.95 paper
An Extension Seminary Primer by Ralph Covell and C. Peter
Wagner. ISBN 0-87808-106-2 1971: 60 pp. $2.45 paper
The World Directory of Theological Education by Extension
by Wayne Weld. ISBN 0-87808-134-8 1973: 416 pp.
$5.95x paper
1976 Supplement only, 1976: 64 pp. $1.95x paper
Writing for Theological Education by Extension by Lois
McKinney. ISBN 0-87808-905-5 1975: 64 pp.
$1.45x booklet

Textbooks and Practical Helps

Becoming Bilingual: A Guide to Language Learning by Donald
   Larson and William A. Smalley.   ISBN 0-87808-718-4
   1974: 455 pp. $5.95x paper
Bibliography for Cross-Cultural Workers by Alan R. Tippett.
   ISBN 0-87808-109-7   1971: 256 pp. $4.95 paper
   ISBN 0-87808-110-0   1971: 256 pp. $5.95 cloth
*Education of Missionaries' Children: The Neglected
   Dimension of World Mission* by D. Bruce Lockerbie.
   ISBN 0-87808-422-3   1975: 62 pp. $1.95 paper
Everything You Need to Grow a Messianic Synagogue by
   Phillip E. Goble.   ISBN 0-87808-421-5   1975: 158 pp.
   $2.45 paper
God's Word in Man's Language by Eugene A. Nida.   ISBN
   0-87808-713-3   1973: 192 pp. $2.95 paper
Manual of Articulatory Phonetics by William A. Smalley.
   ISBN 0-87808-139-9   1973: 522 pp. $4.95x paper
*The Means of World Evangelization: Missiological Educa-
   tion at the Fuller School of World Mission* edited by
   Alvin Martin.   ISBN 0-87808-143-7   1974: 544 pp.
   $9.95 paper
Principles of Church Growth by Wayne Weld and Donald A.
   McGavran.   ISBN 0-87808-108-9   1971: 400 pp.
   $3.95 paper
Readings in Missionary Anthropology edited by William A.
   Smalley.   ISBN 0-87808-719-2   1974: 384 pp.
   $4.95x paper

DATE DUE

APR 1 5 1982			
NOV 2 2 1992			
GAYLORD			PRINTED IN U.S.A